Macmillan Bu

Active Leadership
Enterprise and

(*continued*)

Macmillan Building and Surveying Series
Series Standing Order ISBN 0–333–69333–7

You can receive future titles in this series as they are published by placing a
standing order. Please contact you bookseller or, in the case of difficulty,
write to us at the address below with your name and address, the title of the
series and the ISBN quoted above.

Customer Service Department, Macmillan Distribution Ltd
Houndmills, Basingstoke, Hampshire RG21 6XS, England

Property Investment

David Isaac

Professor of Real Estate Management
Head of Property and Land Management
University of Greenwich

MACMILLAN

First published 1998 by
MACMILLAN PRESS LTD
Houndmills, Basingstoke, Hampshire RG21 6XS
and London
Companies and representatives
throughout the world

ISBN 0–333–69314–0

A catalogue record for this book is available
from the British Library.

This book is printed on paper suitable for recycling and
made from fully managed and sustained forest sources.

10   9   8   7   6   5   4   3   2   1
07   06   05   04   03   02   01   00   99   98

Copy-edited and typeset by Povey–Edmondson
Tavistock and Rochdale, England

Printed in Malaysia

To Joan

By the same author

The Valuation of Property Investments (with N. Enever)
Property Companies: Share Price and Net Asset Value (with N. Woodroffe)
Property Development, Appraisal and Finance
Property Finance
Property Valuation Techniques (with T. Steley)

Contents

Table of Statutes

Preface

This book provides a basis for the study of property investment and will be useful for both students and practitioners. The book has three main sections: principles and markets, appraisal techniques and portfolio analysis. For students it will provide a text at intermediate level (2nd/3rd year undergraduates) in estate management, property, surveying, planning, design and construction disciplines. Those in adjacent areas of study such as housing and economics will find this a useful introduction to the area of commercial property investment. Practitioners involved with property investment, and this includes a wide area of professionals, including surveyors, builders, construction managers, architects, engineers, estate managers and agents will find this a useful overview, perhaps enlightening them to the range of activities involved in the investment process and updating them on contemporary methods of property investment appraisal. Professional advisors such as bankers, financial advisors, accountants, investors, analysts and lawyers should also find this text useful as an aid to their dealings in the property sector.

Where possible I have obtained data and statistics to place property investment appropriately in the wider economic and financial context. I have aimed to reference the material as well as possible but apologise for any omissions. There are relatively few texts in the area of property compared to most other investment sectors and I have tried to reference existing ones as fully as possible to provide additional views and perspectives for the reader in a very complex and difficult area of activity. The art of property investment including appraisal, valuation and analysis has developed enormously over the last twenty years and this book aims to encourage readers to take the development further and consolidate the innovations in research and practice.

Finally, I would like to thank those who have assisted me in writing this book, the late Professor Ivor Seeley, the editor who provided ongoing advice for my writing and encouraged many authors in the property and construction area. Professor Seeley died during the production of this book and he will be sorely missed by both professional and academic colleagues. His contribution to the development of teaching, learning and scholarship in the area of building and surveying has been outstanding. In addition I would like to thank Malcolm Stewart, my publisher who is ever patient and supportive. I would also like to thank Mike Riley and Chesterton International for practical support in my researches. Many colleagues and external organisations have provide me with information and assistance and these are listed in the acknowledgements below. Finally, as ever, I am reliant on the continued support of Professor David Wills, Lewis Anderson and the staff of the School of Land and Construction Management at the University of Greenwich to develop my research and studies and I am grateful for their help.

University of Greenwich   David Isaac
School of Land and Construction Management

Acknowledgements

The author and publishers wish to thank the following for the use of material:

Journal of Property Finance, Journal of Property Valuation and Investment; Journal of Property Research;   Appraisal Journal; CSW-The Property Week, Chartered Surveyor Monthly; Financial Times; S. G. Warburg Securities; UBS; Paribas Capital Markets; Chesterton Financial; Savills Research; DTZ Debenham Thorpe Research; IPD; SPR; the RICS; *Estates Gazette;* and Kogan Page Limited.

Every effort has been made to trace all the copyright-holders, but if any have been inadvertently overlooked the publishers will be pleased to make the necessary arrangement at the first opportunity.

List of Abbreviations

ASB	Accounting Standards Board
ALC	Agricultural Land Classification
ALPTs	Australian Listed Property Trusts
Amt £1	Amount of £1
APT	Arbitrage Pricing Theory
APUTs	Authorised Property Unit Trusts
ASF	Annual sinking fund
ARY	All risks yield
BCIS	Building Cost Information Service
BPF	British Property Federation
CAPM	Capital Asset Pricing Model
CML	Capital market line
COV	Covariance
CSO	Central Statistical Office
DAV	Defined accounting value
DCF	Discounted cash flow
DEFRD	Deferred
DF	Depreciation factor
DHSS	Department of Health and Social Security
DSS	Department of Social Security
DoE	Department of the Environment
DTI	Department of Trade and Industry
EBIT	Earnings before interest and tax
ENPV	Expected net present value
ER	Expected return
ERP	Estimated realisation price
ERV	Estimated rental value
ENPV	Expected net present value
EU	European Union
EUV	Existing use value
FRI	Fully repairing and insuring (lease)
FTSE	Financial Times Stock Exchange (index)
GDO	General Development Order
GLC	Greater London Council
GRC	Gross replacement cost
HITs	Housing Investment Trusts
HP	Hillier Parker
IPD	Investment Property Databank
IPF	Investment Property Forum
IRFY	Inflation risk free yield
IRR	Internal rate of return
ISVA	Incorporated Society of Valuers and Auctioneers

JLW	Jones Lang Wootton
LIBOR	London Interbank Offered Rate
MAFF	Ministry of Agriculture, Fisheries and Food
MBS	Mortgage-backed securities
MCS	Monte Carlo Simulation
MFR	Minimum funding requirement
MGL	Morgan Grenfell Laurie
MPT	Modern Portfolio Theory
MRA	Multi-regression analysis
MWRR	Money-weighted rate of return
NAV	Net asset value
NNAV	Net net asset value
NPV	Net present value
NRC	Net replacement cost
OEIC	Open-ended investment company
OMV	Open market value
OTC	Over-the-counter
PERP	In perpetuity
PICs	Property Income Certificates
PINCs	Property Income Certificates
PPG	Planning Policy Guidance note
PUTs	Property Unit Trusts
PV	Present value
RADR	Risk-adjusted discount rate
RE	Richard Ellis
REITs	Real Estate Investment Trusts
RFR	Risk-free rate
RICS	Royal Institution of Chartered Surveyors
SAPCOs	Single Asset Property Companies
S.D.	Standard deviation
SIB	Securities and Investment Board
SML	Securities market line
SPOTs	Single Property Ownership Trusts
SSAPs	Statements of Standard Accounting Practice
TWRR	Time-weighted rate of return
WGS	Weatherall Green and Smith
YP	Years Purchase
YRS	Years

1 Property Investment

1.1 RATIONALE OF INVESTMENT

Introduction

A property or building can be owner-occupied or rented; the latter being an investment property. In the present market (1996) it may of course be vacant, resulting from being surplus to the owner's requirements or a poor investment! A large proportion of property is owner-occupied but most of the conventional texts and theories in property are applied to the investment market. The investment market for property cannot be seen in isolation from other investment markets. The application of funds to property has to reflect competition from other forms of investment. The decision to invest in a particular area will be a comparison of return and security and thus knowledge of alternative investments and their analysis could be very important. The application of financial techniques to property investment can also be important and this can clearly be seen in the securitisation and unitisation of property which is a key area of development in property investment. Another important point to be made concerns the nature of the lender and the property to which finance is applied. At its simplest, the financial arrangement may deal with an individual purchasing a single property with a single loan, but it is usually more complex. Finance is generally raised by corporate entities, such as property companies, using existing property and other assets as collateral for the purchase of a portfolio of assets which may include property assets but not exclusively. Finally, it is important to realise the significance of property and property investment to the economy. The importance can be shown in three different ways: as a factor of production, as a corporate asset and as an investment medium. As a factor of production, property provides the space in which economic activity and production takes place, and the efficiency and costs of such space will affect the cost of goods and services produced. As a corporate asset, property forms the major part of asset values in companies' balance sheets and the majority of corporate debt is secured against it. As an investment, it is one of the major types of investment held by individual investors and the financial institutions on which pensions and assurance benefits depend (Fraser 1993).

The structure of the investment market

There are three major areas of traditional investment opportunity (ignoring gold, commodities and works of art): these are fixed interest securities, company stocks and shares, and real property. The Stock Exchange provides a market for listed shares and certain fixed interest securities such as those issued by the government, local authorities and public bodies. The market in real property contrasts with that of company shares and other securities. The property market is fragmented and dispersed whilst that of shares and other securities is highly centralised. The London Stock Market is an example of this centralisation. The centralisation of markets assists the transferability of investments, as does the fact that stock and shares can be traded in small units thereby assisting transferability. Compared with other traditional investment opportunities, real property investment has the distinguishing features of being heterogeneous, generally indivisible and having inherent problems of management. The problems of managing property assets may include collecting rents, dealing with repairs and renewals and lease negotiation; these problems may mean that real property is likely to be an unattractive proposition for the small investor. A decentralised market, such as exists for property, will tend to have high costs of transfer of investments and there will be an imperfect knowledge of transactions in the market.

The factors, discussed above, which affect the real property market make property difficult to value. There is no centralised market price to rely on and the value may be to difficult to assess unless a comparable transaction has recently taken place. The problems of valuation relate to difficulties of trying to relate comparable transactions to properties being valued or even trying to assess what transactions could be considered comparable. Because of the nature of the real property market, individual investors have tended to withdraw from the market and this has been reinforced by the channelling of savings into collective organisations, such as pension funds and insurance companies, which has meant that few individuals use their savings for direct investment in the property market.

Qualities of an investment

An investment essentially involves an initial money outlay to recoup a future income stream or future capital repayment. The approach to analysis of what is required of an investment is best done as a check list of questions and answers. The major question is what an investor expects from the investment, to which the answers might be:

(i)   security of capital and also liquidity so that the interest can be disposed of easily;
(ii)   security of income from the capital invested;
(iii)   regularity of income;
(iv)   low cost of purchase and sale of the investment;
(v)   ease of purchase and sale of the investment;
(vi)   divisibility of the investment. Is it possible to sell off parts of it?
(vii)   the security of the investment in real terms. Is the value of the investment increasing in line with inflation?
(viii) the opportunities for growth in value. Is this more than the rate of inflation, i.e. real growth?

These qualities are summarised in Table 1.1, which compares the characteristics to a number of possible investment opportunities. Some investments outperform others in this comparison but these characteristics essentially involve start-up costs and the security of the investment. The additional key variable is the size of return and whether this outstrips inflation, and this is considered in the final row of the table. The real security is considered here, once inflation has been allowed for, in the capital value and income of the investment. That is whether the capital value has not fallen in real value and whether the return is paying off inflation and more. Real values can be thought of in terms of purchasing power; if this declines in terms of capital value or income then the real value return is falling and the investment can be considered inflation prone. The various elements which investors consider in their returns are discussed later in the chapter.

Table 1.1 *The characteristics of investment compared to the type of investment*

Characteristics of investment	Type of investment					
	Vacant house	Tenanted house	Shares	Index linked government stock (ILG*)	Building society accounts	Premium bonds
Security of nominal capital	depends on the market	if tenants vacate, yes, but otherwise ?	? depends on company	yes	yes	yes
Security of income	no	no	? depends on company	yes	yes	no
Regularity of income	no	yes	yes	yes	yes	no
Ease of purchase and sale	no	no	yes	yes	yes	yes
Low cost of purchase and sale	no	no	no	yes	yes	yes
Divisibility	no	no	yes	yes	yes	yes
Real security/ growth (hedge against inflation)	?	?	?	yes	no	no

(ILG*) = Index Linked Gilts

The type of investment chosen is related to a number of factors, and these factors will differ according to the investor. There may be a particular or peculiar arrangement: tax arrangements, for instance, or ethical considerations which may affect investment choice. The quality of an investment from an economic point of view must be a comparison of the return to the risk; the return is not just the cash flow arising but needs to be considered in relation to the original outlay and return on possible sale. So the cash flow needs to be considered relative to the original outlay, ongoing costs and risks involved in future income and capital revenues. A more detailed analysis would look at three prime areas: economic influences, psychic influences and aspects relating to social responsibility. The major influence is the economic one and this relates to the risk/return profile of the investment. There are a number of aspects to this relating to risk and return of capital and income and the associated area of external injections and taxation of income and capital. These matters are essentially financial. Other aspects which affect the risk and return are time matters relating to the incidence of in- and out-flows of income and capital; the life of the asset is associated with this, as is the concept of depreciation in value of the asset. Finally, risk and return are related to the liquidity of the asset and problems of management. There are psychic and social responsibility dimensions to the investment also. To summarise, there are three main qualities related to the property investment medium:

Economic

These relate to financial risk/return and cash flows and are looked at in detail later in the chapter.

Psychic

The psychic effect relates to the 'feel-good factor' associated with land and property, the ability to see 'something concrete' in one's investment like bricks and mortar; the ownership of something tangible, a basic factor of production, in short supply and valued for its own sake especially in heavily populated areas or in areas of natural beauty. There is a status and prestige in the ownership of buildings and this may apply in terms of landmark buildings; large corporations may require flagship buildings for public relations and corporate image reasons.

Social responsibility

The ownership of land is linked with a social responsibility. There is an ethical consideration of investing in property, often the landscapes of property are attractive and treasured by individuals and the community. Development and management proposals can affect flora, fauna and the surrounding environment and buildings. There may be a responsibility in ownership related to the local community and its activities and viewpoints. Thus there are social consequences of the ownership of land; there is status but also a social responsibility. The general and economic qualities of an investment are outlined in Table 1.2.

These economic considerations are now considered in more detail. Overall risk and growth can be divided into two elements: capital risk and growth and income risk and growth.

Table 1.2 *General and economic qualities of an investment*

General qualities of an investment		
Economic	Psychic	Social responsibility

Specific economic qualities of an investment		
	Specific qualities	*Influence of other general qualities*
Economic qualities: risk/return	Overall risk/growth	
	Capital risk/growth	Psychic
	Income risk/growth	
	External capital injection/leakage (subsidies, grants, taxes)	Social responsibility
	Time issues, the timing of cashflow receipts, costs repayments	Psychic
	Life cycle of the investment	Social responsibility
	Depreciation and obsolescence	Social responsibility
	Transferability and divisibility	
	Management problems	Social responsibility

Capital risk and growth

Capital security is important to an investor. Accounts at the bank will not be at risk unless the bank collapses; this is unlikely and, as we have appreciated in recent years, there may still be some form of insurance policy with the government, Bank of England or a consortium of banks available to provide a life-raft. However, in this decade alone the collapse of Barings, the merchant bank, and Bank of Commerce and Credit International (BCCI) shows that even large financial institutions may be at risk. In general terms, however, the capital invested in such institutions as banks and building societies as account monies is unlikely to be at risk, whereas alternative places to put money such as shares or works of art may lead to a partial or complete loss. When the concept of security is being examined, the relationship between security in real terms and in money terms needs to be examined. Money terms ignores inflation whereas in real terms the purchasing power of money is considered. The purchasing power will need to be discounted by the rate of inflation to find the security in real terms. This discount may be offset by interest received on such deposits and such interest may compensate. Real capital growth in property would require the growth in the capital of the asset to outstrip the rate of inflation. However, such an analysis whilst concentrating on inflation ignores those other elements which make up interest rates. Besides compensation for inflation, an interest rate will also need to compensate for delayed consumption and risk. The components of the return on the investment comprise three components: an element which provides compensation for the time preference of money, a second element related to inflation which exists to maintain the real value of the return and finally an element for a risk premium.

Income risk and growth

Most investments involve an initial purchase and a stream of income which provides a return perhaps culminating in a capital receipt on resale. This is a simplification. Investments should generate a return but some may only do so at the end of the holding period; a vintage car is likely to generate a loss of income up until the period of resale. In the property world, investment property companies will receive income periodically from rents as well as capital appreciation but a trading company is likely to rely on the sale of completed project alone. Income is at risk in many investments not just because of absolute changes of income declared by the managers of the investment, for instance a reduction in the dividend, but also because the rate of return for the individual is related to the price paid. In the latter case if a government stock issue price is £100 and the declared nominal rate is 10% then £10 per annum is received. If the stock is purchased at a price higher than the issue price, then, as the £10 income is still paid, the yield is higher. Consider the example in Isaac and Steley (1991):

Example 1.1: Yield on government stock

> 10% 2004 Treasury Stock in May 1990.
> This stock was quoted as:
>
> | | |
> |---|---|
> | Purchase price | £89.625 |
> | Interest only yield | 11.16 |
> | Gross redemption yield | 11.54 |

The gross redemption yield includes the receipt of a capital sum at the end of the life of the investment; this yield can be calculated by using an internal rate of return approach. In this case the stock is purchased in £100 bonds on which £10 will be received annually and the investment will be subsequently bought back by the Treasury at face value in 2004.

$$\text{The initial yield on an interest only basis} = \frac{\text{Income}}{\text{Purchase price}} \times 100\%$$

$$= \frac{£10}{£89.625} \times 100\%$$

$$= 11.16\%$$

Thus the nominal rate was 10% but the existing interest only rate is now 11.16% because of the change in price which will alter to reflect the market structure of interest rates.

Exchange risk can also have effect on the income flows of project funded with foreign currency.

Capital injections and taxation

Net of tax or after tax returns are those which are of interest to investors. Gross funds (pension funds and other investment funds which do not pay tax) would not want to take on income taxed at source as this reduces their return. Where a differential exists between the treatment of capital and income taxes, investors may opt for a low income return but large capital growth. High tax payers would opt for this alternative, for instance. Tax rate differentials between income and capital taxation have now been brought into line but tax allowances may alter actual individual tax rates. Tax shelters from capital allowances in construction or tax relief in certain locations (such as enterprise zones) are important; tax treatment of losses in offsetting profit elsewhere may create a tax shelter and improve returns to a portfolio of investments. Beside enterprise zone tax incentives, there may exist inducements to develop and invest in certain areas and certain industries. These inducements may not only decrease the cost of occupation for an owner-occupier but may also increase investment returns.

Time issues

The timing of receipts is very important especially if an investor is dependent on one or two investments. For a larger investor, a portfolio of investments may balance out the timing of cash flows. Property income is usually paid quarterly in advance and is thus available on a more regular basis than dividend or gilt returns which may be paid half yearly. The importance of timing in investment is to match income with liabilities.

Life cycle of investment

The life cycle of an investment is important. Gilts will have a higher price at the end of their life cycle, all things being equal. As the day nears for repayment of the original sum, however, there is a difference between gilts with a term and those without (such as undated Consols), in the same way as for leasehold and freehold property. A lease will incur great cost at review of the rent or when a lease comes to an end and reinstatement works may have to be carried out under the lease. Freeholders with leases which are not prime property will, in particular, encounter disruption to their income flows as tenancies end and voids increase whilst awaiting reletting.

Depreciation and obsolescence

Depreciation is the wearing out of an asset over time. This wearing out leads to a loss in income as the asset is less attractive to occupiers, and also loss in capital value as it is of less interest to investors. Depreciation may require redevelopment or refurbishment of the asset, a solution requiring capital outlay and loss of income during the reconstruction process. Depreciation can be economical (relating to changes in economic demand), physical (deterioration of the fabric of the building) or functional (relating to the use of the building) or a combination off all three. Land will need to be distinguished from buildings in this analysis as the former will not depreciate generally (unless contaminated or affected by misuse or bad neighbours) but the latter will. Depreciation can be divided into curable and incurable depreciation. Curable depreciation relates to maintenance but incurable relates to obsolescence. Depreciation includes obsolescence which can be further divided into internal obsolescence, such as the outdated design or facilities of a building (the technical and technological changes which render space useless), and external obsolescence which relates to the decay of the environment and economic changes such as changes in the location of industry (Isaac and Steley 1991). A further analysis of depreciation related to the valuation of property and buildings is undertaken in Chapter 7.

Transferability and divisibility

There are higher transfer charges related to the sale and purchase of property assets than in other competing assets classes. There is a time element involved in land transactions also. As well as being costly in terms of accrued interest charged during the period of the transaction, time can also have an adverse effect in situations requiring a forced sale. If the property market is collapsing in a particular sector or location it may be difficult to dispose of the property and the investor may well be left holding an undesirable asset. The complexity of transfer may involve mistakes being made in the conveyance of rights and liabilities over the land, searches made not being done appropriately. Competing investments like gilts and equities can be sold on day-to-day markets, and if markets fall, computer programmes can be triggered at certain points to ensure that the shares are disposed of before the price falls too far. There is a central market in these share assets with publicised prices so there is a knowledge of the net income that will be received. The delay in property transactions and the nature of offers made in property contracts may often lead to terms being renegotiated up to exchange of contracts. In a good market this may lead to a higher return to the vendor, as with gazumping in the residential owner-occupier markets, but generally these situations build in additional risk and uncertainty and lead to abortive costs. Transfer costs on competing investments often amount to only 1% of the price being paid whereas with property transactions it is often 3–4%. The divisibility of property is difficult and this has led to the move in property unitisation to break down the equity investment into smaller parts more acceptable to the purchasing power and risk profiles of a wider range of investors. Stocks and shares can be purchased in small unit sizes and it is easy to build a portfolio of such assets enabling greater diversification and risk avoidance.

Management problems

Even with a full repairing and insuring (FRI) lease, property requires informed and skilled management to deal with the technical and legal aspects, the complex buildings and demanding tenants. There are numerous pieces of legislation to be considered requiring professional advice, and the social aspects of ownership, noted earlier, can add to the problems of management. Maintenance and management problems can be numerous especially when there is not an FRI lease. The problems include risks relating to voids, accidents and liabilities, deleterious substances (like asbestos which may have been used in the construction of the buildings), dangerous structures, nuisance generated by the building, and so on.

1.2   CHARACTERISTICS OF PROPERTY INVESTMENT

An investment is an asset which produces income or capital growth which will convert to income during, or at the end of the life of the asset. The investment market is often considered peculiar to the UK, a situation where investors in property build buildings and others occupy and pay rent. Such a situation may be a product of the development of the landed estates where historically the landed gentry as a class were divorced from those organising and engaged in manufacturing and commerce. Such a debate is beyond the objectives of this book but certainly the landlord/tenant relationship appears peculiar to the UK and the countries of the old commonwealth (even in Hong Kong before its return to China, the land was generally owned by the Hong Kong government). This is not to say that there is little owner-occupation in the UK but considerations of space allocation here relate more to economic factors such as production, labour, profit rather than investment returns arising from property and land.

Darlow (1983) has suggested three major reasons for this situation:

(i)   a high percentage of the savings of individuals (the collectivisation of savings, discussed elsewhere in this book) is channelled through a small number of private sector financial institutions which have to find investments for their resulting cash flows;

(ii)   the tendency among many manufacturers and retailers in the UK to rent rather than own the properties they occupy, thus creating an income producing investment for a potential landlord;

(iii) the planning climate in the UK, which for most of the post war period has kept the supply of good quality commercial property below demand and thus rents have offered protection against inflation because of shortages and capital values have appreciated.

Principles of property investment

As an introduction to property investment it is useful to make comparisons with, for instance, investment in shares. Such a comparison is often applied to the respective returns but the mechanism and structure of investment in the two media is radically different. These initial differences were summarised by Brett (1989) and are shown in Box 1.1.

Property valuation is a means of providing an assessment of the capital value of, or the income arising from, a property investment. There is a range of possible investment opportunities from works of art through oil futures and gold to shares, government stocks and property. The point of investment is that it provides the investor with an income, growth in capital value of the investment, or both.

Principles of property ownership

Property investment is different from other types of investment in that ownership of physical assets like land and buildings is far more complex than the ownership of a share certificate. It also involves the owner in more responsibility and obligations than other forms of investments.

CHARACTERISTICS OF PROPERTY

---

1. Commercial properties are of high value, whereas shares can be broken down to smaller sizes of ownership. Property ownership thus tends to be in the hands of large financial institutions rather than individuals.
2. Property is not a standardised investment; one share in a particular company is the same as another, but properties are not identical.
3. Property is not a pre-packaged investment; with a share you buy the management. With property you will need to manage it yourself or pay someone to do it.
4. Property is an investment that can be improved by active management. You cannot do this with shares. Property investment may require additional new money to restructure leases, refurbish or redevelop buildings, however.
5. Property investment can be created by finding sites, erecting buildings and finding tenants.
6. Points 3–5 show that some expertise is required in investing in and managing property.
7. There is no single market for commercial property, it is a localised market. The time spent in buying and selling is greater than with shares.
8. Market information is often imperfect and the data surrounding transactions is often not available or kept confidential.
9. The income stream from property is often geared to rent reviews in leases and income increases will not be available until the next review, whereas the income stream from share dividends may change half yearly.
10. Property investment can literally wear out (depreciation of buildings) or be made worthless by external activities (as with land).
11. There are a variety of ownerships in land from freehold to leases and licences which affect the value of the interest and level and risk of the income arising.
12. Different interests will be of interest to different types of investor depending on their tax status or investment requirements for income, capital growth or risk avoidance.
13. Different types of property (different sectors like retail, industrial and offices) generate different returns and have different risk profiles so may be chosen by differing investors.
14. Properties also have various risk profiles depending on whether they are prime (best quality) or secondary or tertiary.
15. Property is presented as a long term investment but may not necessarily be so. Most owners do retain their properties for long periods of time.

Box 1.1   *The characteristics of property: a comparison with company shares*

Source: Adapted from Brett (1989).

Economic value

Land is a scarce resource and its supply is limited. Land can change its use to increase supply in the short term but in the long term it is fixed. Expensive projects such as land reclamation or the possibilities of extra-terrestrial colonisation may be feasible in the long term but the effect on the overall supply of land would be marginal. Value, as related to land, was of great interest to the classical economists, who perceived that the supply of land was fixed and used the concept of economic rent to describe payments not only to land but also to any factor involved in the production process which was unable to adjust its supply readily to changes in the level of demand. Economic rent was thus earned in the form of higher prices for land because of its position of scarcity in the short and long term.

Property valuation

The concept of value is a difficult one to comprehend. Economists relate it to utility but this is not of any practical use when determining actual values in the market. A price may be determined in the market but this may not always equate with the value of the property in the market. Problems of the difference of price and value arise because the market place for property is decentralised and fragmented. For instance you can ascertain the price of your British Telecom shares from the morning papers but the price of an office building might be more difficult to determine. It may be that an identical office block has just been sold and this should tell you the price of the block you are looking at. It should do, but it often does not. The problem is one of imperfect markets in that the transaction is difficult to reconstruct and it could well be that the other parties have limited knowledge of the deal that was actually struck. There is a whole number of reasons why premises are sold and the environment in which transactions are taking place is constantly changing.

Besides the problem of assessing the price of a property (its exchange value), there is also a problem of assessing value when a property is not sold (assessing its worth). Property could be valued for a number of reasons; for mortgage, compulsory purchase or tax reasons, for instance. These valuations do not necessarily lead to a transaction which can support or contradict the valuation, thus the valuation of a property is not an exact figure and it is often adjusted according to the purpose it is used. The approach is summed up by the comment made by the estate agent, asked to add 2 plus 2 by a particularity innumerate client, who replied: 'Are you buying or selling?'

Rates of interest and yields

A yield is important to an investor: it indicates level of earnings, it defines money earned over a time period. If 20% is the yield of an investment it means that £20 is earned for every £100 invested. If the yield is 5% then £5 is earned. Thus 20% as a yield is obviously more attractive but the concept is more complicated because the yield also indicates the risk of the investment. Risk is important; some investments involve greater risk than others so a higher return is offered on risker investments to tempt investors away from safe investments. As an example: in drug-smuggling the risk is high and returns are very high. As an outsider in a horse race, the risk of not winning is high, say 100–1 odds. The payback period is a critical element in investment analysis. Yields can be compared simply using payback period analysis. A 20% yield on £100 is £20 p.a.; the purchase cost of £100 is therefore paid back in 5 years (£100/£20 p.a. = 5 years) and this is the payback period. So at a 5% yield the payback period is 20 years. Risky investments tend to have an earlier payback period; there is an early recoupment of the original investment and the rest is profit. This approach ignores the time preference value of money, that is £1 is worth more now than in 1 year's time. The yield that we expect from a property investment will be determined by a number of factors. A greater risk will mean a higher yield and vice versa. The investor will want the highest yield that can be obtained from any one investment and there is therefore a need to look at and compare yields from different investments.

Rates of interest are considered here in the context of nominal rates of interest (a concept introduced earlier in the chapter). That is, if a company sells stock to investors, it needs to have an interest rate to tempt investors, say 10%. So the investor will receive £10 for every £100 of stock owned. For example:

Example 1.2: Nominal interest and market interest rates

At time of stock issue:

nominal rate of interest	10% p.a.
nominal price of stock	£100
thus return is	£10 p.a.

The price of the stock may start at this level but the price will change over a period and if the £10 p.a. return is still offered on the original £100 nominal value of the stock, the rate of interest will change:

price falls to	£80
return still offered	£10
rate of interest (yield) =	£10/£80 = 12.5% p.a.

A £10 p.a. return is still being offered because it is based on the par value of the stock, par value being the original offer price. So the only time when the nominal rate of interest equals yield is at the date of issue. The price of the stock issued will go up and down according to market fluctuations but the nominal rate at which the stock is issued will be based on the base rate in the financial markets. The stock exchange analysis carried out previously gives us a clear relationship between income, yield and capital value. If the rate of interest or yield is 10% and the capital value of the investment is £100, then the expected income is £10 p.a. By working back from this calculation, if an investment produces an income of £10 p.a. and the investor requires a yield of 10% p.a., the price paid by the investor is £100. This is the basis of the investment method of valuation.

The investment method of property valuation

Most investors seek to obtain a return on their invested money either as an annual income or a capital gain. The investment method of valuation is traditionally concerned with the former. Where the investor has a known sum of money to invest on which a particular return is required, the income can be readily calculated from:

$$\text{Income} = \text{Capital} \times \frac{i}{100} \quad \text{where } i = \text{rate of return required}$$

For example, if £1000 is to be invested with a required rate of return of 8% the income will be:

$$\text{Income} = £1000 \times \frac{8}{100} = £800 \text{ p.a.}$$

In this type of problem the capital is known and the income is to be calculated. In the case of real property, the income (rent) is known, either from the actual rent passing under the lease or estimated from the letting of similar comparable properties, and the capital value is usually calculated. The formula above has to be changed so that the capital becomes the subject:

$$\text{Capital} = \text{Income} \times \frac{100}{i}$$

What capital sum should be paid for an investment producing £8000 per annum and a return of 8% is required?

$$\text{Capital} = £800 \times \frac{100}{8} = £10\,000$$

This process is known as 'capitalising' the income, in other words converting an annual income into a capital sum. It is essential that the income capitalised is 'net', that is, clear of any expenses incurred by the investor under the lease, so therefore the formula can be modified to:

$$C = NI \times \frac{100}{i} \qquad \text{where } C = \text{Capital}$$
$$NI = \text{Net Income}$$
$$i = \text{Rate of Return}$$

For given rates of return $100/i$ will be constant; for example:

Rate of Return	$100/i$
10%	10
8%	12.5
12%	8.33

This constant is known as the Present Value of £1 per annum, or more commonly in real property valuation, Years Purchase (abbreviated to YP). The formula can thus be finally modified to:

$$C = NI \times YP$$

Where C is the capital value, NI is net income and YP is the years purchase. The YP, calculated by using $100/i$ will only apply to incomes received in perpetuity which are those received from freehold interests let at a full market rent or rack rent. Incomes to be received for shorter periods use a YP which must be calculated using a more complex formula but tables of constants are available and Parry's Valuation and Conversion tables are most commonly used. The traditional approach of Parry's Tables was to assume that the rental income was received annually in arrear whereas in practice it is received quarterly in advance. Although the tables have been modified much traditional valuation uses the original assumption for simplicity. However, whatever income basis is used the two essential elements required to perform the calculation are: the period of time the investment is to last in terms of years, and the rate of return required, usually known as the all risks yield (ARY).

To summarise, to estimate the capital value of an interest in real property using the traditional investment method, three elements are required:

(i)   The net income to be received.
(ii)   The period for which the net income will be received.
(iii)   The required yield.

(i) and (ii) will be obtained from the lease of the subject property or if the property is unlet; an estimate of the rental value will be obtained from lettings of comparable properties. (iii) will be obtained from analysis of sales of comparable investments. A valuer must therefore have knowledge of two separate markets, the letting and investment markets.

Example 1.3: A basic investment method calculation.

Assume prime shops in Oxford Street have a yield of 4%. The income from the shop you are interested in is £200 000 net p.a. How much would you pay for the freehold interest?

Net Income	£200 000 p.a. ×
Years Purchase @ 4% in perpetuity	25 YP*
Capital Value	£5 000 000

$$*YP = \frac{100}{Yield} = \frac{100\%}{4\%} = 25$$

Characteristics of property as an investment

Property investment is a long-term commitment of funds. Transfer costs and purchase time (up to six months) restrict opportunities for short-term dealings. Investors in property are looking for growth of income and capital. Note that these two aspects are interrelated through the relationship of the all risks yield = income/capital value. In the UK the tradition in the commercial market is for occupiers to lease premises, thus ownership and occupation are split and an investment market in property is opened up. In the US and Europe there is more owner-occupation. In considering the characteristics of property investment it is necessary to look at a number of factors: the property investment market, the nature of income, the rate of return and the level of income.

The nature of the market

The market is fragmented and poorly recorded. There is no central focus for trading either through a central market or by a computerised screen. Property is diverse and each property has unique characteristics so the market is unstructured. The locational characteristics can reduce the size of the market. There is imperfect knowledge in the market (hence the difference between valuation and subsequent analysis). There are no central prices nor registry of transactions as land registry files have only recently been made available to the public. There is restriction of movement into and out of the market because of the constraints of time, legal considerations and financial considerations, so prices stick. In the short run the supply of property is inelastic. This can be seen from Figure 1.1 showing economic supply and demand: the supply S is fixed and if demand is increased from $D1$ to D_2 then the price increases from P_1 to P_2, more than if the supply was elastic (where the s curve would be upward sloping).

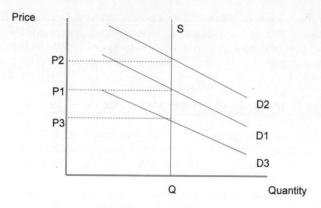

Figure 1.1   *Supply of land*

Nature of the income

The market is made up of a number of types of investment which produce different types of income. For instance: rack rented freeholds, reversionary investments, secure ground rents, short leasehold profit rents, turnover rents and so on. The type of investment will determine the amount and timing of the income stream.

The rate of return

The rate of return can be analysed in its simplified form from an analysis of initial (all risk) yields. An analysis of yield levels over the least 25 years shows that for prime yields (little research has been carried out in areas other than prime properties) there is less variation than in other indices. Since 1977, when the investment market was becoming more settled after the crash of 1974, property yields provided a more stable performance than indices relating to gilt yields or the level of interest rates.

Level of income

Changes in the level of rental value over time show a relationship with the level of inflation. Thus although the money level of rents has varied over the period, the real level of rents shows a real increase based on periods of high inflation. Land is more durable than other commodities. Purchasers buy land for future income or use and thus they forgo present consumption to do this. If purchasers buy properties for personal occupation then they are in the position of receiving an income equivalent to a rent which they would otherwise have to pay if they did not own the property. Property is thus purchased for investment as well as consumption purposes. Land is heterogeneous, each piece is different, each property is unique by location, but properties do have some characteristics in common and one property can be substituted for another. The price of property is high relative to individual earnings and thus people borrow to buy property and the availability and price of credit has an important bearing on demand.

Legal factors have a serious effect on the supply and demand for property. The Rent Acts which controlled income from tenanted property, for instance, restricted the rights to increase the level of rents and thus led to a subsequent decline in investment in the private rented sector.

1.3   PROPERTY INVESTMENT COMPARED TO OTHER INVESTMENTS

Property is only one of a number of competing investment media and investors will put together a portfolio of different investments to reflect their attitudes to risk and return and perhaps other objectives (social and psychological as well as economic, as previously discussed). In 1989 a typical institutional portfolio (pension fund or insurance company) would be UK equities (55%), overseas equities (22%), gilts (12%), property (8%) and cash and other investments (2%) (Dubben and Sayce 1991). This ratio of holdings has varied greatly over a number of years with the property proportion rising to 25% at its peak and falling to around 7% by 1996; this falling-off in the allocation of property in institutional funds' portfolios is of great concern to the property profession. Sweeney (1988) has suggested using a mean-variance technique showing that the inclusion of property in the portfolio reduces risk with examples of low risk portfolios have at least 20% property. These findings are discussed later in the book. Besides property as an investment there are a number of alternatives:

- Bank and building society accounts;
- Articles for use (chattels);
- National savings;
- Guaranteed income and growth bonds;
- Government and public authority shares;
- Company stocks and shares;
- Unit trusts and investment trusts;
- Futures and traded options.

To obtain a balanced portfolio an investor will want a spread of investments similar to the way a unit trust works, but investors will usually chose a mixture of government stocks and company shares as the basis for a portfolio.

What affects property values?

To begin considering elements which affect property values we need to consider the nature of land and buildings. Property consists of two elements, land and buildings, and these need to be separated. Land tends to appreciate but property depreciates so an overall return will need to consider these two opposite elements. The main factors which affect property values are discussed in the following paragraphs.

The international situation can affect levels of confidence in the market but probably not as badly as in the stock market. Interest rates will affect borrowing and therefore activity in the new and second-hand markets for property, that is in the development of new property as well as investment in existing property. The mood of the national economy affects the confidence of investors. The levels of disposable income available affect house prices and the amount available for investment. Government policies affect property values; property is taxed both in terms of capital gains and the income derived from rents; changes in the tax situation can affect the investor's interest. Government legislation can encourage or discourage investment directly or through its fiscal (tax) and monetary (adjustment of interest rates) policy. The local economy can affect land prices; land prices and rents will tend to be higher in areas where the local economy is thriving. This could be shown in the comparison in the 1980s between house prices and industrial rentals in the London suburbs and, say, Teesside.

Physical characteristics and location are also important for value. For instance the most fertile and thus the most expensive agricultural land is located in eastern England. Location is important; an office block may need to be close to a central business area, have transport links and have attractive surroundings. Fashion and local demand can affect price. Trendy recreational/leisure locations and fashionable areas can increase price levels, as can the gentrification of traditional working class districts. Favoured locations may be the spin-off of successful regeneration opportunities like Covent Garden or in areas of historic or interesting built environments like Greenwich. The individual design features of properties can affect value. These may include architectural details, space and design, the scale and nature of the garden and the age and style of the property. Tenure may affect the property price. A property may be freehold or leasehold; this is an important area of valuation analysis and is discussed later. Condition and state of repair will affect value as will the availability of services. The services include the provision of central heating in a house and the installation of air conditioning or computer wiring and trunking in an office building.

The potential for extension, renovation, reuse and redevelopment will affect the value. The ease of purchase and sale, that is the ease of transferability, will affect the property price. Prices will be depressed if a transaction takes a lot time to complete, as property investors are often paying interest on monies used for purchase. Lack of information can affect property price. Because of the nature of the investment, people will not generally buy a property investment unless they have full details of the investment. You would not buy a property, for instance, unless you had carried out the necessary searches of the title and considered any future developments in the area which may affect the property.

Legal interests in land

The two principal interests in land are freehold and leasehold interests. Other legal interests or estates in land are easements, restrictive covenants and licences. Freehold property are properties in which the owners hold ownership absolutely and in perpetuity. The owner is either in possession of the property (i.e. the occupier) or derives rents arising from leases or tenancies granted (an investor). Leasehold properties are subject to legal agreements allowing the lessees rights over the property for a term of years. Freehold and leasehold interests are defined as 'legal estates' by the Law of Property Act 1925 and these are enforceable against anyone. Other interests are termed equitable interests and can be enforced against some people only. Leasehold and equitable interests are carved out of the freehold interest. At the end of a lease there is a reversion to the landlord (that is, the property ownership reverts back). However, this reversion has been restricted by government legislation. For instance, the Rent Acts affected short leases and the Lease-hold Reform Act affected long leases, the Agricultural Holdings Act affected agricultural land and the Landlord and Tenant Act affected commercial property. There are two principal types of lease:

- The *building or ground lease*, where the lessee (the person who takes the lease) erects buildings on the vacant site. These leases tend to be long leases because of the obligation to build, and are usually 99 or 125 years but could be as much as 999 years.
- The *occupation lease*, where the lease is of both land and buildings for occupation. The lease is a medium to long-term one, perhaps say 20 or 25 years, with the rent being reviewed every 5 years.

Subleases are granted by lessees and carved from their leasehold interest. The nature of leases and subleases is shown in Figure 1.2.

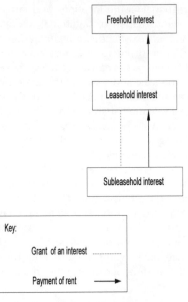

Figure 1.2   *Leasehold interests*

Other interests include restrictive covenants and easements which are restrictions on the use of land by a freeholder or leaseholder. A covenant is a contractual obligation in a deed. An easement is a right under common law which burdens one piece of land for the benefit of another. Easements are such things are rights of way, rights of support and rights of light and ventilation. Interests in land have to be distinguished from permissions to enter upon land such as licences, and this distinction is summarised as follows:

Legal interests	Equitable interests

Legal interests and legal estates such as:
    freeholds
    leaseholds
    easements
    covenants
	Equitable interests, grants under wills or settlements such as:
	    permissions to enter land
	    licences

Legislation on land and premises

Beside the legal interests involved in land, land is also constrained by government statutes. As has been described earlier, the government can intervene in respect of lessees and tenants of certain properties, both to give security of tenure and to control levels of rent. The government also intervenes through its fiscal policy to tax income and capital gains arising from land. Finally the local authorities also have statutory control over the development and use of land through the Town and Country Planning Acts and over the construction of buildings through the Building Regulations. There is a wealth of legislation relating to the use and condition of premises, including the Offices, Shops and Railway Premises Act, the Factories Act, the Fire Precautions Act, the Housing Acts and Health and Safety legislation.

The process of valuation

Valuation is a matter of opinion; it is an individual's subjective assessment of different factors. Different weights can be given to various opinions, and a valuer who has studied the different methods of valuation and who gets his/her valuations to accord with market evidence will be listened to and inform others. Computers can assist with the assembling of market evidence and comparable transactions and they can be used for complex mathematical calculations. In the end, however, it is the art of valuation that counts. A valuer is required to value property, that is to find a market value when a market transaction for the property has yet to take place. This is a responsible and expensive decision if things go wrong. If you put a property up for sale at too low a valuation you are likely to lose money; at too high a valuation the property will stick on the market and take a long time to sell.

1.4   DECISION-MAKING, RISK AND INFLATION

Risk and inflation are important matters for property investors. The yield used by property investors is an interest rate return and interest rates are calculated on the basis of three elements. The components of the interest rate or yield consists of:

- compensation for the time preference of money;
- an inflation allowance to maintain the real value of the return;
- an element for risk-taking.

Time preference element

This element exists as a compensation to the investor who now cannot spend the investment immediately but will need to wait until the investment is sold. The compensation stems from the view that individuals prefer to have money available now rather than later. The money could thus be consumed or invested, allowing for immediate satisfaction from the consumables of income from the investment. The interest rate needs to entice individuals to part with their money and delay consumption.

Inflation allowance

An inflation allowance used in interest rates should be the reflection of the investor's anticipation of the inflation rate and this may differ from economic assumptions held by the government and other investors. At this point the analysis can show the relationship between market rates of interest which are inclusive of inflation and real rates of interest. This is given by the equation:

$$(1 + \text{real rate of interest}) \times (1 + \text{rate of general inflation})$$
$$= (1 + \text{market rate of interest})$$

or $\qquad (1 + i) \times (1 + g) = (1 + e) \qquad\qquad$ (1.1)

so $\qquad\qquad i = \dfrac{(1 + e)}{(1 + g)} - 1$

where i is the real rate of interest, g is the rate of general inflation and e is the market rate of interest, all as decimals. As an example, if the rental growth (at market rate $= e$) is 6% and the rate of inflation (g) is 7% the real rate of growth can be seen to be negative, around -1%, or more precisely:

$$i = \frac{(1 + 0.06)}{(1 + 0.07)} - 1 = -0.0093$$

Risk premium

This is the addition to the risk-free interest rate to take into account the risk of the investment. There is a trade-off between risk and reward. For additional risk a greater reward is expected by the investor and vice versa. This relationship is represented diagrammatically by Figure 1.3 showing the capital market line with $E(R)$ being the expected return and RF the risk free return. Risk, reward and the relationships between them are discussed in detail later in the book. By dividing the real rate of interest into its elements of time preference and the risk premium, the element of the risk premium can be exposed. Thus:

$$(1 + i) = (1 + d)(1 + r) \qquad\qquad (1.2)$$

Inserting into equation (1.1) above:

$$(1 + d)(1 + r)(1 + g) = (1 + e)$$

Here d and r are the time preference and risk elements respectively, rearranging:

$$e = (1 + g)(1 + d)(1 + r) - 1$$

and if the risk element was taken out, a risk-free return (RFR) would be:

$$RFR = (1 + i)(1 + d) - 1$$
$$\text{and} \qquad e = (1 + RFR)(1 + r) - 1$$

Multiplying out:

$$e = 1 + r + RFR + rRFR - 1$$

But *rRFR* will be small and an approximation is $e = RFR + r$, thus the market rate of interest is equal to the risk-free rate plus the risk premium attached by the market.

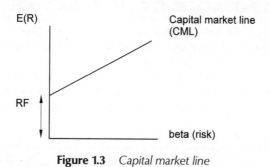

Figure 1.3   *Capital market line*

Property as an inflation hedge

Is property a good hedge against inflation? Matysiak *et al.*(1995) used a multivariate analysis of long-term total returns and inflation data over the period 1963–93. They found no evidence that property returns provide a hedge on an annual basis against expected or unexpected components of inflation. Barkham *et al.* (1995) found a relationship between property and inflation in the short and long term but that the adjustment of property to inflation or vice versa is very weak or slow. They used cointegration techniques and commented that their contribution to the debate is to bring back a longer-term perspective to the argument of the need to supplement property investment in portfolios. Cointegration techniques have been developed to deal with time series where the variables under consideration are non-stationary and therefore this method can be used to test a statistical long-term relationship between property returns and inflation. Nevertheless, the findings from Barkham's study showed that property is not a consistent hedge over the time periods examined.

1.5   THE PROPERTY INVESTMENT MARKET

After the 1989/92 recession and certainly by the middle of 1993, market confidence had increased and had been shown in a number of surveys. Surveys of property lenders showed more inclination to finance non-risky property investment. In addition, by the beginning of 1994, confidence was also returning to business tenants. The Jones Lang Wootton Property Confidence Review (*Property Week* 1994) has recorded the most positive findings in business confidence since the survey began in 1969. A large majority of companies are more confident of their short-term prospects. However, despite this renewed confidence, companies are still disposing of space, although the space shed by companies fell from 0.33 million m² in the six months to July 1993 to 0.11 million m² in the six months to January 1994. Renewed confidence in the investment markets had lowered yields to a level at which, compared to yields for gilts, they were becoming uncompetitive. Property companies in the market had been re-rated, signifying that their market capitalisation as viewed from the share price has increased rapidly, thus enabling property investment and property trading companies to borrow more against their equity.

In the present market (1996) there is a belief that property will outperform both equities and gilts in the short term and research points to a higher level of net institutional investment in 1996. Institutional fund managers are expecting property in 1996 to provide a return of 10.9% against 8.4% for equities and 5.6% for gilts. This renewed interest by institutional investors is a turnaround from the previous attitudes of the pension funds who in the last two years have been disinvesting. Investors are now looking for rental growth and the favourite sector is retail warehousing (Lennox 1996b). This previous disinvestment had led to a fall in net institutional investment in the first two quarters of 1996 from £173m to £71m. The figures for the third quarter are shown in Figure 1.4.

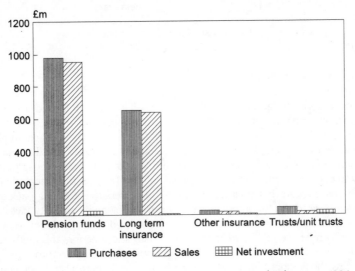

Figure 1.4   *Net institutional investment in property: third quarter 1996*

Other surveys also indicate increased confidence in property investment. The Investment Property Forum/*Estates Gazette* survey of investment intentions indicated a return to favour for property. Property returns had been low for 1995, with the Investment Property Databank (IPD) figures showing a 4.1 % return compared with 28% for equities and 18% for gilts. But the survey indicated a renewed interest in the retail sector with 92% saying they would be buying retail, although with a parallel disinvestment, with 73% saying they would be selling offices. The reasons given for the renewed interest in property is:

(i)   the price of property relative to other assets;
(ii)   better property performance;
(iii)   risk diversification;
(iv)   opportunities for proactive management (Lennox 1996a).

The key areas for renewed interest were retail investment, especially in the regions (North West, Scotland and West Midlands), and secondly industrial investments in the South East and West Midlands. There was a noticeable yield gap developing between primary and secondary property. Current yields (April 1996) are shown in Figure 1.5.

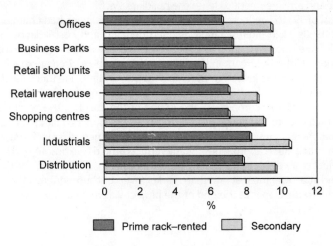

Figure 1.5   *Current yields at April 1996*

1.6   INDIRECT INVESTMENT IN PROPERTY

Background

In the post-war era of the 1950s and 1960s, the modern·style property investors and developers emerged and property companies established themselves. The stimulation for property investment and development was based on the shortage of space following the destruction of buildings in the Second World War and this shortage combined with a period of low inflation. This meant that rental levels of property developments increased dramatically during the period whilst building costs were static. The other major stimulants to property investment and development were fixed interest rates and the ability to finance deals with 100% debt finance without any equity input. The growth of property companies relied on a strategy of refinancing the development on completion with a fixed interest mortgage for 20 to 30 years. Financial institutions also provided finance for the developments during this period and there was a link-up between developers and institutions. Over this period, the institutions, generally insurance companies, started to insist on having a greater share in the equity returns available. They thus purchased shares in the property companies and also made their mortgage debenture loans convertible to shares so that an increased equity stake could be obtained if the development schemes were successful. However, the taxation structure in the late 1960s affected these arrangements. The financial institutions, which were termed gross funds because they did not pay tax, suffered from the taxation of income and dividends under these arrangements and thus new financial structures emerged. In the late 1960s and early 1970s developers began using sale and leaseback arrangements; the project was financed in the development stage using short-term bank finance and was sold on completion. As time wore on, a shortage of schemes became apparent and the institutions (the insurance companies and subsequently the pensions funds) purchased development sites directly from property developers and then tied them to a building agreement and an agreement to lease the buildings back.

The crash of 1974/75 reflected how the economic indications had changed since the 1950s and 1960s. High interest rates, lessened demand and cost inflation meant that profit levels were not maintained as capital costs increased and income voids led to an accumulation of interest arrears. In the 1980s and 1990s the revised approach to funding was that the funder was invited to purchase the site and provide funds for the building contract. Interest would be rolled up during the development period and added to the development costs. On completion and letting of the building, the profit on development was paid over to the developer. On this basis developers built up a large turnover basically matching their site funding and project management skills with the institutional investors' funding. Such approaches greatly reduced the risk exposure of the developer to the project. Forward funding meant that the project was financed for the development period at a lower interest rate than market levels but subsequently the capital sum received by the developer at the end of the project was reduced by valuing at a higher yield to recoup the interest lost.

Property company shares

Property company shares provide a medium for indirect investment in property which deals with some of the disadvantages of direct investment previously outlined. Shares are available in smaller units and can be easily traded. Property shares specifically have been viewed as an effective protection against inflation because of the durability of property. Shares of a property investment company where most of the revenue to the company is derived from rental income also provide the investor with a high degree of income security. Thus property shares traditionally were seen to provide both an element of protection against the effects of inflation and greater security to the investor.

Two types of property company are discernible. The investment company normally holds property for long periods and takes its revenue from rental income. The trading or dealing company will develop and sell property, earning revenues on disposal of the property rather than through income. Because of different tax positions the functions should be kept separate, but the most extensive developers will also often be investment companies which may or may not retain a completed development within the portfolio of the investment company.

Direct versus indirect investment

Long-term savings institutions, the pension funds and insurance companies are the main sources of equity finance in property. The history of the involvement of institutions has been a move towards direct funding of property development and investments. Smaller institutions wanting to take a stake in commercial property but lacking the size of resources to invest direct can use indirect routes into property (see Figure 1.6). The main indirect routes are property company shares, property bonds usually tied to unit linked

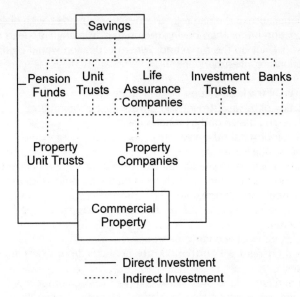

Figure 1.6   *Direct and Indirect Investment in Property*

Source: Brett (1983).

life assurance schemes, exempt unit trusts and managed funds and mortgages and debentures (Brett 1983).

From 1965 on, property bonds were issued. These are insurance linked investments in property aimed at the general public. They were similar to unit trusts but were not allowed to invest in property directly. Pension funds and charities were able to benefit from the formation of property unit trusts and thus tax exempt funds could take property into their portfolio.

Indirect investment vehicles are now seen by institutional investors as a means of enhancing direct property performance in the medium term by creating a diverse market for property investments. This may in the short-term result in diversion of funds from direct property investment but in the longer term as the property market thus becomes more liquid, a large proportion of investment will be drawn in. In DTZ's 1996 report, *Money into Property*, half the respondents to their survey said that indirect vehicles would offer more diversification against equities and bonds than direct holdings in property but only a third said that a successful indirect investment market would lead them to reduce their own property holdings (Lennox 1996b).

1.7   DIRECT INVESTMENT IN PROPERTY

Property investment involves a long-term investment and a commitment because of the nature of the returns and the costs of transferability. Many property investors are also property developers, but they may well keep property development in their portfolio rather than dispose of them as would property traders. Well-selected properties can offer income growth and capital growth over the longer period. Property investment in the UK is strong because of the nature of the investment market, with occupiers taking leases for occupation rather than buying themselves. In many European countries for instance this would not be the norm and owner-occupation would predominate. The main considerations for investment are:

- the nature of the legal interest being acquired;
- the location of the investment and surrounding environment;
- the nature and design of the property itself;
- planning proposals for the area;
- terms of existing leases;
- expectation of income and capital growth from the property investment;
- the level of future demand, both for renting the accommodation and selling the investment at some future date;
- possible future changes in fashion, technology, demography and transportation infrastructure;
- underlying national economic trends;
- structural changes within the industry or sector from where tenant demand originates;
- current and future level of available competitive accommodation;
- government intervention, new legislation and taxes (Darlow 1983).

The acquisition sequence

The sequence of acquisition is shown in Figure 1.7 opposite giving details of the procedures carried out in the acquisition process.

REFERENCES

Barkham, R. J., Ward, C.W. R and Henry O.T. (1995) 'The Inflation-Hedging Characteristics of UK Property', *Journal of Property Finance*, vol. 7, no. 1, pp. 62–76.

Baum, A. E. and Schofield, A. (1991) 'Property as a Global Asset' in P. Venmore-Rowland, P. Brandon and T. Mole (eds), *Investment, Procurement and Performance in Construction*, RICS, London.

Brett, M. (1983) 'Indirect Investment in Property' in C. Darlow (ed.), *Valuation and Investment Appraisal*, Estates Gazette, London

Brett, M. (1989) 'Characteristics of Property', *Estates Gazette*, 21 January, p. 14.

Catalano, A. (1996) 'Property with No Inflation', *Estates Gazette*, 8 June, p. 46.

Currie, D. and Scott, A. (1991) *The Place of Commercial Property in the UK Economy*, London Business School, January.

Darlow, C. (ed.) (1983) *Valuation and Investment Appraisal*, Estates Gazette, London.

Dubben, N. and Sayce, S. (1991) *Property Portfolio Management: An Introduction*, Routledge, London.

Estates Gazette (1996) 'Investment Funds Give Thumbs Up to Property', *Estates Gazette*, 28 September, p. 56.

Fraser, W. D. (1993) *Principles of Property Investment and Pricing*, Macmillan, London.

French, N. (1995) 'Property – Love it or Leave it', *Estates Gazette*, 7 October, pp. 126–7. Hargitay, S. E. and Sui-Ming Yu (1993) *Property Investment Decisions*, E. & F.N. Spon, London.

Isaac, D. and Steley, T. (1991) *Property Valuation Techniques*, Macmillan, London.

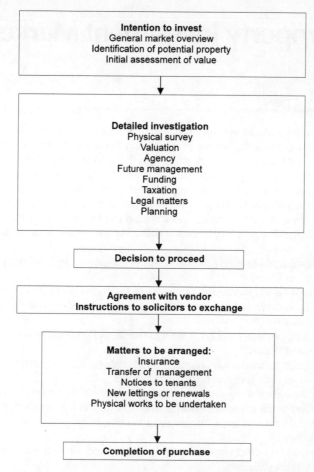

Figure 1.7   *Acquisition sequence (adapted from Darlow 1983)*

Lawson, D. (1995) 'Inflated Opinions: Barber White Inflation Report', *Property Week*, 16 March, pp. 20–1.

Lennox, K. (1996a) 'Thumbs Up for Property: IPF/EG survey', *Estates Gazette*, 20 April, p. 41.

Lennox, K. (1996b) 'Property on the Up', *Estates Gazette*, 7 September, pp. 50–1.

Matysiak, G., Hoesli, M., MacGregor, B. and Nanathakumaran, N. (1995) 'Long-Term Inflation-Hedging Characteristics of UK Commercial Property' *Journal of Property Finance*, vol. 7, no. 1, pp. 50–61.

Property Week (1994) 'JLW Review Reveals Most Positive Business Confidence Since 1989', *Property Week*, 21 April 1994, p. 10.

Sweeney, F. (1988) '20% in Property – a Viable Strategy', *Estates Gazette*, 13 February, pp. 26–8.

Tarbert, H. (1995) 'Is Commercial Property a Hedge against Inflation? A Cointegration Approach' *Journal of Property Finance*, vol. 2, no. 1, pp. 77–98.

2 Property Investment Markets

2.1 INTRODUCTION

The market for commercial property is an established investment market but because there is no central market place for property and because investment properties are unique there is a difficulty in understanding how the market works. This is compounded by the fact that information of the product in the market and the nature of transactions is restricted; information is passed verbally rather than properly documented in the press or reports. The actual detail of the transaction in the market, the details of rents passing, the nature of the lease terms agreed and the yield used in any capital transaction may remain confidential. The property market is thus a dangerous place for the lay person to invest in.

The characteristics of property markets have been summarised by Darlow (1983):

- the market is fragmented, poorly recorded, secretive and generally unregulated;
- there is no central agency or institution such as Lloyds insurance for the insurance industry;
- there is no physical focal point such as the Stock Exchange for the transaction of stocks and shares;
- it is difficult to abstract an aggregation of property transactions;
- the market is diverse and complex in nature;
- there are national, regional and local dimensions to the market; property markets tend to be parochial, disorganised and vary in classification, such as geographical location, type of property, quality of property, value and size of investment;
- there is an imperfect knowledge of the market and within the market there is no central price or listing;
- there is no central registry of transactions which is complete;
- the market is monopolistic, because of the inelastic supply of land;
- there is no freedom of entry and exit from the market because of locational, legal, finance, taxation and other constraints.

The late 1970s was a critical period for property investment; its performance was out-performing inflation. By the early 1980s, average rental growth was under-performing inflation and returns from the capital markets was falling in certain sectors. According to the Richard Ellis Monthly Indices, only since 1986 has property begun to show significant real returns. In the early 1990s, wider performance measures, matched by increasingly sophisticated market research and analysis as property returns fell, produced a much keener understanding of the components of property investment of yield, rent and valuations methods, and by the mid-1980s property was being measured relatively as well as absolutely. In the late 1970s, capital growth was driven by falling yields, in 1987–8, capital growth was generated by rental growth. In 1988 Richard Ellis tested the hypothesis that the property market moves counter-cyclically to equities and gilts and is thus a good prospect for the diversification of a portfolio. This study found:

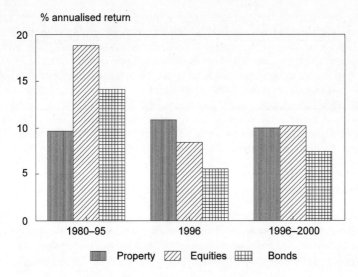

Figure 2.1 *Comparative performance*

Source: Lennox (1996).

(i)   *very limited similarity* between property returns and equities (0.10 correlation coefficient);
(ii)   *no similarity* between property returns and gilts (0.03 correlation coefficient);
(iii) gilts and equity returns were *more in line* (0.44 correlation). (Barter 1988)

The comparative performance of property against other assets over the period 1980–96 and forecast for the period 1996–2000 is shown in Figure 2.1 (Lennox 1996).

If one takes away the sentiment of land and building, then a property investment is basically a flow of income arising from a property asset which can be distributed in many different ways to offer investors differing degrees of risk and thus differing yields and capital values. This is the basis of property securitisation and the innovative forms of property finance which have been developed. These new financial techniques attempt to overcome property's inherent illiquidity and inflexibility. But according to Barter (1988), the key concerns about property as an investment medium remain:

Illiquidity

Properties take 3 months to buy and sell. There is no certainty of price and terms until contracts are exchanged. This problem is acute for properties with capital values above £20 million because of the relatively small supply of potential single purchasers in the market especially when there are no international purchasers. There are problems in appraising and financing the more substantial developments.

Inflexibility

There is a high unit cost with property purchases and little flexibility in the purchase; one needs to buy the whole. There are problems in portfolio diversification and management here. Property shares and property units offer some opportunity to diversify but property companies are taxed in the same way as other companies and unauthorised property unit trusts are only available to pension funds and certain types of charities and cannot be listed. Now there are authorised trusts for the general public but these may remain unlisted and have a corporation tax liability on the income. Some of the problems of illiquidity and inflexibility have been addressed by 'swapping' properties in matched deals. This avoids the exposure and bad publicity of putting properties up for sale in a poor market. A recent example was a swap valued at £34.35m in which the Provident Mutual sold a mixed portfolio of six office, retail and industrial properties to Allied London in exchange for eight retail warehouses, valued at £21.6m, together with £12.75m in cash (*Estates Times* 1993).

Growth of debt finance

There has been a substantial increase in bank lending to the property sector in recent years. This has replaced new equity investment by institutions. This may pose a threat to the property market and is discussed later in the book although the inflow of money into property from banks is now decreasing.

Valuation methodology and precision

Conventional valuation methods are inflexible. The all-risk approach of traditional valuation methods is difficult to apply to more illiquid properties such as major shopping centres and substantial office buildings. A number of cases reflecting errors in the valuation of hotels and restaurants also confirm this. Conventional valuations also have difficulty in the valuation of over-rented property where rents are expected to fall on review.

The future role of the property profession

The liberalisation of the financial markets and the increased importance of debt in property funding require new competencies for chartered surveyors. The demands of the Financial Services Act for those providing information on finance and funding will require different and greater competence in the financial area. In this area and others, the professional institutions are reorientating themselves to the market.

Short-termism

Property is a long-term investment and cannot compete on similar terms with investments that pay off on a much shorter time horizon. Recent attitudes of funders and managers of companies in the UK indicate a short-term approach to investment and performance which may in most cases be a reflection of the recent difficult times in which these companies have had to operate. Companies may in some cases have opted for very short-term investment appraisals and rapid payback. The pressure to perform well has not only led fund managers to increase their activity in managing funds but also led to a short-term perspective for investment. This strategy focuses on the short-term performance of companies in arriving at the valuation of a company's worth with emphasis on current profit performance and dividend payments. This perspective, suggested by Pike and Neale (1993), has many consequences across the spectrum of companies, including:

(i)   The neglect of the long term by management leading to a failure to under-take important long-term investments in resources and research and development.

(ii) The volatility of short-term corporate results becoming exaggerated in securities markets, producing unacceptable fluctuations in share prices.

Because of its long-term production cycle, these consequences are likely to be very damaging to property and construction. A survey carried out by the Department of Industry's Innovation Advisory Board in 1990 concluded that City influence on corporate activity led to companies prioritising short-term profits and dividends at the expense of research and development and other innovative investment and that practices of key financial institutions sustained these priorities. Researchers in the US have concluded that the increasing shareholder power of institutional investors has had a damaging effect on research and development expenditure amongst US firms. The financiers of the City of London reject this criticism by saying that much of the responsibility for the lack of long-term innovation investment is attributable to managers, to their preference for growth by acquisition, their poor record of commercial development and their reward systems based on short-term targets (Pike and Neale 1993). The implications for property in this respect are very clear: property development and the development of its associated transport, social and services infrastructure is a long-term project. Development and refurbishment underpin the property investment market. Projects on difficult town centre sites or involving major infrastructure works encounter problems of risk and uncertainty as they extend into the future. Then there are the problems of high transfer cost and illiquidity in property. To force a sale of a development or investment property at an inappropriate time, for instance halfway through a building contract, could cause a collapse in the price of the asset. This effect is accentuated because of the locational attributes of property; markets are localised and imperfect. The problem of short-term-ism is that such an attitude is inappropriate to property investment where long-term strategy and returns are the key to successful projects.

2.2   PROPERTY CYCLES

The property industry shows a cycle of activity which reflects the general business cycle. This problem, relating to changes in the returns in the market and having a dramatic effect on investment and development activity in the market, is especially evident in the office sector and is discussed in this light in Chapter 4. Recent research by the Royal Institution of Chartered Surveyors (1994) provided some insights into the operation of this cycle. The research looked at the structure of the property industry and found that there were a number of interest groups operating in the market — occupiers, investors and developers. For occupiers the property was an input to their production process, a factor of production for their goods and services; for investors it provided an asset on which returns would be generated and compared to other asset classes; and for developers property was the output of their production process. The interaction between theses groupings gives the indications of how the market operates. In the research, property cycles were defined as recurrent but irregular fluctuations in the rate of all-property total returns. Aggregate property returns were chosen to show the cyclical patterns. Rental performance, yield movements and development activities are linked to the property cycle but these linkages are elastic and flexible. Property cycles were found to be of 4–5 years duration and these cycles match the general business cycle in the economy. The causes of the cycles could be grouped in two areas:

(i)   causes external to the property industry;
(ii)   those produced in the operation of the property industry.

External influences in the occupier markets, cyclical demand factors, GDP, consumer spending, financial and business services and manufacturing demand act as the prime influences on rental values; interest rates and inflation also influence rent values in some markets. In the investment markets the external drivers are bond yields and inflation which have a significant influence on property yields and property investment by UK financial institutions. The internal influences or drivers are the development cycle, the development lag (caused by the inflexibility in the building stock) and rent. Development activity showed internal cyclical supply patterns without even considering the external demand factors.

The formal findings of the survey were that:

(i)   the UK property industry shows a recurrent cycle which meets the qualitative definition applied to economic cycles but cannot be described definitively by statistical techniques;
(ii)   the property cycle is the compounded result of cyclical influence from the wider economy, which is coupled with cyclical tendencies which are inherent in the property market;
(iii)   the critical linkages between property cycles and economic cycles can be captured in simple models.

Further research is thus required into the external and internal drivers to discover whether this impact can be smoothed thus taking away the excesses of the cycle. The property market has integrated with the financial sector and there are wider implications for a market collapse in the sector. In the 1974 collapse it was secondary banks which were involved, but now there is much greater bank involvement. The damage that can be done to the financial system in the event of a collapse will be more general, the so-called contagion effect. The property cycle is related to the business cycle and this can be seen as a series of fluctuations in activity which proceed in an irregular way: depression (low level of consumer demand and economic activity), recovery, boom (industry fully productive) and recession, and so on (*Estates Gazette* 1995) A simplistic property cycle is shown in Figure 2.2.

Richard Barras (1994) has suggested that there are four cycles identified in economic literature and has linked them to the property cycle. These are:

(i)   The classical business cycle of 4–5 years' duration acting on all aspects of economic activity and operating on the property market through occupier demand.
(ii)   Long cycles of 9–10 years' duration which are generated by the exceptionally long production lags involved in property development, creating a tendency for supply to outstrip demand in every other business cycle.
(iii)   Long swings with a period up to 20 years are associated with major building booms: these may occur in every other long cycle of development; they are

typically speculative in nature and of a scale sufficient to generate distinctive new phases of urban development.

(iv) Long waves lasting up to 50 years have been proposed to explain alternating phases of high and low growth in the industrialised world economy, with each new wave being initiated by the adoption of a universal new technology (*Estates Gazette* 1995). A conceptual model proposed by Barras is shown in Figure 2.3.

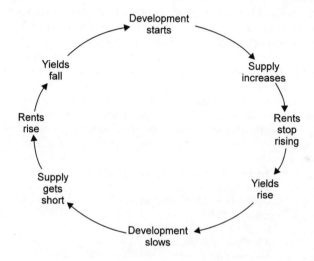

Figure 2.2   *The property cycle*

Source: London (1996).

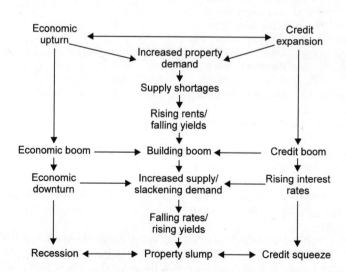

Figure 2.3   *The building cycle*

Source: Barras (1994).

Thus the property slump may last through the next business cycle. Because of the surplus in property there is no shortage in the next upturn. When the next long cycle of development picks up it will tend to be demand-driven with minimal speculative development because the banking system still has debts outstanding from the last boom. Thus another long cycle will need to proceed before the necessary preconditions will be in place for another speculative boom. Barras suggests that this is why the property booms occur in every second long cycle of development and in every fourth short cycle of business activity.

Some original research was carried out by Barber White Property Economics (*CSW- The Property Week* 1993a). They concluded that their research dispelled a number of commonly held views about the nature of the property market. Firstly, although the retail market is the first to recover from recession; it is not the first to fall into recession, a collapse in office rents heralds a recession. Secondly, the property market lags the economy with economic events causing the property cycle. Finally it is wrong to criticise valuers for not paying enough regard to future rental growth prospects; capital value cycles and rental cycles do not coincide and capital value cycles are more frequent than rental cycles. A property cycle route planner conceived by Barber White is shown in Figure 2.4.

1. **Shock moves economy into downturn**
   Office rents collapse
   Construction output declines
   Retail rents fall
   Office and industrial values fall
   Industrial rents fall
2. **Around 2 years later – economy begins recovery**
   Construction output grows
   Office rental fall slows down
   Retail values rise
3. **3–4 years later**
   Retail rents rise
   Industrial values rise
   Office values rise
4. **Beyond 5 years**
   Office rents rise
   Industrial rents rise

Figure 2.4   *The property cycle route planner*

The RICS research explained the three phases of the cycle they perceived (Whitmore 1994). These phases were:

- In the early stages of an economic upturn, rental growth is likely to be dampened by the surplus of space from the recession and the last development boom.
- In the second phase, continued economic expansion faces a shortage of space; rent begin to rise rapidly and trigger development starts. Since these will not reach the market for a year or more, the second phase of rapid rental growth is likely to be as long as a typical economic upswing. Shortage of space will often worsen, and rental growth will accelerate to the peak in the economy.

Developers reacting purely to current market conditions will be encouraged to start more development.

- The third phase is likely to begin with weakening or falling demand, as the recession begins: buildings triggered in the early part of phase two will be completed. The consequent fall in rental values puts a sharp stop to development schemes in the pipeline, although the surplus of newly completed space continues to rise, as the schemes started at the peak of the boom fall into recession.

The research concluded that if the property industry has lacked foresight it is because property cycles are built into the workings of the economy and property directly; they can never be smoothed out, but with a better understanding their impact can be appreciated (McGregor *et al.* 1994).

Property cycles are international in their effect. The nature and significance of cycles varies substantially, with exceptional cycles occurring internationally only occasionally. The increased significance of the cyclicality has been attributed by Pugh and Dehesh (1995) to the decreases in stability afforded by macroeconomic management since the 1970s and they suggest that destabilisation is at the root of many cyclical problems requiring the re-regulation of banking and finance. The effect of property cycles has effect not only on property decisions in the market but also on the decisions of individual investors as Gibson and Carter (1995) suggest. The property cycle imposes a barrier to economic efficiency or represents a wasted investment depending on the point in the cycle. If understanding the cycle is only just emerging in the UK then how can senior managers in major corporations be expected to incorporate property into their strategic plans?

2.3 PROPERTY MARKETS IN THE UK

The post-war property market can be divided into a number of periods (Brett 1990). These are the post-war development boom, the financial boom of 1967–73, the investment boom of the late 1970s and the finance-led development boom of the late 1980s with the subsequent collapse into the 1990s. Differences between the boom periods reflect the different finance sources and methods available during each period.

The post-war boom period

In the post-war boom period immediately after the war there was a shortage of space. This was especially so in the office sector where the shortage of office accommodation was fuelled by the destruction of approximately 750 000 square metres of office space in the Blitz. The economy was growing at a respectable rate against a background of low interest rates and low inflation. Property had been destroyed during the war and space was scarce so this led to a growth in rentals. At the beginning of the 1950s the Conservative government of the time recognised the need for a 'dash for growth' and encouraged a period of rapid economic expansion. Interest rates were low at this time and thus the yields on property investments were higher than long-term borrowing rates. Fixed interest institutional money was available and readily used by the property companies. Financial partnerships between institutions and property companies were frequently established. Financing of property investments could be carried out using long-term mortgage funds at low rates which were fixed. Typically these funds would be provided by an insurance company. Short-term finance for the construction period usually came from bank sources or else from the building contractor. There was an overall attempt by the developer to raise the total funds necessary for the development from lending sources, thus not committing any of its own money. Property developments were thus intended to be 100% debt financed with no equity involvement. Developers held on to their completed developments rather than selling them. Partially this was a response to the tax system as tax was payable on the trading profit, but there was no tax on the surplus created by the developer until the property was sold. Some new funding was achieved by the floating of the property companies on the Stock Exchange in the late 1950s and early 1960s. These flotations achieved cash for new development without the developers having to sell the properties. Developers at this time let their buildings on leases without review and were not concerned with the effects of inflation on their income stream but instead concentrated on income from development profits. Fixed interest financing by financial institutions was standard practice by the 1960s and linked to shareholdings, options and conversion rights taken up in development companies by the institutions. Inflation rose in the early 1960s and the institutions providing finance as mortgages or debentures began to take a share of equity, initially by conversion rights, and then eventually by establishing joint companies with the developers. The insurance companies were especially active at this time. Developers who wanted to retain properties had to give away some equity to ensure finance at lower rates. Sale and leaseback, where the developer offered to sell the proposed building subject to the investor leasing the building back, became the dominant form of funding arrangement. This approach had many advantages including not falling under the government's credit control measures of the time (Savills 1989). By the early 1960s recession affected demand and credit squeezes made short-term financing difficult. The office development boom in London was eventually brought to an end by the Labour Government in 1964 with the Control of Office and Industrial Development Act 1965. This so-called 'Brown Ban', named after George Brown who initiated the legislation, in fact artificially restricted the supply and sowed the seed of the next boom in the 1970s (Fraser 1993).

The financial boom 1967–73

A renewed Stock Market boom commenced in 1967 and lasted until the crash in 1974. Institutional finance was being provided to the property companies in the form of leasebacks. Pension funds in this period joined the insurance companies in buying out completed developments and they dominated the investment market (Cadman and Catalano 1983). New forms of indirect investment such as property bonds and property unit trusts were established. The market was characterised by a series of takeovers in the late 1960s and this activity continued on into the early 1970s. By March 1972 property shares had risen over five times from the low point of 1967 (Brett 1983). The assets of existing property companies were becoming more and more valuable because of the effect of the shortage of investment properties. The value of property companies was thus increasing because of the scarcity of space rather than because of accumulated development profits. Because of inflation in this period rent reviews were introduced, initially on a 14-yearly basis; these reduced to 7-yearly reviews and then to 5-yearly reviews. Between 1964 and 1974 there was a reduction of 40% in the number of quoted companies due to amalgamation and liquidation (Ratcliffe 1978).

To summarise, in the post-war era in the 1950s and 1960s the modern property developer had emerged and property companies had established themselves. The stimulation to development was based on the shortage of property in a period of low inflation. This meant that the rental levels of developments increased dramatically during the period whilst building costs were static. The other major stimulants to the developers were the fixed interest rates and the lack of equity input. The growth of the property developers was on the basis of refinancing the development on a fixed interest mortgage for 20 to 30 years. The institutions were providing finance for the developments and there was some link-up between developers and institutions. Over this period the institutions, generally insurance companies, insisted on having a greater share in the equity returns available. They purchased shares in the property companies and then made mortgage debenture loans convertible to shares so that an increased equity stake could be obtained if the scheme was a success. However, the taxation structure in the late 1960s affected this arrangement; gross funds (not paying tax) suffered from the taxation of income and dividends and new structures of finance emerged. In the late 1960s and early 1970s developers began using sale and leaseback; the property was financed in the development stage using bank finance and was sold on completion. As time wore on, a shortage of schemes became apparent and the institutions (the insurance companies and now pension funds) purchased development sites directly with a building agreement and agreement for lease with the developer. Developers borrowed short term for their developments or to finance acquisitions, because they thought rising asset values would counterbalance the deficit finance. They ignored cash flow and borrowed against the increased value of their properties to meet the income shortfall, between rental and interest payments. The crash of 1974/75 showed how the economic indications had changed since the 1950s and 1960s. High interest rates, lessened demand and inflation of costs meant that profit levels were not achieved because of increased capital costs and income voids during which interest arrears fluctuated. The highly geared property companies had been fuelled by debt finance provided under fairly lax lending criteria. In the aftermath of the oil crisis of 1973, interest rates were raised to a penal level, secondary banks were heavily committed to property and began to collapse. Accounting conventions of the time had disguised the sharply negative cash flow of most property companies with large development programmes. It thus became impossible to sell a property and it was not possible to borrow on it. Property shares collapsed as did the direct market in property (Brett 1990).

The investment boom (late 1970s) and the rental boom (late 1980s)

In the late 1970s the institutions were keen buyers of property and values rose sharply during this period. Large institutions were undertaking direct development or using developers as project managers. Larger companies were borrowing on the hope that the cash flow would be positive at the first rent review. In the 1980s and 1990s the usual approach to funding was that the fund was invited to purchase the site and provide funds for the building contract. Interest would be rolled up during the development period and added to the development costs. On completion and letting of the building, the profit on the development would be paid over. On this basis developers built up a large turnover, basically matching their site funding and project management skills with the institutional investors. Such approaches greatly reduced the risk exposure of the developer to the project. Forward funding meant that the project was financed in terms of the development at a keep rate but generally the capital sum at the end of the project was valued at a higher yield. In the early 1980s the recession and rising unemployment had affected the demand for property and rental increases fell, and yields increased. Property lagged behind the rest of the economy in its recovery. There was not another boom until 1986–7. The institutions were now less important as providers of funds for property and their net purchases dropped as they re-weighed their portfolios towards equities and gilts, disappointed with the performance of their property assets. A development boom, funded by the banks, had begun. The banks were prepared to lend on individual developments and roll up the interest until the property was disposed of. Thus developers were traders rather than investment companies. By the beginning of the 1990s the rental growth had tailed off and the market was collapsing. There were no buyers for the completed developments. The banks had to extend their development loans beyond the development period because there were no institutional funders in the market. Development loans were thus converted to investment loans, committing banks to staying in the market. Innovative financial techniques in the absence of traditional institutional finance were the key developments of the 1980s.

The 1990s

The present players in the lending market include:

Banks	Clearing banks Merchant banks (also providing an advisory role)
Institutions	Insurance companies Pension funds
Investors	Private individuals Overseas investors

At the beginning of 1990 there were 140 banks lending to property companies and developers in the UK, and 40% of these were overseas banks. In terms of bank loans, £30 billion was outstanding to property lending which equates to 7.5% of all bank lending. Lending had increased 20% per annum from 1981 to 1990 and the Bank of England had become concerned. The lending banks' response subsequently has been to reduce loan to value ratios from between 75% and 80% to between 66% and 70%, but they still lent as they had to make profits. Some comparison has been made between the lending crisis of the 1990s and the property crash in 1974 but they are very different. In the 1974 crash, banks were unable to deal with unpaid loans and they had a weaker capital base. There was a weaker tenant demand at the time. The strong investor demand in 1974 was pushing yields down and thus trading profits were based on investor reaction rather than rental growth. The developers had poor covenants. There was poor research by banks and property companies. Nowadays there are better financial controls and banks are taking security (notwithstanding non-recourse deals). The property sector has been driven by tenant demand. Yields have moved but not significantly.

Market model and sectors

A model of the investment market has been provided by Keogh, and this shows that property investment is part of a market which includes a user market, an investment market and a development market. A simple model of the overall property market suggested by Keogh (1994) is shown in Figure 2.5. A schematic model of the property market has also been suggested by Fraser (1996) who suggests that the usual models of the property market concentrate on the interrelationship of the market in the three principle sectors: the letting, user or occupational sector; the investment sector; and the development sector; thus making the property market known as the 'the three ring circus'. Fraser's model has a single ring with three arcs for the principle market sectors. It provides a context of international, national and local economies to the setting of the market and suggests that occupational demand drives the letting sector, investment demand drives the investment sector and development costs the development sector, these three sectors in turn establish the property stock.

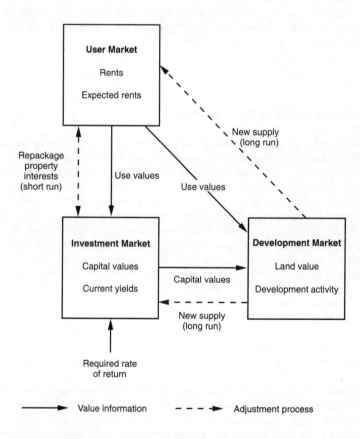

Figure 2.5 *A simple model of the property market*

Source: Keogh (1994).

The other division of the investment market is to look at the types of property involved. The main sectors in the investment market are shops, offices, industrial premises and warehouses, residential, agricultural and leisure. This classification has been complicated by recent developments which include retail warehousing, class B1 developments and mixed developments. Retail warehousing is where the location and structure of the building relates to the warehouse sector, but the economic analysis and financial appraisal of such developments are related more to the retail sector than the warehouse sector. Class B1 use combines office use with light industrial use and also high-tech usage. Mixed developments are particularly workshop conversions which are developed from industrial space but may also include retail and residential space. Details of the sectors are contained in Chapter 4.

Registration of land

Property markets in the UK suffer from lack of information because a Central Land Register did not exist in the UK. Before 1988 the only access to the register was in Scotland and Northern Ireland. The Land Registration Act 1988 made available to the public information on the registration of freehold and leasehold titles in land in England and Wales (*Estates Gazette* 1996).

2.4   THE GLOBALISATION OF INVESTMENT

Financial, capital and money markets have moved from national to international dominance. These markets are globalised, deregulated and freer to operate in. Thus stateless finance, outside the jurisdiction of any one country and its regulatory institutions can manipulate the market. Innovations in the finance of property have been a product of this globalisation. The traditional funding of development projects by short-term bank funding and long-term institutional finance has had to be replaced. Innovations in finance have also had to deal with the inherent illiquidity and lumpiness of property. Investor interest in liquidity, flexibility, the management of risk, yield analysis and portfolio management have been met by new advances of financing property (Pugh 1991).

The background to the finance of property in the 1980s and 1990s is the globalisation of the investment markets of the different asset classes which began to be established after the abolition of exchange controls for investment funds in the late 1980s in the UK. In the mid-1980s, banks became interested in the globalisation; they were following the needs of business occupiers as well as property investors. Property investment globalisation accelerated with the presence of Scandinavians, Japanese and other foreign investment which was having influence in the European markets in the late 1980s (Sieracki 1993).

As investment crosses national boundaries and investors have less and less knowledge of the assumptions that are behind investment decisions, changes are evident. Edgington (1996) in his study of Japanese investment in North America suggested that with the development of the global economy an assumption has developed that property could easily take its place as a globally traded asset and that the specifically locational aspects of property could be ignored. Some analysts call this 'the end of geography' and with the development of telecommunications 'a time-space collapse', but Edgington finds that whilst global factors such as interest rates and surpluses of money capital can be used as explanatory factors for the vast increase in Japanese investment in North American real estate, the specific social and cultural factors cannot be ignored. For instance, investment has ben generally preferred in those centres in North America which were well known in Japan, either as financial centres, important resorts or traditional points of entry for business or immigration.

The decline of institutional investment in property in the late 1980s and the arrival on the scene of foreign money was especially in the form of debt. Cross-border flows of property investment increased at phenomenal rates in the late 1980s due to the removal in the early 1980s of the controls on exporting capital in three countries, USA, Japan and the UK. The increase in global pension fund assets in the 1980s is shown in Table 2.1. The scale of this investment could be seen in the City of London. In 1985 there was no office development over 100 000 m^2 (the largest being the NatWest Tower at 80 000 m^2) but by 1990 there were three schemes over 200 000 m^2 and all involved foreign investment: London Bridge City (Kuwaiti), Broadgate (British but funded by Japanese banks) and Canary Wharf (North American). Another indication was that half the transactions in the City over the period 1985–90 involved foreign buyers. (Schiller 1990) In a study of the role of international property in investment portfolios, Newell and Worzala (1995) found that portfolio diversification was the primary motivating factor of international property investors who also had a high awareness of currency risk considerations.

Table 2.1 *Global pension fund assets 1980–87*

Global pension fund assets ($bn)	1980	1987
Total	760	3645
Held abroad	21	190

Source: Intersec/Schiller (1990).

2.5 MARKET EFFICIENCY

The hypothesis of capital market efficiency says that the prices of securities instantaneously and fully reflect all available relevant information. Capital market efficiency relies on the ability of arbitrageurs (dealers who capitalise on dealing in assets which are over- or under-valued on the market) to recognise that prices are out of line and to make a profit by driving them back to an equilibrium value consistent with available information. In an efficient market securities will be traded at correct prices. This provides confidence to investors and the best allocation of funds.

For a stock market to be perfect, the following conditions need to apply:

(i) The market needs to be frictionless without transaction costs and taxes. No constraining regulations limiting freedom of entry and exit for investors and companies seeking funds. All shares should be perfectly marketable.

(ii) All services in the market should be provided at the average minimum cost, with all participants price takers.

(iii)   All buyers and sellers should be rational expected utility maximisers.
(iv)   There should be many buyers and sellers.
(v)   The market should be efficient from an informational point of view; information should be costless and received simultaneously by all individuals.

No market satisfies all these conditions. It is possible to relax some of the assumptions and still have an efficient market. The assumptions of costless information, a frictionless marketplace and many buyers and sellers are not necessary conditions for the existence of an efficient capital market. The capital market approach used in finance theory is important in respect of financial decisions made; the approach is only tenable if markets are efficient. If markets are efficient then the market prices will reflect the effects of decisions made in the market. The market price is the present value of future returns expected by the participants in the market discounted at a rate which reflects the risk free rate and an appropriate risk premium. The stock market is essentially a secondary market – a place to buy and sell established securities. The influence of the market on sources of new capital is very high. The conditions necessary for efficiency in the capital markets are not as stringent as those defined by a perfect capital market. The efficient market requires that dealing costs are not too high so there is easy access in and out of the market. In addition, the relevant information for dealing should be available to a large number of participants. Finally, no individual should dominate the market.

If people disagree on individual judgements on future returns, this will lead to transactions. The sum of the transactions process will produce unbiased valuations in an efficient market. Such a market is a 'fair game' one. If it is a fair game then ex *post* gains or losses cannot be predicted ex *ante*. Efficient markets suggest that current market prices reflect available information. If valuations are a good proxy for prices then valuations should reflect all known information (Brown 1991). There are several forms of market efficiency: weak form, semi-strong and strong. If markets are efficient, they can process the information available and the information is incorporated into the price of the security. Thus systems for playing the market cannot succeed, abnormal returns cannot be expected. The definition of the types of market depends on the information the market uses to determine prices:

- *Weak-form* – incorporates the past history of prices and is efficient with respect to these prices. So stock selections based on patterns of past stock price movements are no better than random choice.
- *Semi-strong form* – this market makes use of all publicly available information. This is reflected in the price of stocks, thus investors will not be able to outperform the market by using the same information.
- *Strong-form efficiency* – the market has available all information and uses all the available information that anyone knows about the stocks, including inside information to price the stocks.

Evidence from different financial markets supports the weak-form and semi-strong efficiency but not the strong form. Therefore it is still not possible for the investor to use available information to beat the market, the share prices thus conform to a 'random walk'. Efficient markets enable us to say something about the way assets should be priced. If the market is a fair game, investors should be compensated for that part of the total risk that cannot be reduced by diversification. An efficient market implies valuers are doing a good job impounding information into valuations (Brown 1991).

2.6 CAPITAL MARKETS

Capital Market Theory relates to the Capital Asset Pricing Model and to Arbitrage Pricing Theory. The theory is about discounting risky cash flows. The theory has a number of important aspects which are covered point by point:

(i) *How is risk measured?*
The risk is related to an asset (we can use a company stock for ease of understanding). It relates to the variability of returns, measured by their variance or standard deviation. This is applicable to a single asset or security.

(ii) *How is risk measured in a portfolio of securities?*
Investors generally hold diversified portfolios, we are thus interested in the contribution of a security to the risk of the entire portfolio. Because a security's variance is dispersed in a large diversified portfolio, the security's variance/standard deviation no longer represents the security's contribution to the risk of a large portfolio. In this case, the contribution is best measured by the security's covariance with the other securities in the portfolio.
For example , if a stock has high returns when the overall return of the portfolio is low and vice versa, the stock has a negative covariance with the portfolio. It acts as a hedge against risk, reducing the risk of the portfolio. If the stock has a high positive covariance, there is a high risk for the investor.

(iii) *What is the measure of diversification?*
β (beta) is the appropriate measure of the contribution of a security to the risk of as large portfolio.

(iv) *What are the criteria for holding an investment?*
Investors will only hold a risky investment if its expected return is high enough to compensate for its risk. There is a trade-off between risk and reward. The expected return on a security should be positively related to the security's beta:

Expected return on a security = Risk-free rate+

(beta × (Expected return on market portfolio − Risk-free rate)).

(Ross *et al.* 1993)

The term in brackets is positive so the equation relates the expected return on a security as a positive function of its beta. This equation is the basis of the Capital Asset Pricing Model (CAPM). The Arbitrage Pricing Theory (APT) also derives a relationship between risk and return but not in this form. The APT draws basically the same conclusions but makes assumptions that the returns on securities are driven by a number of market factors.

Capital asset pricing model

$$\bar{R} = R_F + \beta(\bar{R}_M - R_F)$$

where $\bar{R}_M$ is the expected return on the market, $\bar{R}$ is the expected return on the security, R_F is the risk free rate and beta is the measure of risk. Beta is a measure of the security's sensitivity to movements in an underlying factor, a measure of systematic risk. Systematic risk affects a large number of assets and is also called market, portfolio or common risk. Diversifiable risk is a risk that affects a single asset or small group of assets; this is also called unique or unsystematic risk. The total risk for an individual security held in a portfolio can thus be broken down as follows:

Total risk of individual security =

Portfolio risk + Unsystematic or diversifiable risk.

Total risk is the risk borne if only one security is held. Portfolio risk is the risk still borne after achieving full diversification. Portfolio risk is often called systematic or market risk. Diversifiable, unique or unsystematic risk is that risk which can be diversified away in a large portfolio. Finance uses the capital market approach as the basis for decision-making. Such an approach is only useful if the capital markets are efficient.

The point made by the theory discussed previously on efficient markets is that in efficient markets, investors cannot consistently achieve above-average returns other than by chance. In October 1987, on 'Black Monday', there was a sudden and dramatic fall in share prices on most of the world's stock markets, with share prices falling by 30% or more. Had this been triggered by a particular event, shareholders' reaction could have been explained as the efficient market reacting to new information. However, this collapse was not due to external events but rather a recognition that the bull market had ended and the speculative share price bubble had burst. The equity returns in US markets were out of alignment compared to returns on government stocks, and there was a sharp international adjustment starting with this realisation and accentuated by futures dealing and 'program trading' which triggered sales of stocks and shares automatically as prices fell. This crash brought into question the validity of the simple efficient markets hypothesis and a view developed that there may not be a single 'true' value for the level of shares but a range.

Pike and Neale (1993) suggest that there are a number of implications for managing investment which arise from market efficiency:

(i)   Investors are not easily fooled by glossy financial reports or 'creative accounting' techniques which boost corporate reported earnings but not underlying cash flows.

(ii)   Corporate management should endeavour to make decisions which maximise shareholders' wealth.

(iii)   There is little point in bothering with the timing of new issues. Market prices are a 'fair' reflection of the information available and rationally evaluate the degree of risk in shares.

(iv)   Where corporate managers possess information not yet released to the market (termed 'information asymmetry') there is some opportunity for influencing prices. Release of this information can be done strategically, as when an unwelcome takeover bid occurs.

Capital structure and gearing

Money lent to a business by third parties is debt finance or loan capital. Most companies borrow money on a long-term basis by issuing stocks or debentures. The supplier of the loan will specify the amount of loan, rate of interest, date of payment and method of repayment. The finance manager of a firm will monitor the long-term financial structure of the firm by examining the relationship between loan capital (where interest and loan repayments are contractually obligatory) and ordinary share capital (where dividend payment is at the discretion of the directors). This relationship between debt and equity is called gearing (known in the USA as leverage). Strictly, gearing is the proportion of debt capital to total capital in the firm. The capital structure of a property company is a key factor in how a company is viewed in terms of its attractiveness for an investor or lender. The property sector is characterised by a high level of gearing due to the availability of fixed interest finance during the first post-war boom from 1954 to 1964. This availability led to many property companies being highly geared. High gearing is of benefit when property values are rising ahead of interest charges but can be dangerous if the real rate of interest is rising at a greater rate than property values.

2.7   LEASES AND LEASE STRUCTURES

The institutional lease has been the backbone of the investment market in the UK and is a reflection of the power of the financial institutions in the market. In the words of Michael Mallison, the author of the report on commercial property valuations:

> *The profession has been overly solicitous toward financial institutions – a rich source of their fees. Their initially cheap capital was offered at the price of unattractive features such as institutional leases, stereotyped physical structures and minimal landlord management. (CSM 1995, p.48)*

The institutional lease relies on a 25-year term with 5-year rent reviews and is a fully insuring and repairing lease. Thus the landlord has no expenses but receives a net income for 25 years with upward-only rent reviews at each review. Not only that, but prior to the recent legislation on privity of contracts they also had the right to pursue assignors for the debts and loss of rent incurred from assignees. The lease structure has now changed and the privity of contract has come to an end by legislative changes. There has been some comment that this would lead to higher rentals being asked but there is little evidence of this in the market. The other main area of change is the breakdown of the institutional lease. Leases are becoming shorter although rent review periods are not lengthening or lessening. There was a period in the 1970s and 1980s when 9-year leases were being granted on 3-year rent review patterns but the strength of the landlord in this case was such that it was a mechanism for frequent rent reviews in a period of inflation. The breakdown of the institutional lease has been due to stronger tenant negotiation, the need for a strong covenant and thus the acceptance of negotiation on the key points of the lease. It has also been due to the influence of foreign tenants and investors unused to the hegemony of long lease terms. Finally, pressure has come from occupiers who have to trade and make profits in volatile and rapidly changing markets under adverse economic conditions.

Research carried out by Drivers Jonas suggested that the average lease length has decreased from 21 to 9 years over the period 1984–94 and that 12% of all leases have tenants' break clause options, although this figure fell to 2% in London and the South East. This research is contained in the *City Research Project*, which provided a final report at the end of 1995 (*Estates Gazette* 1996a). One cannot overemphasise the importance of the traditional UK property lease as an attraction to bank lending on property with its upward-only reviews, the 25-year term and the privity rules maintaining the original tenant's liability. The loss of this privity under the Landlord and Tenant (Covenants) Act 1995 must logically remove a layer of security from the bank's security. But Taylor (1996) suggests that in some ways there may be benefits. Taylor sees winners and losers in the revised privity situation. The winners will be true speculative lenders who can take real property risk and those with an established borrower base; also those who lend on portfolios and multi-income properties. Those who will lose by the new arrangements are the 'bond' property lenders, those that purely seek to lend on an undoubted income flow. Those who are new entrants to the lending market will also find difficulties, as will those lenders with a large overseas borrowing base and those who are risk averse and tend to lend on new properties let on long leases to high-profile tenants. Research has shown that the days of the 25-year lease are numbered: major occupiers will not take the responsibilities of the institutional 25-year lease. Although 95% of property owned by UK institutions is let on 25-year leases, (UBS Phillips & Drew/CSW 1993a), major companies have suggested in the same article that they would not sign a 25-year lease. The Property Director of BP, for instance, was quoted as saying he was happy to sign a 10-year lease and would consider terms up to a maximum of 15 years but with a break clause after 5 years; if the only option was a long lease he would prefer owner-occupation.

2.8   ECONOMIC AND MARKET ANALYSIS

Market research

The increasing fragmentation of the property market means that a higher level of skill is required in discovering and exploiting the profitable location. Research is necessary into the likely scale, design, layout, occupancy, tenure and service requirements of prospective purchasers. Market research is an important area which would aim to establish the current demand and supply of property within the area to ensure that the property could be sold or let. The estimation of current demand may include the estimation of the current total market potential which is the maximum amount of sales that might be available to all competing firms during a given period in a given market segment under a given level of marketing.

Estimating current demand in market research will involve the estimation of:

(i)   The total market potential.
(ii)   The territorial potential.

Having established the market potential, the management decision will be to decide how much of that market a product can gain and how much effort is needed to gain it. The product seller wants to know if the market is large enough to justify participation. The formula for the estimate is $m = n \times q \times p$ where m is the total market potential, n is the number of buyers in the specific market, q is the quantity purchased by an average buyer and p is the price of the average product. For instance, if there are two hundred high-technology companies who wish to buy a new production facility every five years and the average price of the facility is say £200 000 for an average floor space of 500 square metres, then the total market potential is approximately £40 000 000 over a five-year period. The difficult component to calculate is the number of buyers in the market in a given time period (Cleaveley 1984). A variation of the formula above is called the chain method, based on the premise that it is easier to look at each component of magnitude rather than at the magnitude itself. So, for instance, the current demand for high-tech buildings can be built up as being equal to the number of high-tech companies in the UK times the average percentage of those without spare capacity on site, times the average percentage of those companies who need specialised premises, times the average percentage of those companies who would pay the current market rent for high-tech buildings.

Economic analysis

Property traditionally operates in a demand-led market where, because of the inadequacies in the market and restrictions on supply caused by controls and procedures of obtaining planning permission, property developers, except in periods of slump, have managed eventually to dispose of their properties. Since the late 1960s, owner-occupiers have been much more explicit about their requirements and thus market research, economic analysis and proper marketing of the product is much more necessary. There are three steps that can be used, for instance, in the market research of a shopping centre. This retail analysis will include firstly background analysis, secondly market analysis and thirdly an estimation of the size of the project:

The *background analysis* will include the geographical extent of the urban area, the road pattern, the population and growth areas, the level of employment and key employers, retail sales patterns and per capita income by sector.

The *market analysis* will look at the site, its suitability, size and location, its access by roads and transport facilities, its trade or catchment area. This catchment area is defined by natural boundaries, access times, competition and size. The market analysis also includes population growth and income and buying power per capita and per family. The analysis involves the consideration of competition from other sites and an estimation of the sales potential which is the potential population times expenditure for each store type. The residual sales for the site to be developed is this level of potential less an allowance for the competing sites.

The *recommended size* of the project can be estimated by taking the level of population and multiplying it by the per capita expenditure within that type of shopping centre. Assuming a share for the location, this total expenditure can be reduced by that share and also by an additional share for competition. This then gives a figure for the potential within that town centre location which is unsatisfied. The judgement then has to be made as to what proportion the project will take of this unsatisfied potential.

The approach to the analysis for a retail development is summarised in Box 2.1.

Thus economic analysis concerns three factors: supply and demand; changes in the environment; and changes in technology.

Supply and demand

Price rises in a market are generally an indication of a shortage of supply of that type of space, but this conclusion may require further analysis. An estimate of the supply of space will involve the calculation of the existing stock on the market and an analysis of the type of product. There is a need to assess the existing vacant space and the rate of take-up. Finally a calculation will be required of the space to be released on to the market by new development or the release of existing premises.

ECONOMIC ANALYSIS

1. Background
    - geographical extent of the urban area
    - road pattern
    - population and growth areas
    - employment and employers
    - retail sales pattern
    - per capita income by sector
2. Market analysis
    - site – size, suitability, location
    - access – roads and transport
    - trade (or catchment) area: natural boundaries, access times, competition, impact zone
    - population growth
    - income and buying power per capita, family expenditure
    - competition
    - sales potential: population × expenditure for each store type (population based on total less that attracted by competition or assumed share of total market).
3. Recommendations
    - Recommend size of project based on sales potential, provide brief to designer, detailed financial analysis of potential.
    - Calculation: population × per capita store expenditure × percentage captured by town centre stores minus effective competition = town centre potential. The project share taken as a percentage of this.
    - Recommended area schedule will divide up total space into percentages for each user depending on expenditure: i.e. food, chemist, department store, furniture, eating, etc.

Box 2.1   *An approach to a retail economic analysis*

The calculation is:

$$\frac{EV + ND_t + NV_t}{TU_t}$$

where: EV is existing stock

ND_t is new development for the coming year (say)

NV_t is existing space becoming available over the year

TU_t is the take-up rate assessed on an historic analysis and projected forward.

If TU_t is less than $EV + ND_t + NV_t$, then the calculation represents so many years' supply of property on the market. The equilibrium position is 1 year in this case.

Changes in the environment

The strength of the local economy, planning proposals for the development of open space and general economic conditions are of relevance here.

Changes in technology

Technology changes may lead to changes in the demand for space, changes in user requirements and redundant space. Homeworking or teleworking, where employees work full-time or for part of the week at home, will affect demands for space, as will desk sharing or desk renting where exclusive work space is not allocated on a regular basis to employees.

The RICS has summarised the influences on occupier demand as:

(a) location of property;
(b) access;
(c) availability of transport routes;
(d) car parking facilities;
(e) amenities attractive to tenant and/or purchasers;
(f) size of development in terms of lettable packages;
(g) form and specification of development;
(h) market supply, including actual or proposed competing developments.

(Royal Institution of Chartered Surveyors 1995)

Potential users of space

In order to assess demand, the key element will be to analyse the potential users of space. These will essentially be of four types: firstly, companies moving into an area either to open new facilities, branch offices etc. or because of a complete relocation of the business operation; secondly, expansion of the existing requirement by established firms in the area; thirdly, small space requirements by business start-ups; finally, companies moving into an area to rationalise space, change location or move to updated premises.

Market research procedure

Cleaveley (1984) suggests that there are five steps in setting up the operation of a market research project and these are applicable to the property industry. The first step is the defining of objectives. Here the research objectives or the subject to be investigated is defined. A clear direction of research activities is required to ensure that the results come from a right target market and that sufficient valid data is obtained.

(i) *Designing the research methodology*: Decisions must be taken about the appropriate method of obtaining data. These may be, for instance, desk research, the study of published information or in-house information from appropriate agents. It may come from observation or finally by survey research which may consist of face-to-face interviews, self-completing questionnaires, interviewing by telephone, or group discussion where opinion leaders are drawn together to discuss markets under the direction of the trained group leader which can be very effective in finding out a general consensus of viewpoints.

(ii) *Sampling*: Because of the costs of analysing the total target market, most research programmes will focus upon samples of that market. Larger samples obviously give more reliable data but the degree of accuracy must be related to the amount being spent on the research project. Most research projects begin with a pilot survey which will evaluate the procedure which is intended to be carried out and also the design of the research method and the level of response to the method carried out. Random sampling is effective and easy to administer but structured sampling or non-random methods have also been designed to achieve maximum statistical reliability from the results.

(iii)   *Fieldwork*: Trained interviewers or executives can be employed to carry out the fieldwork to provide the information on the research project. The supervisor to the project will need to monitor closely what is happening in terms of the fieldwork and ensure that it is completed accurately without bias and on time.

(iv)   *Data analysis*: The analytical techniques used in the data analysis can vary from simple statistical techniques to a very complex regression analysis. The extent of the analysis should be agreed with the client before the research is entered into.

(v)   *Presentation of report*: The results of research and any conclusions are shown in a comprehensive report which should have clear recommendations so that the findings of the research can be translated into action by the client.

REFERENCES

Barras, R. (1994) 'Property and the Economic Cycle: Building Cycles Revisited', *Journal of Property Research*, vol. 11, no. 3, winter, pp. 183–97.

Barter, S. L. (1988) 'Introduction' in S. L. Barter (ed.) *Real Estate Finance*, Butterworths, London.

Bowie, N. (1988) 'More Thoughts on the Market', *Estates Gazette*, 3 December, pp. 26–8.

Brett, M. (1983) 'Growth of Financial Institutions', in C. Darlow (ed.) *Valuation and Investment Appraisal*, Estates Gazette, London.

Brett, M. (1990) *Property and Money*, Estates Gazette, London.

Brown, G. R. (1991) *Property Investment and the Capital Markets*, E. & F. Spon, London.

Cadman, D. and Catalano, A. (1983) *Property Development in the UK – Evolution and Change*, College of Estate Management, Reading.

Chartered Surveyor Monthly (CSM) (1995), 'Mallinson Delivers a Yorker', *CSM*, November/December, p. 48.

Cleaveley, E. S. (1984) *The Marketing of Industrial and Commercial Property*, Estates Gazette, London.

Copeland, T. E. and Weston, J. F. (1988) *Financial Theory and Corporate Policy*, Addison-Wesley, Wokingham.

CSW-The Property Week (1993a), '25 Year Lease', *CSW-The Property Week*, 10 June, pp. 24–5.

CSW-The Property Week (1993b), 'New Research Reveals Market Pattern', *CSW-The Property Week*, 28 October, p. 13.

Darlow, C. (ed.) (1983) *Valuation and Investment Appraisal*, Estates Gazette, London.

Debenham, Tewson and Chinnocks (1984) *Property Investment in Britain*, Debenham, Tewson and Chinnocks, London.

Edgington, D. (1996), 'What Drives Japanese Property Investors?', *Chartered Surveyor Monthly*, March, p. 32.

Estates Gazette (1995), 'Property Cycles Explained', *Estates Gazette*, 25 November, pp. 147–8.

Estates Gazette (1996), 'Tenants are Lukewarm on New Lease Code of Practice', *Estates Gazette*, 6 January, p. 40.

Estates Times (1993) 'Swaps Not Cash', *Estates Times*, 19 November, p. 24.

Fraser, W. (1996), 'A Schematic Model of the Commercial Property Market', *Chartered Surveyor Monthly*, January, pp. 32–3

Fraser, W. D. (1993) *Principles of Property Investment and Pricing*, Macmillan, London.

Gibson, G. and Carter, C. (1995) 'Is Property on the Strategic Agenda?', *Chartered Surveyor Monthly*, January, pp. 34–5.

Isaac, D. and Steley, T. (1991) *Property Valuation Techniques*, Macmillan, London.

Keogh, G. (1994) 'Use and Investment Markets in UK Real Estate' *Journal of Property Valuation and Investment*, vol. 12, no. 4, pp. 58–72.

Lennox, K. (1996) 'Thumbs Up for Property: IPF/EC Survey', *Estates Gazette*, 20 April.

London, S. (1996) 'Lure of the Property Magnet', *Financial Times*, 23 September.

McGregor, B., Nanthakumuran, N., Key, T. and Zarkesh, F. (1994) 'Investigating Property Cycles', *Chartered Surveyor Monthly*, July/August, pp. 38–9.

Newall, G. and Worzala, E. (1995) 'The Role of International Property in Investment Portfolios', *Journal of Property Finance*, vol. 6, no. 1, pp. 55–63.

Pike, R. and Neale, B. (1993) *Corporate Finance and Investment*, Prentice Hall, London.

Pugh, C. (1991) 'The Globalisation of Finance Capital and the Changing Relationships between Property and Finance', *Journal of Property Finance*, vol. 2, no. 2, pp. 211–15 and no. 3, pp. 369–79.

Pugh, C. and Dehesh, A. (1995) 'International Property Cycles: The Causes', *Chartered Surveyor Monthly*, January, p. 33.

Ratcliffe, J. (1978) *An Introduction to Urban Land Administration*, Estates Gazette, London.

Ross, S. A., Westerfield, R. W. and Jaffe, J. F. (1993) *Corporate Finance*, Irwin, Boston.

Royal Institution of Chartered Surveyors (1994) *Understanding the Property Cycle: Economic Cycles and Property Cycles*, RICS, London, May.

Royal Institution of Chartered Surveyors (1995), *Valuation of Development Land*, RICS, London, January

Savills (1989) *Financing Property 1989*, Savills, London

Schiller, R. (1990), 'International Property Investment: The Importance of Debt', *Estates Gazette*, 24 February, pp. 22–4.

Sieracki, K. (1993) 'U.K. Institutional Requirements for European Property', *Estates Gazette*, 17 July.

Taylor, S. (1996), 'Privity and Property Lending', *Estates Gazette*, 2 March, pp. 119–20.

Whitmore, J. (1994), 'RICS Identifies the Property Cycle', *Property Week*, 12 May, p. 4.

3 Investors

3.1 TYPES OF INVESTOR

The main investors in the market are: financial institutions, overseas investors and property companies. The financial institutions are the pension funds and the insurance companies. Other investors are High Street clearing banks, foreign banks, building societies, merchant banks and finance houses. In their recent report on the sources of money flowing into property, DTZ Debenham Thorpe and the Central Statistical Office provided the figures shown in Table 3.1.

Table 3.1 *New money into property*

			(£ million)			
	Pension funds	Insurance companies	Banks	Property companies	Overseas	Total
1980	908	855	72	147	100	2 082
1981	843	1 073	469	97	70	2 552
1982	797	1 059	822	263	120	3 061
1983	680	845	934	83	85	2 627
1984	997	744	963	237	65	3 006
1985	590	815	1 691	344	90	3 530
1986	434	821	2 224	737	150	4 306
1987	240	755	3 998	2 300	290	7 583
1988	312	1 102	7 954	761	1 897	12 026
1989	92	1 510	10 622	1 647	3 267	17 138
1990	−491	1 080	7 066	164	3 269	11 088
1991	467	1 483	678	1 352	1 551	5 531
1992	349	600	−1 708	212	1 232	685
1993	299	232	−3 248	2 022	1 514	819
1994	−325	2 708	−2 077	1 848	1 740	3 894
1995	−16	283	−1 093	1 146	1 790	2 110
1996[a]	154	70	−120	261	689	1 054

Note: [a] *1996 first two quarters only.*
Sources: Evans (1993), CSO (1994, 1996), DTZ Debenham Thorpe (1996).

In the market, the main sources of equity are long-term institutions (pension funds and insurance companies), property companies, private investors and others. Institutions and property companies are examined in this chapter together with private investors and others who can be owner-occupiers, overseas investors and construction companies.

3.2   INDIVIDUAL AND CORPORATE INVESTORS

Private investors are excluded from participation in many areas of the property market because of the large sums involved in purchase and transaction costs. Some funds have been established for groups of investors with a single specific purpose. Authorised unit trusts are one means of access and are discussed later. In the lower end of the market with high yielding secondary and tertiary property, individuals do play a part; this is a significant sector. However, generally the role of the private investor in the property market in the UK is smaller than elsewhere.

Other sources of finance may be owner-occupiers. Commercial owner-occupiers are in operation to earn a profit and therefore will compare rental payments with the opportunities for owner-occupation. The benefits of purchase mean that the asset base of the company is extended, and if the cash flows have been worked out correctly, there may be net savings in occupation costs. However, if the company has to borrow to purchase the property, the debt will need to be shown on the balance sheet. In the 1960s and 1970s, there were a number of sale and leasebacks where owners disposed of their freehold interests in land and took on occupational leases. There appears to be a reversal of this in recent years because of the disadvantages of the standard institutional lease. These disadvantages are:

(i)   the length of lease and difficulties of assignments; privity of contract pre- viously meant liability for the full term whether assignment takes place or not;
(ii)   because of regular rent reviews which may have been upward only, no equity can be built up in the property asset;
(iii)   lease terms, besides the rent review terms and length of lease, can be onerous in terms of repairing, use and other obligations and damaging to the cash flow (Mallinson 1988).

Construction companies may also provide equity in property. This is likely to be short- term development finance and may be provided as a package to the developer to ensure a building contract. Some construction companies will participate over a longer period as partners or joint venturers but these interests are usually held in property company subsidiaries. Department stores in particular may participate in partnerships in major development schemes. Equity in specific individual investments can take a number of forms; for instance:

(i)   finance from the developer's own cash and resources;
(ii)   partnership funds where another party joins in to share the risks and rewards of the enterprise;
(iii)   financiers providing equity against which collateral or debt can be raised. The money is thus not used in the development nor is a joint company formed. A form of guarantee is provided;
(iv)   forward funding by an institution. The institution may meet the costs of development including the acquisition costs of the site, construction fees, interest and letting fees. The institution may provide these monies at a lower interest rate but may require purchase of the completed development at a lower price.

Direct versus indirect funding

Long-term savings institutions, the pension funds and insurance companies are the main sources of equity finance. The history of the involvement of institutions has been a move towards direct funding of property development and property investments. Smaller institutions wanting to take a stake in commercial property but lacking the size of resources to invest direct can use indirect routes into property (see Chapter 1, Figure 1.6).

There are a number of indirect routes into investment in property. The main ones are: property company shares; property unit linked life assurance schemes (so-called 'property bonds'); exempt unit trusts and managed funds; mortgages and debentures (Brett 1983). Within this scheme of things, shares are generally available to a wide range of investors whereas bonds are an investment medium for an individual. Exempt trusts and managed funds, on the other hand, often provide an indirect investment vehicle for pension funds and charities. The property company, unlike the other indirect routes, is a corporate body with its shares quoted on the Stock Exchange. The value of its shares bears some relationship to the value of the property it owns and the income it derives from property operations, but the link is not a direct one. Property company shares will fluctuate on the market depending on the value of property owned, but the stock market will also tend to discount expected economic and financial events before they happen. An investment trust is a company which holds a portfolio of shares.

Property bonds, exempt property unit trusts and managed funds work on a different principle. The value of the unit in the fund is determined directly by the valuation of the property portfolio of the fund. Thus the value of the portfolio is divided by the number of units held in the fund, and after allowance for the fund's expenses this value becomes the unit price of the fund. The managers of the fund then operate the market at this price by sale of units whose owners wish to dispose, and by issue to new investors. There is obviously a margin between offer and bid prices to cover costs of transfer of the units and there is also a need for some liquidity in the system as sales will not equal purchases in the short term. If demand exceeds supply then new monies can purchase new investments which are added to the fund. If sales are not matched by new demand for units, then assets have to be disposed of.

Funds operating on the unit principle are 'open ended' in the sense that the number of units in existence can increase or decrease. Share capital is fixed (the company is 'close ended') apart from new issues authorised by shareholders or capital reductions. Direct and indirect reductions in capital are closely governed by statute and case law and the doctrine of share capital maintenance distinguishes between the income and capital of a company. There are two basic forms of funding for development: corporate finance and direct project funding. In the 1980s, because of the exempt or partially relieved tax status of the principal financial institutions and the landlord and tenant system established in this country which encouraged the investor rather than the owner-occupier, the long-term funding of most commercial developments was usually project based rather than through the stock market or the company share medium.

An avenue of property development finance was the Business Expansion Scheme. This scheme provided tax concessions involved in development but as an opportunity for investment with tax relief. This avenue was closed by the 1985 Budget which excluded certain property development companies from the scheme and further by the 1986

Budget which excluded high asset-back activities and effectively closed a loophole previously exploited by several property based activities.

It is difficult to analyse precisely the proportion of new development attributable to property companies, as it is hard to distinguish between investment funds used for existing and for new development. From statistics available it is possible to distinguish broadly the amount of funds available for direct and indirect funding by institutions. Studies in the mid-1980s (Woodroffe and Isaac 1987) show in 1983 £1498 million was invested in property (other than house mortgages) by the institutions; banks advanced £969 million to property companies. However, as will be shown in the next section, new development represents a small proportion of the overall investment and the major problem related to funds is how much of the direct and indirect funding relates to new property. At the beginning of 1983 the total market value of the 42 major property companies was in excess of £4274 million. Again, it is difficult to analyse the amounts of internal capital available for corporate funding of property but the figures produced by Rowe and Pitman at the beginning of 1983 show a total retained profit of the order of £65 million. Looking globally at these figures it was evident that property companies are playing a significant role in property investment and funding. Using the outline figures mentioned earlier it may be shown that in 1983 property company investment was running at 70% of institutional funding (there were £969m of bank loans to property companies together with £65m retained profit compared to institutional investment of £1498m).

Direct property investment

Property investment is a long-term commitment of funds. Transfer costs and purchase time (up to six months) restricts opportunities for short-term dealings. Investors in property are looking for growth of income and capital, but note that these two aspects are interrelated through the relationship: all risk yield = income/capital value. In the UK, the tradition in the commercial market is for occupiers to lease premises, thus the ownership and occupation are split and an investment market in property is opened up. In the US and Europe there is more owner-occupation.

The most notable change in the investment market, as far as funding is concerned, is the narrowing between the yield and interest rate gap. Rising property yields and falling interest rates now mean that many investments are close to self-funding. The difficulty for many funders is that there is not enough investment product to place with the banks, with most of the prime investments being snapped up by the institutions. There is a 'flight to quality' in investment lending. Increasing company failures have left banks with substantial problems in this sector, and they are now suspicious of anything but the highest quality tenants. For any secondary investments, the banks will look very closely at the financial strength of the borrower and probably lend more onerously, reducing the loan to value exposure they are prepared to consider, and pushing up the interest margin they would expect the borrower to pay. Banks are also looking at the level of interest cover provided by rental income. Previously, banks were happy for rental income to cover interest payable on a ratio of 1:1 or even deficit fund whilst rents were rising sharply. Today, however, banks will require rental cover more in the order of 1:1.2 or 1:1.25 taking the view that there may be little or no rental growth at next review. (1:1.2 means that every £100 of interest payable, say on a monthly basis, will have to be matched by £120 of rental income for the same month.)

The two main markets which are easier to find funding in are, firstly, investments let to blue chip covenants where funding is arranged at 85% of the purchase price, at fixed rates of interest from 2 to 20 years; secondly, on secondary investments bought on high yields with a good spread of tenants regardless of their covenant strength, and in these instances funds can be arranged at up to 75% of purchase price and again on fixed rates of interest from 2 to 20 years.

Market players

In the 1990s property came to be regarded as an investment comparable to other investment media and there was a need to compare the characteristics of property with other investments such as government stocks (gilts) or ordinary shares (equities) especially in respect of the returns arising. There was thus a realisation in the property profession that to enable financial specialists to compare these returns they would need some understanding of property and, in turn, the property adviser will need to be able to analyse returns from other investments. The idea was created, following the deregulation of the financial markets in the 1980s, of a one-stop shop, where the City security houses could merge with surveyors and the same company could provide property expertise, banking and stock market advice. The idea of the one-stop shop has not really materialised but the smaller and medium-sized surveying practices have been taken over by financial institutions to integrate the financial functions. This has mainly taken effect in respect of commercial rather than residential property. The development in the commercial property area has been that the financial groups in the City have tended to develop in-house expertise in commercial property (Brett 1990). Larger estate agencies have set up financial services subsidiaries employing ex-bankers. The banks have now begun to apply the innovative techniques of financing derived from applications to corporate bodies in the trading area and also those techniques introduced from the USA. The traditional institutions, the insurance companies and the pension funds have become less important as a source of finance for commercial property and the banks have become more important. Traditionally in development property, the surveyor has been the intermediary between the property developer and institutions. The combination of the factors above have deprived agents and surveyors of their most profitable business: the securities and bank markets.

The insurance companies and pension funds are traditionally long-term owners of commercial investments. The life assurance and the general funds both have control of long-term investment monies and in this respect property always appeared to be a suitable home for them. Both are investing their own funds rather than borrowed funds, so for these funds the element of capital appreciation as opposed to income generation is important. There are no problems of an income deficit which may be a problem, for instance, to property owners reliant on borrowed money. In the traditional approach to property development the property developers relied on bank lenders for short-term finance during the development with a buy-out by the institution enabling repayment of the short-term bank debt. Now the institutions are taking out a much smaller proportion and there has been a change to other more innovative forms of finance.

3.3   OVERSEAS INVESTORS

Overseas purchasers are generally institutions, property companies or construction companies. They tend to deal in London and are cautious small players often seeking

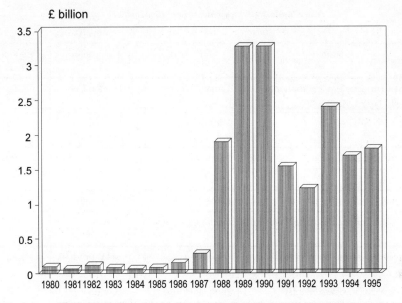

£ billion

Figure 3.1   *Overseas direct investment in property 1980–95*

partnerships with UK developers. The scale of overseas investment is estimated at £1.5–£2 billion for 1993; this is down from £3 billion in 1989/90. The overseas investment is concentrated in central London. German investors have led the market with Middle Eastern and Asian investors following (DTZ Debenham Thorpe 1993). The scale of overseas direct investment is shown in Figure 3.1.

In 1995 the US investors dominated the investment scene and invested some £760m. The Germans however have invested more in the 4 years to 1995 (Catalano 1996, based on research by DTZ: *Overseas Investment in the UK Property Market, Special Report January 1996*). In 1995 the Germans invested £370m. Buyers from other European countries also feature in 1995, accounting for 19% of the total foreign investment. Swedish investments were prominent, investing more than £50m. Of the rest, Middle Eastern and Far Eastern investors account for large investments. Middle Eastern money has been the most consistent over the period of record of investment by DTZ in the seven years up to 1995. The major deals in 1995 associated with foreign investment are shown in Table 3.2. In their report *Money into Property*, DTZ Debenham Thorpe (1996) reported that the key overseas players in the five-year period to 1996 had been German investors. The £370m of investment in 1995 accounted for nearly a fifth of all overseas purchases, bringing their cumulative total of purchases since 1989 to £2.73 billion. In the first six months of 1996, they purchased a further £336m of investments. The countries represented by overseas investors are shown in Figure 3.2.

3.4   FINANCIAL INSTITUTIONS

Institutional investment

The financial institutions consist of the insurance companies and pension funds, the two principal channels for the nation's savings. Because of the nature and risks of the real

Table 3.2 *Major investment deals in 1995*

Source	Property	Location	Reported price (£m)
US-led consortium (International Property Corporation)	Canary Wharf	London E14	780
German (DEGI)	Portfolio	Central London	125
German (CGI)	Plumtree Court	London EC4	90.2
German (CGI)	One Curzon Street	London W1	55
US/UK (Teachers/Haslemere)	Kinnaird Park	Edinburgh	55
US/UK (Whitehall Fund/Bourne End)	Marlowes Centre	Hemel Hempstead	45
Malaysian (Millennium Group)	Leavesden Aerodrome	Nr Watford	40
French (Bail Investissements)	Templar House	London WC1	33
US (General Electric Pension Trust-half share)	Cannon Bridge	London EC4	32
Hong Kong (Adrian Fu)	15 Appold Street	London EC2	31.3
German (Despa)	100 Ludgate Hill and D'Arcy House	London EC4	45.3
Danish (PFA)	Aliffe House	London E1	26.75
German (CGI)	10 George Street	Edinburgh	20.5

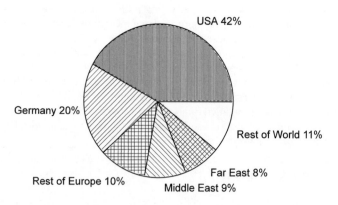

Figure 3.2 *Foreign investment in the UK by nationality 1995*
Source: DTZ Debenham Thorpe Research.

property market and because of the larger lot size, individual investors have generally withdrawn from the market, also the channelling or collectivisation of saving into financial institutions is more tax effective than direct investment.

Financial institutions, beside the pension funds and insurance companies, also include the unit trust funds and investment trusts which are dealt with later. In addition there are also the traditional institutions such as the church, the crown and local authorities who own a large portfolio of investment land from bequests, death intestate and government purchase. These lands are generally considered operational lands and are now subject to normal investment performance criteria. Landed estates are also significant property owners and the Grosvenor Estate is a major property developer and investor. Baum and Schofield (1991) carried out a survey of UK institutions in a questionnaire, and found that the reasons for holding property were listed as risk/return characteristics, liability matching, and inflation hedging, and also the respondents invested in property because their competitors did!

The financial institutions dominated the funding of development properties in the late 1970s and early 1980s. The traditional approach adopted for development finance was to obtain short-term finance to complete a development and then arrange a buy-out by an institutional investor. The dominance of the financial institutions has since declined. Since 1985, the important new money into commercial property has been from banks, property companies and through overseas investors (Evans 1992). Thus the growth of financial institutions, evident from the expansion of their development activity in the post-war period, has now abated and resulted in a significant move away from property investment and funding by institutions (Woodroffe and Isaac 1987). The decline of the institutions in the commercial property market has been matched by an increase in indirect investment in property companies by way of bank advances. Outstanding bank loans to property companies increased from £5 billion in 1985 to just over £40 billion in the second quarter of 1991 and have declined only slightly since, to £36.8 billion at the beginning of 1993; by the second quarter of 1994 they had declined to £32.5 billion (CSO 1994). Between 1986 and 1992 institutions' purchases have generally exceeded their sales but their net property investment has been a declining share of the total. Institutional net property investment is shown in Table 3.3.

Table 3.3   *Institutional net property investment 1986–94 (£ million)*

	1986	1987	1988	1989	1990	1991	1992	1993	1994[a]
Insurance companies:									
Life funds	789	726	1008	1090	946	1493	668	452	2024
General insurance	32	29	94	420	134	−10	−68	−220	−156
Total insurance companies	821	755	1102	1510	1080	1483	600	232	1868
Pension funds	434	240	312	92	−491	467	349	299	−282
Property unit trusts	−101	−516	99	31	−61	19	−12	92	89
Total	1154	479	1513	1633	528	1969	937	623	1675

[a] First 2 quarters 1994 only.
Sources: Evans (1993), CSO (1994).

From 1984 there was thus a noticeable fall in the availability of long-term institutional funding and the reaction of the City to the shortfall was to turn to innovative financing methods. Out of necessity developers turned to alternative finance sources to complement institutional finance (Richard Ellis, 1986). Money flowing into property from investors during the early 1980s increased from £2 billion to £4 billion in the period 1980–6. Between 1986 and 1989 there was a rapid increase to £14 billion. It then tailed off to £8 billion, £4 billion and finally £0.5 billion in 1992. Of the financial institutions, the pension funds' involvement had been relatively static but decreased in the late 1980s. The insurance companies have been more stable investors with an increase in investment in the period 1989–91. The Stock Exchange has not been a significant contributor except in 1987, 1989 and 1991. Banks rapidly increased their involvement between 1986 and 1991 but this has since decreased quite dramatically.

Property as a proportion of overall institutional investment has been falling in recent years. The Investment Property Databank Annual Review for 1993 suggests that the best end-of-year figures for the proportion of property in institutional portfolios as at December 1992 showed a fall to 7% from the figure in December 1991 which was 9%. The bulk of the drop can be explained, however, in terms of the differential price movements between the different asset classes held in the portfolio. Net property investment by institutions is still positive but as at 1993 was the lowest recorded level since 1980 (Investment Property Databank 1992). Twenty years ago 22% of pension fund investment was in property but by 1996 this had fallen to about 5% of pension fund assets. This has been due to disappointing returns and increased range of alternative investments, such as overseas investment and index linked bonds. There is now a need to create a property investment vehicle with tax concessions. Without institutional investment in property, commercial concerns will keep their capital tied up in bricks and mortar without being able to invest it elsewhere. The problem of property investment for the institutions are:

(i)   Illiquidity: it takes time to sell property and this can be especially difficult for an investor in a falling market.

(ii)   The cost of trading: a 'round trip' selling one building and buying another costs about 4% of the amount reinvested including agents and legal fees and stamp duty. These aspects are poor compared to competing assets like equity or gilts.

(iii)   Less secure leases: tenants are no longer prepared to enter into institutional leases, i.e. 25-year leases with 5-year rent reviews.

(iv)   Returns: in the 10 years to 1995: commercial property delivered an annual total investment return of 9.1% against 12% for gilts and 14.7% from equities (London 1996).

The percentage of the average pension fund invested in property has declined over the years, as shown in Figure 3.3.

New pension legislation will be introduced in April 1997 and pension schemes will have to show they are holding enough assets to met their obligations. This new minimum funding requirement (MFR) will have an effect on funds' investment policies but it is not felt that it will affect property investment. Property was regarded as a good diversifier because of low volatility of returns and low correlation with other asset classes. Regulations issued by the Department of Social Security mean that property will be valued on an open market basis for MFR purposes, not forced sale, as some thought and which

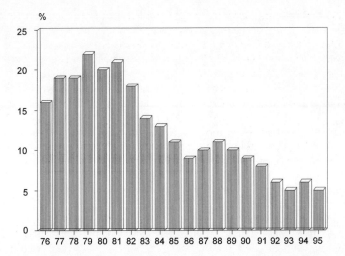

Figure 3.3   *The average percentage of pension fund assets invested in property*

Source: London (1996).

would have had negative effect (Catalano 1996b). The Pensions Act 1995 sets out the new test of the minimum funding requirement. It basically tries to make sure that pension trustees are holding the appropriate assets and if they are not, that they are aware of the financial responsibilities of a mismatched fund. Assets and liabilities must be valued annually by an actuary and if the fund's assets are less than 90% of its liabilities, the company sponsoring the fund must inject additional contributions to restore the 90% ratio. If the ratio is between 90 and 100% the sponsor must take action to bring the funding level to 100% in 5 years. The benchmarks for valuing assets and liabilities are set out in statutory regulations issued by the Department of Social Security and in guidance notes from the Institute of Actuaries. Assets are valued using current market values, thus the open market value for the property assuming a willing seller and buyer. No more than 5% of the total assets for MFR purposes can be held in land or buildings occupied by the sponsoring company. The current level of liabilities, which is the aggregate value of all the current and future pensions that a fund is committed to paying, is calculated using solely the returns from UK gilts and equities as a benchmark. Other assets classes such as property or overseas equities are excluded from the benchmark (Catalano 1996c). Institutional net investment in property 1985–94 is shown in Figure 3.4, and a comparison of institutional investment and bank finance in property is shown in Figure 3.5.

History

In the early post-war period the insurance companies in particular played an important role in property financing by lending long-term fixed interest funds. This approach was useful immediately after the war when inflation was low and thus the returns were not eroded.

Financial arrangements between developers and property companies were encouraged because of the shortage of supply of commercial space, the heavy demand and the resultant rental grown and capital value gain. When inflation established itself, the

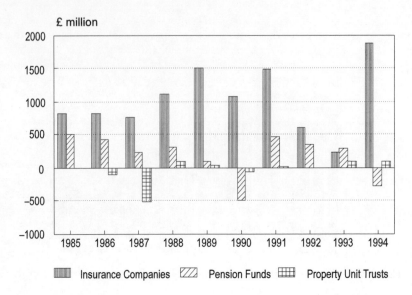

£ million

Insurance Companies   Pension Funds   Property Unit Trusts

1994 First 2 quarters only

Figure 3.4   *Institutional net investment in property 1985–94*

Sources: Evans (1993), CSO (1994).

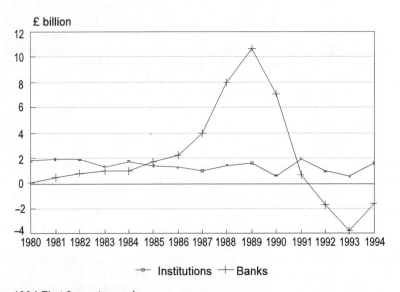

£ billion

Institutions   Banks

1994 First 2 quarters only

Figure 3.5   *Institutional investment and bank finance in property 1980–94*

Sources: Evans (1993), CSO (1994).

fixed interest approach was no longer attractive to the institutions, and insurance companies which had previously had financial arrangements with major developers broke these arrangements and moved into providing funds for sale and leaseback or situations where they could obtain some share in growth. Eventually the institutions carried out their own direct development, funding the developer in an arrangement whereby the developer received a project management fee with some additional incentives. The good performance of equities in the 1980s was matched by a poor performance in property. The demand for development sites by the institutional funds increased land values and capital values of completed developments; the level of income arising from the developments in terms of rentals was over-exaggerated and thus the yield was poor. The insurance companies had been more firmly established in the development markets and the decline in activity affected them less. The pension funds, except for a few larger ones, cut back their portfolios quite drastically. As has been said, new purchases were still made but marginal or poor performing properties were removed from portfolios. In 1990 the property holdings of the insurance companies (life and general companies combined) reached £42 billion with pension funds having holdings of £22 billion (Brett 1990).

Partnership arrangements

The larger insurance companies and the very large pension funds have sizeable departments specialising in property. These departments have sufficient expertise and resources to carry out development themselves as well as advising on the purchase and management of completed investment properties. Smaller funds may choose alternative approaches to investment in property, by indirect investment in unauthorised property unit trusts for instance. Conventional mortgage finance was replaced by direct development by institutions in the 1980s, as mentioned previously. Alternatively the institution would find a sale and leaseback; this involved the sale of the freehold of the property to the institution and the taking back of a long lease by the developer who then sublet the development to occupying tenants on conventional 25-year occupational leases. Early deals had no provision for rent reviews, but in the late 1960s and early 1970s as shorter and shorter review periods became the norm, so these interests provided an appropriate inflation-proofed equity investment, at the same time minimising any management problems (which were taken on by the developer). Equity sharing sale and leaseback arrangements are extremely complex and relate to the balance of risk and return of the parties involved.

The power of the institutions in the UK securities markets can be seen from the fact that one institution alone, the Prudential, controlled 3.5% of the UK equity market in 1990 (Baum and Schofield 1991). The institutions which are commonly regarded as pension funds, insurance companies, property unit trusts and others control one-third of the commercial property market. These were major players in the UK property market in the 1970s, investing up to 19% of their total assets in 1981. The average UK institutional portfolio had fallen back to 12% by 1990 basically on the back of falling values. Whilst transactions in good quality investments were being made there was a disinvestment of poorer performing property assets. The proportion has now fallen to around 9%. The institutions are unlikely to act as major developers again and are more likely to fund property companies to carry out such development and rely on income from investment in property and active management of those investments. Baum and Schofield (1991) in their analysis of institutional investment conclude that:

(i)   institutional investors now have a much greater variety of domestic and over-
        seas investment vehicles to choose from;

(ii)   the property industry generally lacks the tools needed to market property
        successfully to institutional investors who have a choice of many assets types;
        these tools are basically the ability to analyse appropriately the risk and
        returns;

(iii)   there is a great concern in the UK amongst commercial property agents
        regarding the continued decline of institutional commitment to property.

Pension funds

Pension funds are established to meet the future pension liabilities of the employees of a
particular organisation. Occupational pension schemes have grown rapidly in the UK
with half the UK working population being members. There is a clear distinction between
'insured' and 'self-administered' schemes. The former is normally managed on behalf of
the trustees by a life office which will bear the actuarial risk. The latter carries the risk
itself with the management carried out in-house or contracted to an external fund
manager.

Occupational pension schemes may be either funded or unfunded. The former
involves the setting up of an investment fund whilst the latter provides benefits directly
out of current contributions from existing employees. Most UK occupational schemes
are funded.

Funded schemes are categorised into 'immature' and 'mature' funds. An immature
fund is where the net contributions made by the existing employees match or exceed
the payments to be made to retired members. Thus there is a surplus of contributors'
income each month for the fund to invest, and investment income from existing investments is added to this current income. The objective of an immature fund is to invest in
assets which will provide future income flows, matching liabilities which occur as the
fund matures, thus reducing the contribution rate as far as possible.

There are difficulties in measuring the maturity of a pension fund and the scheme's
trustees and actuaries retain influence over this question through exercise of their policy.
An immature fund is more likely to exist in a growing industry. The top funds are quoted
by Baum and Schofield (1991); there are 20 quoted with funds above £2 billion, categorised as manufacturing, energy or services. Pension funds in the traditional manufacturing sectors like ICI and British Steel are likely to be more mature as the employment
shifts from the traditional manufacturing sector. Energy funds are also mature but the
service sector is growing rapidly and these are less likely to mature in the future. These
cover areas such as banking, air transport and education.

As we have noted, pension funds invest the contributions from members to produce
sufficient cash for retirement benefits. The pension fund is managed by trustees and the
relative power of the trustees is determined by the trust deed. The deed normally
provides for employers of the organisation or company associated with the fund to be
appointed to the board of trustees with whom the investment policy for the fund rests.
Usually in the investment market, investors will try to maximise their returns and this
may be a combination of increased dividend to shareholders, increase in share price or
greater capitalisation to enable the company to borrow further capital or distribute
retained earnings through a rights issue, but this approach is not possible for a pension
fund (Dubben and Sayce 1991). With a pension fund each fund operates in a different

way investing members' contributions and the monetary value of these contributions can be accurately calculated. The calculation is based on the age of the present fund members, the probable future age structure of the firm or industry associated with the fund and the probable wage rates of retiring members in the future, on which their pensions will be based. Charities are tax exempt. Pension funds avoid risk and in reality maximise returns in the short term, say 1–3 years, although they should be geared to the achievement of pension levels at a future date. The majority of the pension funds' investment is in equities and they own 40% of the stock in London Stock Market. The recent years of a bull equity market and low inflation has meant that they have con-centrated more on equities; property investment is seen as illiquid, difficult to value and expensive to manage and is a considered a long-term investment in comparison with equities. In March 1986, the Chancellor of the Exchequer imposed a 5% ceiling on pension fund surpluses which before were not controlled. The surpluses are used to improve the benefits to members; members' contributions to the fund can be reduced or excess capital can be withdrawn from the fund. If the fund continues to make a surplus greater than 5% then the fund is no longer exempt from taxation.

Insurance companies

The insurance companies are limited providers of property funds. They do, however, offer the attraction of long-term, fixed rate funds which are priced over gilt rates and which can be useful in certain transactions. Insurance companies must keep their long-term activities and general insurance separate by law. Life assurance is part of the long-term business, accumulating funds over a long period of time. Life assurance funds are either with profits or without. The former guarantee a base pay-out which must be met by the insurance company and entitles the insured to a share in profits. The latter has the pay-out determined and fixed in advance. General insurance includes policies such as fire, accident, household and motor insurance, which by nature represents short-term liabil-ities. Insurance companies aim to spread risk over time or between policy holders or both; each fund must have regard to nature, mix and term of relative liabilities.

The insurance companies have payment liabilities which are based on the actuarial table uses of their commitments. General funds do not invest in the same investments as the life funds, as they have to respond to possible claims from policyholders over the shorter term, say less than 12 months. Life insurance companies have had a long history of investment in property and their investment has been greater than the pension funds. Dubben and Sayce (1991) suggest this is because of three reasons:

(i)   Insurance companies have in-house experts and many take direct responsi-bility for decisions on property investment, whereas pension funds entrust management to outside managers who may have little understanding of the property market but lots of the equity and money markets.

(ii) Pension funds in old established industries mature in the medium term which mitigates against long-term property investment.

(iii) Unit linked insurance policies require a short-term return as opposed to endowment policies issued by the insurance companies which require long-term growth.

An example of the portfolio of Norwich Union is outlined in Box 3.1.

NORWICH UNION PORTFOLIO

Norwich Union had a £2.75 billion portfolio at the time of writing. Since the peak of the market the property weighting in the portfolio has been halved to 15% of total assets. They took a strategic positioning in property believing it to be about 2% overweight. Norwich Union was overweight in City offices and did well in the 1980s but was affected by the downturn in the 1990s. There is an exposure to shopping centres with investments in the Bentall Centre in Kingston and Queensgate in Peterborough. Policy is to restrict sector weightings to within 5% of the average Investment Property Databank fund's average; fund managers are specialist to particular sectors

Total assets are: 25% fixed interest securities, 60% equities and 15% property. The property portfolio (based on £2.5bn assets) is 51% offices, 41% retail, 6% industrial and 2% international.

Box 3.1 *Norwich Union Portfolio*

Source: Lennox (1995).

Other financial institutions

High Street clearing banks

The big four are Lloyds, Barclays, National Westminster and Midland. These are probably the first port of call for people looking for loans, especially if they have established relationships. However, they are conservative and may view new transactions related to property in a cynical way. Smaller High Street banks such as the Royal Bank of Scotland, the Bank of Scotland, Yorkshire Bank and the Clydesdale Bank may be more useful potential funders. The smaller banks are likely to have less of a bad debt problem and may want to increase market share. The larger banks are burdened at the moment by over-exposure to the property sector; the emphasis at the present time is on debt repayment rather than new lending. British clearing banks' exposure to the property sector at the critical period to the end of the 1980s is shown in Figure 3.6. Total bank lending as at June 1996 was £30.6 billion down from £32.2 billion in June 1995 (Bank of England 1996). Bank lending by clearing banks is shown in Figure 3.6, bank lending to property companies is shown in Figure 3.7.

Foreign banks

The foreign banks tend to be more aggressive sources of property finance, or were in the early 1990s, but by 1993 they were showing less interest. They are useful sources of funding particularly for quality and corporate transactions. The collapse of BCCI may make borrowers wary of dealing with foreign banks. The collapse of a bank halfway through a development may mean that it could take years to unwind the legal problems and thus would put the borrower's own financial position at risk.

Building societies

The building societies fared badly in the recent slump in the property market. In the late 1980s, their inexperience and desire for market share in commercial property lending led

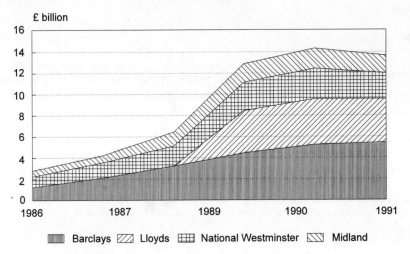

**British Clearing Banks
UK Property Lending**

£ billion

Barclays   Lloyds   National Westminster   Midland

Figure 3.6 *UK clearing banks: UK property lending*

No figures for Lloyds 1986–88.

Source: IBCA/Scott (1992).

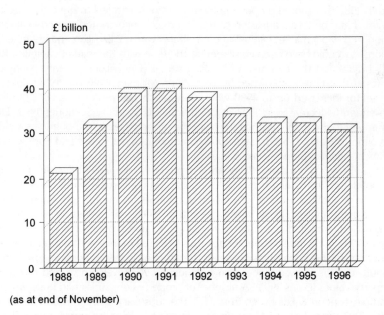

£ billion

(as at end of November)

Figure 3.7 *Bank lending to property companies*

Sources: CSO (1996), Bank of England (1996).

to substantial bad debt. They are now putting their respective houses in order with more qualified staff and are likely to be an important source of commercial finance in the future.

Merchant banks

Merchant banks rarely lend their own money but act as advisers and especially concentrate on large corporate transactions. They are unlikely to be interested in ordinary debt transactions because there would be little opportunity to use their expertise and add value to such a transaction.

Finance houses

In essence, the finance houses have been the principal providers of funding to the secondary leisure and retailing markets, providing finance for the purchase of freehold shops, pubs, restaurants and hotels. Their small trader exposure has made them particularly vulnerable to this latest recession which has resulted in most of them leaving the market.

3.5   PROPERTY COMPANIES

Property business is defined as extraction of value from land and buildings such that the landlord takes a creditor's view rather than an equity holder's view of the occupiers. In March 1988 the quoted property company sector (this refers to quoted property companies, that is ones that are listed on the Stock Exchange) owned property valued at £17 billion, and had a market capitalisation of shares worth £13 billion and net assets of £14 billion. This could have been compared at the time with the market capitalisation of BP (£15 billion) and the commercial banking sector (£16 billion). Seventy percent of the shares at that time were owned by institutions (Millman 1988). The total book assets of the sector increased up to 1990 when they reached a peak of nearly £30 billion but subsequently decreased in 1992 to £25 billion (S. G. Warburg Securities 1993). Debt has continued to rise in the balance sheets of the property sector, although less rapidly than the period to 1992. Table 3.4 sets out a summary of asset values and borrowings in the balance sheets of property companies.

In 1993 there was a dramatic re-rating of property companies because of a major shift in confidence. In the first half of 1993, equity and convertible issues raised by property companies totalled around £1.3 billion. Capital issues raised subsequently showed a rapid expansion (see Figure 3.8). To the end of 1993, share prices rose so strongly that they no longer traded at a discount to net asset value. Property companies were, at the end of 1993, in the rare position of being able to raise money without significant dilution of net asset value or earnings. However, the situation in 1993 was marred by a continued fallout from the consequences of over-lending, over-development and much reduced property values (Evans 1993). A number of property companies had huge writeoffs. For example, London & Edinburgh Trust (LET), the subsidiary of the Swedish Company SPP, had a 1992 pretax loss of £449m against a loss of £138m in the previous year. SPP bought LET in 1990 for £491m. By 1994, property companies' shares were again being traded at a discount to net asset value. Table 3.5 gives a sample of the main quoted property companies on the Stock Exchange and their market capitalisation.

Table 3.4 *Quoted property companies: balance sheets, gearing and financing*

	Total book assets (£m)	Total borrowings* (£m)	Cash (£m)	Debt† as % of book assets	Short-term borrowings (£m)	Short-term borrowings (as % total)
1986	11 298	3 087	437	24.4	1 075	34.8
1987	15 172	4 254	722	24.4	1 506	35.4
1988	19 862	4 988	1 407	19.4	1 748	35.0
1989	27 055	6 939	1 716	20.6	2 648	38.2
1990	30 933	8 590	1 453	24.2	3 642	42.4
1991	27 992	10 132	1 223	32.7	4 374	43.2
1992	25 462	11 130	1 278	38.7	5 218	46.9

Notes: * Total borrowings include convertible loan stocks and bonds.
† Debt is net of cash.
Short-term borrowings are less than 5 years and also include convertible loan stocks and bonds.

Source: S. G. Warburg Securities (1993).

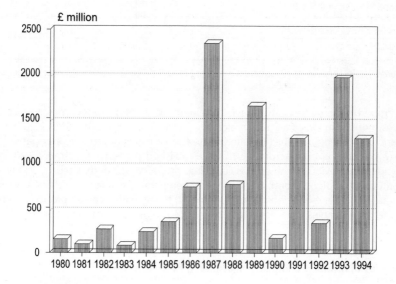

1994 to September only

Figure 3.8 *New capital issues by property companies*

Sources: Evans (1993), CSO (1994).

Table 3.5   *Major quoted property companies*

Company ranking by market capitalisation: UK property sector, January 1995		
Company	*Share price (p)*	*Market capitalisation (£m)*
Land Securities	572	2915.8
MEPC	384	1560.8
British Land	359	1100.6
Hammerson	323	913.7
Slough Estates	220	858.1
Capital Shopping	190	691.6
Great Portland	177	572.7
Brixton Estate	176	409.7
Bradford	178	260.0
Chelsfield	158	247.1
Burford	83	245.3
London Merchant (Ord)	94	228.2
London Merchant (Def'd)	53	40.9
Bilton	241	211.5

Source: UBS (1995) as at 19 January (Only those in FT-SE 100 Index and FT-SE Mid 250 quoted)

Property companies often have development arms as subsidiaries. In fact, most investment companies are also major developers and it is better to distinguish investment and trading activities to differentiate the activities of property companies. Large firms of building contractors have also established property investment and trading companies. Previously the market for prime property was dominated by the financial institutions who could outbid the property companies by finance and tax advantages. Institutions do not have borrowings compared to the highly geared property company. Property companies have also begun to finance themselves through retained profits and rights issues.

Features of property companies considered by an investor

The property companies listed on the Stock Exchange offer potential investors a range of different opportunities. The main features of a property company to be considered by an investor are:

(i)   *The quality of assets in the portfolio*: the age, location and tenure of individual properties will be important as well as the investment's relative importance in the portfolio. The different types of property and the proportion of overseas investment in the portfolio should also be considered.

(ii) *The perceived quality of management in the company*: this perception is very subjective and is often restricted to the market's view about single individuals in the company.

(iii) *The sources of income of the company*: these will vary between well-established property investment companies relying on rents for income, and property trading companies whose income arises from selling on completed developments.

(iv) *The capital structure and gearing of the company*: a highly geared financial structure is more appropriate for established companies deriving a large proportion of revenue from rental income rather than for trading companies dependent on less secure trading profits. The nature of debt is also important.

The summary for a successful property company from an investor's viewpoint is shown in Box 3.2.

WHAT MAKES A SUCCESSFUL PROPERTY COMPANY?

1. Ability to understand and forecast external influences.
2. Reputation, track record, style.
3. Links with other developers.
4. Links with financiers.
5. Exploitation of competitive advantages.
6. Efficient use of resources.
7. Management structure.
8. Market leaders rather than pack followers.

Box 3.2 *Criteria for a successful company*

Property shares

Property companies hold all or most of their assets in property; their shares are thus a surrogate for property. There should be a close correlation between share prices and property value. Shares are more favoured than direct property because of the general rising share market; because of gearing which can increase returns to equity; because of the benefits of stock selection; and because of the perceived dynamic management of property companies (Barter 1988). The drawback of share ownership as against direct property investment is the incidence of tax. This affects the returns compared with direct property investment, as the shareholder is in effect double taxed (see Box 3.3).

Thus property company shares offer the investor four main features:

Management

Shares take away the direct problems of management and offer specialist management and entrepreneurial skills.

Gearing

Gearing (debt to equity as a percentage is used here which is common in the market, but as mentioned earlier in the book debt to total capital is usually used in economic texts) of the larger quoted companies at January 1993 varied quite dramatically. For instance, Speyhawk (before its demise) had a negative equity of £105m, Stanhope had a gearing of 600% whilst Bradford and Warnford had no borrowing. Land Securities had a gearing of 54% (S. G. Warburg Securities 1993). As well as the level of debt, the type of debt is important; whether it is fixed or variable rate, short or long-term is important. Gearing can increase the equity return but can lead to problems of insolvency if overall returns fall.

Liquidity

The market in shares has a central price and there is a speed of entry and exit in and out of the market.

Other participants

Liquidity exists because there are other participants in the share market. Institutional investors hold a high percentage of shares. Usually the shares are held as part of an equity rather than a property portfolio and thus are managed in the more market-led style of equity shares rather than the more asset-led style of direct property (Mallinson 1988).

EXAMPLE: CAPITAL GAINS TAX:
DISADVANTAGE OF OWNERSHIP THROUGH A CORPORATE ENTITY

A property is purchased in 1965 for £4m, had £6m spent on it and was sold in 1982 for £40m. Consider the different tax position of direct ownership against purchase by a UK holding company, which is sold after sale of the property to put its shareholders in funds:

	£m
Sale proceeds	40
Cost	(10)
Gain	30

	Holding company	*Direct ownership*
Gross gain	30	30
Tax on capital gain	(9)	
Available to shareholders	21	

	Tax on capital gain	*Net proceeds*	*Tax on capital gain*	*Net proceeds*
UK gross funds	–	21	–	30
Non-resident	–	21	–	30
UK tax-payer	6.3	14.7	9	21

Box 3.3   *Capital tax disadvantages of the corporate structure*
Source: Millman (1988).

Discount on net asset value

Property investment companies as opposed to property trading companies are valued on the basis of their net assets rather than the income produced. A feature of the market in property in property investment shares is that they trade at a discount to the net assets held. This may not be in cases of a very bullish market and over longer periods for exceptional performers but generally this discount appears to be around 20%. The average discounts on net asset value for property investment companies 1977–94, as analysed by S. G. Warburg Research, are shown in Figure 3.9.

Property share price
discount to net asset value

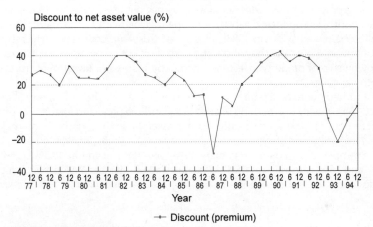

As at December and June. Projected
figures for December 1993 and 1994

Figure 3.9   *Average discount on net asset value 1977–94*

Source: S. G. Warburg Research (1993).

The discount is measured as:

$$\frac{\text{Net Asset Value per share (NAV/share)} - \text{Share price}}{\text{NAV/share}} \times 100\%$$

This means that the underlying assets are undervalued because of this discount. Three reasons are commonly given for the existence of the discount:

(i)   the problems of possible loss on the forced sale of the company's assets;

(ii)   tax liabilities, being the capital gains tax liability on disposal of the properties in the company's portfolio and the tax inefficiencies of holding shares as opposed to direct investment;

(iii)   disquiet over the quality of valuations carried out by surveyors on the underlying property assets.

Recent research is inconclusive as to the precise reasons for the discount but this situation has an effect on financing and activity in the sector. Assets are undervalued because of the discount and this discourages the growth of property companies through equity expansion and forces them into borrowing to expand. This leads to companies being highly geared (having a high ratio of borrowed capital to total capital). It discourages takeovers within the sector because takeover situations raise share prices and narrow the discount. Subsequently, following takeovers, the share price will tend to fall to a realistic discount as perceived by the stock market. On the other hand, property investment companies could be vulnerable to takeover by firms from other sectors where discounts do not exist (Woodroffe and Isaac 1987). Contingent capital gains tax on property investment companies prior to the 1988 budget (which moved the base date for capital gains tax forward from 1965 to 1982) probably amounted to about 20% of net asset value but subsequently this has fallen to probably 10%. There is an argument for valuing property investment companies by net net asset value (NNAV) which takes into account the contingent liability for capital gains tax. On this basis the discount would be narrowed (Millman 1988). Investment trusts are companies which hold their investments in shares and they also suffer from discount on net asset value in respect of their ownership of property investment company shares, but investment trusts are not liable to capital gains tax.

1994 turned out to be a poor year for the property sector. The FT Property Share Index fell by 21.5%, mainly due to rising interest rates, and the projected forecast for premiums on share prices in the sector relative to net asset values was dashed. The majority of companies by the end of 1994 were again standing at a share price discount to net asset value. Examples of discounts in January 1995 were British Land at 18.3%, Greycoat at 23.5% and Land Securities at 16.3% (Paribas Capital Markets 1995a). Net asset values and discounts for key companies in the property sector in March 1995 are shown in Table 3.6.

Table 3.6   *Net asset values and discount on major quoted property companies: UK property sector, March 1995*

Company	Share price (p)	Current net asset value (NAV) (p)	Discount to current NAV (%)
British Land*	363	424	14
Brixton Estates	179	214	16
Burford Group	94	92	(2)
Capital SC	193	221	13
Great Portland	170	215	21
Hammerson	319	390	18
Land Securities	586	689	15
MEPC	387	489	21
Slough Estates	227	289	21

Source: Paribas Capital Markets (1995b) as at 8 March.

* adjusted for current open offer.

Over the past decade UK investors have continued investing abroad. This expansion has been encouraged by the need to increase the performance of the property portfolio and reduce market risk through diversification. Hedging techniques are available to these companies through foreign exchange futures, options and swap contracts, but a recent study (Dawson 1995) found that 72% of property companies, institutions and fund management groups with overseas property exposure did not avail themselves of this protection thus leading to lower returns on the portfolio. The extent of the dispersion of the top 5 quoted companies who invest abroad – Hammerson, MEPC, Slough Estates, Brixton Estates and British Land – is shown in Figure 3.10.

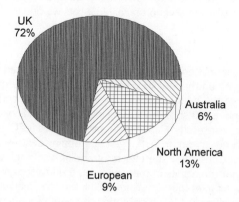

Figure 3.10 *Top five investors' overseas portfolios: breakdown of 1994 property assets by country*

Source: Dawson (1995).

Corporate capital structure

The question of an optimal capital structure for a particular company is a question which has aroused much debate and this is especially important in property companies where there may be high levels of debt. The problem is the choice of the best mix of debt (loans, debentures) and equity (ordinary shares, reserves and retained profits). The following factors ought to be considered, but assessing the weight to be given to each one is a matter of judgement:

Cost

The current and future costs of each potential source of capital should be estimated and compared. The costs of each source are not independent of one another. It is generally desirable to minimise the average overall cost of capital to the company.

Risk

It is unwise to place a company in a position where it may be unable, if profits fall, to pay interest as it falls due or to meet redemptions. It is equally undesirable to be forced to cut or omit the ordinary dividend to shareholders.

Control

Except where there is no alternative, a company should not make any issue of shares which would have the effects of removing or diluting control by the existing share-holders.

Acceptability

A company can only borrow if investors are willing to lend to it. Few listed companies can afford the luxury of a capital structure which is unacceptable to the main institutional investors. A company with readily mortgageable assets will find it easier to raise debt.

Transferability

Shares may be listed or unlisted. Many private companies have made issues to the public so as to obtain a listing on the Stock Exchange and improve the transferability of their shares. A summary of the performance of the major property companies is shown in Table 3.7; the year end results show how rising investment yields have hit most investors for the 1995 end-of-year results. Capital Shopping Centres (CSC) have done relatively well based on a high-quality portfolio of regional shopping centres; other retail investors also benefited. The returns show the effects of adding value through active manage-ment; by stripping out the results of management, the Investment Property Databank (IPD) have created a 'market index' (Lennox 1996); thus the market return in 1995 was 3.2% against the benchmark 4.1%, highlighting the positive influence that active man-agement can have in protecting investment returns from the worst effects of falling values.

3.6   AUTHORISED PROPERTY UNIT TRUSTS

The use of unit trusts to encourage investment in property has already been discussed as well as the difficulties related to setting up an authorised unit trust. On 15 July 1991, the Securities and Investments Board issued regulations enabling authorised property unit trusts (APUTs) to invest directly in property. Thus APUTs will allow the investors to enter the commercial property market in exactly the same way as the unit trusts offer investors exposure to shares. Prior to the change in regulations, unit trusts were not permitted to invest directly into property. This meant that unauthorised property unit trusts were only open to exempt funds such as pension funds and charities.

There are tax advantages of investing in an APUT. Corporation tax is paid at the base rate level of 25% on net income instead of the full rate of corporation tax at 33%. A distribution made by an APUT to its unit holders will be treated for tax purposes as dividends. Individual unit holders will received a tax credit of 25% on those distributions and will only be liable for higher rate personal tax. Corporate investors who pay corpora-tion tax at the small companies' rate of 25% will also have the whole of their liability to tax arising from APUT covered by the tax credit. An APUT, in addition, is entirely free from capital gains tax arising on the disposal of property. Unit holders will, however, remain subject to any capital gains tax arising from the disposal of their units unless, of course, they are tax exempt. Set against these tax advantages, APUTs will have to comply with many regulations imposed by the Securities and Investment Board (SIB) to protect

Table 3.7 *Property company performance 1995*

Company	Year-end pretax (£m)	Pretax % (+/−)	Portfolio (£m)	Valuation (%) (+/−)	NAV (p)	NAV (%) (+/−)	Share price (p)
Argent	13.6	+400	275.6	+0.4	287.0	+7.0	350
Asda Property	8.9	+7.0	214	0.0	130.0	+1.0	144
Bilton	18.2	−2.0	306	−2.5	315.0	−3.3	224
Bourne End	1.0	+23.0	169.1	−4.3	81.2	−12.7	44
Brixton Estate	25.1	+7.9	932	−4.9	188.0	−6.9	180
Brightstone	0.3	+123.0	13.9	n/a	149.0	−7.0	103
Burford	11.7	−20.4	385.3	+3.0	104.3	+16.0	126
Capital & Regional	4.7	+14.0	159.3	−1.3	186.2	+1.5	185
CSC	46.4	+72.0	1 260	+12.8	254.0	+16.0	282
Chelsfield	10.6	+4.0	653.3	n/a	190.2	+6.0	276
City Site	0.5	+322.0	111.5	−3.0	30.0	−54.5	32
Clarke Nickolls	1.5	+25.0	25.5	−2.6	9.5	+1.4	8
CLS	8.2	−32.5	335.4	−0.6	130.5	−1.0	101
Derwent Valley	4.4	−30.2	224.8	+5.0	340.0	+9.0	363
English & Overseas	(0.6)	−163.0	34.1	n/a	31.9	−8.8	19
Estates & General	(1.8)	−5.0	68.3	−1.6	n/a	n/a	5.5
Fiscal Properties	1.6	+800.0	83.9	+2.4	78.4	−2.0	56
Green Property	Ir6.4	+58.2	Ir165.8	n/a	Ir202.0	+9.8	242
Hammerson	57.7	−46.3	1 785.3	−0.6	376.0	+0.3	376
Helical Bar	9.2	+12.0	180.8	−1.5	368.0	+1.0	373
Hemingway	2.8	+4.0	171.6	n/a	37.3	+8.7	28
London & Associated	1.7	+1.0	71	n/a	50.2	−4.3	34.5
St Modwen	10.0	−12.5	83.7	+0.5	53.0	+8.2	60
Moorfield	0.6	−47.9	44.5	−8.0	37.0	−18.0	31
Newport Holdings	0.2	+212.0	27.1	n/a	115.0	+2.7	80
Olives Property	0.7	+19.8	23.5	n/a	38.7	+6.8	28
Premier Land	(5.6)	−17.9	82.1	−3.8	n/a	n/a	3.7
Rugby Estates	1.0	−57.0	21.1	−10.0	n/a	n/a	84
Slough Estates	70.7	+10.5	2 008.6	−3.1	267.0	−3.6	222
Speciality Shops	0.9	−19.8	45.5	−3.0	134.0	−5.0	101
Wates	0.6	+249.0	213.7	n/a	79.6	+4.6	67.5

Source: Lennox (1996).

non-institutional investors from the risks involved in property investment. These pro-blems include the lack of liquidity of property, a unit price based on possible subjective valuations, changes in values and the actual market for the units themselves (Ryland 1991; Baring, Houston and Saunders 1991). The regulations are as follows:

Structure

The structure of an APUT is similar to existing unit trust schemes with a trustee and a manager. The manager is responsible for the day-to-day management of the scheme, with the trustee and manager owing a fiduciary duty to the unit holders.

Investment characteristics

(i)   A fund must attain a value of £5m within 21 days. Thereafter between 20% and 80% of its funds must be invested in property or property related securities. These investments can be in EU member states and a number of other countries like the US and Canada.

(ii)   Up to 10% of the portfolio may be invested in unlisted property shares.

(iii) 20%–30% may be invested in cash or near cash (government securities or quoted property company shares).

(iv)   It can only invest a maximum of 15% of value of fund in any one property. This maximum value may increase to 25% once the property has been included in the portfolio. No more than 20% of the gross rental income may come from the tenant and only 25% of the fund may be invested in vacant or development properties.

(v)   APUTs may borrow against properties, up to a maximum of 30% of each property's value or 15% of the whole portfolio.

Valuation

The value of an APUT is strictly controlled with a full independent valuation once a year, carried out by a qualified surveyor in accordance with the Royal Institution of Chartered Surveyor's guidelines. In addition, to keep unit prices current, there will be an 'armchair' valuation at least once a month to review the last full valuation. Any new purchases must not exceed 105% of the valuation.

Redemptions

Units will normally be redeemed within four business days after the valuation following the request for redemption. In certain circumstances, a manager may suspend redemp-tion rights for a period up to 28 days subject to trustee approval and the SIB being advised.

Potential

APUTs offer a good opportunity of gaining exposure to the property investment market. By the end of 1991 only two APUTs had been established, as substantial commitment is required from the institution or funder to establish an APUT. The APUT has achieved more acceptance in the market than securitisation vehicles (see Chapter 12) but APUTs are not a direct alternative to these vehicles; APUTs invest in smaller-sized properties which already has a broad market appeal among investing institutions, not large illiquid properties (Sexton and Laxton 1992).

3.7 INVESTMENT TRUSTS AND UNIT TRUSTS

Investment trusts are companies which own shares in other companies. They suffer from the problems of discount on net asset value which are described in the context of property companies earlier in this chapter. As an example of a property investment trust, Banque Paribas announced in October 1993 the setting up of a £50 million property investment trust on the Stock Exchange. The trust is called the Wigmore Property Trust and will concentrate on the share of small companies with a market capitalisation of less than £250m. The trust will invest in mainly quoted ordinary shares and focus on invest-ment companies. It may also have up to 20% of its net asset value in special situations which could mean finance for corporate restructuring and acquisitions (Catalano 1995). The Trust is a quoted company and closed-ended unlike a unit trust. Exempt property unit trusts (PUTs) are designed for non-taxpaying investors like pension funds and cha-rities. The market in these units is illiquid. They are valued at the underlying net asset value with no discount. Exempt PUTs are open-ended.

A unit trust is a legal claim to a fractional part of a trust's portfolio. It allows a small investor to benefit from full portfolio diversification and specialist management without requiring the individual expertise and financial resources if investing directly in the same investment portfolio. A property unit trust or PUT invests solely in property but holding units differs from holding shares in a property company. The former is subject to trust law, the latter is subject to company law. A PUT is generally open-ended; it can contract or expand according to demand and supply. Units in PUTs are not marketable in a second-ary market and can only be acquired or redeemed through the unit trust, while company shares are traded on the Stock Exchange. Whilst property companies are highly geared, the borrowing of PUTs is usually small. PUTs are tax transparent but companies usually pay dividends out of taxed profits. PUTs have traditionally been unauthorised so that they cannot be marketed direct to the public. This is now changing although the essential function of the PUT (to provide a medium which enables tax exempt pension funds and charities to invest in property without taking excessive risk) will ensure their continuation. The problems associated with being open ended will need to be remedied.

APUTs as discussed above are also open-ended. The manager has to be in a position to liquidate part of the trust's investment at any time to redeem units that investors wish to sell. The market price of APUTs is again the net asset value without discount. The experience of Rodamco in Holland has shown the shortcomings of open-ended funds which invest in illiquid assets; this is treated as a brief case study in Box 3.4. There is a liquidity problem with APUTs (Venmore-Rowland 1991).

Australian PUTs and US real estate investment trusts (REITs) are close-ended trusts. The REIT market is a useful comparison for developments in unit trusts and securitisation. The REIT market started in the US in 1960; the laws allowed certain companies (REITs) to own property and mortgages and to pay dividends without prior deduction of corporate taxes. Of the REITs in existence in the US now, 50% are mortgage REITs and 40% are equity REITs, (which derive their income from rent); the remainder are hybrids. There were

RODAMCO: A CASE STUDY

The principle

Rodamco was established in 1979 as an open-ended fund. Rodamco forms one of the main investment vehicles within the largest Dutch investment fund management group. To investors, the vehicle appeared a safe and highly liquid exposure to direct property. It attracted the interest of institutional and private investors who formed, initially at least, 80% of the shareholders. Such companies expand by issuing new shares when demand exceeds supply, but as the company stands in the market it also has to repurchase shares when no other buyer can be found. The shares were thus considered a low-risk investment. Stock market transactions took place at prices close to the net asset value of the company and the net asset value was recalculated each day. This situation requires the company to maintain substantial cash balances but at the same time there was little dilution of assets or earnings per share from share issues. This enabled the company to expand without the need for increasing bank debt to any significant level.

The reality

The fund grew rapidly by way of share placings in 1980. This expansion led to a series of acquisitions especially in the UK and US. In 1986, Haselmere Estates was acquired in the UK and Hexalon Real Estate in the USA. In 1988 it mounted a bid for Hammerson but was outbid by Hammerson's major institutional shareholder. The downturn in 1990 in the US and UK markets led to investors selling the Rodamco stock. This was easy for investors to do as the company stood in the market and bought in the shares offered at the daily quoted net asset value price. The company's shares were suspended in September 1990 and the company changed to being 'close-ended', that is to have a fixed number of shares in issue. On being relisted the share price fell sharply (around 20%), prompting additional selling of the stock before settling at a more normal, in UK terms, discount to net asset value.

Box 3.4   *Rodamco: a case study of an open-ended trust*

Source: Paribas Capital Markets (1993a).

some mistakes in the issues during the period 1985–6 which affected the confidence in the market. Now there is better gearing in these companies and management is better trained to deal with investment decisions especially in the specialist investment areas (Jennings 1993). A property unit trust could be used with securitised property (SPUTs; see Chapter 12 for developments in the area of securitised property).

REFERENCES

Albert, D. and Watson, J. (1990) 'An Approach to Property Joint Ventures', *Journal of Property Finance*, vol. 1, no. 2, pp. 189–95.

Bank of England (1994a) *Quarterly Bulletin*, vol. 34, no. 3, August.

Bank of England (1994b) *Quarterly Bulletin*, vol. 34, no. 4, November.

Bank of England (1996) *Quarterly Bulletin*, vol. 36, no. 4, November.

Baring, Houston and Saunders (1991) *Property Report*, London.

Barkshire, R (1986) *The Unitised Property Market*, Working Party of the Unitised Property Market, London, February.

Barter, S. and Sinclair, N. (1988) 'Securitisation', in S. L. Barter (ed.), *Real Estate Finance*, Butterworths, London.

Barter, S. L. (1988) 'Introduction', in S. L. Barter (ed.), *Real Estate Finance*, Butterworths, London

Baum, A. E. and Schofield, A. (1991) 'Property as a Global Asset', in P. Venmore-Rowland, P. Brandon and T. Mole (eds), *Investment, Procurement and Performance in Construction*, RICS, London.

Beveridge, J. (1988) 'The Needs of the Property Company', in S. L. Barter (ed.) *Real Estate Finance*, Butterworths, London.

Bramson, D. (1988) 'The Mechanics of Joint Ventures', in S. L. Barter (ed.), *Real Estate Finance*, Butterworths, London.

Brett, M. (1983) 'Indirect Investment in Property', in C. Darlow (ed.), *Valuation and Investment Appraisal*, Estates Gazette, London

Brett, M. (1990) *Property and Money*, Estates Gazette, London.

Catalano, A. (1995) 'Property Paper Chase', *Estates Gazette*, 1 July.

Catalano, A. (1996a) 'MFR threat to property overdone, says research', *Estates Gazette*, 13 January, p. 57.

Catalano, A. (1996b) 'Property in the pensions balance', *Estates Gazette*, 13 January, p. 62–3.

Catalano, A. (1996c) 'Foreign wallet open in the UK', *Estates Gazette*, 27 January, pp. 66–7.

Central Statistical Office (CSO) (1994) *Financial Statistics*, CSO, November.

Central Statistical Office (CSO) (1996) *Financial Statistics*, CSO, November.

Chesterton Financial *Internal uncirculated reports*, Chesterton Financial, London.

Colliers (1987) 'Unitisation: Elaborate Experiment or Worthwhile and Much Needed Solution?', *International Review*, no. 20, Colliers International Property Consultants.

Dawson, A. (1995) 'Finance: Picking a Path Through the Hedges', *Estates Gazette*, 11 March, pp. 46–7.

Dubben, N. and Sayce, C. (1991) *Property Portfolio Management*, Routledge, London.

DTZ Debenham Thorpe (1993) *Money into Property*, DTZ Debenham Thorpe, London, August.

DTZ Debenham Thorpe (1996) *Money into Property*, DTZ Debenham Thorpe, London, September.

Evans, P. H. (1992) 'Statistical Review', *Journal of Property Finance*, vol. 3, no. 1, pp. 115–120.

Evans, P. H. (1993) 'Statistical Review', *Journal of Property Finance*, vol. 4, no. 2, pp. 75–82.

Fraser, W. D. (1993) *Principles of Property Investment and Pricing*, Macmillan, London.

Gibbs, R. (1987) 'Raising Finance for New Development', *Journal of Valuation*, vol. 5, no. 4, pp. 343–353.

Investment Property Databank (1992) *Annual Review 1993*, IPD, London, December.

Isaac, D. (1986) 'Corporate Finance and Property Development Funding: An Analysis of Property Companies' Capital Structures with Special Reference to the Relationship between Asset Value and Share Price', Unpublished thesis, Faculty of the Built Environment, South Bank Polytechnic, London.

Isaac, D. and Steley, T. (1991) *Property Valuation Techniques*, Macmillan, London.

Isaac, D. and Woodroffe, N. (1987) 'Are property company assets undervalued', *Estates Gazette*, London, 5 September, pp. 1024–6.

Isaac, D. and Woodroffe, N. (1995) *Property Companies: Share Price and Net Asset Value*, Greenwich University Press, London.

Jennings, R. B. (1993) 'The Resurgence of Real Estate Investment Trusts (REITs)', *Journal of Property Finance*, vol. 4, no. 1, pp. 13–19.

Lennox, K. (1995) 'Moving with the Times', *Estates Gazette*, 27 May, pp. 50–1.

Lennox, K. (1996) 'Valuations – Winners and Losers', *Estates Gazette*, 27 April, p. 60.

London, S. (1996) 'Lure of the Property Magnet' *Financial Times*, 23 September, p. 19.

Mallinson, M. (1988) 'Equity Finance', in S. L. Barter (ed.) *Real Estate Finance*, Butterworths, London.

Maxted, B. (1988) *Unitisation of Property*, College of Estate Management, Reading

McIntosh, A. and Sykes, S. (1985) *A Guide to Institutional Property Investment*, Macmillan, London.

Millman, S. (1988) 'Property, Property Companies and Public Securities', in S. L. Barter (ed.) *Real Estate Finance*, Butterworths, London.

Orchard-Lisle, P. (1987) 'Financing Property Development', *Journal of Valuation*, vol. 5, no. 4, pp. 343–53.

Paribas Capital Markets (1993a) *European Equity Research: Rodamco*, Banque Paribas Nederland N.V., October.

Paribas Capital Markets (1993b) *Monthly Property Share Statistics,* Banque Paribas, November.

Paribas Capital Markets (1995a) *Prospects for the Property Sector,* Banque Paribas, January.

Paribas Capital Markets (1995b) *UK Property Sector Review 1,* Banque Paribas, March.

Peat, M. (1988) 'The Accounting Issues', in S. L. Barter (ed.), *Real Estate Finance,* Butterworths, London.

Pike, R. and Neale, B. (1993) *Corporate Finance and Investment,* Prentice-Hall, London.

Richard Ellis (1986) 'Development Finance', *Property Investment Quarterly Bulletin,* Richard Ellis, London, April.

Royal Institution of Chartered Surveyors (1985) *The Unitisation of Real Property,* RICS, London.

Rydin, Y., Rodney, W. and Orr., C (1990) 'Why Do Institutions Invest in Property', *Journal of Property Finance,* vol. 1, no. 2, pp. 250–8.

Ryland, D. (1991) 'Authorised Property Unit Trusts', *Estates Gazette,* London, 9 November, pp. 163–4.

S. G. Warburg Securities (1993) *U.K. Property: Review of 1992 and Prospects for 1993,* S. G. Warburg, London.

S. G. Warburg Research (1993) *U.K. Property: Monthly Review,* S. G. Warburg, London, November.

Savills (1989) *Financing Property 1989,* Savills, London.

Savills (1993) *Investment and Economic Outlook,* Savills, London, Issue 3, October.

Scott, I. P. (1992) 'Debt, Liquidity and Secondary Trading in Property Debt', *Journal of Property Finance,* vol. 2, no. 4.

Sexton, P. and Laxton, C. (1992) 'Authorised Property Unit Trusts', *Journal of Property Finance,* vol. 2, no. 4, pp. 468–75.

Temple, P. (1992) 'How to Beat a Hostile Takeover', *Journal of Property Finance,* vol. 2, no. 4, pp. 476–83.

UBS Global Research (1995) *U.K. Property Service: Company Ranking by Market Capitalisation,* UBS, London, January.

Venmore-Rowland, P. (1991) 'Vehicles for Property Investment', in P. Venmore-Rowland, P. Brandon and T. Mole (eds), *Investment, Procurement and Performance in Construction,* RICS, London.

Woodroffe, N. and Isaac, D. (1987) 'Corporate Finance and Property Development Funding', Working Paper of the School of Applied Economics and Social Studies, Faculty of the Built Environment, South Bank Polytechnic, London.

Yuen Ka Yin, McKinnell, K. and Isaac, D. (1988) 'The Unitisation of Real Property in Hong Kong', Unpublished research paper, Hong Kong University/University of Greenwich.

4   Types of Investment

4.1   TYPES OF INVESTMENT

The established classification of property investments changed in the 1980s with the addition of high-tech developments, retail warehouses, retail parks, mixed used developments and speciality shops. Workshop conversions with residential or studio space also created an innovative sub-sector. Some of these new categories were encouraged by the changes in planning controls. The Town and Country Planning Use Classes Order 1987 lists the categories of property use and within each classification it is possible to change use without any additional planning consent. This legislation established the class B1, which is a business class allowing movement across the divide from light industrial use to office use. This change caused a remarkable shake-up in the office sector but more so in the industrial sector. Business space became a recognised sector of the investment market dealing with B1 properties, and in addition the concept of business parks was established as opposed to dealing with a block of offices or an industrial estate. The legislation allowed this change of use within the band of uses as long as substantial external physical alterations were not required. However, any change of use which required movement between one class and another required specific consent. Class B1, as well as combining office use with light industrial use, also generally indicated a high-tech usage or specification to the building.

Additional developments in industrial space saw the use of retail warehouses, a retail outlet forming part of a warehouse facility either being a small part of activity, like a trade counter, or the main activity, as with a DIY store or furniture warehouse. With retail warehousing, the location and structure of the building is related to the warehousing sector but the economic analysis and financial appraisal used in such developments relates more to the retail sector. The leisure industry has also followed this trend with 'leisure boxes' enabling flexible use of the facilities. 'Dinosaur World' near Newhaven is an example of a warehouse accommodating a plant nursery and garden centre being extended to include a Dinosaur museum, an extensive botanical garden, miniature village and amusements.

The traditional classes of investment however, remain:

- Retail and retail warehousing
- Offices and business space
- Industrial and warehouse
- Agricultural land and woodland
- Leisure and healthcare
- Residential

The main areas of investment activity are retail, offices and industrial space but, in the past, agricultural estates have formed a major proportion of portfolios. In the leisure and residential sectors, owner-occupiers rather than investors predominate. Dubben and Sayce (1991) quote research carried out in late 1985 which asked pension fund portfolio managers to indicate their ideal portfolio of property assets. The respondents chose 50%

retail, 30% office and 20% industrial. The IPD Annual report for 1995 showed the average property portfolio to account for just 6% of total assets and was split 44% retail, 39% offices, 14% industrial and 3% other. The returns for the sector are set out in Table 4.1. The retail sector provides the best performance and has done so for 4 years previous to the 1995 figures. The office sector under-performed the rest of the market in all but four of the previous 15 years. The industrial sector has shown the sharpest fall in values and the poorest return of the three sectors but 1995 performance is its best for ten years. In terms of income security, in the retail sector 90% of the current income is backed by market rents but in the office sector 30% of income is at risk because of overrenting. The overrenting problem is less serious in the industrial sector but still higher than in retail (Lennox 1996).

Table 4.1   *Returns in the property sector 1995*

Sector	Total return (%)	Capital growth (%)	Rental value (%)
All property	3.2	4.2	0.1
Retail	3.4	−3.2	1.2
Office	2.8	−5.0	−1.3
Industrial	2.7	−6.1	−1.5

Source: IPD/Lennox (1996).

Retail, offices and industrial premises when let are collectively known as business premises and fall within the legislation of the Landlord and Tenant Act 1954 (part 2) and its associated legislation. Under the provisions of the Act, the occupying lessee has the right on the expiration of the lease to be granted a new lease at a market rent, unless the landlord can prove certain grounds for possession, such as redevelopment or tenant/ lessee breach of contract. The law of 'Landlord and Tenant' has provided an unchanging legislative framework over a period of time in which the contractual arrangements between investor and occupier can operate. A recent case of dispute has arisen over privity of contract, where the balance of security and risk between the business tenant and landlord has been changed in the tenant's favour and this is discussed elsewhere in the book.

4.2   DESIGN IMPLICATIONS AND COST

Design and layout of property investments are very important, from an aesthetic, economic, functional and qualitative point of view. The economic viewpoint would consider that a high quality building of good design would be both more efficient and innately more valuable; this would add to the value of the completed development. An efficient building may be economic relative to the cost of construction but also economic in terms of minimising costs in use over the life of the building. The principal constraints on the layout and design of the building are:

(i)   the site and its surroundings;
(ii)   the budget or economic limits on construction;

(iii)   planning permission, building and fire regulations and layout standards laid down by the planning authorities;

(iv)   the users' requirements; and

(v)   legal constraints, such as easements or restrictive covenants.

The designer/architect has to seek a solution to satisfy both the client and the local authority who may act as planning authority and agent for the enforcement of the Building Regulations and other legislation. The client has to be satisfied in respect of the budget, the space and layout, finishes, services, appearance, access and open space and daylighting. The local authority will have to be satisfied as to planning and highway considerations, building regulations and fire precautions. Finally, the architect/designer may have to convince other consultants within the development process that the design is appropriate. This includes the financier who is providing the funding for the scheme. Some of the aspects relating to these constraints are now considered.

The site

The designer of the development will need to know the load-bearing capacity of the subsoil to determine the substructure. The designer or design team will also need to know if there are any restrictions on the legal ownership of the site which might affect the design including easements and restrictive covenants. Planning authorities are sensitive to the effect of height, mass and materials on the street scene, particularly in areas of historic character.

Project or economic limits

The designer should aim to increase the value of the completed development by reducing the costs in the design. The value on completion can be increased by enlarging the floor space but this obviously adds to cost as well. The capital value of the completed development can also be improved by a more economic layout defined by the efficiency ratio and also by low costs in use and high quality finishes. The shape of a building is an important consideration and, from analysis, it is evident that the shape closest to a cube gives the greatest economy in terms of external surface, but there are difficulties in dealing with this shape: firstly, the site and aesthetic considerations; secondly, lighting and ventilation would be difficult in such a shape, as permanent artificial lighting and air conditioning may need to be considered. The efficiency ratio is termed the relationship between gross internal floor area and net usable space; the difference between the two is the space used for internal access areas (stairs, lifts and passageways), toilets and plant rooms. Open-plan offices reduce the space used by internal divisions. A fairly optimum efficiency ratio for an office is about 80% but shops should give at least 90%. In covered shopping centres, non-retail space will need to be allowed for malls and arcades and for servicing, plant rooms, offices for the manager and communal toilets.

The type of construction will also affect the budget, and cost considerations include the structural frame; for instance, a steel frame and precast concrete floors may be more expensive than a cast *in situ* reinforced concrete frame. Column spacings vary according to the use to which the property is put. For shops, a six metre grid is conventional; offices are built to twelve metres with factory and warehouse construction at eighteen metres. Large clear spaces can be achieved but at a cost in terms of roof members, roof depth and loadings on the columns and foundation pads. External cladding can directly affect the costs of construction; the cladding will also need to satisfy thermal insulation and noise insulation requirements. In terms of internal finishes, suspended ceilings are now frequently installed for concealing service runs and also suspended flooring. Commercial space may be let in a shell form in which the tenants fit out the space and finishes to their particular requirements.

Town planning and layout criteria

The planning authority may inhibit the amount of development that can be carried out on a site. These inhibitions can be categorised as follows:

Plot ratio

This is a device used by planning authorities to determine the maximum gross area of building space to be allowed on a site to be developed. It is used for commercial or industrial purposes. The ratio is a ratio of the gross area of the building to the area of the site which may include half the width of adjoining roads. Office schemes seldom exceed a plot ratio of 3½:1 and warehouse industrial developments are usually 1:2 or coverage of half the site.

Daylight

For traditional buildings, simple daylight angling tests were originally used for planning considerations. Modern daylighting standards apply tests based on percentage of total light from an unobstructed sky.

Car parking

Local authorities are generally concerned about the extent of car parking. However, owner-occupiers generally require on-site car parking and lack of provision may prevent sale or letting. One car parking space per 50–100 square metres of gross built space may be a typical provision but this will depend on circumstances. The need for parking spaces for shopping facilities is very important, This may amount to three spaces per 100 m^2 of gross retail floor space.

The users' requirements

Users' requirements relate to the future tenants' requirements but sight should not be lost of the need to accord with the requirements of future owners, investors and financiers. If institutional investors are going to buy the development, they will have certain criteria for design, including floor loadings, ceiling or eaves heights, plot density and size of units. For industrial and warehousing premises, the location may need to be close to the transport infrastructure. Manufacturing premises will need to be convenient for a workforce including transport and community facilities. A developer will usually provide various sizes of buildings in a typical commercial estate to cater for different demands. The site layout of industrial and warehouse estates is also important. The units can be terraced to achieve economies in cost and maintenance. Adequate turning spaces need to be provided for the manoeuvring of heavy goods vehicles. Car parking requirements may vary considerably depending on the numbers of staff employed and the customers and visitors calling at the premises. In terms of eaves height, for ware-housing an economic height is usually about six metres. For manufacturing, this is generally four metres. Ancillary offices for industrial and warehouse premises are gen-erally provided at no more than 10% of total space but with high-tech premises this proportion could be much higher. Offices should have some form of central heating and be insulated from noise from the manufacturing areas. In terms of construction, with a minimum floor loading of 2500 kg per m^2, the cost could be £400/m^2 (1995), but building prices vary considerably because of constructional, site and locational variations (Seeley, 1996).

For business parks and science parks the location is very important, with good access needed to road, rail and air transport. These developments should be low density and of higher quality with good landscaping and good car parking. In addition, in science parks the use of the unit should be restricted to research and development activities and exclude conventional production uses. A dynamic relationship between the entrepre-neurs on the site and researchers and staff of an academic institution is useful. There are few physical differences between business park and science park developments and both uses are classified as B1 under the Town and Country Planning Use Classes Order 1987. Buildings defined as high-tech normally cater for advanced technology companies. Car parking standards for business and science parks are much higher than for tradi-tional industrial estates. Most schemes will want to provide space at the ratio of one space per 20 m^2 of lettable industrial space.

Specific types of property

In shopping centres the chief design criteria is to achieve concentrated pedestrian flows in the malls and arcades. The selection of key tenants and the overall tenant mix is the second most important ingredient of success. To attract shoppers, the magnet or anchor stores should be located where they will draw people along the malls. Careful siting and management of car parks is essential. Tenant mix should include a balance of trades to meet shoppers' requirements. Restaurants, play space and seating help towards the attractiveness of the shopping centre. Malls and arcades should be wide enough for pedestrian traffic, but not too wide to lose the window shoppers' attention (15 metres for the mall but 6 metres for the arcades with a height of 4.5 metres). Shopping units will vary in size from the department store (up to 25 000 square metres), to specialist stores (6000 square metres), supermarkets (around 2000 square metres) and the majority in the 100 to 400 square metres range. These areas are all measured in gross internal floor areas (between the internal surfaces of the external walls).

Retail warehousing is a recent introduction to the retail scene. A great number of these retail warehouses, either individually or in a communal park, have been developed since the mid-1980s. Location is the most important criteria; they can be located in or out of town but need to be close to centres of population and major road networks. In many cases, in order to provide economic buildings, the retailers deliberately avoid high specifications. A range of units within a park may be from 500 to 5000 square metres. The frontage to depth ratio is at least 1:2. Surface parking is essential for a non-food store, ideally at a ratio of one space to 20 m^2 of gross floor area.

For offices, there are a number of considerations that need to be observed, including the lettable area, column spacing and ceiling height, access, including the approach and entrance halls, the quality of finish and the services. Column spacing at 6 metres is reasonably economic, ceiling height minimum should be about 2.8 metres. Floor loading should be based on a institutional requirement of 3 kN per m^2 (a kN is a measure of force roughly equivalent to a mass of 1000kg).

Summary

The architectural design of buildings is influenced by a number of basic factors which the designer needs to be aware of in providing a design solution. These include:

(i)   geographical location;
(ii)   occupier or user requirements – from corporate requirement to individual office worker;
(iii)   economics of development – for the owner-occupier and speculative developer;
(iv)   legislative control – town planning, building regulations and similar legislation;
(v)   construction – constructional techniques, materials, components and the use of sophisticated equipment;
(vi)   aesthetic or architectural design – the 'creative ingredient' based on local characteristics, climate, materials, sense of identification, architectural 'fashion'.

Geographical location

This is determined by economic/organisational factors. For instance, decentralisation of organisations has thrown up demands for building in the suburbs or in regional towns and cities where previously office buildings were rare. It is also determined by the existing character of the town. This may be a significant factor in architectural design: for instance a positive style in an industrial town to enliven the environment or a low-key building in traditional materials in an historic town centre. The siting within a town is also important. A self-contained office on its own detached site poses a different architectural and planning problem from one that is an element of a comprehensive development with shopping and car parking. Problems of precedence in mixed developments of office as against retail use in terms of entrances, layout and servicing will be important.

User requirements

The needs of users, not the prestige or whim of the architect/developer, are of most importance. Owner-occupied buildings need to be built with specific occupiers' requirements in mind. There is a need here to establish user requirements before design is commenced (involvement of the design team at an early stage in conception of project). It is important that the architect's brief is drawn up in response to client's requirements, not written in isolation. Generally, the user/developer should write the brief.

Clients' brief

This will cover elements like the number of people to be accommodated; what activities will be carried out in the building; where activities will be carried out and how they will be organised; the working conditions, environment and welfare and amenity facilities required. The brief will also cover special technical requirements (computer systems, etc.), budget cost and the date for completion.

Legislative controls

This is concerned with maintaining town planning and building regulations. Planning controls will examine issues like: plot ratio (the ratio of gross floor area to actual site area, i.e. 1:1); daylighting angles; car parking requirements; planning agreements; and height massing and aesthetic design.

Constructional techniques, materials and equipment

The design of structure will have effect on: method of construction; time for construction; and aesthetic appearance. The choice of external materials will depend on: cost; ease of construction and manufacture; ability to be weatherproof; weathering; maintenance costs; and appearance. The choice of internal materials will depend on durability, ease of cleaning, appearance. The provision of facilities in the building will depend on the developer's provision rather that actual tenant need. Other factors to be incorporated in the design include: air conditioning which is an integral part of structure and layout; a flexibility of layout for changing office arrangements; floor loadings to take office machinery; and the spacing of columns. The spacing is a trade-off between flexibility and cost.

Aesthetic design

The design should be the most appropriate and suitable, given the client's brief. The relationship and scale to adjoining buildings will be important. The materials should be sympathetic to, but not necessarily the same as, the surroundings.

4.3   RETAIL INVESTMENTS

Retail investments are regarded as the best performing property sector in the property portfolio. The yields that investors are willing to purchase at are accordingly lower than most other forms of investment. The reason for investors bidding down yields reflects the fact that the retail sector is based directly on the spending of the consumer population. Increases in consumption are quickly relayed to High Street and other shop spending. Thus retail occupiers are able, in the appropriate circumstances, to pay higher rents and may be more able to increase rents at review, thus allowing for rental growth. Of course, we are talking here about the prime retail sector; in the secondary and tertiary sectors investments would be very difficult indeed to manage. The structural changes in the retail markets and consumer preference in shopping activity has put paid to many traditional areas of retail activity.

Morgan and Walker (1988) identify the main types of retail development as:

(i)   Infill developments in existing high streets.
(ii)   Covered or open shopping malls as extensions to existing shopping centres.
(iii)   District shopping centres in new suburban locations, usually based upon a large supermarket or superstore with ancillary shops and surface car parking.

(iv)　　Regional and sub-regional out-of-town shopping developments, ranging in size from 20 000 m^2 to 200 000 m^2 based on comparison shopping with extensive car parking.

(v)　　Free-standing superstores and hypermarkets.

(vi)　　Free-standing retail warehousing ranging in size from 1000 m^2 to 20 000 m^2.

(vii)　　Retail warehouse parks ranging in size from 10 000 m^2 to 20 000 m^2.

(viii)　　Speciality centres comprising small units sited off existing high streets with a total size between 1000 m^2 and 25 000 m^2.

(ix)　　Festival centres.

Ignoring the non-prime areas of the retail market (the mixed developments, the corner shop and the suburban parade), the main areas of interest for the investor in retail sector are high street shops and shopping centres, superstores and retail warehouses in non-central, suburban and out-of-town locations and out-of-town shopping centres. There is a hierarchy here of location, and as the activity moves away from the central shopping areas, there is also a hierarchy of scale; the movement out leads to less centralisation of different outlets which are then again consolidated in out-of-town centres. Finally there is a difference in activities in centres. Shopping centres will have a range of outlet providing consumer goods, food and durables; in superstores and retail warehouses there is a differentiation between food based and consumer durable activities. Factory outlets are an extension of the retail warehouse concept and are based on clothing and household goods.

High street shops and central shopping centres

Shops in prime positions such as shops in suburban locations are usually owned by small investors or are owner-occupied. Shops in these locations traditionally will have residential or storage space above. Where the floors above are owned by the ground-floor retailer, there may be little opportunity for letting because of security problems or difficulties with joint access and services. The space is often left vacant, used for poor quality staff rooms or storage rather than being let to residential or commercial users. This eventually leads to a waste of space and the upper floors add little to the overall investment. An RICS research project found evidence of much of the space above conventional shops in poor locations was left vacant.

Location is very important for high street shops; income to the shopkeepers and thus rental levels are based on customer spending and thus a position which is convenient to shoppers and a layout which encourages sales is important. An investor will be looking at a good position primarily in a major shopping locality with good quality neighbouring lettings and convenient pedestrian flows past or through the shop premises. The location is also important with respect to the town or city in which the shop is situated: is this a location of growth; is it likely to be troubled by the development of competing shopping areas nearby; is it a locality or a town in a region with good spending power? Shops need to be of reasonable size; the market has moved against the traditional high street department stores in a multistorey building and these are less favoured, some being subdivided into smaller units or redeveloped.

Town centre schemes incorporating shopping malls were a product of post-war developments, starting off in a basic open format and gradually developing into the covered mall with high quality finishes, facilities and climate control. Centres have required constant refurbishment or 'retro-furbishment' to enable the established centre to adapt to modern demands and match competing centres. Many in-town centres are partnerships between local authorities and developers. The local authorities often own land and have responsibilities for encouraging the rejuvenation of the local economy as well as providing shopping facilities. Town centre schemes may also have problems of related traffic congestion which may require alleviating by the local authority. The success of shopping schemes generally relate to location, access and spending power. The Glades shopping centre in Bromley, Kent is an example of how a shopping development can be skilfully constructed in an area of affluence and high spending power which ensures good retail sales. The development is matched with extensive car parking, pedestrianisation of the high street and good bus and train links to the high street. On the other hand the classic failure of a shopping centre in the past has often been quoted as the Elephant and Castle. This case has been well documented in the book *The Property Boom* (Marriott 1962). The concept of establishing the centre in this location was a good one, based on an existing thriving centre known as the 'Piccadilly of South London' before the Second World War. The awful traffic congestion at the Elephant and Castle junction, where five major roads met, led the Greater London Council (GLC), after the war, to construct a road scheme of two linked roundabouts to deal with the traffic problems; the scale of the redevelopment was assisted by the destruction of the area during the Blitz. The development of the shopping centre came as an afterthought and elements of the shopping provision were split by the road system, access to the central shopping area being through gloomy pedestrian underpasses. The scale of shopping provided was such that the upper shopping floors were partially empty from the beginning, the scale of the centre being based on an unrealistic catchment calculation which stretched across the River Thames to the more affluent and culturally separate area of Pimlico. Subsequent ground lessees of the development from the GLC dealt with the problems as best they could, with Land Securities Investment Trust, besides letting the central office block above the centre to the then Department of Health and Social Security (DHSS), also converting the upper shopping floor to office use.

To be a success, then, a shopping centre must have a good location and a good catchment. By location we can suggest a particular position with reasonable access, with car parking facilities and public transport. The design must also incorporate appropriate pedestrian flows and provide back-up services such as leisure and restaurant facilities to encourage shoppers. The design must be attractive and innovative, creating an impression to shoppers which is pleasing and complementary to the activities of the shoppers. The area must be based on a strong local economy and be of an appropriate size, providing transport facilities appropriate to the catchment area. This provision of transport facilities may involve a possible trade-off between private car parking and the provision of public transport, depending on the analysis of the socio-economic groups involved in the shopping activities and the level of car ownership. A further point to be made is that the shopping centre must be managed effectively. Developers should do this in conjunction with local authorities to ensure, for instance, that adjoining streets are appropriately clean and that the concourse is properly policed. Cleanliness and appearance are important in the presentation of the centre to shoppers. The malls need to be secure for the benefit of shoppers and shopkeepers. Good property management will keep rents up and provide good value for money for the tenants of the centre. Fashion retailing is one of the key activities in high street shopping and is characterised by intense competition between retailers and different shopping centres. The key players in

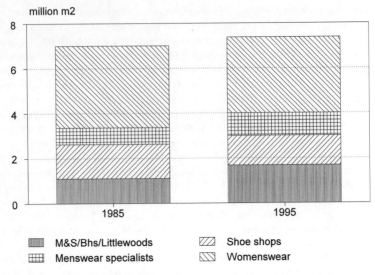

Figure 4.1   *Retailers' space 1985 and 1995 (million m²)*

Source: Verdict space 2000/department and variety stores, *Estates Gazette* (1996a).

1995 were Marks & Spencer (14.7% market), department stores (various, 10%), Burton Fashion (5.2%) and C & A (4.1%); the retail floorspace occupied by the various sectors is shown in Figure 4.1.

To summarise, the important aspects of shopping mall development, based on the findings of Morgan and Walker (1988) were:

  (i)   location;
  (ii)   design;
  (iii)   scale: the development had to achieve a critical mass;
  (iv)   anchor tenants: retail shops so well known and used by shoppers that their presence helps to assure the success of the development;
  (v)   linking-in: how the developments links in with existing shopping and other facilities including infrastructure;
  (vi)   unit sizes around 290 m² but larger sizes essential for fashion retailers;
  (vii) car parking provision: 10 per 100 m² of floor space ideal, 4.5–5.5 per 100 m² usual in USA, 2.5 per 100 m² common in the UK. Multistorey parking provision is very expensive.
  (viii) tenant mix.

Hillier Parker Research have provided a hierarchy of shopping centres based on the location of multiple retailers. Evidence from these studies indicates that town-centre ranking has been influenced more by town-centre developments than out-of-town competition, concluding that out-of-town durable development is dispersed and its effect gradual, whereas town-centre development has immediate and direct effect (Schiller 1996). Table 4.2 shows the effect of major recent schemes on town-centre ranking.

Table 4.2   *The effect of major schemes on town centre ranking*

Town centre	Rank 1984	Rank 1989	New scheme	Rank 1995
Aberdeen	26	33	Bon Accord – 1990	9
Bromley	37	48	The Glades – 1991	24
Kingston	31	29	Bentalls – 1992	18
Watford	39	59	Harlequin – 1990	33
Woking	137	153	The Peacocks – 1992	96

Source: Schiller (1996).

Superstore and retail warehouses

Superstores are built in suburban or edge-of-town locations, or out of town but usually away from conventional shopping areas. They are usually single large stores but occasionally a few small units may be built with the store. They are an enlarged version of the traditional town centre or suburban supermarket, built on a grander scale (2500–10 000 m^2) but dependent on car-user customers. The stores sell foodstuffs and household commodities but some have additional sales in clothes (especially childrenswear), kitchenware and toys. Superstores tend to be developed by owner-occupiers for their use and thus the design will incorporate the house style. In the foodstuffs sector, all the major operators, Sainsburys, Tesco, Safeway and Waitrose, are involved in superstore developments. Institutional investors have become more interested in developments as the trend to superstore development has established itself. Access is all important to the site as customers will be arriving by car generally, thus close and easy proximity to major roads, good signage and easy traffic flow to the site are essential. Bus routes nearby or a shoppers' bus service will allow non-car-borne customers to come. If a possible retail development site is close to a rail line and station then the catchment is improved and all types of shopper can be catered for in terms of transport; these sites may be rare but surplus railway land may provide a good site. The Waitrose stores at Beckenham Junction in South East London and in Chichester are good examples of sites close to stations with easy access and also clearly visible from the trains passing. On the other hand, because of the demand from car-borne shoppers, the retail site will need to be large enough to accommodate an effective traffic flow system and sufficient surface car parking. Traffic flows are important in minimising the conflict between pedestrians and cars moving in and out of parking areas; the conflict, besides being dangerous, will slow the movement of traffic. The Tesco store at Ruxley Corner in Sidcup, Kent has an unfortunate traffic flow. It is adjacent to a busy road with one access; the topography of the site provided the main inflow and outflow to run to the front of the store with outgoing traffic running to the front of the main entrance and exit.

The recent publication of the revised Planning Policy Guidance Note 6 (PPG6) will increase pressure on grocery retailers to revise their out-of-town building programmes, although it is expected that three-quarters of new stores built in 1996 will be superstores above 2500 m^2 (*Estates Gazette* 1996b). The larger grocery operators are shown in Table 4.3 together with an analysis of the number of superstores owned.

Table 4.3   *Comparison of total grocery stores versus superstores*

Operator	Total number of stores	Total number of superstores	Superstores' sales area (000 m²)	Superstores' share of total sales area (%)
Tesco	527	266	968	75.4
Sainsburys	358	211	635	72.6
Asda	194	184	722	97.4
Safeway	374	125	348	46.5
Co-operative stores	2150	80	288	27.1

Source: IGD Stores Database, *Estates Gazette* (1996c).

Retail warehouses are much like superstores in that they depend on the car-borne shopper and so again location is very important with good road access and infrastructure, prominent location to attract passing traffic and sufficient car parking facilities to accommodate shoppers' cars. The developers are usually the owner-occupiers but investors are taking more interest in the sector; the unit size of such development can be larger, the superstore perhaps up to 4000 m². The retail warehouse will be less well fitted than the superstore especially in terms of finishings and services; many will be built in the style of ordinary warehousing, possibly steel framed with steel profile walls and roof and with partial brick or blockwork-built walls. Retail warehouses sell a wider range of goods than a superstore and may be based on electrical goods (Currys), DIY (B&Q), motor accessories (Halfords), carpets, furniture (IKEA) and so on. They may form part of an existing industrial estate or, unlike superstores, may be built as retail warehouse parks with a number of retail warehouses up to 7500 m². Investors have become more interested in retail warehouses because the range of tenants on any particular development will be varied and this diversification thus lessens risk. Factory outlets are an extension of retail warehouse activities, an invention from the US; outlets provide the retail outlets from a particular manufacture and carry stocks of overruns and perhaps discontinued lines. These outlets are especially popular for clothing and kitchenware, and parks consisting of a number of these outlets have been established.

Out-of-town shopping centres

Before discussing the investment potential of out-of-town shopping centres one must be aware of the continued planning debate on the establishment of out-of-town shopping centres, the effect on existing nearby High Streets and the effect on the local economies based on the High Street. PPG6 gives guidance on the development of these centres and the move by government is certainly against them being built on a grand scale. Out-of-town centres are duplicates of the town-centre shopping malls and provide a full range of goods and services associated with town-centre shopping. These will differentiate their activities from superstores and retail warehouses. Beside consumables and durables, services like financial services and banking, restaurants and leisure services will also be provided. In out-of-town centres, unless there is an established public sector transport

infrastructure, like a nearby bus terminus or railway station, the shoppe
car and thus ample surface car parking or multistorey provision will be
access and car parking the centre will be fitted to a high specificatior
malls, lift and escalators, ornamental features and atria and planting. The services will be
expensive, providing the heating and air conditioning necessary for appropriate climate
control and the avoidance of noxious fumes, and also providing a well-lit, welcoming
area. Leisure facilities will be generally provided and will be an important part of the
provision, acting as a public service and encouraging additional and extended visits to
the centre.

As an investment, the out-of-town shopping centre does not have the same degree of
diversity that exists with retail warehouse developments. In addition, the scale of development together with the costs associated with finishes, design and services would not
be attractive to investors unless a successful return could be guaranteed. Major out-of-
town centres include Lakeside in Thurrock, the Metrocentre in Newcastle and Meado-
whall near Sheffield. The government's Planning Policy Guidance Note 6 (PPG6) on out-of-
town development has resolved the previous situation in which there was a complete
ban on out-of-town development and has provided a more flexible approach to car
parking. However, there may be problems caused by the introduction of the concept
of a 'sequential approach' in PPG6 by which the developer of an out-of-town location
has to demonstrate that all potential town-centre sites have been thoroughly assessed.
PPG6 thus limits out-of-town developments; developers must basically build in town or
city-centre sites before edge-of-town sites. If out-of-town development is unavoidable
then PPG13 (relating to car use) comes into force and states there should be a choice of
public transport in serving the site. PPG6 has led to a fall in out-of-town developments in
the pipeline with renewed development interest in town centres (*Estates Gazette* 1996e).
In order to examine out-of-town development more closely, a case study of Bluewater
Park, Dartford, Kent is discussed in Box 4.1.

4.4   OFFICE INVESTMENTS

A recent survey by Chesterton reveals 437 000 m^2 of office space under construction or
near to construction in London. There is a demand for a new generation of office space
from newly restructured businesses. New patterns of working are determining new
requirements and the need to keep operating costs low is paramount. Office buildings
represent the second largest expense after staff salaries, amounting to 10–20% of
revenue, and now need to be used more efficiently to increase competitiveness (Davis,
Langdon and Everest 1996). The increase in the service sector in the UK along with other
developed countries has been due to a decline in the traditional manufacturing base
which has been parallelled by an increase in the service sector, thus increasing relative
demand for office space, especially from the financial services sector. This movement has
seen a decline in both industrial space for manufacturing and in warehousing space due
to more efficient storage. It has also led to a decline in the financial services sector
operating from retail premises. This may or may not lead to an overall increase in office
space as many technological changes are also affecting the use of offices. The traditional
9 a.m to 5 p.m. routine is definitely changing as a mode of working, but whilst the
economy has restructured it still seems to have left many of those remaining in work in
the services sector with ever-lengthening hours. The approach to office use is now one of
flexibility. There are large costs involved in occupying prime office space for working and

---

BLUEWATER PARK, DARTFORD

Blue Circle Properties have extensive land ownerships in the north-western part of Kent due to the land being used for mineral extraction. They have constructed the Crossway Business Park near to junction 1a of the M25 just outside Dartford. The aim of the park is to provide large-sized units with good access to the M25 whilst allowing easy internal movement for large trailers up to 3.7m. Thus the centre is attractive for distribution companies. Existing office tenants include Woolwich Building Society, Honeywell Regis and Colorcon. A major distribution depot has been erected for Fyffes as well as for Gefco (the logistics arm of the PSA Peugot Citroen Group) who have a 3200 m^2 distribution centre which acts as the southern freight terminal for pan-European distribution: their building offers cross-docking and sorting procedures, two floors of offices, driver facilities and training rooms but minimal storage facilities.

Close by, Blue Circle is building a shopping centre, Bluewater Park, which will be completed in April 1999. The cost of development is £350m and key tenants who have already signed agreements to take space include Marks & Spencer, John Lewis, and House of Fraser. The scheme is a mixed retail and leisure development of nearly 150 000 m^2. The three anchor tenants are taking space as follows: John Lewis & Partners 37 000 m^2, Marks & Spencer 18 600 m^2 and House of Fraser 12 100 m^2. Other tenants include C & A, W. H. Smith and Boots. There will be 10 flagship stores of 465–13 000 m^2 and 260 shop units spread across 3 malls arranged in a triangular shape. The tenant mix is being planned over a period of 12–15 months. The catchment area includes 9.6 million people within one hour's drive time.

The retail activity in Dartford town centre has suffered in recent years because of the effect of the Bluewater Park scheme. Zone A retail rentals stand at £345/m^2 at October 1996 compared with £700/m^2 at the height of the market.

Box 4.1   *Case study: Bluewater Park, Dartford*

Sources: Freedman (1996b), Jack (1996), Cavanagh (1996).

---

if this is unnecessary, people can do routine business from home or a back office in a less prestigious location. There are social costs and personal costs involved in tiresome journeys to work which may be unnecessary. The application of technology in the development of office systems and communications means that employees can be linked to a central database from home or car, at conferences or when visiting clients. The need for formal desk areas to sit at is thus reduced. The use of information technology and communications has lessened the need for administrative and clerical staff who traditionally would have dealt with matters to do with handling the paperwork. This leads to flat structures with top management and executives with their own computer technology and database, word processing and spreadsheet/accounting skills. Financial and clerical administrators are not required to do the work of recording and storing information but only in small numbers to manage the data systems. The amount of floorspace used per employee in the clerical office sector is thus lessened, and prime space is only used for important meetings. Employees 'hot desk': they share desks and book meeting-rooms to optimise space, and their records are contained in a lap-top computer and the central database. Employees can send in material from home, by teleworking, communicating by E mail, fax and telephone, so that unnecessary journeys and use of space in the central office location is lessened. Paperless offices prevent the need for excessive files and storage of paperwork and also the machines associated with paper – typewriters, photocopiers, shredders, cabinets, in-trays, and so on, which occupy valuable space. Lesser activities relating to administration, if not done at home, can be done in less expensive locations with an efficient communication system with the head office. Thus the decline in the use of office space can be computed from three variables: the decline in the number of office workers employed; the change in the ratio of floor space occupied per worker; and finally the efficiency of use of the space.

Thus the location of offices will be important but only for certain types. For the central head office a prestigious location may be useful, certainly a position where meetings with professional advisors and clients could be facilitated easily. This will depend on the nature of the business, but for investment purposes, locations in Central Business Districts or conventional locations on major access routes, preferably uncongested, with a good transport infrastructure will be important. For back-room uses a location with good access but perhaps in an area of available labour, or where government financial support is provided, may be appropriate. International organisations in the City of London, following the deregulation of the Stock Exchange (or 'Big Bang') in 1968, created additional demand for large banking floors but as the initial panic subsided so these spaces were left vacant. Space is now more likely to be required on a cellular basis for smaller professional firms and advisors, so the key point of design should be flexibility.

Out-of-town or suburban office parks offer flexible working space to occupiers and this appears to be the demand of the future. This may put an end to the need for the traditional city-centre office building and this is an area of constant debate. The main reasons for companies moving from town or city centres used to be cost but this factor has now been superseded by others: the flexibility of office space to incorporate information technology and personnel requirements resulting from changing company structures; proximity of an appropriate labour force; parking and transport provision and enhancements such as on-site childcare and leisure facilities. Arguments in favour of town-centre locations are still, however, evident, including the need for a prestigious address, the proximity to clients and access to a concentrated and diverse workforce. A number of major companies for instance have in 1996 made major investments in expansion in the City of London, including Deutsche Bank, Morgan Grenfell, Chase Chemical and Merrill Lynch Smith Newcourt. London is seeing companies relocate to the suburbs rather than out-of-town locations, for example Hillingdon (Uxbridge/Heathrow) and Hammersmith to the West of London and Docklands to the east; these include occupiers such as Coca-Cola, Disney, Seagrams, Readers Digest, Morgan Stanley and BZW (Hiatt 1996).

The design of offices is varied and analysis of the footprints of recent developments will provide a range of shapes sometimes related to the site, topography, planning or architectural nature of the development. As suggested above, a most important feature would be flexibility in major office development to accommodate different tenants and use, especially the ability to open up banking floors or open plan space or close it down into cellar offices. For smaller offices for which the investment demand is less, there is a great variety including offices above shops and areas ancillary to manufacturing and warehouse premises. Offices are not so dependent on passing pedestrian flows and therefore their location can be more varied. The essential ingredient is transportation infrastructure, either a railway station, good local bus route and/or ample car parking on the premises. Table 4.4 shows the influences of design and working patterns on the offices of the 1990s.

Table 4.4   *Offices of the 1990s*

Changes to building design	
Conventional	*New*
Deep plan	Medium-depth plan
Single occupation	Multiple occupation
Sealed box	Opening windows
Maximised net lettable area	Efficient lettable area
Flexibility for growth	Flexibility for change
Extensive services distribution	Structured services distribution
Ceiling and floor voids	Single services void
Centralised building management system	Local simple building management system
Fitted out	Shell and core
Changes to pattern of working	
Conventional	*New*
Routine, individual tasks	Creative, group tasks
Isolated activity	Interactive activity
Owned space	Shared space as needed
Low space use	High space use
Single work setting	Multiple, varied work setting

Different office layouts	High autonomy	Low autonomy
High interaction	Den	Club
Low interaction	Hive	Cell

Source: Davis, Langdon and Everest (1996).

The impact of office design is evident in information received from key occupiers who in general are concerned about flexibility of layout, quality of the environment within a building and quality of location. Flexibility has meant moving people to desks not desks to people and using plug-in plug-out task orientated workstations (Freedman 1996a). The debate on teleworking suggests it could lead to a fall in office requirements, and possible changes in the office environment have been noted by recent surveys including that undertaken by King Sturge & Co. which was summarised in *Property Week* (Hunt 1996) and is outlined in Figure 4.2. This research shows the facilities already presently offered by employers which have an impact on the debate.

As Morley (1996) has noted, there has been economic growth since the official end of the recession in 1992, yet there is still a vacancy rate of 10% in the main office centres, higher than in the recessions of the 1970s and 1980s. Investment Property Databank (IPD) figures have shown a negative growth in office rentals since 1990.

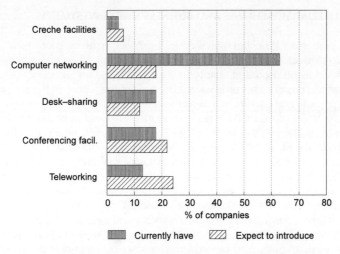

Figure 4.2   *The changing office environment*

Dubben and Sayce (1991) suggest the following criteria for investing in office premises:

(i)   *lettability*: dependent on location, size, architecture, quality, facilities, finishes and running costs;

(ii)   *rental growth*: dependent on appropriate rent review clauses and lease structures, a good office location, reasonable cost in use and a reasonable size. Offices over 10 000 m² are viewed as having few potential lessees.

(iii) *relettability* at the end of the lease: this is related to the problems of obsolescence and depreciation accelerating. Premature obsolescence is due to inflexibility of design.

(iv)   *the ratio of gross to net area*: building costs are estimated on gross areas and rents on net lettable areas; the higher the ratio of net area to gross the better, from a valuation point of view.

The office market has provided a good example of the property cycle in operation, Since the 1960s if the office market is divided into 5-year periods from 1960 to 1980, there has been a peak in each period (Darlow 1983). The sequence of the cycle involves a period when business expectations improve and so does the demand for good quality office space to rent, but on the supply side it takes a minimum of 2 years to respond with new space. By this time demand is in decline and the supply floods the market; rental growth is reduced as the market becomes imbalanced. The office market is underpinned by inflation but is cyclically out of phase. The problem of oversupply can be seen in the problems faced by the Canary Wharf development in the London Docklands in the 1990s. The concept appeared a good one when the building was first mooted; there was a demand after 'Big Bang' and the restrictive planning of the City of London prevented expansion. The idea of a new office city in Docklands providing large areas of space for cheaper rents was attractive. Two problems then occurred. The City of London took fright at their new competitor and relaxed planning restrictions, encouraging more development in the City. Secondly, the property market collapsed and rents fell in the City to the existing levels in Dockland. The financial problems that Olympia and York, the owners of Canary Wharf, had then become very difficult to solve.

4.5   INDUSTRIAL, WAREHOUSE AND BUSINESS SPACE INVESTMENTS

Industrial properties have been viewed by investors as being more risky and more susceptible to decline in the local and national economy. The effect is twofold. The premises tend to be used and adapted for a specific use and if economic conditions change and the premises become vacant because of the nature of the premises which tend to depreciate and become obsolete, they are difficult to relet. In these situations the void risk is a major problem. Premises such as industrial and warehouse buildings have be subject to shorter and shorter life cycles. The traditional 60-year cycle often not only leaves a property obsolete but also the site possibly contaminated or in the wrong location due to changes in the location of industry, the labour force or the transport infrastructure. Redevelopment cycles are being reduced to as little as 20 years depending on the value of the site, development or the depreciation of the existing building. The sector is divided into three main areas: the industrial core, with its subdivisions of heavy, general and light industrial, the warehousing sector, and the business space sector which consists of upgraded warehousing or industrial space set in landscaped parks and involves more of an office orientation to the basic space. Variants of this can be seen in new developments such as science parks, and high-tech or business parks, where users are often high-technology companies or high value-added industries. In these parks the surroundings will be landscaped, have a high office content together with the light industrial space, have good quality finishes and services relative to shed construction (the typical industrial space) and involve specialised space such as workshops or laboratories and perhaps a retail outlet. In refurbished premises there may be more of the bringing together of manufacturing, storage, research, office and reception space into a single location which may be suitable to new embryo firms or small business enterprises and start-ups.

The criteria for good investments are basically the same for this sector as have been mentioned for previous sectors discussed; that is location, communications and size. Location is important from the point of view of the market which is being serviced. Communication and access will be important for customers, staff and vehicles. The local economy, its buoyancy and markets will be important. A prominent location may be a necessity for flagship buildings or head offices. Size could be a problem on initial letting and reletting. Large units may have to be subdivided, and may have problems of lack of diversity. On the other hand a sizeable site will allow for expansion of the premises and can accumulate possible changes in technology.

The Thames Valley has long been a favoured area for industrial and warehouse location as well as fortunate in attracting many new business parks schemes. The valley is centred in an area of strong economic diversity with major markets in London and the south-east of England as well as reasonable access via the M5, M3 and M40 to the M25 and Europe and the two major UK airports. As well as easy access to the channel ports, access to the north is also convenient. The local labour force is skilled and the area is attractive for potential inward investors.

Industrial

Heavy industry and much general industry will rely on specialised plant and companies will thus own the assets and property unless some financial leasing arrangement has been made. Needless to say this is unlikely to be an area for the property investor unless there is mileage in relocation or redevelopment or surplus property for reuse. Heavy industry will be in one-off ownerships, although perhaps in a group because of the general location of industry. Light industrial premises will be developed on estates and this is the likely area for investment. Industrial estates take many forms, from the basic shed structure, indicated earlier in the chapter to the business park development. Investors in industrial estates may work the investment by sale of large sites, the building of premises for sale and the erection of perhaps smaller units for letting. The variations in use, size, tenant and cash flow reduce the risk involved in the venture.

The design of the traditional shed used for industrial or warehouse purposes is a steel portal frame structure with lower sections in brick or blockwork to 2 m and the roof and remaining walls in steel profile sheeting; the property will usually be single storey with appropriate insulation given the nature of the materials. Floor loadings will be 2500 kg (say 2.5 kN) per m^2 with heating, sprinklers and 3 phase power; ancillary offices and toilets are incorporated. The eaves height will depend on use but 4–6 m is usual but perhaps higher for warehousing with a corresponding increase in the floor loading. The office provision is traditionally 10% but the extent of the office space will determine, amongst other things whether the design is a business park one; this office content could be as much as 25%. Units will vary in size but layout is important for access, parking and loading and general circulation on the site, including fire exits and access for emergency vehicles. Unit size may vary from small or nursery units in the 200 m^2 range to conventional estate units of 500 m^2 to 2000 m^2. The degree of landscaping, services and finish to the buildings and the common areas will determine whether the development is classed as a traditional industrial or warehouse, business or high-tech space; the rental levels and capital value will increase accordingly.

Warehouse units

Warehouse units are used for storage and distribution but may occupy the same premises as industrial users. As said above, however, there may be a demand for higher eaves heights and thus a greater floor loading. The location of warehousing units will also differ; by their nature the immediate local economy may not be relevant. What is important is the communication infrastructure and access both to the adjoining roadways and internally to the buildings involved. Close proximity to channel ports, airports or the motorway infrastructure will thus lead to additional value. In terms of design the eaves height may need to be increased to over 7 m with additional floor loading to 3000kg/m^2. Warehousing units are used to centralise production for distribution and therefore offset the need for storage facilities in retail outlets or in the manufacturers' premises. The management of the space should thus be flexible to accommodate change if distribution strategies should be considered. Clear space is required internally to allow the movement of stored products into and around the premises. Owner-occupiers, because of the nature of the market, will tend to be involved in the market but smaller estates of warehouses are developed by investors.

Melzack (1990) suggests the following investment characteristics which need to be taken into account for warehousing:

(i)   Age, construction, maintenance: access for repairs is important as well as avoiding obsolescence in design.

(ii) Height to eaves and floorloading: preferred height 8–10 m, more than 14 m can be a liability.

(iii)   Floorloadings: loadings of 3000 kg per m^2 are not unusual but 1500 may be suitable for 6 m height.

(iv)   Columns, pillars: absence for use of forklift trucks.

(v)   Loading bays: need good facilities with covered loading bays and tailboard-high loading.

(vi)   Yard space: for manoeuvring heavy goods vehicles and articulated lorries and for staff parking.

(vii)   Office space: 5–10% overall space.

(viii)   Heating and ventilation.

(ix)   Ready accessibility: good access to roads.

(x)   Public visibility: added value if premises advertise to passers-by.

(xi)   Security: well fenced and of substantial construction.

(xii)   Size and location: access to motorways and main ports, no ideal size for warehousing but demand (1990) was greatest for 1000 m^2 to 8000 m^2, if premises are large the ability to subdivide is important.

Business space

Business parks are upgraded industrial estates although at the top end they are not recognisable as such. These developments are the product of the boom in science park developments originally conceived by Cambridge University but also further developed by regenerating sites in inner urban areas such as at Aston Science Park in Birmingham. The linkage here is between universities' and technological firms' research and development activity in the parks which may require the consultancy and research output of the nearby academic institution. The management of such parks should encourage advice and technology transfer between companies and the umbrella academic institution. New ideas and the nurturing of embryonic development companies and production lines are an important aspect of their development. Much development is now in the service sector and it has led to an increase in demand for service uses but scientific developments in bio-technology and electronics are important. The units on business park estates are generally well serviced and well landscaped. The internal atmosphere may require appropriate controls (especially with regard to climate and dust) in the spaces devoted to the production of computers and other electronic devices. There is an integration of space so the product development and manufacturing space may be side by side with offices, meeting-rooms or even a rudimentary retail outlet. There needs to be good access and car parking to the premises. In developments like this, although location with respect to communications is important, it is the labour force which is necessary, both skilled people for product development and the 'movers and shakers' who provide the innovations to develop new products. Areas such as 'Silicon Valley' in California are based on the concept that different firms will share the skills of the local labour force and perhaps provide a synergy in research and production which may not be attainable by a single company in isolated production.

The 1987 Town and Country Planning Use Classes Order defined a new use class for the B1 or business space user. The quality of the premises in many cases is more like office space than industrial, and the landscaped campus and parking provision is also like office space with 1 parking space per 25 m^2 of floorspace as a norm. Larger developments require leisure facilities to be incorporated to attract the best tenants and rentals. Firms on these sites may be growing rapidly and they may need to expand and perhaps exchange their premises for larger ones. The landlord will then have to make provision for additional space, which may be wasteful, or allow for flexibility in leasing. This will be so especially with international, and especially US tenants, who will be used to more flexible leasing structures, either a shorter lease (a 5-year rather than a 25-year institutional lease), a more flexible rent review structure or break clauses to allow a get-out.

4.6 LEISURE INVESTMENTS

The range of leisure investments is quite varied and this sector has been the subject of increased investor interest. The sector should include healthcare as well as leisure and there has been increased interest in this area also. The sector is varied and may be based on land, sport activities or accommodation. Land-based activities include theme parks, country and wildlife parks. Sports includes pools, golf and vacation centres based on sports activities, such as Center Parcs, a Dutch leisure development concept of indoor pools and restaurants and sport facilities in a central dome area immune to the vagaries of the British climate. Other activities are more traditional and will involve theatre and cinemas including cinema complexes which are fast becoming a part of out-of-town shopping developments together with other leisure facilities. Hotels, restaurants and public houses have seen a re-emergence of interest. Finally there has been the development of the concept of the leisure box, a shed on an industrial estate but with the potential for a number of different leisure and recreational uses such as bowling alleys, fitness centres, discotheques, night clubs, wine bars and theatrical workshops, markets and amusement arcades. Leisure is a distinct property use but its life cycle and the involvement of rapidly changing technology in the sector has led to conflicts with the traditional 25-year lease pattern, thus turnover rents and flexible lease structures are likely to become more significant (*Estates Gazette* 1996b). The government policy on out-of-town development (PPG6) recommends that entertainment development be built in city centres where possible.

Leisure has tended to be a high risk investment because of problems of keeping the profit up. The value of the property is in the profit. Leisure properties are valued by the traditional profits method and thus variations in profit will have a major effect on value. However, investors are forced into leisure investment because more mixed schemes involve leisure uses. Major industrial, or retail schemes may need to include leisure facilities to be of interest to tenants, employees and to obtain local authority planning permissions. Leisure interests may complement other activities such as retail and extend shopping times. They may complement other activities by the use of premises at unconventional times, shared car parking for instance; for shops by day and cinema by night. Leisure input also diversifies the risk in the investment as its income is likely to vary differently from conventional rentals in the retail and industrial sectors.

4.7 AGRICULTURAL INVESTMENTS

Agricultural land is bedevilled by legislation and valuation is based often on ability to achieve vacant possession rather than on any inherent income flow arising. Farmland is graded by the Ministry of Agriculture, Fisheries and Foods (MAFF) into 5 grades known as the Agricultural Land Classification (ALC) and this will determine the value of the land along with the usual aspects of location and buildings, etc. The ALC is based on three elements, climate, topography and soil. Grade 3 is the broadest grade of land incorporating nearly 50% of agricultural land in England and Wales. Investment in agricultural land may arise from the income from letting or may be farmed by a manager or contractor or in an in-hand farming agreement. Contract farming and other arrangements including share farming have provided a vehicle for landowners to farm 'land in hand' land and this has come about mainly because of the restrictions of the Agricultural Holdings Act 1986. The fear of creating secure tenancies on land benefiting from vacant possession is removed by a properly constructed contract farm agreement. However, with the introduction of the Agricultural Tenancies Act 1995 there is a new option, a freedom of contract between the parties is now available subject to certain caveats (Cox 1996). There are a number of advantages of investing in farming in land, there is the potential from redevelopment, changes in income are likely to be different to other investments and thus add to the diversification of the portfolio. Finally there are subsidies and psychic benefits from the ownership of land.

4.8   RESIDENTIAL INVESTMENTS

It is outside of the range of a book like this to cover the vagaries and complexities of the residential sector in any detail. Needless to say, it is complex; it is a source of much economic analysis and the market is dominated by legislative intervention and prejudice. The residential market had developed from a situation where major landowners owned most residential land and rented houses and tenements, to a situation where local authorities took responsibility for housing, and legislation was introduced which decimated the private rented market. This led finally to a situation where there is now legislation to encourage reletting and more flexible use of residential premises, which will possibly lead to the recovery of the private rented sector. Owner-occupation has contributed to growth but many local authority estates have been transferred to housing associations to manage. Investors in the residential market have generally been in the luxury end of the market where legislation has not been involved; recent development of shorthold and assured tenancies has encouraged the market in lesser properties. Another area of interest would be in mixed developments, especially in inner-city refurbishment in economic regenerating areas. Residential space may be mixed with studio, retail or workshop space, a Covent Garden type scenario, to provide a reasonable investment. Riverside developments in Docklands, following on from previous successes in Baltimore, New York, Boston and San Francisco, have added to this interest; Chelsea Harbour is another example.

4.9   OVERSEAS INVESTMENT

In 1996 the four big property companies with substantial commitments to continental Europe reassessed that commitment. Two of these major players, MEPC and Brixton, decided to withdraw from Europe; the other two, Hammerson and Slough Estates, decided to continue operations. Catalano (1996) carried out some interesting analysis on their opposite strategies which provides an introduction to this section. Hammerson had invested £185m in France in 18 months to the beginning of 1996. This formed a major part of a £375m holding in continental Europe which was concentrated, as with most continental portfolios, in France, Germany and Spain. Hammerson viewed the strategy as one of maximising growth potential. In contrast MEPC were withdrawing and selling their £179m portfolio; MEPC's continental portfolio was only 9% of its £3.4 billion world-wide portfolio and its continental holdings were concentrated on the cities of Frankfurt, Hamburg, Paris, Stuttgart and, interestingly, Vienna. This portfolio consisted mainly of offices which were developed in the 1980s. MEPC's withdrawal from Europe is based on a strategy to concentrate on other parts of the worldwide portfolio, in Australia and the USA, where it expects better performance. Slough Estates' and Brixton Estates' activities in Europe have been as developers since the 1970s. Slough's stock in Europe is only 4% of a £1.7 billion world-wide holding with Belgium as the main location for investment in Europe followed by Germany and France. Brixton Estates is also in Belgium and Germany with a small holding in Paris; they own five industrial estates mainly around Dusseldorf.

Overseas investment in general has caused some property investors much grief (Plender 1994). Investment in US real estate for the five years to the end of 1990 led to foreign companies investing $5 billion in US real estate which then suffered a loss in the market collapse of 1990. Foreign owned property companies have lost money every year after 1985 culminating in $10.1 billion of pre-tax losses in 1990–2. US commercial values fell 31% in the period 1990–3 but the losses will be greater because of the extent of debt leverage. The collapse of the dollar in the period also led to currency losses. In principle, the international diversification of a portfolio reduces risk for a given level of return provided the investor takes into account or insures against country-specific shocks. Real estate is a particularly attractive vehicle for such diversification, as bond and equity market returns tend to equalise as cross-border capital flows increase the efficiency of securities markets in the developed world. Only the emerging markets offer a low correlation against markets in richer countries. But property needs a long-term commit-ment, and as the bigger property companies already act as intermediaries for investing institutions in overseas investment in real estate, overseas investment will only appeal to the financial institutions if their fund managers can demonstrate skills in judging the timing of the property cycle in any investee country. The diversification of existing UK property companies does not offer enough exposure to the high-growth markets where diversification would be fruitful, and these countries are difficult for institutional investors to invest in directly.

Sieracki (1993) has suggested that in order for institutions to invest internationally, they need to know how property assets are performing in both absolute and in real terms. For instance, where measures are taken of performance, is account taken of loan and tax liabilities; is the property assessed on a property basis, that is income and capital, and is account taken of the voids, management costs and indexation of rent? Or alternatively, are calculations worked out on a balance sheet basis (debtors and creditors) which looks at all the hidden costs (including those of different property vehicles, required in Eur-opean countries), which can erode the return? Are the returns considered on a real or nominal basis and are the returns in local currency or sterling? Sieracki suggests that the framework required for a European property strategy for institutional investors has a number of gaps including an appropriate performance analysis, a relevant index, eco-nomic and demographic data, supply data and pricing information.

Recent research into international investment has been carried out by Worzala (1994) and the research shows that the benefits of including property investment in portfolios has been inconclusive. Worzala looked at a group of 43 funds mainly insurance compa-nies and pension funds. These included Dutch, German, US, Japanese and Swedish funds as well as British ones. The research found that allocations of overseas investment ran up to 65% of the portfolio and some of the findings were:

- The funds used less sophisticated techniques of analysis. When presented with a ranking of several different techniques – general diversification; simple correlation of returns; mean-variance/Markowitz asset allocation; and index models (such as CAPM) – the fund managers opted for the generalised techniques.
- The holding period of overseas assets was generally 10 years, similar to domestic assets.
- Most respondents calculated returns in local currency and on a currency adjusted basis, but many only reported their investments on a currency adjusted basis, thus exposing these investments to translation risk. For these funds, reported returns incorporated the full impact of currency fluctuations in the way returns are calculated. This translation adjustment is inappropriate since properties are held for a longer time period than is used for reporting purposes.
- Suitable vehicles for overseas investment were considered to be equity joint ventures with other institutional investors, a wholly owned equity investment or a joint venture with a property company.
- The reasons for overseas investment were given as diversification, lower risk, higher yield and lack of opportunities in the domestic market. When ranked in detail these were, in order: returns having low to negative correlation suggesting diversification benefit, and secondly, diversification to a different economic and political environment. Less important reasons were given as currency strength; the ability to invest in country-specific features different from domestic opportunities; and, finally, lack of domestic investment opportunities and the ability to match investment to liabilities.
- There was little interest in currency risk or hedging the risk.

REFERENCES

Adams, A. (1996) 'What Differentiates Grades of Agricultural Land?', *Chartered Surveyor Monthly*, July/August, p. 43.

Catalano, A. (1996) 'Different Strokes', *Estates Gazette*, 9 March, p. 139.

Cavanagh, E. (1996) 'Design: Hot Tin Roof but Not a Cat in Sight', *Estates Gazette*, 2 November, pp. 108–9.

Cleaveley, E. S. (1984) 'The Marketing of Industrial and Commercial Property', *Estates Gazette*, London.

Cox, C. (1996) 'Contract Farming or Letting with a Farm Business Tenancy', *Chartered Surveyor Monthly*, July/August, p. 44–5.

Darlow, C. (ed.) (1983) *Valuation and Investment Appraisal*, Estates Gazette, London.

Davis, Langdon and Everest (1996) 'Cost Model: Offices of the Future' *Procurement, Building*, September, pp. 13–20.

Dubben, N. and Sayce, S. (1991) *Property Portfolio Management: An Introduction*, Routledge, London.

Edwards, M. (1996) 'PPG6 and the Future of Retail Development', *Estates Gazette*, 29 June, pp. 126–7.

Estates Gazette (1996a) 'Industry Profile: Fashion Retailing', *Estates Gazette*, 6 July, pp. 58–60.

Estates Gazette (1996b) 'Leisure Development', *Estates Gazette*, 20 July, pp. 103–5.

Estates Gazette (1996c) 'Industry Profile: Food and Drink Industry', *Estates Gazette*, 27 July, pp. 41–2.

Estates Gazette (1996d) 'Teleworking Threat to Office Demand', *Estates Gazette*, 31 August, p. 28.

Estates Gazette (1996e) 'PPG6 Causes Drop in Retail Park Proposals', *Estates Gazette*, 21 September, p. 41.

Freedman, C. (1996a) 'Design for Life' *Estates Gazette*, 14 September, pp. 122–3.

Freedman, C. (1996b) 'Local Loyalties' *Estates Gazette*, 5 October, pp. 104–5.

Guy, G. (1994) *The Retail Development Process: Location, Property and Planning*, Routledge, London.

Hiatt, C. (1996) 'Irresistible Lure of Green Fields', *Estates Times*, 21 June, p. 13.

Hunt, J. (1996) 'Teleworking Poised to Rise Sharply by 2000', *Property Week*, 1 June, p. 7.

Jack, S. (1996) 'Ever Increasing Circles', *Estates Gazette*, 5 October, pp. 108–9.

Lennox, K. (1996) 'IPD Annual Index: Down But Not Out', *Estates Gazette*, 30 March, p. 52.

Mackmin, D. (1994) *The Valuation and Sale of Residential Property*, Routledge, London.

Marriott, O. (1962) *The Property Boom*, Hamish Hamilton, London.

Melzack, H. (1990) 'Sheds Checklist', *CSW Business and Industrial Space Supplement, Chartered Surveyor Weekly*, 26 July, p. 42.

Morgan, P, and Walker, A, (1988) *Retail Development*, Estates Gazette, London.

Morley, S. (1996) 'The Future for Offices', *Estates Gazette*, 3 August, pp. 76–8.

Plender, J (1994) 'Exploring Foreign Markets', *Estates Gazette*, 26 November, p. 68.

Property Journal (1996) 'PPG6 Makes Progress But Introduces New Problems Says BPF', *Property Journal*, British Property Federation, July, p. 3.

Schiller, R. (1996) 'Town-Centre Winners and Losers', *Estates Gazette*, 13 July, pp. 134–5.

Seeley, I. H. (1996) *Building Economics*, Macmillan, London.

Sieracki, K. (1993) 'UK Institutional Requirements for European Property', *Estates Gazette*, 17 July, pp. 116–18.

Simmons, M (1996) 'My perfect office', *Estates Gazette*, 14 September, pp. 108–110.

Taylor, N. P. (1991) *Development Site Evaluation*, Macmillan, London.

Worzala, E. (1994) 'Overseas Property Investments: How Are They Perceived by the Institutional Investor?', *Journal of Property Valuation and Investment*, vol. 12, no. 3, pp. 31–47.2

5 Property Investment Appraisal Techniques: Introduction

5.1 CAPITAL APPRAISAL TECHNIQUES

Investment appraisal systems need a clear criterion on which to measure the proposals for investment in a project. The appraisal can only deal with money considerations; items can then be quantified in cash terms. It cannot deal with qualitative assumptions, thus the criterion is measured on a cash yard stick. The method used must also allow other alternative investment projects to be measured against one another. In this section we look at the development of capital appraisal techniques in the business sector for comparison with methods in the property sector. Just as in the property field there is a comparison of traditional methods of appraisal with discounted cash flow approaches; the development of capital appraisal techniques in business mirrors this. The traditional methods in business, however, are more basic than those in the property field. Property valuation methods take into account the concept of discounting income and costs in the future, which illustrates the time value of money in the sense that a £1 available today is worth more than a £1 in a year's time even ignoring an inflation effect. This is because if a £1 is immediately consumed, the benefit is obtained a year earlier or the £1 can be invested and earn interest over the year. In property valuation the traditional Years Purchase approach takes into account the time value of money, whereas in business valuation traditional methods ignore this. The more advanced approaches of discounted cash flow involving net present value (NPV) and internal rate of return (IRR) are dealt with later in this chapter. The two basic approaches discussed first are the payback period method and the rate of return on investment method.

Payback period method

This method involves the calculation of the number of years that it takes to pay back the original investment in a project. The important criterion is the length of time; the shorter the period the better the project (see Example 5.1).

Thus on this basis either project A or B could be chosen and there is no way to distinguish between these in the analysis. Time in this analysis is used in a crude way as it does not take into account the timing of the cash flows: for instance high cash flows in the early years (in projects B and C compared to A) and also the cash flow after the payback period (project C). The advantage of such an approach is in its simplicity and its ability to recognise the time factor, although in a crude way, but no account is taken of the timing of the cash flows and cash flows occurring after the payback cut-off point and thus it ignores the overall profitability.

Example 5.1

	Projects		
	A	B	C
Investment	£10 000	£10 000	£10 000
Cash Flow (£)			
Year 1	£1000	£7000	£7000
Year 2	£9 000	£3 000	0
Year 3	£2000	£2000	£3 000
Year 4	0	0	£7000
Total cash inflow	£12 000	£12 000	£17 000
Payback period	2 years	2 years	3 years
Ranking	equal 1	equal 1	3

Rate of return method

This approach expresses a rate of profit as a percentage of the cost of an investment:

$$\frac{\text{Profit}}{\text{Cost}} \times 100\%$$

The cost figure is calculated by the capital employed in the project. A target return is set and if the profitability exceeds this figure then the project is acceptable. This is a replica of the basic traditional all risks yield in perpetuity:

$$\frac{\text{Net income}}{\text{Capital value}} \times 100\%$$

Note, however, that the capital value in this context is the price paid or cost and the yield is an initial yield. This appraisal is thus a form of a market valuation rather than an analysis of the investment. In business finance the calculation can be done on various bases including: profit before tax (PBIT = profit before interest and tax) or after tax. Profit figures can be for the first year, the maximum annual figure over the project life or the average figure over the project life. The latter is usually considered the most suitable. Interest is the interest outstanding on debt raised by the company. The capital employed may be shown gross or as an average figure over the life of the asset deducting each year for depreciation.

Example 5.2

Investment	£8 000
Cash inflows (£)	
Year 1	£4 000
Year 2	£6 000
Year 3	£4 000
Year 4	£2000
Total cash inflow	£16 000

Assuming there is no resale or scrap value to the investment then the original £8000 is lost at the end of the investment period and the depreciation on the investment is £8000.

$$\text{Average profit is:} \quad \frac{£16\,000 - £8\,000}{4 \text{ years}} = £2\,000$$

Return on the investment before tax and any interest payment is:

$$\frac{£2\,000}{£8\,000} \times 100\% = 25\%$$

Depreciation in the calculation is taken as a straight line approach for an equal amount of the total depreciation per year. The advantage of this method is that it uses the same criterion related to profitability both for projects and the overall business. The choice of target rate could be the same rate as the firm sets for overall profitability. The disadvantage of using this method is that it again ignores the time value of money. The use of a straight line approach to depreciation may not realistically reflect the timing of any negative flows. In answer to the deficiencies of the traditional approaches in respect of their inability to take into account the time value of money, business has adopted the discounted cash flow techniques outlined in the following section.

Discounted cash flow techniques

Discounted cash flow (DCF) techniques are an important aid in the evaluation of investment proposals. The overriding advantage of the DCF techniques is that they recognise the time value of money. It should be remembered that DCF analysis is only as accurate as the data that are put into the calculation. Where a rate is used in a DCF calculation, it is more useful as a yardstick than those approaches which use the traditional methods of payback period and return on investment. The evaluation of capital investment techniques has two difficulties. Firstly, costs and revenues arise at different times and this means that they are not directly comparable; this problem is handled by discounted cash flow analysis. The second problem is that the future is uncertain and that forecasted cash flows may not arise as predicted. The discounted cash flow approach appears to give a clear indication of the accept/reject decision for project appraisal and this works well when there is only one project being considered in isolation. In reality the project will face competition arising from the investor not having sufficient funds to accept all projects indicated as acceptable under the analysis. This is a problem of capital rationing and involves a restriction of choice when resources are limited. The second problem is where two competing projects fulfil the same objective and only one is required. These problems can be analysed by NPV and IRR analysis but the literature shows clearly that the NPV approach is preferred. This analysis concerns individual projects but it may also be necessary to consider investment opportunities as part of a portfolio of investments and this is dealt with later in the book.

This chapter has considered the major alternative investment techniques available in the commercial world and the choices that may be made between them. It is also necessary to look at investors and investment companies themselves because such investigation will bring to light how capital appraisal techniques are used in the corporate sector and how cash flows are generated. There are rules governing the generation of the cash flows. These are related to the accounts of the company. In order to understand the financial affairs of a company the appraiser must be aware of its financial standing and, if advising on investment in property assets, the appraiser must know about the company's cost of capital. The cost of capital could affect the target discount rate used in discounted cash flow calculations.

The investment method

In Chapter 1 we looked at the constant known as the Present Value of £1 per annum, or more commonly in real property valuation, the Years Purchase (abbreviated to YP). The formula was given as:

$$C = NI \times YP$$

where C is the capital value, NI is net income and YP is the Years Purchase. The YP was calculated by using $100/i$ and only applied to incomes received in perpetuity, which are those received from freehold interests let at a full market rent or rack rent. Incomes to be received for shorter periods use a YP which must be calculated using a more complex formula, but tables of constants are available and *Parry's Valuation and Conversion Tables* (Davidson 1989) are most commonly used. In order to understand the basis of the traditional method and the calculation of compounding and discounting factors in investment calculations, we need to consider the tables which underpin the appraisals. In dealing with investment situations, we are considering the purchase of an asset to generate an income stream over a period of time. Thus we are converting the value of an income stream in the future into a present capital sum. The basis of the traditional approaches, the tables used in *Parry's Tables*, is about the conversion of present and future sums and the conversions of capital and income streams. The tables deal with the process of compounding and discounting; for instance, the Amount of £1 table will add compound interest to an initial sum to give a future capital sum. The six main options of conversion are:

- Capital to income and vice versa
- Present sums to future sums and vice versa
- The compounding of sums into the future, and discounting back to the present

Summary of the valuation tables

Amount of £1

This table provides the amount £1 will accumulate to over n years at an interest rate of i% pa. It thus compounds up from a present capital sum to a future capital sum. The approach is commonly known as compound interest and the formula is A (Amount of £1) $= (1 + i)^n$.

PV of £1

The present value of £1 gives the sum which needs to be invested at the interest rate i to accumulate to £1 in n years. i discounts a future capital sum to a present capital sum; it is the process of the Amount of £1 in reverse and the formula is $1/A$.

Amount of £1 p.a.

This is the amount to which £1 invested annually will accumulate to in n years. It is thus compounding a present income stream to a future capital sum and the formula is $(A-1)/i$.

Annual sinking fund (ASF) to produce £1

This is the amount which needs to be invested annually to accumulate to £1 in n years at an interest rate i%. It thus discounts back the future capital sum to a present income stream. The formula is $i/(A-1)$.

Annuity £1 will purchase

This is the income stream that will be generated over n years by an original investment of £1. The income produced will be consumed as part capital and part interest on capital. Assuming the rates of consumption are the same, a single rate approach gives an equation $i/(1-PV)$. If the rates differ, then the formula $(i+s)$ needs to be used, where s is the annual sinking fund formula above at a different interest rate from i. Note that this is the way a mortgage is calculated: the Building Society provides the initial capital sum and expects repayments of equal amounts throughout the loan period (assuming fixed rate money), but the repayments consist of interest and capital (that is, the sinking fund).

PV of £1 p.a.

The present value of £1 p.a. is the present value of the right to receive £1 p.a. over n years. The future income stream is discounted back to the present value and is the opposite of the annuity calculation. Thus the formulation for a single rate is $(1-PV)/i$ or for the dual rate, $1/(i+s)$, where s is the annual sinking fund at the sinking fund rate. This approach is commonly known as the Years Purchase and gives the present value of a future stream of rental income.

As a summary we can see that the valuation tables may have a number of different uses in the analysis of investments; for instance:

Capitalising an income

As in the investment method of valuation:

> Income × YP = Capital value
> i.e. $i = 10$%, $n = 10$ years, income = £10 p.a.
> YP = 10 years @ 10 % = 6.1446
> £10 × 6.1446 = £61.46
>
> YP compounds then discounts
> i.e. PV of £1 p.a. =
> Amt of £1 p.a. in 10 years @ 10%   £15.9374
> × PV £1 in 10 years @ 10%   ×   .3855
>   _____
>   £6.1439

Summary table

Option	Cash flow		Formula
	Now	Future	
Amount of £1 (A)	Capital sum	Capital sum	$A = (1 + i)^n$
	compounding >		
PV of £1 (PV)	Capital sum	Capital sum	$PV = \dfrac{1}{A}$
	< discounting		
Amount of £1 p.a.	Income	Capital sum	$\dfrac{A - 1}{i}$
	compounding >		
ASF to produce £1 (ASF)	Income	Capital sum	$ASF = \dfrac{i}{A - 1}$
	< discounting		
Annuity £1 will purchase	Capital sum	Income	$\dfrac{i}{(1 - PV)}$
	compounding >		
PV of £1 p.a. (YP)	Capital sum	Income	$YP = \dfrac{(1 - PV)}{i}$
	< discounting		(single rate)

Discounting costs

Cost	£100
PV £1 in 10 years @ 10%	.3855
Amount to be invested now	£38.55

Sinking funds

Estimating the contingency to be put away each year to pay for a future cost:

Future cost	£100
ASF 10 years @ 10%	.0627
Annual sinking fund (ASF)	£6.27 p.a.

Mortgage instalments

The mortgage tables are base on the annuity £1 will purchase. The annuity represents mortgage payments that are made up of instalment of interest and capital.

Discounted cash flow

These tabes are used in investment analysis as already discussed:

PV of £1 is used to discount capital sums.
PV of £1 p.a. is used to discount incomes.

Annual equivalents

The tables can also be used for working out annual equivalents of capital sums, either capital costs or capital receipts (premiums).

5.2   YIELD AND DISCOUNTED CASH FLOW (DCF) APPROACHES

Discounted cash flow appraisal

Comparison of investments is not so simple when the alternatives being considered have varying costs and incomes generated over different periods of time. A technique used to overcome this difficulty is known as 'discounting', that is to bring all future amounts, revenue and expenditure, to present-day values using a given rate of interest known as the 'discount rate'; by so doing, a cash flow becomes a 'Discounted Cash Flow' (DCF). DCF is a technique developed by financial appraisers as a tool to assess the overall profitability of a project. Increasingly, the technique is being used by property valuers and analysts, very largely because as financial institutions became more involved in property development and investment they found the traditional approach of surveyors to be unacceptable on its own. It complies with incomes and expenditures varying in amounts and in time periods (that is, yearly, monthly or for alternative periods); in other words, the 'time value' of money is taken into consideration. It can also be used to compare capital projects, but there is some evidence to suggest that in practice simpler methods are often used (such as payback).

As stated above, the technique is based on calculating the present worth of future sums of money, either income or expenditure, a technique not unknown to valuers who are familiar with using Present Value of £1 and Present Value of £1 per annum tables from *Parry's Tables*, which are the same as other tables published under the title 'DCF Tables'. Indeed the traditional investment method estimates the present value of future periodic incomes and therefore 'DCF' is just what valuers have been doing for years. It is true that the traditional method and DCF both find the net present value; however, the important difference lies in the thought processes involved in using the technique and the variation possible to the inputs of the DCF, particularly the rate of interest used.

To produce a DCF, the valuer has at least three forms of discount rate to choose from:

(i)   The rate which has to be paid for borrowing capital – the borrowing rate.
(ii)   The rate which could be earned if the capital was invested elsewhere – the opportunity cost rate.
(iii) The rate of return which the investor requires to compensate for the risk involved, the loss of immediate consumption and inflation – the target rate.

In investment appraisal and analysis it is the target rate which is most commonly used. It could be related to Government stock rates.

Example 5.3

Consider an asset A purchased for £20 000 which will generate the following estimated incomes: year 1, £3 000; year 2, £5 000; year 3, £6 000; year 4, £3 000; year 5, £6 500; year 6, £5 750; year 7, £3 000. In year 4, maintenance costs will be £1000 and at the end of year 7 the asset will be disposed of for £1500. If a borrowing rate of 10% per annum is required, the discounted cash flow will be:

Year	Cash flow	Present value of £1 (PV £1 @ 10%)	DCF
0	−£20 000	1	−£20 000
1	3 000	0.909	2 727
2	5 000	0.826	4 130
3	6 000	0.751	4 506
4	3 000		
	−1000	0.683	1 366
5	6 500	0.621	4 037
6	5 750	0.564	3 243
7	3 000		
	1500	0.513	2.309
	Net present value @ 10% discount rate		£2 318

The DCF is positive and thus the asset purchase is worthwhile; at a 10% target threshold it will earn in excess of 10%. At this rate it would provide a £2 318 contribution to profit. The use of a DCF approach when considering a single project is useful; however, the technique can be invaluable when alternative investments are to be compared.

Thus there are two forms of DCF used in investment analysis:

- Net Present Value (NPV)
- Internal Rate of Return (IRR)

Net present value (NPV)

This is the form of DCF demonstrated above, namely the result of discounting to the present day all sums of money, incoming and outgoing, which the investor incurs.

For single sums, the Present Value of £1 Table can be used, or it can be calculated by using the formula:

$$\frac{1}{(1+i)^n}$$

This will be seen to be the inverse of the Amount of £1, or compound interest formula, discussed earlier.

Where the same amount is being received or spent for a series of years, then the Present Value of £1 per annum can be used; this is more familiarly known as the Years Purchase (YP). It can be seen that it is simply the sum of a series of individual Present Values. For example, using the rate of 8%:

PV £1	1 year @ 8%	0.9259
PV £1	2 years @ 8%	0.8573
PV £1	3 years @ 8%	0.7938
PV £1	4 years @ 8%	0.7350
YP	4 years @ 8%	3.3120

As stated above, the discount rate can be: (i) the borrowing rate, (ii) the opportunity cost rate, or (iii) the target rate. Whichever form of rate is used, when a positive NPV is obtained then the project will be worthwhile. However, other criteria may need to be considered.

Internal rate of return (IRR)

NPV is most frequently used in investment appraisal for acquisition purposes, but it can also be used for analysis on a trial-and-error basis. More often, though, analysts require to know the actual return on capital to be obtained from an investment. This is the rate generated internally from the income and expenditure incurred, and therefore it is known as the Internal Rate of Return (IRR). It is the discount rate at which the NPV of income equals the NPV of expenditure, or in other words the rate which produces a nil NPV. In the example discussed earlier, if the target rate had been 10%, and it produced a positive NPV, it means that the asset was generating returns about the target rate. A negative NPV would have indicated that the target rate would not have been achieved.

The IRR may be obtained by use of a computer, programmable calculator or *Parry's Tables*. In the event of none of these being available then it can be calculated by use of a formula or graph. Both methods require the selection of two discount rates by trial and error, one giving a positive NPV, the other a negative NPV, and then interpolating between the two.

Example 5.4

Asset A (from Example 5.3)

Year	Income	PV £1 @ 10%	DCF	PV £1 @ 14%	DCF
0	−20 000	1	−£20 000	1	−£20 000
1	3 000	0.909	2 727	0.877	2 631
2	5 000	0.826	4 130	0.769	3 845
3	6 000	0.751	4 506	0.675	4 050
4	3 000				
	−1 000	0.683	1 366	0.592	1 184
5	6 500	0.621	4 037	0.519	3 373
6	5 750	0.564	3 243	0.456	2 622
7	3 000				
	1 500	0.513	2 308	0.400	1 800
		NPV @ 10%	£2 317	NPV @ 14%	−£495

As the NPV at 10% is positive and at 14% is negative, and the IRR is the rate at which NPV is zero, then IRR will be at a rate between 10% and 14%. It can be calculated by linear interpolation which can be undertaken by using the formula:

$$R_1 + \left[(R_2 - R_1) \times \frac{NPV\ R_1}{NPV\ R_2 + NPV\ R_1} \right]$$

where R_1 = lower rate; $NPV\ R_1$ = NPV lower rate;
          R_2 = higher rate; $NPV\ R_2$ = NPV higher rate;
          in both cases, the + or − signs are ignored.

Inserting the data from above:

$$10 + \left[(14 - 10) \times \frac{2317}{495 + 2317} \right] = 13.3\%$$

Further examples of discounted cash flow approaches applied to property investments are set out below.

Example 5.5

The NPV of a project is to be calculated using a purchase price of £10 000. The subsequent cash flows are set out below. Assuming a discount rate of 10% calculate the net present value (NPV).

	Cash flow (£)
Year 1	2 000
Year 2	5 000
Year 3	4 000
Year 4	2 000

Year	Cash Flow (£)	PV £1 @ 10%	Present Value (£)
1	2 000	0.909	1 818
2	5 000	0.826	4 130
3	4 000	0.751	3 004
4	2 000	0.683	1 366
			10 318
		less outlay	10 000
		NPV	318

Note:
(i)   Cash flows are best estimates and may be net or gross of tax.
(ii) The discount rate is a target rate, so the NPV is positive, the profit is made and the target is reached and passed.
(iii) The target rate may be based on: the cost of borrowing; the rate of return on other projects; or, the rate on government stock (not equities as equity yields are low to take into account future growth and may have a risk adjustment).

If the NPV is positive than the investment is worthwhile. If a number of projects are chosen, the one with the highest NPV is chosen, provide the capital outlay is the same. If the capital outlay differs one needs to calculate the benefit:cost ratio

$$= \frac{\text{discounted PV of total benefits}}{\text{discounted PV of total costs}}$$

That with the highest ratio is chosen.

Example 5.6

Using the cash flows from the previous example calculate the internal rate of return (IRR).

Year	Cash flow (£)	PV of £1 @ 11%	Present value (£)	PV £1 @ 12%	Present value (£)
1	2 000	0.901	1 802	0.893	1 786
2	5 000	0.812	4 060	0.797	3 985
3	4 000	0.731	2 924	0.712	2 848
4	2 000	0.639	1 278	0.636	1 272
			10 064		9 891
		less outlay	10 000		10 000
		NPV	64		(109)

At 11% a positive NPV is produced and at 12% a negative one, whereas the IRR is that rate which produces a NPV of zero. Therefore the IRR lies in the range of 11 to 12%. If the NPVs are plotted on a graph against discount rates, a curved line results from which may be read intermediate points to determine the exact IRR. An alternative, slightly inaccurate, short-cut is to assume a straight line relationship in which a change in discount rate produces an exactly proportional change in NPV. This is known as linear interpolation, and the IRR may be derived by this method using the following formula as shown previously:

$$R_1 + \left\{ (R_2 - R_1) \times NPVR_1 / (NPVR_2 + NPVR_1) \right\}$$

where R_1 is the lower rate and R_2 is the higher rate, and the signs $(+ \text{ or } -)$ of the NPV are ignored. Thus in the example, the correct rate is:

$$11 + \left\{ 1 \times (64/173) \right\} = 11.37\%$$

Property valuation assesses the advantages and disadvantages of an interest in property and expresses them in money terms. DCF techniques facilitate comparisons but IRR techniques do not give the value of the property; only the NPV approach will do this.

Example 5.7

Value the income flow for the next four years of £10 000 p.a. payable in arrears from a freehold property if the property is considered an 8% risk.

Net income	£10 000 p.a.
YP for 4 years @ 8%	3.3121
Capital value	£ 33 121

YP = PV of £1 p.a. = the addition of PV of £1 for each of the years under consideration. Thus:

First year's income:
£10 000 × PV £1 in 1 year @ 8% = £10 000 × 0.9259 = £9 259

Second year's income:
£10 000 × PV £1 in 2 years @ 8% = £10 000 × 0.8573 = £8 573

Third year's income:
£10 000 × PV £1 in 3 years @ 8% = £10 000 × 0.7938 = £7 938

Fourth year's income:
£10 000 × PV £1 in 4 years @ 8% = £10 000 × 0.7350 = £7 350

£33 120

In this example the income is broken up into a series of cash flows; the YP groups cash flows for a number of periods, the DCF enables annual cash flows to be discerned. The layout usually use in DCF approaches to property calculations is set out in Example 5.8.

Example 5.8: Calculation of net present value (NPV)

End of year	Particulars	Outflow	Inflow	Net flow + or −	PV of £1 @ 12%	Net outflow	Net inflow
0	Purchase price	100 000					
	Purchase costs	8 000		(108 000)	1	108 000	
1	Rent		11 000	11 000	0.8928571		9 821
2	Rent		11 000	11 000	0.7871939		8 769
3	Rent		11 000	11 000	0.7117802		7 830
4	Rent		11 000				
	Sale proceeds		140 000				
	Sale costs	6 000		145 000	0.6355181		92 150
						108 000	118 570
						NPV	10 570

Target rate + 12%, NPV @ target rate = £10 570

Example 5.9: Calculation of the internal rate of return (IRR)

End of year	Particulars	Outflow	Inflow	Net flow + or −	PV of £1 @ 15%	Net outflow	Net inflow
0	Purchase price	100 000					
	Purchase costs	8 000		(108 000)	1	108 000	
1	Rent		11 000	11 000	0.8695652		9 565
2	Rent		11 000	11 000	0.7561437		8 769
3	Rent		11 000	11 000	0.6575162		7 233
4	Rent		11 000				
	Sale proceeds		140 000				
	Sale costs	6 000		145 000	0.6355181		82 904
						108 000	108 020
						NPV	20

Rate at which NPV = 0 is the IRR, here it is approximately 15%, thus the IRR is approximately 15%.

Example 5.10: Investment valuation using DCF

Investment valuation: DCF						
Purchase price £	50 000 000		Sale price £			72162144
Rent passing £	4 000 000		Est rent on sale £			4329729
Initial yield %	8		Est exit yield %			6
Fees on purchase %	2.75		Fees on sale %			2.75
Rental growth %	2					
Holding period years	5		NPV @ discount rate £			8236908
Discount rate %	10		IRR %			13.7843
Rent receivable annually in arrears						

Period	Income	Capital	Fees	Cash flow	DCF	
0	0	−5000000	−1375000	−51375000	−51375000	
1	4080000			4080000	3709091	
2	4161600			4161600	3439339	
3	4244832			4244832	3189205	
4	4329729			4329729	2957263	
5	4416323	72162144	−1984459	74594008	46317010	
				NPV	8236908	

The DCF calculation is long and tedious but can be represented by the equation, which assumes constant rental growth:

$$k = \frac{e[(1+e)^n - (1+p)^n]}{(1+e)^n - 1}$$

where k = Initial (all risks) yield expressed as a decimal
  e = Cost of capital expressed as a decimal
  p = Rental growth p.a. (expressed as a decimal)
  n = Number of years between rent reviews

This equation is derived in Darlow (1983) and is set out in form of a cash flow statement as below. The assumptions are:

Cost of capital = $E\%$ (or e expressed as a decimal)
Rental growth = $P\%$ (or p when expressed as a decimal)
Initial yield with rent reviews every n years = $K\%$ (or K when expressed as a decimal)
Period between rent reviews = n years
Total time period = xn years

Discounted cash flow statement

Year	(a) Rental P% p.a. growth (Amount of £1)	(b) YP n years @ E% (YP single rate)	(c) PV £1 @ E% (PV £1)	(d) = b × c YP defrd @ E%	(e) = (a × d) = (a × b × c) Capital value
0	1	$\dfrac{(1+e)^n - 1}{e} \times \dfrac{1}{(1+e)^n}$	1	b × c	$\dfrac{(1+e)^n - 1}{e} \times \dfrac{1}{(1+e)^n}$
n	$(1+p)^n$	$\dfrac{(1+e)^n - 1}{e} \times \dfrac{1}{(1+e)^n}$	$\dfrac{1}{(1+e)^n}$	b × c	$\dfrac{(1+p)^n[(1+e)^n - 1]}{e(1+e)^{2n}}$
xn	$(1+p)^{xn}$	$\dfrac{(1+e)^n - 1}{e} \times \dfrac{1}{(1+e)^n}$	$\dfrac{1}{(1+e)^{3n}}$	b × c	$\dfrac{(1+p)^{xn}[(1+e)^n - 1]}{e(1+e)^{(x+1)n}}$

The NPV equals the sum of the cash flows in column (e). This is a geometric progression with a constant term of $\dfrac{(1+e)^n - 1}{e(1+e)^n}$ (i.e. YP single rate @ $E\%$)

The summation of column (e) can be expressed in the form;

$$S = a + ar + ar^2 + ar^3 \ldots ar^n,$$

multiply by r: $Sr = ar + ar^2 + ar^3 \ldots ar^n + ar^{n+1},$

subtract Sr from S: $S(1 - r) = a - ar^{n+1},$

$$S = \frac{a(1 - r^{n+1})}{1 - r}$$

i.e. $S = \dfrac{1 - \left(\dfrac{1+p}{1+e}\right)^{(x+1)^n}}{1 - \left(\dfrac{1+p}{1+e}\right)^n} \times \dfrac{(1+e)^{n-1}}{e(1+e)^n}$

The geometric progression is to be calculated in perpetuity (as we consider rent being received in perpetuity); then as x tends to infinity so $(x + 1)^n$ tends to infinity. As e is $> p$,
$$\frac{1+p}{1+e} < 1.$$
Therefore the expression

$$\left(\frac{1+p}{1+e}\right)^{(x+1)^n}$$

tends to 0.

So to simplify the equation:

$$\frac{1}{1 + \dfrac{(1+p)^n}{(1+e)^n}} \times \frac{(1-e)^{n-1}}{e(1+e)^n}$$

$$= \frac{(1+e)^n}{(1+e)^n - (1+p)^n} \times \frac{(1+e)^{n-1}}{e(1+e)^n}$$

$$= \frac{(1+e)^{n-1}}{e[(1+e)^n - (1+p)^n]}$$

$$= \text{capital value}$$

as interest yield $= \dfrac{\text{income}}{\text{capital value}}$, then if income is £1

$$\text{yield} = \frac{K}{100}$$

$$= \frac{e[(1+e)^n - (1+p)^n]}{(1+e)^n - 1}$$

5.3   TRADITIONAL VALUATIONS

There are a number of approaches to valuation. These include:

- Comparison method
- Profits method
- Contractors method
- Investment method
- Residual method

The comparison method compares the capital values and rents of properties which have recently been sold or let with the subject property. The profits method is based on the assumption that the value of a property is based on the profit produced and is used to value hotels for instance. The contractors approach is based on the cost of construction and is used where there is no market in the type of property being valued. The investment method is used to value capital investments in property and the approach to this form of valuation (including the use of the Years Purchase to capitalise rental figures) has been examined earlier. The residual method is used in development situations and is based on a calculation of value less cost and profit and provides a residual sum which is the amount available to purchase the land. Thus in the use of valuation methods, there are three bases, as shown in Table 5.1.

Table 5.1   *Bases of valuation*

Value		*Cost*		*Profit*	
based on:	value	based on:	cost of construction	based on:	profit from accounts
use:	Comparison method Investment method Residual method	use:	Contractors method	use:	Profits method

For existing property and new development the approaches may also require different methods, as shown in Table 5.2.

Table 5.2   *Valuation for new and existing property*

For existing property	*For new development*
Use: Comparison method Investment method	Use: Comparison method Investment method or development value less cost, the Residual method

The comparison method will give rent and capital value, the investment and residual valuations will give capital value. In an investment valuation some important factors should be noted. Firstly, even in owner-occupied property, a notional rent equivalent to a market rent is assumed to be passing, thus a rental value can still be assessed even if no rent is passing. Secondly, the full rental value is also termed a rack rental: this is the maximum rent for which a property can be let on the open market for a given set of letting terms; the more usual term is now ERV or estimated rental value. Thirdly, the letting terms are an important consideration for the valuation. If a tenant is responsible for all repairs and insurance then the rent will be less than if the landlord is responsible. The usual situation is that tenants enter into lease where they have to (in the terminology: 'they covenant to . . .') pay for repairs and insurance. So the tenant covers all outgoings and this is called a fully repairing and insuring lease (a FRI lease). The landlord therefore does not have any outgoings and the rent is the net income. The rack rental on FRI terms is called the net rack rent.

The comparison method will give rent and capital value, the investment and residual valuations will give capital value. The investment method thus converts the income from a property into a capital sum:

Income × Years Purchase (YP) = Capital value

Income/Capital value = Yield

Yield = 1/YP

Letting terms

This is an example of a lease on FRI term showing tenants outgoings:

Rent	£10 000 p.a. (rack rent)
Repairs @ 15%	£1 500 p.a. (estimate of repair cost p.a.)
Insurance @ 2.5%	£250 p.a. (estimate)
Outgoings	£11 750 p.a.

Therefore the tenant's outgoings are £11 750 p.a. Other outgoings are rates and water rates for which the tenant is usually responsible except in multiple letting situations where the landlord pays, apportions the cost between tenants and recovers the apportionment. Following is an example of a lease on internal repairing terms (so the landlord is responsible for external repairs and insurance and the tenant is responsible for internal repairs). For instance, what rent would the landlord expect to put him in the same position as an FRI lease?:

Net income, rent	£10 000 p.a. (rack rent)
Repairs allowance	£1 500 p.a. (estimate of repair cost p.a.)
Insurance @ 2.5%	£250 p.a. (estimate)
Management fee	£1 175 p.a. (10% gross rent which includes repairs and insurance)
Expected rent	£12 925 p.a.

Rental value

At stages during the lease, the rent could be reviewed. The normal lease is a 20- or 25-year lease with 5-year reviews, but reviews could be 3, 5, 7, or 25-yearly. The longer the review period, the higher the rent at review (because you have to wait a long time before you can review it again). To work out the rental value you need to compare the property you are working on with a comparable property using the comparison method. To compare properly you need to assess on a unit of comparison. The unit of comparison for most commercial properties is per square metre of space which is lettable space; for shops it could be per metre frontage and for land it could be per hectare. In the assessment of rental it is important to get to a net figure. In valuing an interest we are interested only in the net income (the income after outgoings have been paid) to the landlord. If rent contains amounts for outgoings, they should be deducted. So rent less outgoings equals net income.

Outgoings

Outgoings are repairs, insurance premiums, general rates, water rates, general services and management costs.

Repairs

Usually the landlord will get the tenant to do all the repairs. If the landlord is responsible, he may only have to deal with structural or external repairs. Repair costs should be costed but can be assessed as a % of rack rent, e.g.:

	external %	internal %
Offices and commercial	10	5
Shops	5	5
Residential	30	10

Insurance

The property has to be insured for fire insurance which is based on the cost of the building (the reinstatement cost is based on the area of the building × the cost of construction per m^2). The premium is a percentage of the reinstatement cost but a rough approximation is 2.5% of rack rent.

Rates

Usually the liability of the tenant. The rates payable are the rateable value (RV) of the property, times the rate in the £.

Management charges

These are made when there is a need to have a rent collector and to check that the tenant is in occupation under the terms of the lease (i.e. is abiding by the terms). If a net income is being received by the landlord (i.e. on an FRI lease), sometimes a deduction for management is not made. The charge is 10% of the rack rent but this may be reduced to 7.5% on property which is easy to manage.

Valuation of freehold interests

The freehold interest is perpetual. The leasehold interest is for a number of years during which the lessees or tenant has right to occupy and enjoy the property. The method used is the investment method as set out earlier, where:

>Capital value = net income per annum × Years Purchase
>Net income = rent received per annum less outgoings.
>Years Purchase = 1/yield (as a decimal)

Examples of yields (yields for freehold interests let on a full rental basis)

	Yield%
Houses, poor	10–12
good	8–10
Flats	5–8
Factories/warehouses	6–14
Offices	4–9
Shops	4–9
Agricultural land	3–6
Ground rents with reviews	5–7
(Millington 1984).	

These are examples of historic ranges of yields; the up-to-date yield structure for property sectors was discussed in Chapter 1.

The basic tables used generally in valuations are summarised as:

(i)   Years Purchase single rate
(ii)   Present value of £1
(iii) Years Purchase of a reversion in perpetuity

The method of valuation depends on whether the income is perpetual, variable or deferred. A perpetual income occurs where a freehold property is let at the full rental value. If we take a freehold shop let on full repairing and insuring terms at a rack rent of £5000 p.a., the net income is £5000 p.a. This is already net because the tenant does all the repairs and pays the insurance. The income is received in perpetuity. The yield is assumed to be 7%. The lease will not have rent reviews but we do not need to take into account rent growth if rent is at the full rack rent; the yield allows for the growth:

Net income	£5000 p.a.
YP in perpetuity @ 7%	14.286
Capital value	£74 430
	say £75 000

Example 5.11: An investment valuation

Value the freehold interest in an office block of 50 m² at 1 High Street which is vacant. 2 High Street is a block of offices of 100 m² just let at £10 000 p.a. on internal repairing terms. (The landlord is responsible for external repairs and insurance.)

Assumptions: office yield 7%
                  lease to be on FRI terms

Approach:
step 1:   capital value = net income × YP; we know yield so we can calculate the YP (1/yield);
step 2:   we need to find the net income; the offices are not let so this will be based on the rental of the adjoining property;
step 3:   analyse comparable, find rent per m^2 on FRI basis (net income);
step 4:   do valuation.

Analysis of comparable 2 High Street:

	£	£
Rent received		10 000 p.a.
less:		
external repairs @ 10%	1 000 p.a.	
insurance @ 2.5%	250 p.a.	
management fee @ 5%	500 p.a.	
total outgoings		1 750 p.a.
net income		8 250 p.a.
net income per m^2		/100 m^2
net income		82.5 per m^2

Valuation of 1 High Street:

	£
Net income:	
£82.5 × 50 m^2	4 125 p.a.
YP in perpetuity @ 7%	14.286
Capital value	58 929
	say £59 000

If 2 High Street had been sold at £137 500, then this would alter the valuation because the analysis would show that:

	£
Net income:	8 250 p.a.
YP in perpetuity	x
Capital value	137 500

$$YP(x) = \frac{137\,500}{8\,250} = 16.76$$

Yield = 1/YP = 6%

The valuation would then be redone at a 6% yield.

Asset valuation

Valuers are required to produce valuations for company purposes. These purposes are, firstly, for asset values to be incorporated in the financial accounts of the company. Under the Companies Act, the company must produce, at the end of the accounting year, a balance sheet, a profit and loss account and a Director's report. Secondly, to value a company's assets for incorporation into a prospectus when a company is going public, that is selling shares to the public. This is a rule of admission of the company to the stock exchange, through which the public flotation takes place. Thirdly, to value a company when subject to a takeover bid. Finally, to value assets for property bonds and trusts and general investment purposes.

Up until 1974 there were no guidelines. In 1974 the RICS set up the Asset Valuation Standards Committee and in 1976 it issued its Asset Valuation Guidance Notes. The Asset Valuation Guidance Notes rejected the use of a going concern valuation. This is the idea that the assets of the company are more valuable to the company as a going concern than in the open market because of the elements of goodwill which are attached to the assets. The basis of valuation is thus open market value (see Guidance Note A2). Open market value as defined in guidance note D1 is:

> *the best price at which an interest in a property might reasonably be expected to be sold by private treaty at the date of valuation, assuming:*
>
> (a)   *a willing seller (same as compulsory purchase assumptions);*
> (b)   *a reasonable period within which to negotiate, taking into account the nature of the property and the state of the market;*
> (c)   *that values remain static through the period in b);*
> (d)   *the property will be freely exposed to the market (i.e. marketed and advertised);*
> (e)   *no account be taken of any additional bid by a special purchase (e.g neighbour's bid).*

The definitions of open market value have been revised in the new 'Red Book' issued by the RICS (1995) and this will be discussed later in the chapter. Practice Statement P5 of the RICS guidelines concern valuation for company accounts and financial statements. The Accounting Standards Board advocates the use of a 'value to the business' model in determining values in the balance sheet. Value to the business of an asset is the lower of its net current replacement cost and its recoverable amount. The recoverable amount is the higher of 'value in use' and 'net realisable value'. The net current replacement cost is the cost of purchasing, at the least cost, the remaining service potential of the asset at the balance sheet date. Value in use is the maximum amount recoverable from continuing ownership and ultimate disposal of the asset. Net realisable value is the estimated proceeds of sale of an asset less the selling cost. Continuing enterprises would normally have their assets valued to net current replacement cost (RICS 1995).

So: value to business = lower of: net current replacement cost or
                                         recoverable amount
         recoverable amount = higher of: value in use or
                                           net realisable value

5.4   A CRITIQUE OF UK TRADITIONAL METHODS OF VALUATION

The distinction between valuation and analysis

The property crash in the early 1970s focused attention on valuation methods used in the profession. Over the period since then there have been a number of pressures on valuation professionals to improve the quality and standard of the valuations produced. This has arisen for a number of reasons. Large scale investment for instance has taken place in recent years and the investment advisers acting for the institutions and investors are looking for more analysis in the valuations which have been carried out. Because of situations which have occurred in the past involving institutional investors, where actual returns on property investments have not reflected target returns set out in accordance with the price paid, there has been much debate about the validity of the methods used. There is also much more awareness in the market now, in terms of the responsibilities of the professional to clients' demands, that the property professional should not just act as an agent but provide during the buying and selling process some idea to the client of the forecast of income arising from the investment in the future.

This added awareness and monitoring of valuation procedures has been a subject of debate in the professional institutions as well as in the market place. Recent suggestions by leading members of the RICS are that valuations should try to reflect a view of the future movement of prices and forecast potential supply and demand situations which may affect price levels. The findings of the 1994 Mallinson Report on commercial property valuation suggested that the valuer should get clearer instructions from the client and should more clearly explain the valuation of property in company accounts. In addition, the report suggested that there should be more comment on valuation risk factors, price trends and economic factors and use of more refined discounted cash flow techniques. The recent debate and the earlier debate have combined to demand that, in what has previously been called property valuation, a more extensive service of property analysis be provided. Generally the approach that should be taken (see Baum and Crosby 1995) is that the overall property appraisal should be clearly divided between property valuation for purchase, that is the valuation for market price, and the subsequent analysis of performance. In the first case, this is defined as valuation and in the second case it is defined as analysis. The overall process is generally termed 'property appraisal'. Thus the valuation of a property, that is the calculation of the exchange value of property, is different from the subsequent analysis of the performance of the investment which is the appraisal of its actual worth. Calculations before and after purchase will not agree because of the lack of perfect knowledge in the market at the time of the transaction and the inability to predict future changes in the cash flow and the risk profile of the investment accurately. Thus the techniques discussed later on in this book can be used to anticipate the market value or else to record and analyse the progress of the investment subsequent to purchase. However, it is still important to understand the difference between these two approaches.

The argument of using DCF approaches against the traditional 'Years Purchase' investment method is extensive. Problems arise because the price paid in the market may not reflect the present worth of the future cash flow, and these problems relate to the fact that property appraisal needs to distinguish between the valuation for purchase price and the analysis of the worth of an investment. A DCF approach appears to be the only realistic approach to dealing with over-rented property where existing contractual rents under a lease which have been agreed in the past are now higher than those generally evident in the market for equivalent properties. In the present UK recessionary market, the use of traditional techniques may no longer be defended. The traditional methods may not be able to cope with issues such as rent free periods, reverse premiums, tenant incentives, bad debts, negative growth and over-rented properties. However, the use of the DCF is paramount and it needs to be applied appropriately. The DCF approach may be no more consistent than the conventional method and both approaches require some modification to be used in a way which is compatible with basic economic concepts (French and Ward 1995).

The application of valuation methodology requires the definitions to be clear, and only on the basis of these definitions can the debate between the various methodologies be clarified. The distinction between market price, valuation and worth must be clarified in this context. Baum *et al.* (1996) suggest the following approach:

- *Market price* is the recorded consideration paid for a property.
- *Valuation* is the estimate of the most likely selling price, the assessment of which is the most common objective of the valuer. This 'most likely selling price' is commonly termed 'open market value' in the UK but is different from the concept of worth.
- *Worth* is the underlying investment value and consists of two aspects. Firstly, *individual worth* is the maximum bid price of an individual purchaser. Such a bid would take into account the appropriate use of all available data relating to the individual, the property and the market. Secondly, *market worth* is the price at which an investment would trade on a market where buyers and sellers were using all available information in an efficient manner.

The application of these different concepts leads to adoption of different valuation approaches. Peto *et al.* (1996) have suggested that, in terms of market value, the valuer should adopt a model that gives most help in adjusting evidence for the inherent differences between one property and another and gives the client the level of detail required. In this consideration they adopt a strategy covering the all risks yield, the short-cut DCF and the full DCF:

All risks yield

In most cases, they argue, the all risk yield approach concentrating on the initial yield is still the most acceptable approach. It is based on comparable evidence and thus, in markets where there is sufficient evidence, it can give the best indication of market sentiment.

Short-cut DCF

For more complicated situations, or as a check to the all risks yield approach, a short-cut DCF approach may be appropriate. This makes more rational use of comparable evidence, its most obvious being in reversionary situations whether over- or under-rented.

Full DCF

The full DCF may also be used as a check on traditional methods. As a valuation method the DCF is most appropriate for very complex properties such as shopping centres, where there are many variables to be taken into account. Having carried out the DCF, the valuer should check if the resulting initial yield is acceptable and sustainable in market terms. In assessing worth for investment property the DCF technique is the only acceptable method.

5.5 MARKET VALUATION AND THE 'RED BOOK'

A revised definition of market value came into effect from 1 June 1992. The principal change is that the 'reasonable period' for marketing the interest is now assumed to have taken place before the valuation date which in turn is assumed to coincide with the date of completion of the sale. To meet the point that, in practice, a purchase price is usually fixed not on the date of completion of the sale, but on an earlier date when unconditional contracts were exchanged, the valuer is required to assume that circumstances, values and market conditions at the date of contract were the same as those prevailing at the date of completion (i.e. the date of valuation). Thus there can no longer be an assumed marketing period following the date of valuation and so the provision that 'values will remain static' disappears. The 'reasonable period' in normal circumstances should not exceed a few months. The sale of an interest is assumed to have been completed unconditionally for a cash consideration. The valuer may not assume deferred completion, stage payments or consideration in terms of shares or an exchange of land. 'Proper marketing' means the most appropriate method to effect a disposal at the best price.

There has been some debate recently over the role of the mortgage valuation. It is generally accepted by the RICS/ISVA guidance notes for valuers that the valuer should not make a recommendation as to the amount or the percentage of mortgage advance or as to the length of the mortgage term. The mortgage valuation has been the subject of debate in two areas. Firstly, in new house valuation where new house premiums may be taken into account. The premium relates to the fact that, as soon as the property is sold second-hand, there is likely to be a discount. A solution has been suggested that the valuations be carried out on the basis of a new house with the premium, provided that it is stated that on immediate resale the value will be reduced by a certain amount. The second debate on mortgage valuation relates to whether a warning should be given to the lender when valuing in a falling market. This would be especially important when valuing a property in the process of construction when only a small amount of building work had been carried out.

Recent criticisms and court cases reflecting the alleged negligence of professional valuers has led to some reconsideration of the advice given to purchasers. The problem may, of course, relate to a decline in the market whereby mistakes related to the calculation of market value at the time of transaction are not upheld by subsequent evidence. The Mallinson Report commissioned by the RICS and properly called the President's Working Party on Commercial Property Valuations reported in March 1994. The Chairman suggested that there were four key areas which are described as needs or requirements of the valuer undertaking commercial property valuations. These needs are:

(i)   Valuers need to be able to demonstrate to clients that, although there are many valuers who would make different judgements, all work is within a common body of knowledge, application and expression. Differences will therefore be as narrow as possible, and where they occur they will be reasonable and explicable, not perverse or chaotic.

(ii)   Valuers need to demonstrate that the profession is regulated, not in a purely bureaucratic sense, but that valuers perform their task in an organised manner, not in a maverick or inspirational way, that they take care to educate themselves, and that they are subject to discipline.

(iii)   Valuers need to be able to express more clearly what they do and what they do not do. It is not possible to 'make clients understand', nor is it tenable to urge that 'clients should be educated'. Care and precision in explanation will do much to achieve both ends.

(iv)   Valuers need to improve the technical element of their skill, updating and extending their mathematical models, their access to and use of data, and their expression of the relativities of their judgement. They should not assume their task to be limited to the production, as if from a hat, of a final figure.

The main proposals of the Mallinson Report are that there be a greater dialogue between valuers and their clients leading to clearer instructions, a summary of which would accompany the valuation figure. A second proposal is the right for valuers to ensure that shareholders receive the statement explaining property valuations in company accounts. In addition, the report proposes closer liaison between valuers and auditors, with direct access to audit committees. It also proposes that there be increased investigatory powers for the RICS in cases of public concern or at the client's request. The report recommends that valuations need to contain more comment on valuation risk factors, price trends and economic factors. Refined discounted cash flow techniques and research on concepts of 'worth' need to be developed. Finally, the report also suggests that there be a wider availability of data which is necessary for valuations and that the definition of open market value should be retained but its title changed to 'defined value' or 'defined notional price'. The report embraced open market value (OMV) and estimated realisation price (ERP) and suggested a new possible basis of defined accounting value (DAV). This latter definition was rejected by the RICS group who prepared the new 'Red Book' (see below) although both concepts of OMV and ERP are embraced (Rich 1994). It is hoped that these proposals would go some way towards dealing with the disquiet which has arisen over a number of cases. It is to be noted that this is not just a problem of valuation in the UK, as can be noted from the collapse of the Jurgen Schneider Property Group in Germany in 1994 and which is likely to have a lasting effect on the German property market because of the size of the collapse. Some of the blame relating to this collapse has been put on the poorly trained and organised German valuers whose valuation methods and education were suggested to be below those of the international standard. A German society of valuation surveyors has been formed to correct this.

The Mallinson Committee report advised that the previous 'Red Book' (guidelines used for valuing assets) and the 'White Book' (guidelines used for mortgage valuation and other specialist areas) should be merged. In September 1995, the Royal Institution of Chartered Surveyors' (RICS) *Appraisal and Valuation Manual* was published, this manual provides the minimum required standard and is mandatory from January 1996 onwards for members of the appropriate valuation institutions (the RICS, the Institute of Valuers and Auctioneers and the Institute of Revenue Rating). The new 'Red Book' is in two parts: the Practice Statements and the Guidance Notes. The Practice Statements apply to all types of valuation and are mandatory along with the appendices. The Guidance Notes are not mandatory but provide information on good practice. The 'Red Book' contains a number of definitions, including:

- *Appraisal:* the written provision of a valuation, combined with professional opinion or advice on the suitability of the subject property for a defined purpose.
- *Estimation of worth:* the provision of a written estimate of the net monetary worth of the subject property to the client.
- Valuation: the provision of a written opinion as to the price or value of the subject property on any given basis. It is specifically not a forecast which in turn is defined as the prediction of the likely value on a stated basis at a future specified date. The complexity of the number of valuation definitions now being used is shown in Table 5.3 overleaf.

These valuation bases are agreed with the client prior to the valuation and should be appropriate to the client's needs but cannot override statutory definitions. If ERP is required it is also necessary to provide market value or open market value. The calculation of worth is distinguished from calculations for market value or open market value. Open market value starts from the assumption that parties to the transaction acted knowledgeably, prudently and without compulsion. Market value appears the same as open market value but appears as the definition used by the International Valuation Standing Committee (*Estates Gazette* 1996). The 'Red Book' defined open market value as:

An opinion of the best practice at which the sale of an interest in property would have been completed unconditionally for cash consideration on the date of valuation, assuming:

(a) *a willing seller;*

(b) *that, prior to the date of valuation, there had been a reasonable period (having regard to the nature of the property and the state of the market for the proper marketing of the interest, for the agreement of the price and terms and for the completion of the sale;*

(c) *that the state of the market, level of values and other circumstances were, on any earlier assumed date of exchange of contracts, the same as on the date of valuation;*

(d) *that no account is taken of any additional bid by a prospective purchaser with a special interest; and*

(e) *that both parties to the transaction had acted knowledgeably prudently and without compulsion.* (RICS 1995, Practice Statement 4.2.1, p. 4)

The 'Red Book' is divided into the following practice statements and guidance notes. Practice Statement 1 covers appraisal and valuations for all purposes including Home Buyers Reports and mortgage valuations. Practice Statement 2 relates to the requirement to understand the needs of the client and sets down the basic criteria that the valuer would need to identify, such as the basis of valuation, the subject property, the purpose of the valuation, any assumptions to be made and the date of the valuation. In addition, it should be clear, firstly, whether information will be required from the client for the valuation to be made, secondly, the currency of the report, and thirdly, the limitations to third party use and restrictions on publication. Practice notes 5–7 go on to examine special circumstances related to the report, database of comparables and record of analysis, and finally, the minimum requirements of the reports (for instance the need to check if the valuation report is being included in company accounts). Statements 8–22 list special requirements for reports if these conflict with the general guidance given.

Table 5.3 *Valuation bases under the 'Red Book'*

Application of valuation bases			
Base definition	*Rental value*	*Plant and Machinery*	*Other*
Market value (MV)			
Open market value (OMV)	Open market rental value (OMRV) (1). Valuer assumes the grant of a new lease not a renewal.	Open market value for plant and machinery (OMVPM)	
Existing use value (EUV). Existing use value is OMV subject to additional assumptions as to use.		Valuation of plant and machinery to the business (VPMB) (2)	Existing use value for registered housing associations (EUVRHA)
Estimated realisation price (ERP) (3)	Estimated future rental value (EPRV) (1)	Estimated realisation price of plant and machinery (ERPPM)	
Estimated restricted realisation price (ERRP) (4)		Estimated restricted realisation price of plant and machinery (ERRPPM)	Estimated restricted realisation price for the existing use as an operational entity having regard to trading potential (ERRPEU)
Depreciated replacement cost (DRC)			

Notes:

(1) New valuation bases

(2) Value of plant and machinery to the business is approximately the same as EUV.

(3) Estimated realisation price requires the valuer to consider what changes are likely to occur in the market for the property during the marketing period, this includes external factors such as quality of the location etc. It is the open market value but with completion assumed after the date of valuation and where the valuer is required to specify an appropriate marketing period.

(4) Estimated restricted realisation price is not forced sale value (which should not be used in any circumstances) but is where the estimate is subject to a marketing period defined by the client which does not allow for proper marketing.

Table 5.4 *A comparison of open market value and revised ERP*

Open market value	Revised ERP (from 1 January 1996)
Sale . . . completed . . . at the date of valuation **plus** proper marketing, agreement of price etc. prior to the date of valuation	Opinion as to . . . consideration on the date of valuation . . . . Completion of sale on a future date specified . . . following the period of marketing
Both parties had acted knowledgably, prudently and without compulsion (with effect from 1 January 1996)	Both parties *will* act knowledgeably, prudently and without compulsion

Source: Law and Gershinson 1995.

There is a continuing debate about estimated realisation price (ERP) and whether it will resolve or compound problems of credibility which gave rise to the need for the Mallinson report in the first place. A view is that need for the valuer to look forward in providing valuation advice has been imposed on the profession by lending institutions and could result in more rather than less claims for negligence against valuers. The change for the profession relates to the way the old 'Red Book' referred to relevant experience whilst the concentration in the new 'Red Book' is on knowledge, understanding and skills (*Estates Gazette* 1996). The new definition of ERP was needed following pressure from secured lenders who believed that the existing definition of open market value required the marketing period to be retrospective, ending at the date of valuation and expecting the valuer to look backwards. The valuer was therefore telling the lender only what, in effect, he already knew and did not supply what he wanted to know which was an assessment of the security provided by the property in the future. The key differences are indicated in Table 5.4. It is apparent in the market that some valuers are looking to forecast in situations where they may not have the skills and knowledge to do so. Law and Gershinson (1995) suggest that a valuation report should be an appraisal with emphasis on the risks attached to the performance of the property during the period of the loan. However, one has to assume a static market unless the valuer or market as a whole is aware of factors which may affect the market, and if this is so then surely the market would have taken this into account. There may be concern that some valuers are forecasting valuation figures in the future, making assumptions regarding changes in the market which did not reflect the worth of the property at the date of valuation. The advice concerning the new ERP is to respond to the question of how much do you think the property can be sold for, commencing the selling process at the date of valuation, whilst indicating how long it will take.

In the light of the new regulations, the Appraisal and Valuations Board of the RICS suggested the following vital questions for the professional valuers to ask themselves before proceeding with an instruction:

- Do I know whether the mandatory requirements of the manual apply to the sorts of valuations I do?
- If I work regularly for the same client, do I have standard conditions of engagement which comply with Practice Statement 2?
- Have I prepared revised standard terms of business?
- Am I satisfied that I meet the qualification requirements in Practice Statement 5?

- Am I aware of the valuation bases to be adopted, and of the changes in some of the titles and the definitions? Have I put in hand amendments to my software?
- If my reports are to be referred to in published documents am I ready to provide a draft statement for the purposes with my report, in accordance with Practice Statement 7.10?
- Do I know what service my client requires of me? (see Practice Statement 2.1) (CSM 1995b).

A recent joint study between the City University Business School and the Universities of Reading and Western Sydney, on valuation reports and their format and information provided, concluded that UK clients were generally satisfied with the quality of valuation reports received from external valuers but a common criticism was that valuers do not provide sufficient information on valuation methodology and the state of property and wider markets. The research noted that, in respect of the response from bankers, 77% wanted more professional/industrial guidelines – this, despite the introduction of Valuation Guidance Note 12 (VGN 12) in the new 'Red Book', already discussed, which gives detailed guidance to valuers on loan valuations (CSM 1996).

REFERENCES

Baum, A. and Crosby, N. (1995) *Property Investment Appraisal*, Routledge, London.

Baum, A., Crosby, N. and MacGregor, B. (1996) 'Price Formation, Mispricing and Investment Analysis in the Property Market. A Response to 'A Note on "The Initial Yield Revealed: Explicit Valuations and the Future of Property Investment"', *Journal of Property Valuation and Investment*, vol. 14, no. 1, pp. 36–49.

Chartered Surveyor Monthly (CSM) (1995a) 'Finding Your Way into the New Red Book', *CSM*, October, p. 22.

Chartered Surveyor Monthly (CSM) (1995b) 'Finding Your Way into the New Red Book', *CSM*, November/December, pp. 20–22.

Chartered Surveyor Monthly (CSM) (1996) 'The Variable Value of Property Investment Valuation Reports', *CSM*, April, pp. 38–9.

Crosby, N. (1992) 'Reversionary Freehold; UK Market Valuation Practice', Research paper, RICS, London.

Darlow, C. (ed.) (1983) *Valuation and Investment Appraisal*, Estates Gazette, London.

Davidson, A.W. (1989) *Parry's Valuation and Investment Tables*, Estates Gazette, London.

Estates Gazette (1996) 'The New Red Book', *Estates Gazette*, 6 January, pp. 96–7.

French, N. (1994) 'Editorial: Market Values & DCF', *Journal of Property Valuation and Investment*, vol. 12, no. 1, pp. 4–6.

French, N and Ward C (1995) 'Valuation and Arbitrage', *Journal of Property Research*, vol 12 no 1, pp 1–11, Spring.

Jenkins, S. (1996), 'Valuations still highly variable', *Estates Times*, 15 March, p.2.

Law, D. and Gershinson, J. (1995) 'Whatever Happened to ERP?', *Estates Gazette*, 16 September, pp. 164–5.

Millington, A. F. (1984) *An Introduction to Property Valuation*, Estates Gazette, London.

Peto, R., French, N. and Bowman, G. (1996), 'Price and Worth Development in Valuation Methodology', *Journal of Property Valuation and Investment*, vol. 14, no. 4, pp. 79–100.

Rich, J. (1994) 'The Wonderland of OMVs, ERPs and DAVs', *Estates Gazette*, 26 November, pp. 153–5.

Royal Institution of Chartered Surveyors (RICS) (1995) *RICS Appraisal and Valuation Manual*, RICS, London.

Wright, M. G. (1990) *Using Discounted Cash Flow in Investment Appraisal*, McGraw-Hill, London.

6 Property Investment Appraisal Techniques: Applications

6.1 INTRODUCTION

This book is concerned with property investment and it is not intended to go into great detail on appraisal techniques. However, this chapter and the next will look at issues related to conventional and contemporary appraisal techniques. For a more detailed exposition of the fundamentals, you are referred to Enever and Isaac (1995) and Isaac and Steley (1991). This chapter looks at reversionary property, leasehold interests, growth and inflation and valuation accuracy.

6.2 REVERSIONARY PROPERTY

In his RICS research, Crosby (1992) suggests that the major criticism of contemporary approaches is that they do not forecast growth and that they subjectively choose a discount rate. He suggests that using implied rental growth rate analysis will reduce the subjectivity. There is a debate between academics over which type of model makes the best use of available evidence: the growth explicit model using comparable transactions to assess an implied growth rate after subjectively choosing a discount rate or, alternatively, the growth explicit model using the objectively found equivalent yield from comparable transactions and then applying it subjectively to properties to be valued. In Baum and Crosby (1988) the view is that the subjective element in contemporary methods has less effect on the possible range of solutions than the subjective element in conventional approaches; this is still, however, a minor view in the profession. The market valuation of reversionary freehold property is generally carried out by conventional growth implicit techniques but the research showed that not all were using the same conventional approach. Crosby, in his paper, indicates that in the future he perceives a demise of the traditional term and reversion approach. Reversionary property is valued in a traditional approach without an explicit growth allowance. Crosby discovered that of the reversionary techniques used in practice, the traditional term and reversion was not dominant but that the layer approach (also known as the hardcore method) and equivalent yield were also used. There was an even spread across these three approaches. Example 6.1 will show the application of these three methods in a simple valuation.

Example 6.1

A freehold shop is let at an existing rent of £50 000 net. The estimated full rental value (ERV) is estimated at £100 000. The capitalisation rate at full rental value is 5%. There are 3 years left on the lease to run. Calculate the capital value.

Term and reversion:

Term rent	£50 000	
YP 3 years @ 4%	2.7751	
		£138 755
Reversion to ERV	£100 000	
YP in perp. @ 5% ×	20.000	
PV £1 in 3 years @ 5%	0.8638	
		£1 727 600
Capital value		£1 866 355

Note: The yield on the term is reduced to reflect the security of the income.

Hardcore or layer approach:

Term rent	£50 000	
YP in perp. @ 5%	20.000	
		£1 000 000
Reversion to ERV	£100 000	
Less term rent	£50 000	
Top slice	£50 000	
YP in perp. @ 6% ×	16.667	
PV £1 in 3 years @ 6%	0.8396	
		£699 681
Capital value		£1 699 681

Note: The income stream is split horizontally.

Equivalent yield:

Term rent	£50 000	
YP in perp. @ 5%	20.000	
		£1 000 000
Reversion to ERV	£100 000	
Less hardcore rent	£50 000	
Top slice	£50 000	
YP in perp. @ 5% ×	20.000	
PV £1 in 3 years @ 5%	0.8638	
		£863 800
Capital value		£1 863 800

Note: The income stream may be split vertically as in the traditional term and reversion or horizontally as in the layer method. As the yield rates for the term and reversion are the same in this calculation it does not matter.

6.3   LEASEHOLD PROPERTY

In traditional leasehold valuations the leasehold yield is derived from the freehold yield and adjusted for tax and a sinking fund to replace the asset on expiration of the lease. There has been much debate about the relevance of both the sinking fund and the tax adjustment and critics have suggested that an appropriate approach would be to value without the sinking fund adjustment or even without both. This section shows the conventional approach and a valuation without adjustment.

Example 6.2

A leasehold interest in a shop is subject to a head rent of £50 000 net. The estimated full rental value (ERV) is estimated at £100 000. The capitalisation rate at full rental value is 5%. There are 3 years left on the lease to run. Calculate the capital value of the leasehold interest.

Dual rate, with sinking fund tax adjusted:

ERV	£100 000	pa	
Less head rent	£50 000	pa	
Profit rent	£50 000	pa	
YP 3 years @ 6% + 3%(40p tax)	1.6688		
Capital value			£83 440

Note: The criticism of this approach relates to how the leasehold rate is assessed from the freehold, the tax rate is an individual calculation and not a market one and the renumeration rate used at 3% is low.

Single rate

ERV	£100 000	pa	
Less head rent	£50 000	pa	
Profit rent	£50 000	pa	
YP 3 years @ 6%	2.6730		
Capital value			£133 650

Note: The yield could be increased in this calculation to provide a similar answer to the dual rate calculation.

6.4   OVER-RENTED PROPERTY

The layer approach used above can also deal with situations where properties are over-rented. That is where the property is let at a rental value higher than the estimated rental value and thus where the rental will fall at the next review. The over-rented layer of rent (the overage) is thus treated differently from the core which represents the estimated rental value; see Example 6.3.

Example 6.3

A freehold shop is let at an existing rent of £100 000 net. The estimated full rental value (ERV) is estimated at £50 000. The capitalisation rate at full rental value is 5%. There are 3 years left on the lease to run. The lease has 10 years to run with upward-only rent reviews. Calculate the capital value of the freehold.

Hardcore or layer approach

Core rent		
ERV	£50 000	
YP in perp. @ 5%	20.000	
		£1 000 000
Top slice		
Rent passing	£100 000	
Less ERV	£50 000	
Overage	£50 000	
YP 10 years @ 10%	6.1146	
		£305 730
Capital value		£1 305 730

Notes: The calculation assumes that the full rental value will be less than the rent passing for the duration of the lease and beyond. By using implied growth to the rental level, the precise time can be found when the ERV has grown to the same level as the rent passing. Assuming this is in 5 years' time, then the overage can only be valued for the five year period. The problem of this method is that the rental growth is double counted in the valuation of the core income and in the overage. This can be overcome by valuing as a term and reversion for the 10-year period; see Example 6.4.

Example 6.4

Term and reversion

Term rent	£100 000	
YP 10 years @ 10%	6.1146	
		£611 460
Reversion to ERV	£50 000	
YP in perp. @ 5% ×	20.000	
PV £1 in 10 years @ 5%	0.6139	
		£613 900
Capital value		£1 225 360

6.5   GROWTH AND INFLATION

Growth can be built into DCF cash flows so that the IRR of the calculation represents the equated yield: that is, the yield with an explicit growth or inflation rate. The NPV which arises from such a calculation thus will take into account the growth in rental levels; this is shown in the calculation of the equated yield set out below.

Equated yield

The technique of equated yield analysis is as follows:

(i)   Assume a growth rate in the rental per annum. Apply this to the original income using the Amount of £1.
(ii) Insert the income with growth into the DCF analysis. Once the IRR has been found, this is the equated yield.

Example 6.5: Calculation of equated yield

A freehold investment has been purchased for £100 000; it has been let at a rental value of £5000 p.a. It is let on a lease for 25 years with 5-year rent reviews. Assuming rental growth of 10% p.a., determine the equated yield. The layout used below is a possible presentation of the calculation, if a computer spreadsheet were to be used.

Capital value	£100 000	
Initial rent	£5 000 p.a.	
Initial yield/YP	5%	20 YP
Trial equated yields	14%	15%
Rent review frequency	5 yearly	
Growth rate p.a.	10% compound	
YP for the review period at the trial rate	3.43081	3.352155

(These YPs are based on the YP for 5 years, the review period, at the trial rates of 14% and 15% as above).

Period (years)	Amt £1 @ 10%	Cash flow	PV £1 @ 14%	Deferred YP	PV of slice
0	n/a	−100 000	n/a		−100 000
1– 5	n/a	5 000	n/a	3.433081	17 165
6–10	1.610510	8 053	0.5193687	1.783035	14 358
11–15	2.593742	12 969	0.2697438	0.9260523	12 010
16–20	4.177248	20 886	0.1400965	0.4809626	10 046
21–25	6.727500	33 637	0.0727617	0.2497969	8 403
26–30	10.83471	54 174	0.0377902	0.1297367	7 028
31–perp	17.44940	87 247	0.0196270	0.3925405	34 248
				Net present value	3 258

Period (years)	Amt £1 @ 10%	Cash flow	PV £1 @ 15%	Deferred YP	PV of slice
0	n/a	−100 000	n/a		−100 000
1–5	n/a	5 000	n/a	3.352155	16 761
6–10	1.610510	8 053	0.4971767	1.666614	13 420
11–15	2.593742	12 969	0.2471847	0.8286015	10 746
16–20	4.177248	20 886	0.1228945	0.4119614	8 604
21–25	6.727500	33 637	0.0611003	0.2048176	6 890
26–30	10.83471	54 174	0.0303776	0.1018306	5 517
31–perp	17.44940	87 247	0.0151031	0.3020611	26 354
				Net present value	−11 708

$$IRR = 14 + \left(1 \times \frac{3\,258}{14\,966}\right) = 14.22$$

Notes to the calculation:

(i) Because the rent review period is for 5 years, the calculation deals with the cash flows in slices of 5 years as the income cannot change within the 5-year period.

(ii) The cash flows for each period have been inflated by the amount of £1 at the growth rate of 10% to the beginning of each period, showing the rent with growth at each review.

(iii) The deferral rate is calculated for each cash flow period for each trial rate (PV £1 for deferred period at 14 and 15%). This is multiplied by the PV £1 column to give the deferred YP.

(iv) The period cash flow is valued by capitalising at the trial rates for the 5-year period (YP 5 years at 14 and 15%). This is multiplied by the PV £1 column to give the deferred YP.

(v) The deferred YP at the trial rates is multiplied by the inflated cash flow to give the value of the deferred slice. The values of the deferred slices are added together to give the net present value.

(vi) To calculate the equated yield which is the IRR of the calculation, we need to arrive at a positive and negative NPV and interpolate between them to obtain the point where the NPV = 0; this is then the yield which is the IRR.

(vii) The calculation could go on indefinitely but cash flows after 30 years because of the deferral factor make much less difference to the calculation; after this, no growth is added to the income and thus the initial yield is used for the trial rates. In this case the initial yield is 5% and the final deferred YP is YP in perpetuity @ 5% deferred 30 years. In view of the problems of predicting growth over the longer period it may be more desirable to restrict the analysis to 20 years.

An alternative way of arriving at the equated yield is to use the equation which underpins the calculation. The equated yield equation is:

$$k = e - e\left[\frac{(1+g)^n - 1}{(1+g)^n - 1}\right]$$

where: k is the initial or all risks yield $= \dfrac{\text{rack rent}}{\text{purchase price}}$ when the property is freehold

or let at the rack purchase price rent or full rental value. The yield is expressed as a decimal in the equation not a percentage.

e is the equated yield as a decimal.

g is the annual growth rate in rental income compounded as a decimal

n is the rent review period in years.

This equation which lies behind the DCF calculation used above can be used directly to compute the growth rate and this is shown in Example 6.6, the calculation to find the implied growth rate.

Implied growth rate

There are a number of ways of obtaining this as shown in Example 6.6.

Example 6.6

A freehold shop is let on a 25-year lease with 5-year reviews at the full rental value of £100 000. The property has been sold for £500 000. What is the implied rental growth rate?

Capitalisation rate $(k) = \dfrac{£100\,000}{£500\,000} = 0.05 = 5\%$

Target rate of return (assumed) $(e) =$ 15%
Rent review period $(t) =$ 5 years
Implied annual growth rate (g) is calculated from the formula:

$$k = e - \frac{e\left[(1+g)^t - 1\right]}{(1+e)^t - 1}$$

$$0.05 = 0.15 - \frac{0.15\left[(1+g)^5 - 1\right]}{(1+0.15)^5 - 1}$$

$$g = 0.1085 = 10.85\%$$

An alternative formula on the same basis is:

$$(i+g)^t = \frac{\text{YP perp. @ } k - \text{YP } t \text{ years @ } e}{\text{YP perp. @ } k \times \text{PV } t \text{ years @ } e}$$

Equated rents

The valuation of equated rents or constant rents relates to the adjustment of comparables for non-regular rent review patterns. K, the constant rent factor is based on the formula:

$$K = \frac{A - B}{A - 1} \times \frac{C - 1}{C - D}$$

where: A is the Amount of £1 @ $R\%$ (the equated yield) for L years (the actual abnormal review period);
B is the Amount of £1 @ $G\%$ (the growth rate for property of this type) for L years;
C is the Amount of £1 @ $R\%$ for Z years (normal rent review pattern);
D is the Amount of £1 @ $G\%$ for Z years.

Example 6.7

Calculate the rent appropriate on rent review for a lease with 21-year rent reviews. The lessor's required return on capital is 15% (equated yield) and the growth rate anticipated is 8%. The estimated full rental value is £10 000 p.a. on a normal rent review pattern of 5 years.

$$K = \frac{\text{Amount of £1 @ 15\% for 21 years} - \text{Amount of £1 @ 8\% for 21 years}}{\text{Amount of £1 @ 15\% for 21 years} - 1} \times$$

$$\frac{\text{Amount of £1 @ 15\% for 5 years} - 1}{\text{Amount of £1 @ 15\% for 5 years} - \text{Amount of £1 @ 8\% for 5 years}}$$

$$= \frac{18.8215 - 5.0338}{18.8215 - 1} \times \frac{2.0114 - 1}{2.0114 - 1.4693}$$

$$= 1.443$$

Thus the rent appropriate on review is:

$K \times$ rent on normal review $= 1.443 \times £10\,000$ p.a. $= £14\,430$ p.a.

6.6   VALUATION ACCURACY

The *Estates Times* of 15 March 1996 proclaimed 'Valuations still highly variable'. This headline was the findings of a piece of RICS research involving teams of researchers from the Universities of Aberdeen and Ulster. These teams asked local and national firms of surveyors to value hypothetical properties in 14 UK locations and then calculated the variation from the mean valuation. For rack-rented property, only 57% of office and industrial valuations and 70% of retail valuations showed a variation of less than 10%. For reversionary property, 60% of industrial valuations, 73% of retail and 74% of office valuations were in the 10% band. These results were based on prime properties only; presumably the variation would have been higher with secondary properties. The reason for the divergence appeared to be accounted for by lack of data. The methods of valuation used also caused some concern, with only one of the 446 valuations submitted being based on DCF techniques (Jenkins 1996). However, over 80% of the total valuations produced a variation from the mean of less than 20%, and in the case of reversionary investments over 90% were in that range, but, generally, commenting on the research project, Hutchinson concluded: 'The results of this research do not inspire confidence that valuers would produce accurate valuation in stable conditions' (Hutchinson 1996, p. 41).

Scarrett (1991) gives recent examples of the range of accuracy acceptable. For instance in *Singer and Friedlander Ltd* v. *John D Wood and Co*, the valuation error was in respect of development land and the finding was for a valuation 10% either side of the 'accurate' figure and in exception circumstances 5%. The test by Hager and Lord (1985) used 5% variation. In the Oldham Estate valuation quoted by Scarrett, one firm valued the portfolio at £581m, whilst another acting for the bidder valued it at £436m, a 25% variation on the previous figure. In this latter case, the RICS found that the valuations were within acceptable professional standards.

The issue of accurate performance measurement is dependent on accurate valuations and the crucial point is whether valuations act as good proxies for prices. This issue was highlighted in a paper by Hager and Lord (1985) in which a limited experiment, involving the valuation of two properties by a team of valuers, was undertaken. The authors wished to test the hypothesis that the range of valuations for any particular property would be about 5% either side of the average. When results of the test failed to confirm the hypothesis, the authors proceeded to counsel caution about the accuracy of property valuation. Using a random sample of 29 properties, Brown (1991) also tested the hypothesis that valuations act as good proxies for prices. The test produced a regression coefficient of 1.02, statistically significant at the 99% level. While acknowledging the limited sample size, Brown offered the test as empirical evidence suggesting that performance measurement based on valuations is as valid as using prices.

A major drawback to the use of valuation based property indices (discussed in Chapter 10) is whether valuations are a good proxy for prices. IPD tested 1400 sales between 1980 and 1988, and taking into account the lags between the valuation date and the sale date, valuations accounted for all but 7% of the difference in agreed sale prices. On average valuations have been considered a good proxy for prices in the strong market of the 1980s but may be less applicable in the thin markets of the early 1990s (Godson 1991). This survey was carried out in conjunction with Drivers Jonas and two tests were carried out using regression techniques (Drivers Jonas/IPD 1988). The first test was based on the valuation surveyor's ability to assess the current level of the local property market through the measure of capital value as an estimate of subsequent sale prices, and Drivers Jonas suggested a 93% success rate here with a suggestion of a slight bias of conservatism. The second measured the investment surveyor's ability to forecast both the direction and subsequent rate of rental growth levels in the local property market. The sample consisted of around 1600 properties which had been in single institutional ownership between 1981 and 1987. The results confirmed a negative relationship between yield and rental value growth. This indicated that investment surveyors are able to impound a very rough measure of future rental growth into their yield. Many predictions were successful; about one-third of valuation yields fixed in 1984 predicted to within plus or minus three percentage points of the subsequent annual growth rate. A subsequent study by Divers Jones and IPD also concluded that valuers were providing accurate valuations. These studies have been the subject of some debate in terms of their methodology (Lizieri and Venmore-Rowland 1991).

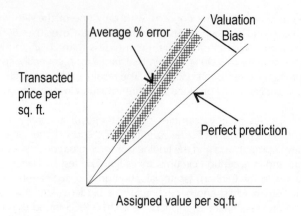

Figure 6.1   *Bias and error in price estimation*

Source: Drivers Jonas/IPD (1988).

A diagram showing the difference between bias and error is taken from the Drivers Jonas/IPD research and is shown in Figure 6.1. Error is a random discrepancy around the line of relationship between value and price, bias is a systematic difference one way or the other to the ideal relationship. The Drivers Jonas test used regression techniques; in Figure 6.1, if valuations were perfect predictors of prices for all transactions, each deal would lie on the 45% line. The regression method allows us to establish what bias, if any, is built into the valuations, by measuring the angle of the line which best fits the actual relationship between values and prices. It also tells us how close the fit is (irrespective of the bias) by measuring the correlation between values and prices. The error estimate derived in this way is indicated by the dashed lines in the figure. In order to take out the effect of size variation, the tests were performed in each case using prices and values on a per square foot basis. Herein lies the criticism of Lizieri and Venmore-Rowland; the error term must have a constant variance for all observations, known as homoscedasticity (Brown 1991). This means that the disturbances around the regression line must be the same for small values of x as for large; if not they would be heteroscedastic and the shaded area in the diagram would increase or decrease along the regression line and would be cone-shaped rather than enclosed in parallel lines (Watson *et al.* 1990). The issue of bias has been taken up by Gallimore (1996). He defines bias in terms of a deviation from a prescriptive mode of behaviour, and in his study he looked at the existence of confirmation bias in property valuation: that is, the tendency for valuers to look to confirm their opinions rather than objectively set them to the test. In his survey Gallimore found that there was little evidence to support the view that confirmation bias is a dominant factor in the working procedures of valuers.

REFERENCES

Baum, A. and Crosby, N. (1988) *Property Investment Appraisal*, Routledge, London.
Brown, G. R. (1991) *Property Investment and the Capital Markets*, E. & F.N. Spon, London.
Crosby, N. (1992) 'Reversionary Freeholds; UK Market Valuation Practice', Research paper, RICS, London.

Drivers Jonas/IPD (1988) *The Variance in Valuations*, Drivers Jonas Research Department, London, Autumn.

Enever, N. and Isaac, D. (1995) 'The Valuation of Property Investments', *Estates Gazette*, London.

Estates Gazette (1996) 'The New Red Book', *Estates Gazette*, 6 January, pp. 96–7.

French, N. (1994) Editorial:'Market Values & DCF', *Journal of Property Valuation and Investment*, vol. 12, no. 1, pp. 4–6.

Gallimore, P. (1996) 'Confirmation Bias in the Valuation Process: A Test for Corroborating Evidence', *Journal of Property Valuation and Investment*, vol. 13, no. 4, pp. 261–273.

Godson, V. (1991) 'Methods of Portfolio Analysis', in P. Venmore-Rowland, P. Brandon and T. Mole (eds), *Investment, Procurement and Performance in Construction*, E. & F.N. Spon, London.

Hager, D. P. and Lord D. J. (1985) *The Property Market, Property Valuations and Property Performance Measurement*, Institute of Actuaries.

Hutchinson, N. (1996), 'Variations in the Capital Values of UK Commercial Property', *Chartered Surveyor Monthly*, April, pp. 40–1.

Isaac, D. and Steley, T. (1991) *Property Valuation Techniques*, Macmillan, London.

Jenkins, S. (1996), 'Valuations Still Highly Variable', *Estates Times*, 15 March, p. 2.

Lizieri, C. and Venmore-Rowland, P. (1991) 'Valuation Accuracy: A Contribution to the Debate', *Journal of Property Research*, vol. 8, pp. 115–22.

Scarrett, D. (1991) *Property Valuation: The Five Methods*, E. & F.N. Spon, London.

Watson, C. J., Billingsley, P., Croft, D. J. and Huntsberger, D.V. (1990) *Statistics for Management and Economics*, Allyn and Bacon, Boston.

7   Contemporary Investment Appraisal Techniques

7.1   DISCOUNTED CASH FLOW MODELS

Explicit DCF models can be developed using growth in the calculation and discounting using the investor's target rate or equated yield. Freehold property requires an infinite cash flow and this means the process needs to be shortened. This can be done by assuming a certain holding period and then resale of the investment at the initial capitalisation rate.

Example 7.1: Shortened cash flow model

Shortened cash flow model (spreadsheet layout)					
Freehold shop					
Lease	25	years	5	year reviews	
Existing year of lease			0		
Years to review			5		
Equated yield			15.00%		
Market capitalisation			5.00%		
Net rental value	£		100000	pa	
Implied rate of growth			10.86%		
Period	Amt £1 @	Cash	PV £1 @	Deferred	PV of
(years)	10.86%	flow	15.00%	YP	slice
0–5	1	100000	1	3.352155	335216
6–10	1.674238	167424	0.497177	1.666614	279031
11–15	2.803073	280307	0.247185	0.828601	232263
16–20	4.693012	469301	0.122894	0.411961	193334
21–25	7.85722	785722	0.0611	0.204818	160930
26–30	13.15486	1315486	0.030378	0.101831	133957
31–perp	22.02436	2202436	0.015103	0.302061	665270
			Capital value		2000000

Notes to Example 7.1 spreadsheet:

1. The deferred YP is the YP for 5 years at the equated yield times the PV in the previous column
2. The deferred YP for the years over 30 is YP in perpetuity at the market capitalisation rate times the PV in the previous column

An alternative would be to use the equation discussed earlier, which is the DCF model:

$$YP\ n\ \text{years} = YP\ t\ \text{years} @ e \times \frac{1 - (1+g)^n/(1+e)^n}{1 - (1+g)^t/(1+e)^t}$$

where the income is £1 per annum, the total term is n years, the rent review period is t years, the equated yield is $e\%$ and the growth rate is $g\%$ p.a.

By formula (spreadsheet layout)				
$YP\ n\ \text{years} = YP\ t\ \text{years} @ e \times \dfrac{1 - (1+g)^n/(1+e)^n}{1 - (1+g)^t/(1+e)^t}$				
Here $n =$	perpetuity and thus $(1+g)^n/(1+e)^n$ will tend to 0			
$t =$	5	years		
$e =$	15.00%			
$g =$	10.86%			
YP in perp $=$		3.352155	×	1
				0.167608
	$=$	20		
Valuation:				
ERV		£100 000	pa	
YP whole term		20		
Capital value			£2 000 000	pa

7.2   A REAL VALUE/EQUATED YIELD HYBRID

A conceptual weakness of the approaches adopted in traditional reversionary approaches or where the capitalisation rates are marginally varied according to the security in money terms, is that the degree to which the various tranches or layers of income are hedged against inflation is not explicitly reflected in the valuations. An alternative approach would be to regard the term income as similar to a fixed interest security and capitalise at an appropriate rate. The reversionary income would then need to be treated as a growth investment and capitalised either using an overall all risks yield or by using an even more explicit DCF approach whereby the future income is enhanced to reflect anticipated value changes, and is then capitalised at a rate appropriate to a growth investment but discounted at a rate appropriate to a fixed interest security. This latter part of the procedure is needed to avoid double-counting the growth (Enever and Isaac 1994). This approach is shown in Example 7.2.

Example 7.2: Real value/equated yield hybrid

Value the freehold interest in a factory built and let on a 42-year lease with 14-year reviews which now has ten years unexpired on the lease without review. The current net rent passing is £60 000 and the estimated net full rental value is £90 000. 10% is considered an appropriate equivalent yield rate but similar investments let at the full rental value produce an 8.5% yield.

Term and reversion:

Term rent	£60 000	
YP 10 years @ 11.5%	4.8765	
		£292 590
Reversion to ERV	£ 90 000	
YP in perp. @ 9% ×	11.1111	
PV £1 in 10 years @ 9%	0.4224	
		£422 400
Capital value		£714 990

Alternative approach

Term rent	£60 000	
YP 10 years @ 11.5%	4.8765	
		£292 590
Reversion to ERV	£90 000	
Amt £1 in 10 yrs @ 2%	1.219	
Estimated ERV with growth	£109 710	
YP in perp. @ 8.5%	11.76	
Capital value on reversion (allowing for growth)	£1 290 190	
PV £1 in 10 years @ 11.5%	0.327	
		£422 410
Capital value		£715 000

The approach suggested above has come to be known as the short-cut DCF approach and the full calculation would involve the calculation of the growth rate used in the approach. For instance the growth rate can be calculated from the growth equation:

$$\text{The growth rate per annum} = \sqrt[n]{\left[1 + \frac{E - I}{AF}\right]} - 1$$

where n = number of years between reviews
      E = equated yield rate
      I = initial yield rate
      AF = annual sinking fund for review period at rate e

In the example, $n = 14$
                  $E = 11.5\%$ (this is the yield used for the term income and deferral)
                  $I = 8.5\%$
                  AF = the annual sinking fund at 11.5%
                  thus the growth rate = 4.83%

Another approach uses the implied growth rate formula is outlined later in the chapter.

DCF approaches

The short-cut DCF approach was discussed earlier. The DCF approaches are alternatives to the traditional term and reversion. The DCF approach has been examined in Chapters 5 and 6; here the approach can be extended by the use of term and reversionary rents for the time periods and a growth rate applied to the reversion. A distinction has to be made here between the short-cut DCF used above and the real value/equated yield hybrid which is based on the real value approach suggested by Ernest Wood but developed by Baum and Crosby (1995). The short-cut DCF is:

> Term rent
>   × YP n years @ $e\%$
> plus
> Reversion to ERV
>   × amount of £1 for n years @ $g\%$
>   × YP in perp @ $k\%$
>   × PV for n years @ $e\%$

where n = number of years to rent review
  $e\%$ = equated yield rate
  $k\%$ = all risks yield of comparable
  $g\%$ p.a. = the implied rental growth per annum

The equated yield is used to capitalise the rent passing over the term and also to discount the capital values over this period. This is because the rent passing is fixed and does not reflect market conditions. The full rental value is inflated to the time of the reversion at the implied growth rate and then capitalised at the all risks yield. The short-cut DCF does not inflate the rent through the reversion period, thus the discount rate for the all risks yield is used on the reversion. The following example shows the application of the short-cut DCF approach; in this example a situation of over-renting exists where the rent passing is higher than the estimated rental value.

Example 7.3: Short-cut growth explicit DCF

Stage 1. Calculate implied rental growth:							
$(1+g)^t = \dfrac{YP \text{ in perp } @ \ k - YP \text{ for } t \text{ years } @ \ e}{YP \text{ in perp } @ \ k \times PV \text{ for } t \text{ years } @ \ e}$							
where g = Implied rental growth p.a. (%)							
e = Equated yield (%)					=	12%	
t = Rent review pattern of the comparable (years)					=	5	
k = All risks yield of comparable (%)					=	7%	
$(1+g)^t =$	14.2857	–	3.6048	=	10.6809		
	14.2857	×	0.5674		8.1061		
$(1+g)^t =$	1.3176						
$g =$	0.0567	=	5.67	%			
Stage 2. Valuation							
Assume:	Rent passing				220000		
	Full rental value				200000		
	Rent reviews				14		
	Term to reversion				14		
	All risks yield at full rental value				7		
	Equated yield				12		
Valuation							
Term:	Rent passing					220000	
YP	14	years @	12	%		6.6282	
							1458197
Reversion to Full Rental Value					200000		
Amt £1	14	years @	5.67	%		2.1649	
							432975
YP	in perp	@	7	%		14.2857	
PV £1	14	years @	12.00	%		0.2046	
						2.9231	
							1265648
							2723845

The real value/equated yield hybrid suggested by Baum and Crosby involves the calculation of the IRFY (inflation risk-free yield) which is the real interest rate (the market rate with inflation taken out). This approach to the reversionary calculation is the same as the short-cut DCF except that the reversion is not inflated. Values are discounted at the IRFY rather than the equated yield, thus the calculation is:

> Term rent
> × YP *n* years @ *e*% (same as above)
> Plus
> Reversion to ERV
> × YP in perp @ *k*%
> × PV for *n* years @ *IRFY*

The calculation of IRFY comes from the general calculation of interest rates (see Isaac and Steley 1991):

$$(1 + e) = (1 + g)(1 + i)$$

where *i*% is the all risks (initial) yield.
> *g*% is the growth rate
> *e*% is the equated yield.

here   *i*% is the IRFY

thus

$$i = \frac{(1 + g)}{(1 + e)} - 1$$

To find *g*, Crosby's calculations use the implied rate of rental growth formula which is stated as:

$$(1 + g)^t = \frac{YP \text{ in perp @ } k\% - YP \text{ for } t \text{ years @ } e\%}{YP \text{ in perp @ } k\% \times PV \text{ for } t \text{ years @ } e\%}$$

where *g*% p.a. = the implied rental growth per annum
> *e*% = equated yield
> *t* = rent review pattern of comparable
> *k*% = all risks yield of comparable

It is suggested that using this valuation approach, there may be some under-valuation because the deferment of the reversion is at a yield which reflects that rental values will grow periodically every five years over the reversionary period whereas they actually grow continuously.

Calculation using the real value/equated yield hybrid approach

The real value/equated yield hybrid approach is:

$$YP \text{ of the whole } (n) = YP\ t@e \times \frac{YP\ n\ @\ i}{YP\ t\ @\ i}$$

where i = the inflation risk-free yield (IRFY) $= \dfrac{1+e}{1+g} - 1$

e = equated yield
t = rent review period
n = valuation term

Example 7.4: Real value/equated yield hybrid approach

A freehold property was recently let at £100 000 p.a. on a 5-year rent review pattern. Assume growth rate to be 10% and the equated yield to be 15%. Value the freehold interest.

Thus: $e = 15\%$, $g = 10\%$, n is in perpetuity, $t = 5$.

Calculate i:

$$i = \frac{1+0.15}{1+0.10} - 1$$
$$= 0.04545 = 4.545\%$$

Calculate YP:

$$YP \text{ in perp} = YP\ 5 \text{ yrs } @ 15\% \times \frac{YP \text{ in perp } @\ 4.545\%}{YP\ 5 \text{ yrs } @\ 4.545\%}$$

$$= 3.522 \times \frac{22.0022}{4.3845}$$

$$= 16.8219$$

Valuation:

ERV	£ 100 000	pa
YP in perp	16.8219	
Capital value	£1 682 190	

The calculation of a leasehold interest using the real value/equated yield hybrid approach is in two parts: the valuation of the right to receive the rent from the sublessee is found and the capital value of the liability to pay the ground rent is deducted. This head lessee's valuation is calculated at the risk rate for the head lessee's net income. The valuation is thus:

Calculate IRFY:

$$i = \frac{1+e}{1+g}$$

where $i = $ IRFY

$e = $ equated yield of head lessee's interest

$g = $ growth rate p.a.

Valuation:

Value of rent received

$= $ rent received $\times$ YP t years @ $e\% \times \dfrac{YP \ n \ \text{years @} \ i\%}{YP \ t \ \text{years @} \ e\%}$

less

value of rent paid $=$ rent paid $\times$ YP n years @ $e\%$

where: $i = $ inflation risk-free yield

$e = $ equated yield of head lessee

$n = $ length of lease

$t = $ rent review period

7.3   OVER-RENTED FREEHOLD PROPERTIES

Problems of over-rented freeholds

In a falling market there arise cases of overage. Overage means that the rent passing is higher than the rack rental in the market. This can occur in two particular cases: firstly, where the rent passing is greater that the rent on a normal rent review because of the absence of rent reviews; secondly, it can occur because of a fall in rental values since the last rent review. In the year to end of March 1991 the All Property Rental Growth Index fell 2.4% (Crosby 1991). The problem of falls in rental values has meant that in many cases the rent passing is less than the current open market value, and this, as indicated above is defined as overage or froth. Overage can also occur when the property is let on abnormally long rent reviews but here the term 'overage' is misleading as really it is an open market value put on different terms. Therefore, overage is best defined as the excess rent over open market rental value on a normal rent review pattern of five years. Crosby and Goodchild in their analysis of the problems of over-renting came to the conclusion that valuers must now use explicit growth calculations and cannot use the top slicing approach employed in the hardcore method which had become popular in the 1970s. These authors in their research consider the need to adopt a growth explicit cashflow approach for both the market valuation and the subsequent appraisal of worth in over-rented situations (Crosby and Goodchild 1992).

Overage related to abnormal review patterns

Crosby and Goodchild (1992) suggest five approaches to dealing with this:

(i)   ignore and value at the full rental value;

(ii)   ignore overage as an addition, value the full rental and add the overage; this is then valued to rent review at a higher yield;

(iii) include overage as an addition as previously mentioned, but adjust the all risks yield on the core income at a higher yield;

(iv)   value as a conventional term and reversion, valuing the term at a higher yield with a reversion at the rack rent;

(v)   use a short-cut growth explicit DCF (see later example).

Crosby and Goodchild suggest that conventional approaches may overvalue the term and undervalue the reversion. In the short-term growth explicit DCF, the valuation allows the fixed term to be specifically dealt with.

Overage caused by rental value reduction

In this case the additional income is a bonus until the next rent review and the issue is how this is to be treated. The use of a conventional and a growth explicit calculation are given below.

Example 7.5: Over-rented property

A property has a yield at a rack rent of 5%. It was let one year ago at a rental of £150 000 and thus has four years unexpired. The full rental value at present is £100 000 per annum. A conventional approach would value the core income and overage separately.

Traditional/hardcore approach:

Core income:			
	Full rental value	£100 000	
	YP perp @ 5%[1]	20.00	
		£2 000 000	
	Overage:		
	Passing rent	£150 000	
	less Full Rental Value	£100 000	
		£50 000	
	YP 4 years @ 14%[2]	2.9137	
			£145 685
	Capital value		£2 145 685

Notes:
1. The initial yield (i) used on the core income is 5%.
2. The return on the overage is assessed as 14%.

The debate on the use of this valuation relates to the security of the core income and the overage, and how the reduction of this overage should be treated on the assumption that rents may grow until the overage is eliminated at a subsequent review. In a growth explicit DCF calculation the equated yield of 12% or target yield is assumed. The growth rate will need to be calculated using:

$$(1 + g)^t = \frac{YP \text{ in perp @ } k\% - YP \text{ for } t \text{ years @ } e\%}{YP \text{ in perp @ } k\% \times PV \text{ £1 for } t \text{ years @ } e\%}$$

where $g\%$ p.a. = the implied rental growth per annum
$\quad$ $e\%$ $\quad$ = equated yield
$\quad$ t $\quad\quad$ = rent review pattern of comparable
$\quad$ $k\%$ $\quad$ = all risks yield of comparable

Here the growth rate calculation gives the growth rate ($g\%$) as 7.64%.

where $e\%$ $\quad$ = 12%
$\quad$ t $\quad\quad$ = 5 years
$\quad$ $k\%$ $\quad$ = 5%

Example 7.6: Growth explicit approach

Term:	Rent passing	£150 000		
	YP 4 years @ 12%[1]	3.0373		
				£455 595
	Reversion to Full Rental Value	£100 000		
	Amt of £1 in 4 years @ 7.64%[2]	1.3422		
		£134 220		
	YP in perp @ 5%[3]	20.0000		
	× PV £1 in 4 years @ 12%[4]	0.6355		
			12.7104	
				£1 705 936
				£2 161 531

Notes:
1. Based on a target equated yield of 12% but may be varied intuitively; may be higher to accord with the hardcore valuation as set out earlier.
2. Growth rate as calculated.
3. All risks yield.
4. Equated yield.

The use of DCF techniques in the form of a short-cut or modified DCF is being adopted by the profession to deal with over-renting, and thus knowledge of the application of the techniques is vital.

7.4   TREATMENT OF INDUCEMENTS

The definitions of expressions used in this section are summarised in Box 7.1:

DEFINITIONS USED IN RENTAL INDUCEMENTS
Headline rent: the rent payable after inducements etc. have expired
Equivalent rent: the rent adjusted to take inducements into account also known as the core rent

Box 7.1   *Definitions used in rental inducements*

Source: RICS (1995).

Inducements such as rent-free periods reduce the rent actually paid below the headline rent which is the rent set out in the lease. An example would be a new lease of 10 years with a 5-year rent review which is upward only. The first year is rent free and the rent for years 2–5 is £50 000. Four approaches have been suggested in this situation, as shown in Example 7.7 (*Estates Gazette* 1995).

Example 7.7: Treatment of inducements

Approach 1:
£50 000 may be the true FRV (full rental value) if the rent-free period is merely an incentive to attract a tenant offering a good covenant who might otherwise have been reluctant to enter into a long-term commitment.

Approach 2:
Calculate the total rent over the first 5 years and divide by the years to the first review. The present value is then discounted over the period to review to find its annual equivalent value.

$$\text{Rent} = £50\,000 \times 4 \text{ years} = \frac{£200\,000}{5 \text{ years to review}} = £40\,000$$

$$= \text{Equivalent rent}$$

Valuation:
Equivalent rent   £40 000 pa
YP 5 years @ 9% (more secure)
Reversion to FRV (£50 000) defrd 5 yrs @ 10%

Approach 3:
The same as 2 but the rental payment is discounted to find the present value.

Valuation:

Rent passing		£50 000 pa
YP 4 years @ 8%	3.31	
x PV £1 @ 8%	0.926	
		3.06506
Capital value		£153 253
divide by YP 5 years @ 8%		3.993
Equivalent rent		£38 400

Approach 4:
This valuation is as for 3 but recognises the upward-only review and the relatively low rates of rental growth. The headline rent may be at market rent at review, thus the contractual rent stays the same. The equivalent rent therefore has to be discounted over the longer period of the whole tenancy. For rent to exceed £5000 at first review, the average annual growth rate needs to be greater than 5%.

Valuation:

Rent passing		£50 000 pa
YP 9 years @ 8%	6.25	
x PV £1 @ 8%	0.926	
		5.7875
Capital value		£289 375
divide by YP 10 years @ 8%		6.71
Equivalent rent		£43 125

Approaches 3 and 4 are arithmetically identical to 2 of the approaches adopted in the RICS consultation paper on lease inducements (RICS 1995) which calculates the annual equivalent of the present capital value of the incentive to adjust the headline rent to the equivalent or core rent:

$$\text{Incentive} = \frac{£50\,000}{5\text{ yrs @ 8\%}} = \frac{£50\,000}{3.993}$$

Equivalent rent = headline rent less incentive

$$= £50\,000 - \frac{£50\,000}{3.993} = £38\,500$$

7.5   DEPRECIATION

Depreciation has been defined as:

> *the measure of wearing out, consumption or other loss of value of a fixed asset whether arising from use, effluxion of time or obsolescence through technology or market changes.* (Bowie 1982, p. 405)

Accountants will charge depreciation to an asset and simply by looking at the purchase price and sale price or scrap value, they will write off the value over the life of the asset. Example 7.8 is a simple case of this.

Example 7.8: Straight line depreciation

A car is purchased for £10 000. It is estimated that it will last 4 years before being resold for £2000. The car can be written down in accounting terms using a straight line method (there are other approaches), thus:

purchase price	£10 000
less resale price	£2 000
amount to be written off	£4 000
life of asset	4 years
depreciation per year	£2 000

The impact of depreciation is in the reduction in rental value of a property, the increase in the all-risks yield thus affecting capital value also and in additional costs for repair, maintenance and insurance. The main approaches to obsolescence are Bowie's all-risk approach which is essentially hypothetical and Salway's explicit approach using empirical evidence of depreciation; both are discussed here (Bowie 1982, and Salway 1987).

Depreciation and obsolescence

The problems of depreciation and obsolescence are incorporated in the cost approach to valuation, but they are of importance generally in looking at the valuation of property in the market. Techniques can make allowance for depreciation and there have been a number of suggestions as to how this can be done. Depreciation can be divided into curable and incurable depreciation. Curable depreciation relates to lack of maintenance, but incurable depreciation relates to obsolescence. Obsolescence can be further divided into internal obsolescence, such as the wearing out of a building (the technical changes which render space useless), and external obsolescence which relates to the decay of the environment such as changes in the location of industry. It is possible to make an adjustment to the yield on a property so as to estimate the true depreciated yield. Writers distinguish between functional, physical and economic obsolescence. Baum (1988) defines depreciation as the loss in the real value of property, whilst obsolescence is defined as one of the causes of depreciation, a decline in utility not directly related to physical usage or the passage of time. Baum finds it useful to consider only two types of obsolescence: aesthetic obsolescence and functional obsolescence. The calculation of the true depreciated yield is shown in Example 7.9.

Example 7.9: Depreciated yield

Assume a building has a 40-year life span. When the building is new, the land content is 20% value and the initial yield is 7.5% for each £100 invested:

	£
Total investment	100
less land value	20
Building value	80

Depreciated over a 40-year life = £2 p.a. = 2% of £100 invested.
Thus true depreciated yield = 7.5% − 2% = 5.5%

Salway (1987) suggests that there are three methods of investment appraisal which can allow explicitly for an analysis of building depreciation:

(i)   Treat the built element as a leasehold interest.
(ii)   Use a cost base approach.
(iii)   Use an explicit DCF appraisal over the life of the building.

Salway uses the latter approach to develop a DCF appraisal over a limited time period which equates to the anticipated life of the building in its existing form. Allowance is made for the effects of depreciation in two ways. Firstly, the appraiser chooses a new building growth rate and then specifies the percentage of the new-building rental value expected to be achieved at each successive rent review. Secondly, the terminal capital value is taken to be the estimated residual value of the property for refurbishment or redevelopment. This is based on present-day prices inflated over the time period at a new building growth rate. The DCF is used to provide a NPV given a discount rate and a projected net of depreciation growth rate, or a discount rate or net of depreciation growth rate given the other two variables. The terminal value is represented by the site value, the residual value on refurbishment or the investment value if relet. If there is uncertainty about the outcome then probability techniques can be used.

Example 7.10: Depreciation and probability

The probability of the terminal outcome of a property asset is assessed as follows:

Outcome	Value	Probability
Site value	£300 000	0.2
Residual value on refurbishment	£400 000	0.5
Investment value, relet unimproved	£450 000	0.3

Terminal value $= (£300\,000 \times 0.2) + (£400\,000 \times 0.5) + (£450\,000 \times 0.3)$
$= £395\,000$

Baum has developed Salway's work (Baum 1988) and incorporated depreciation in the basic explicit property appraisal. Using a comparison of implicit and explicit appraisal models:

$$y = r - g$$

all-risks yield $=$ *overall return* $-$ *income growth*

The overall return consists of a reward for losing the use of capital or liquidity preference (l), a reward to compensate for inflation (i) and a risk premium (p), thus:

$$r = l + i + p$$
$$\therefore \quad y = l + i + p - g$$

It is usual that property analysis uses nominal returns and thus *i* is not exposed, so the model becomes:

$$y = (I + i) + p - g$$

$(I + i)$ is a risk-free inflation prone opportunity cost rate (*c*); this is derived from the redemption yield on conventional gilts. Thus:

$$y = c + p - g$$

p and *g* are the variables requiring explanation, *p* is a property risk premium over gilts, *g* is the estimated rental growth, the most difficult variable to handle, *y* and *c* can be derived from market evidence. If we assume *p* and solve for *g* then for any investment *g* is net of depreciation and the all-risk yield (*k*) of a property is thus:

$$k = c + p - (g_m - d)$$

This leaves three variables exposed for analysis: the rental premium (*p*), the rental growth in a sample of new building (g_m) and the average depreciation in the rental value of the subject property (*d*).

Baum's study provides the regression equation:

Depreciation = £1.16 + 0.431 age

$R^2 = 67.26\%$ (significant @ 95% level)

To test the importance of building quality in Baum's study, shortfalls in rental value below a prime rent (depreciation) were related to shortfalls in each measure of quality (maximum 5). These qualities were configuration, internal specification and external appearance (obsolescence factors) and physical depreciation. Physical depreciation was not significant in the regression equation at the 95% level; other factors such as obsolescence are much more important than physical deterioration as a cause of depreciation. Scarrett (1991) has stated that the discrepancy between the rental value of a modern building and one 20 years old, when the higher yield required by investors is taken into account, means that the older building will be worth little more than half of its new counterpart. He quotes from his research the annual rates of depreciation in rental values in Table 7.1

Table 7.1   *Annual rates of depreciation*

Years	Offices (% p.a.)	Industrial (% p.a.)
0–5	3.3	3.1
5–10	3.4	3.9
10–20	2.7	3.2
0–20	3.0	3.3

Source: Scarrett (1991).

Scarrett uses the following equation to calculate the depreciated rental value as:

$$R_n = R_0(1 - d)^n$$

where R_n = rental value of a building n years old
R_0 = rental value of a building 0 years old
d = annual rate of depreciation in rental value
n = number of years

The effect of depreciation on the value of property is reflected generally in the effect of quality on value. In his research in this area, Baum (1994) looked at the effect of quality on property performance; he defined quality in property as the resistance of a building to physical deterioration (interior and exterior) and resistance to obsolescence. High quality property, he found, generated better returns but design factors were more important than durability. For income and capital return through rental growth, configuration of the property is the single most important factor.

REFERENCES

Baum, A. and Crosby, N. (1995) *Property Investment Appraisal*, Routledge, London.
Baum, A. (1994) 'Quality and Property Performance', *Journal of Property Valuation and Investment*, vol. 12, no. 1, pp. 31–46.
Baum, A. E. (1988) 'Depreciation and Property Investment Appraisal', in A. R. MacLeary and N. Nanthakumaran (eds) *Property Investment Theory*, E. & F.N. Spon, London.
Bowie, N. (1982) 'Depreciation: Who Hoodwinked Whom?', *Estates Gazette*, 1 May, pp. 405–11.
Brown, G. (1987) 'A Certainty Equivalent Expectations Model for Estimating the Systematic Risk of Property Investments', *Journal of Valuation*, vol. 6, no. 1, pp. 17–41.
Brown, G. R. (1991) *Property Investment and the Capital Markets*, E. & F.N. Spon, London.
Butler, D. and Richmond, D. (1990) *Advanced Valuation*, Macmillan, London.
Byrne, P. and Cadman, D. (1984) *Risk, Uncertainty and Decision Making in Property Development*, E. & F.N. Spon, London.
Chapman, C. B. (1991) 'Risk', in P. Venmore-Rowland, P. Brandon and T. Mole (eds), *Investment, Procurement and Performance in Construction*, RICS, London.
Crosby, N. (1991) 'Over-rented Freehold Investment Property Valuation' *Journal of Property Valuation and Investment*, vol. 10, no. 2, pp. 517–24.
Crosby, N. and Goodchild, R. (1992) 'Reversionary Freeholds: Problems with Over-Renting', *Journal of Property Valuation and Investment*, vol. 11, no. 1, pp. 67–81.
Enever, N. and Isaac, D. (1994) *The Valuation of Property Investments*, Estates Gazette, London.
Estates Gazette (1995) 'Rent-Free Periods and Valuations', *Estates Gazette*, 13 May, pp. 143–4.
French, N. (1994) Editorial: 'Market Values and DCF', *Journal of Property Valuation and Investment*, vol. 12, no. 1, pp. 4–6.
Isaac, D. and Steley, T. (1991) *Property Valuation Techniques*, Macmillan, London.
Lumby, S. (1991) *Investment Appraisal and Financing Decisions*, Chapman & Hall, London.
Royal Institution of Chartered Surveyors (RICS) (1995) *Rental Valuation of Commercial Lease Inducements*, Consultative Document, RICS, London.
Salway, F. (1987) 'Building Depreciation and Property Appraisal Techniques', *Journal of Valuation*, vol. 5, no. 2, pp. 118–24.
Scarrett, D. (1991) *Property Valuation: The Five Methods*, E. & F.N. Spon, London.

8 Cash Flow Approaches and Risk

8.1 USE OF CASH FLOW METHODS

Introduction

This chapter looks at cash flow methods in property investment appraisals. Cash flows into the future are forecasts, but valuations and forecasts are fundamentally different. This aspect has been discussed to a degree in Chapter 5, but essentially the valuation is about market price as a snapshot in time. It may be based on assumptions as to what will happen in the future but it is not a forecast A forecast will be concerned entirely with the future. In development appraisals assumptions need to be made about project costs and future rents, and potential changes can be incorporated. Formal forecasting is used in property development, but its overall lack of use is based on the problems of risk and uncertainty in the development process (Schiller 1994). Cash flow approaches are aided by computers, and the use of spreadsheets for calculations involving cash flow statements is vital. Some texts suggest the use of bespoke computer programs (Darlow 1988); these bespoke programs can examine the answers relating to changes of inputs into the calculations, but it is difficult to examine the changes in detail as they occur, and for this a spreadsheet is more useful. The computer spreadsheet is a useful tool for investment appraisals and the examples in this book have been calculated using this software.

The traditional method of investment valuation is the most commonly used approach in the financial analysis of investment proposals. However, the increasing complexity of investment markets and the size and complexity of investment properties have required more sophisticated techniques for analysis. As with investment markets, much of the push for greater detail and analysis in appraisal lies with the demands and example set by the major funders of schemes, the financial institutions: the insurance companies and the pension funds. They make demands for better analysis when they are providing funds and offer an example in the quality of analysis used in-house when they are project managing or dealing with their own portfolio. In addition, other lenders – banks, individuals and organisations in joint ventures – have established their own standards to ensure that their money does not get into trouble. The financial sector and the investment market deal internationally and with a number of asset classes, so techniques have been adopted from experiences in the US, and the use of analysis in investment appraisal has been utilised from examples used in the management of portfolios of shares and gilts. Economic analysis, providing a wider setting to the micro-economic financial analysis used in property development, has been applied, established both in the valuation to ensure the outcome is appropriate to the market and in the subsequent analysis of the investment. These developments are reflected in the move in property appraisal in the UK, from the traditional definition of open market value to the concept of estimated realisation price and the need for more explicit forecasting.

At a basic level, the traditional valuation can be developed by using a cash flow approach which divides up the time scale of investment into periods to which the interest periods can be more precisely applied. Cash flows can also enable more explicit assumptions to be put into the appraisal: changes over time, for instance changes in rents or yields, can be accommodated. These changes cannot be accommodated in the 'snapshot' traditional investment valuation. In a period of inflation, allowance can be made for inflation in revenue and costs in the calculation; growth and inflation can be applied to various revenues and rents. The cash flow can make allowance for the timing of possible one-off payments or allow for deductions or allowances based on the size of the various elements, tax deductions and capital allowances for instance. The argument about using cash flow approaches (including discounted cash flow) against the traditional Years Purchase approach of valuation is extensive. Problems arise because the price paid in the market may not reflect the present worth of the future cash flow and these problems have been discussed earlier when it was suggested that appraisal needs to distinguish between the valuation of a purchase price and the analysis of the worth of an investment. A discounted cash flow approach appears to be the only realistic approach to dealing with over-rented property (where the rent passing under the lease is higher than the existing market rental), and this also has been discussed earlier in this book. In the present recessionary market, the use of traditional techniques may no longer be defended. Thus traditional methods may not be able to cope with issues such as rent-free periods, reverse premiums, tenant incentives, bad debts, negative growth and over-rented properties (French 1994).

Development appraisal: the use of cash flows to improve the traditional residual approach

This section shows the application of cash flows. This uses the development appraisal as a vehicle and the application can be seen very clearly dealing with costs as well as values as inflows and outflows to the calculation. Using this approach it is therefore easy to apply the method to the investment appraisal, as shown in Chapters 5 and 6. Cash flows can assist in the calculation of costs over the development period for development appraisal. The basic residual method is unaltered but the cash flow approach gives a more detailed calculation of the scheme's total costs and thus the finance costs. In the cash flow approach, all development costs are divided into monthly (or quarterly or annual) amounts. The net cash flows are calculated and short-term finance allowed for each period. Cash flows deal more accurately with the build-up of total construction costs over the period. In Figure 8.1 the build-up of costs can be seen and, depending on the shape of the S curve, the simplified example shows that over the period to the halfway stage only 40% of the contract value may have been spent. There are two errors in the traditional residual. Firstly, it assumes that the total money borrowed will bear interest over half the building period. This is inaccurate, because it bears no relation to the actual incidence of costs which may differ from month to month over the period and also interest compounds monthly or quarterly over the period, depending on the arrangements with the lender; the simple interest formula of the traditional residual, or even compounding interest annually is an over-simplification. The second error arises from the build-up of building costs because, as shown in the S curve, the costs are loaded to the end of the building period. In the example only 40% of the costs are incurred halfway through the period. This may be because ground and initial works may

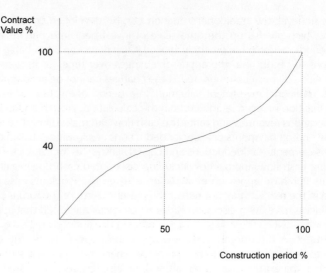

Figure 8.1   *S curve of building costs*

be cheaper. This will depend on circumstances but in many cases this is a fair assumption. Any building with complex service provision in the form of lifts or air conditioning or with expensive finishes will exaggerate this tendency. The traditional method will thus allow for too much interest. To summarise, cash flow statements are useful in certain situations:

(i)   in showing the effect of inflation in rents and building costs over time;
(ii)   in sensitivity analysis, to examine the effect of changes on the elements of cost;
(iii)   when including tax in the calculation;
(iv)   when taking into account a phased acquisition or development and partial disposal;
(v)   in showing the debt outstanding at any point; and,
(vi)   in showing the time of peak cash outlay.

Cash flows are a necessity for certain developments, for instance in residential estates with phased disposal or for complex central area shopping schemes with phasing and funding related to the phases. The cash flow approach is also essential for appraisal on industrial estates or business parks with a program of disposal of sites and completed buildings to minimise cash outlay. Finally a cash flow approach will be essential in new-town developments with a phased implementation of schemes to develop infrastructure and social provision. When considering the finance of a project, discounted cash flow techniques can be useful if the scheme is to be retained and financed by mortgage and leaseback, as the net return can be seen. Morley (1988a) suggests three general approaches to the use of cash flow statements. These are: the period-by-period cash flow, net terminal value approach and a discounted cash flow approach. The advantages and disadvantages of the three approaches are summarised in Box 8.1. Example 8.1 sets out a calculation in a spreadsheet format using these three approaches.

CASH FLOW APPRAISAL

PERIOD BY PERIOD	NET TERMINAL VALUE	DISCOUNTED CASH FLOW
Interest accrues quarterly according to how the bank charges or monthly for payments to the building contractor. Interest on the previous quarter is added to the next.	Like the residual valuation, it adds interest on the outstanding amount to the end of the construction period.	It converts the period payments to present-day value.
Advantages The debt is shown for each period; it copes with interest rate changes.	Quicker, logical extension to the traditional residual.	Quickest approach; the internal rate of return is calculated.
Disadvantages Laborious	Not flexible	Not related to how cost is evolved. Does not show the total debt.

Box 8.1 *Cash flow appraisal: alternative approaches*

Example 8.1: Cash flow methods

Value a site for development. Outgoings, buildings costs and fees breakdown as follows, excluding finance:

Year 1	£		Year 2	£	
Ist quarter	90 000		5	120 000	
2	50 000		6	160 000	
3	120 000		7	170 000	
4	140 000		8	150 000	

The builder is usually paid monthly, so a monthly cash flow is needed for this; the developer uses a quarterly cash flow as interest is usually charged on a quarterly basis. Income from the scheme is £200 000 and it could be sold at a 8% yield for £2 500 000 on completion of the works. Finance is 4% per quarter (17% p.a.). The return for risk and profit is 20% capital value.

TRADITIONAL RESIDUAL						
				£	£	£
Income				200 000		
YP perp @	8	%		12.5		
Gross Development Value					2 500 000	
less costs:			£			
Building cost + fees			1 000 000			
Finance @	17	% for 1/2				
costs for	2	years	170 000			
Total costs				1 170 000		
Return for risk and profit						
20	% capital value			500 000		
Costs plus profit					1 670 000	
Site value on completion					830 000	
PV £1	2	years @	17	%	0.730514	
Site value today					606 326	
(including purchase costs)						

PERIOD BY PERIOD CASH FLOW						
Period	Total	Income	Net flow	Capital	Interest	Capital
3 months	costs £	£	£	outstanding	@	outstanding
				from	4.00%	
				previous		
				period	(on d)	
	a	b	$c = b + a$	d	e	$f = c + d + e$
1	−90 000	0	−90 000	0	0	−90 000
2	−50 000	0	−50 000	−90 000	−3 600	−143 600
3	−120 000	0	−120 000	−143 600	−5 744	−269 344
4	−140 000	0	−140 000	−269 344	−10 774	−420 118
5	−120 000	0	−120 000	−420 118	−16 805	−556 922

6	−160 000	0	−160 000	−556 922	−22 277	−739 199
7	−170 000	0	−170 000	−739 199	−29 568	−938 767
8	−150 000	0	−150 000	−938 767	−37 551	−1 126 318
					£	
Capital value					2 500 000	
less: Outstanding debt				1 126 318		
and return for risk and profit						
20	% capital value			500 000		
Costs plus profit					1 626 318	
Site value on completion					873 682	
PV £1	2	years @		17	%	0.730514
Site value today					638 237	
(including purchase costs)						
NET TERMINAL VALUE						

Period	Net flow		Interest until		Net outlay	
	as above		completion @		on completion	
	£		4.00%		£	
			% (see below)			
1	−90 000		1.315932		−118 434	
2	−50 000		1.265319		−63 266	
3	−120 000		1.216653		−145 998	
4	−140 000		1.169859		−163 780	
5	−120 000		1.124864		−134 984	
6	−160 000		1.0816		−173 056	
7	−170 000		1.04		−176 800	
8	−150 000		1		−150 000	
					−1 126 318	

This gives the same answer as above. Interest on completion is the Amount of £1 for the remainder of the project; in period 1 it is the Amount of £1 in 7 quarters @ 4%.

DISCOUNTED CASH FLOW						
Period	Net flow		PV £1 @		PV of	
	as above		4.00%		cash flow	
	£		%		£	
1	−90 000		0.961538		−86 538	
2	−50 000		0.924556		−46 228	
3	−120 000		0.888996		−106 680	
4	−140 000		0.854804		−119 673	
5	−120 000		0.821927		−98 631	
6	−160 000		0.790315		−126 450	
7	−170 000		0.759918		−129 186	
8	−150 000		0.73069		−109 604	
Total cost					−822 990	
− Profit	−500 000		0.73069		−365 345	
+ Value	2 500 000		0.73069		1 826 726	
			Site value today		638 391	

Present value of £1 is based on the PV £1 @ 4% for the period shown in the first column: i.e. for period 1 is $1/((1+0.04)^1)$; in this case value and profit are discounted back to the present time, this means that the site value calculated is already at the present.

The main differences between the approaches can thus be summarised:

Period-by-period

1. The interest is assessed quarterly on the outstanding amount from the previous quarter.
2. This is a more accurate statement of cost plus interest. The total cost is deducted from the gross development value to get to the site value.
3. The site value needs to be discounted back to the present in this calculation.

Net terminal value

1. The interest per quarter is assessed to the end of the project.
2. and 3. As above in the period-by-period cash flow approach.

Discounted Cash Flow

1. The cost and interest is present valued for the period involved.
2. The value and profit is present valued and the site value worked out.
3. The site value is already at present value.

The used of predicted values and costs in development appraisal

Current estimates can easily be overtaken by time. The research by Marshall (1991) suggested that in the late 1980s the bullish market used growth figures to increase rental values in the calculation of the gross development value. The use of predicted values in the calculation by the application of inflation to the cost figures and forecasted growth rates for the rental levels are subject to the risk of errors in estimation. This risk may be less than the equivalent risk of using current figures in an environment of change where approaches to the prediction of that change can be made. Estimates of the future and consideration of risk and the probability of outcomes are discussed later in the chapter. Property developments, as with other major investment projects, have a long time scale. The environment is changing with ever-increasing rapidity, and the danger will be that the estimates will be inaccurate. But consider the danger of taking no action. Many business and personal decisions involve the need to take decisions. The decisions may turn out to be more or less a success or a disaster, but not to make a decision in a rapidly changing environment is surely to court the certainty of disaster. The explicit approach of looking to the future and making adjustments accordingly may be flawed but is likely to be the only option. The problems of forecasting changes can be alleviated by the application of better techniques, the use of data arising from extensive research and the use of computing hardware/software to handle the demands of the techniques and the weight of data. Strictly speaking, if a market rate of interest is used to discount and compound the elements within the residual valuation, then these elements should be at market rates. A market discount rate will include an inflation element and therefore should be applied to a current cost, not an historic one envisaged at the original time of appraisal. The current cost will have the inflation allowance built in.

Morley (1988a) looks at the prospects for forecasting costs using an historic analysis of changes in building cost inflation using data provided by the Building Cost Information Service (BCIS), and also the prospects for rental forecasting using an example from the retail sector (the Hillier Parker forecast of shop rents). An approach to building predicted costs and values into the cash flow would involve the cash flow being broken down into its elements of cost and appropriate inflation rates applied. These total costs can then be increased by the interest charges to completion. Finally, the building and finances costs can be incorporated into a residual valuation with a rental figure in which a growth rate has been applied. This approach is shown in a simplified example in Example 8.2. There will need to be a refinement in the cash flow to allow for the delay in payment of the contractor (say 4 weeks) and a retention allowance of 3–5% deducted from each monthly payment with half repaid on completion and the other half six months after completion.

Example 8.2: Cash flow with inflated costs and expected rents

Assume a project with the following criteria:

Gross development value:

Full rental value	£ 100 000
YP @ 5%	20YP
Capital value	£2 000 000

Period of development: 1 year, cash flow divided into 4 quarters.

Costs:		Building cost	Fees
		£	£
Period	1	200 000	
	2	200 000	
	3	200 000	50 000
	4	200 000	50 000

Growth rate for rent:	1% per quarter
Inflation rate for building costs:	3% per quarter
Inflation rate for fees:	2% per quarter
Interest rate:	4% per quarter

Step 1: Apply inflation to costs (£)							
Period	Current estimate: building costs	Inflation @ 0.03 per quarter	Inflated cost: building costs	Current estimate: fees	Inflation @ 0.02 per quarter	Inflated cost: fees	Total cost
1	200 000	1	200 000				200 000
2	200 000	1.03	206 000				206 000
3	200 000	1.0609	212 180	50 000	1.0404	52 020	264 200
4	200 000	1.092727	218 545.4	50 000	1.061208	53 060.4	271 605.8

Assumes costs incurred at the beginning of the period, thus inflation applied to remaining periods: e.g. for period 1 inflation $= (1 + i)^n$ where i is the growth rate per quarter, n is existing period less 1.

Step 2: Include interest								
Period	Total	Interest	Cost to					
	cost	@ 0.04	completion					
		per						
		quarter						
1	200 000	1.124864	224 973					
2	206 000	1.0816	222 810					
3	264 200	1.04	274 768					
4	271 605.8	1	271 606					
		Total	994 156					

Step 3: Valuation with growth rate applied to rent:								
				£				
Present estimated rental				100 000				
Rental growth 4 quarters @			0.01	1.040604				
Future estimated income				104 060				
YP in perpetuity @	5		%	20				
Capital value				2 081 208				
Less cost and finance			994 156					
Risk and profit @		0.2						
	capital value		416 242					
Total				1 410 398				
Site value				670 810				
PV of £1 in 4 quarters @			0.04	0.854804				
Site value today (including acquisition costs)				573 411				

This calculation is taken from a spreadsheet. Note the layout and note that there may be rounding differences as the spreadsheet is working to more precise figures not visible on the display.

8.2   COMPUTER SPREADSHEETS

Computer software is critical for property investment appraisal. In addition to databases to provide the evidence and analysis for valuation and property transactions, the spreadsheet is also an important tool to be used by valuation surveyors in calculations. The spreadsheet was introduced generally into business at the beginning of the 1980s. The spreadsheet consists of a computer program which displays on the computer screen a number of cells. Each cell is given location coordinates, rather like a map reference, and these coordinates provide an address in which to put input data and a means by which the relationship between each of the cells can be described. By knowing the addresses of the various cells, by installing data within the cells and by instructing the computer in a relationship between the cells, it is possible to build up a complex calculation across a number of cells and obtain an answer to the calculation. The power of the spreadsheet is its ability to recalculate instantly when one or a number of the inputs into the cells are changed. The investment calculation can thus be changed to allow access of a number of 'what if' scenarios. It may also be used with the input of very simple data to ensure that the calculation process that has been put into the spreadsheet is correct before elaborate calculation. The use of the spreadsheet comes into its own when dealing with complex valuation methods, particularly when dealing with discounted cash flow calculations and attempting to apply growth rates or risk probabilities to variables, as discussed earlier. The development of the spreadsheet came mainly in the area of accounting, where it can be seen that the tool was very powerful in managing the complex financial transactions as contained in the accounts of companies and being able to give solutions for the final accounts.

Spreadsheets used to facilitate investment appraisal

A spreadsheet is the equivalent of a piece of paper divided into a grid of rows and columns. In a computer, it can be considered as an electronic grid. The rows and columns are either number or lettered and each box formed by the grid is known as a cell and will have a unique reference. The size of the grid will depend on the spreadsheet program, and that can be considerable, enabling quite extensive and complex calculations to be undertaken. Where calculations such as a valuation or viability statement will follow a structured format, templates can be set up in the program; all that needs to be done is for the relevant data to be inserted in the appropriate cells and the required result is immediately obtained. Although data can be over-written in any cell, it is possible to lock cells containing essential formulae in the program thereby preventing any accidental alteration to the structure of the program. There are differences in the figures produced from the spreadsheet and those in other worked examples because the spreadsheet is capable of greater accuracy in the calculation.

The spreadsheet has the ability to calculate 'what if' calculations. This is because, as is appreciated in investment valuations, relatively minor changes in any one of the input variables can produce considerably greater change in the resulting final answer. Appraisers therefore need to pose questions such as: what if the interest rate changes? what if the rents increase? Formerly, it would have been necessary to undertake a series of repetitive manual calculations, changing the data each time to produce answers to these questions. It can readily be seen that the spreadsheets allow such data changes to be made, instantly producing answers to 'what if' problems (Isaac and Steley 1991). An example of a spreadsheet which was used to develop a cash flow analysis is shown in Example 8.3. Here a sensitivity analysis was used, for instance in repetitive calculations where the outcomes were tested with a range of yields between 7 and 10%. It is not intended to describe the elements of this spreadsheet in detail but to give examples of its use. For instance, in the spreadsheet it can be seen that variables can be altered over the life of the cash flow; for eample the growth rate of the rents has been changed over the periods. Also the spreadsheet can incorporate quite complex calculations in a single cell; the figure for the capital value of the term and reversion involves the term and reversion calculation in a single cell.

Example 8.3: Example of the use of spreadsheet analysis

BUSINESS PARK EQUITY SCHEMES: INVESTMENT SCENARIO 1							
Initial yield		9.00%		Reversion yield			7.50%
Loan:value ratio		70.00%		Rental per m^2			£75.00
Property:		PHASE 1					
Gross area:		4000	m^2				
Rent p.m^2.:		£75.00					
Rental value:		£300 000					
Yield:		9.00%		Reversion yield			7.50%
Capital value: £		3 333 333		Loan:value ratio:			70%
Sale year		3					
Rent review year:		5					
Total costs: £		3 082 893					
YEAR			92/93	93/94	94/95	95/96
CAPITAL GROWTH							
Growth rate of rent				−3.00%		6.00%
Amount of £1				0.97	0.97	1.0282
Rent with growth				291 000	291 000	308 460
Yield:						7.50%
Capital value of term and reversion:						4 105 128

Example continued overleaf

INTEREST						
Investment loan interest rate				14.50%	14.50%	14.50%
Investment loan b.f.			(2 333 333)	(2 333 333)	(2 371 667)	(2 415 558)
Loan interest			0	(338 333)	(343 892)	(350 256)
Rental income			0	300 000	300 000	300 000
Investment loan balance			(2 333 333)	(2 371 667)	(2 415 558)	(2 465 814)
Interest on cost shortfall				16.00%	15.00%	14.00%

CASH FLOW Year end March			92/93	93/94	94/95	95/96
Total b.f.			0	(749 560)	(876 879)	(1 015 996)
Interest on Shortfall			0	(127 319)	(139 117)	(149 883)
Construction costs			(3 082 893)	0	0	0
Sale of investment						4 105 128
Loan Capital (Repayment)			2 333 333			(2 465 814)
Total c.f.			(749 560)	(876 879)	(1 015 996)	473 435
Cash flow for NPV			0	0	0	473 435

Net Present Value @ 17% = £295 599

This compares with a net value at the present time of:

£3 333 333 less total costs £3 082 893 = £250 440

Notes:

1. The present capital value is based on the rental of £7.50 per m^2 capitalised at 9% yield.
2. The sale price at the end of year 3 is based on the capital value of the term and reversion assuming a 5 year rent review. The reversionary yield is 7.5% and the income has been inflated at the anticipated growth rates to year 3.
3. Debt interest is compounded quarterly. It is assumed that 70% of value is charged at the lower rate and the balance of interest less rental income is rolled up to year 3.
4. The remainder of the debt is charged at the higher rate and also rolled up to year 3.
5. The net present value of the net income in year 3 is discounted back at 17%, an opportunity cost rate.

8.3   SENSITIVITY ANALYSIS AND RISK

Risk is related to return but it is important to distinguish between risk and uncertainty. Whereas risk can be assessed in terms of its probability and therefore insured against or allowed for, this is not possible with uncertainty. Risk also needs to be distinguished in its application to an individual asset or to a portfolio of assets. Risk relating to a portfolio is more concerned with investment strategy and portfolio analysis, and this is discussed later. Allowance for risk can be applied in a number of ways. Firstly it can be applied to the discount rate used in the calculation, or secondly it can be applied to the cash flow which arises from the investment. In the first case, for instance, if a risk-free rate is 5% and the risk premium is 2% then this premium could be added to the risk-free rate to give a discount rate of 7% which is therefore appropriate for the risk taken. If the risk is applied to the cash flow, then this flow has to be varied within a range of acceptable values, and thus the output of the calculation can be assessed accordingly. The result can be found by using a statistical analysis assigning probability to the incidence of the cash flows, and therefore the result can be even more accurately defined.

Sensitivity analysis

The aim of sensitivity testing is to examine the effects of changes in variables on the final value, and the basic method involves changing one variable at a time, recalculating the value and analysing the result. The percentage change in the variable is compared with the percentage change in the final value. If a small percentage change in the variables produces a large percentage change in the final value then this variable is very sensitive. Sensitivity analysis has been developed as a means of identifying the independent variable which causes the greatest change in the dependent variable (Baum and Crosby 1988).

Examples of approaches to sensitivity analysis are now considered. These approaches require repetitive calculations and therefore will need computer assistance, for instance a spreadsheet. The medium of a book such as this to indicate approaches makes it difficult to show these approaches properly; the presentation of a number of different calculations would make reading the text particularly difficult. So it is pointless setting out the figures to a particular example in the cases provided. The reader will learn about the approach by carrying out the calculations alone and will learn about the construction of the appraisal by constructing the appraisal method on a spreadsheet.

Simple sensitivity testing

Here the individual variables are changed one at a time and the effect of these changes on the result is seen. Percentage changes in the result or output can be seen relative to the changes in the input variables. A simple sensitivity test would be to draw up a matrix of capital values for different variables as shown in Example 8.4.

Example 8.4: Simple sensitivity testing I

Variable 1: Investment capitalisation rate		5%	6%	7%
Variable 2: Estimated rental value	£100/m^2	capital value 1	capital value 2	capital value 3
	£110/m^2	capital value 4	capital value 5	capital value 6
	£120/m^2			etc. . .

Or alternatively, the approach which shows which variables to focus on is set out in Example 8.5.

Example 8.5: Simple sensitivity testing II

Change in variable, say +10%	Change in capital value	Change in income
Rental growth	+x%	+y% etc . . .
Investment yield		
Refurbishment costs		
Finance cost		

A spider diagram will show changes in the variables plotted against the capital value or level of investment yield, for instance, see Figure 8.2 for an example.

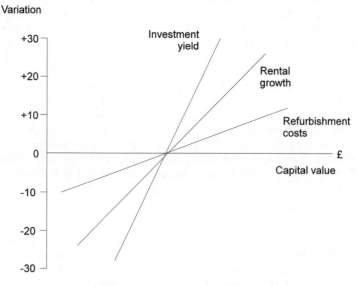

Figure 8.2   *Spider diagram*

Scenario testing

This involves changing a combination of a number of inputs, and the output then is calculated with this combination of changes. This can be done in a number of ways; for instance, a combination of factors which are the expected variables can be used, such as the expected rental and yield of a future deal. In addition to this expected or realistic outcome, an optimistic scenario and a pessimistic scenario taking more optimistic or less optimistic outcomes can also be assessed, as in Example 8.6.

Example 8.6: Scenario testing

VARIABLE	Optimistic	Expected	Pessimistic
Rental growth	e.g. 7%	5%	3% etc . . .
Investment yield			
Refurbishment costs			
Finance costs			
EFFECT ON			
Income			
Capital Value			

Probability

Where a model for appraisal contains several or many uncertain inputs, predicted output is problematic and sensitivity analysis is of limited use. The output will be a range rather than a single value, and the problem is how to define the range and distribution; this is done by probabilistic modelling (Mollart 1994). In a more sophisticated form of sensitivity analysis, probability can be taken into account. This assesses the probability of the inputs being at a certain level and therefore can provide an even more sophisticated result. The probabilities are assigned to the input variables according to how likely these variables will be at certain levels. For instance, if there is a 50% chance of the rent being say £120 per m^2, then the probability is assigned at 0.5 and included in the calculation accordingly. By running a computer program with the assigned probabilities which picks up the inputs on the basis of the probability, for instance a 50% chance of picking a rent of £120, and then by running the program a number of times, an average output can be assessed. This approach is called a Monte Carlo Simulation (for more information on sensitivity analysis, see Morley 1988a and Byrne and Cadman 1984). A basic approach to probability would look like Example 8.7.

Example 8.7: Probability analysis of rental growth

Probability of rental growth:

Rental growth	(a)	7%	5%	3%
Probability	(b%)	10%	60%	30%
Chance	(b)	0.1	0.6	0.3
Expected outcome	(a × b)	0.7	3.0	0.9

The weighted probability of rental growth = 0.7% + 3.0% + 0.9% = 4.6%. This figure can then be used in the scenario test in the previous section instead of the single estimate figures (Isaac and Steley 1991). Analysing risk requires that the distribution of returns be defined in some way, and this requires that the range and distribution of the inputs must be defined and incorporated. The analysis used is probabilistic modelling;

where the value of a variable cannot be predicted with certainty it is usually possible to set a range within which it will almost certainly fall; furthermore it will be possible to say that some values for the variable are more likely than others. This identifying of the range and associated probabilities for the values of variables typifies probability analysis (Mollart 1994).

Probabilistic modelling generally falls into two categories: algebraic and simulation. The algebraic approach normally used is the Hillier method, but this has severe limitations, and simulations are more useful in this analysis. Monte Carlo Simulation (MCS) is the simulation model most referred to and these routines can be run on a spreadsheet. Previously these were crude, but with the advent of a spreadsheet add-in, @RISK, this enables the simulation to be more easily carried out (Mollart 1994). The key feature of the Monte Carlo Simulation is that input variables which cannot be stated with certainty are treated as distributions of some sort. When the simulation is run, a value for each variable is selected at random from the range of possible values, which are then fed into the appraisal model being used to give a possible value from the output. Through a process of iteration this is repeated many times thus simulating the range of possible outcomes. So long as sufficient iterations have been undertaken, a distribution of the possible outcomes can be produced to provide a measure of risk for the project.

Simulation

To summarise the use of simulation, the computer valuation is run like a Monte Carlo Simulation which picks up the variables at random but within a range according to the probability ascribed to the variable; the simulation may then be run 1000 times. This then gives a range of results, say for the residual value or profit. The mean is then calculated for the value or profit and the standard deviation is calculated. Assuming that the range of results is a normal distribution in statistical terms, there is a 95% likelihood that the result will fall in the range of the mean ±2 standard deviations. The standard deviation is an indication of the variability of the results and therefore represents risk. The developer may choose to avoid the risk by choice of variables, if risk-averse, to limit the downside possibilities – that is, the result falling below an acceptable range of values. Aspects of risk are discussed in the next section. The use of computers to handle the analysis can save a lot of time. @RISK is a spreadsheet add-in which is available for the major spreadsheets. @RISK adds-in a number of facilities to enable the simulation to be carried out easily:

- it enables input variables to be specified as distributions instead of single point estimates;
- using a simple execute command, it performs as many iterations as specified, i.e. 1000;
- it carries out a detailed statistical analysis of the resulting distribution;
- it generates a graphical output in a range of formats (Mollart 1994).

Risk

The decision-maker's attitude to risk can be seen in terms of the utility function of the individual/corporate entity (see Figure 8.3).

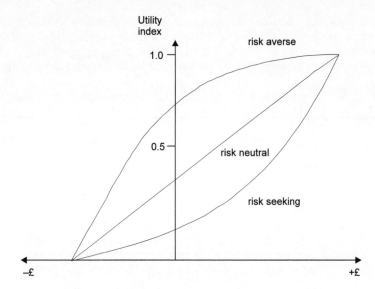

Figure 8.3 *Utility functions illustrating attitudes to risk*

Source: Lumby (1991).

The risk-averse investor will require more reward for more risk than the risk-neutral investor, and much more than the risk-seeking investor. These curves all represent risk avoidance in the sense that all require more reward for more risk, but the classification is determined by the extent of the additional return required. Generally most investors are considered to be risk-averse, that is preferring less risk to more risk and there is evidence to suggest that all investors are risk-averse when making important investment decisions (Brown 1991). The risk profiles of investors will change over time and will change relative to the project being considered. The risk-indifference curves shown in Figure 8.3 can be adapted to show the return expected in the market and the actual trade-off of risk and reward as shown in Figure 8.4.

Baum and Crosby (1995) have adopted DCF approaches to analyse property investments; however, many international investment markets are still reliant on basic initial yield analysis. Baum and Crosby recognise three levels of analysis: first, the individual investment or project return using NPV or IRR techniques (NPV is better: see Baum and Crosby 1995 or Hargitay and Yu 1993); the second level is calculation of the individual risk; and the third is portfolio risk. The analysis of return without consideration of risk is pointless; the return will vary with risk and expected return will be higher in a risky situation. Individual risk will need to be considered, and also the influence of choosing a particular investment or project relative to the rest of the portfolio of investments/ projects held (portfolio risk). To summarise, the levels of analysis suggested by Baum and Crosby are thus:

(i) calculation of NPV or IRR;
(ii) calculation of individual risk;
(iii) portfolio risk.

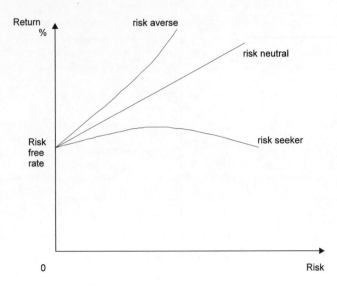

Figure 8.4   *Risk/return trade-off*

Definition of risk

Investment and development are considered risky because the investor/developer is unsure about the actual return which will be realised from the investment, so that risk is related to the uncertainty of future returns from an investment. There is a spectrum of uncertainty (see Figure 8.5).

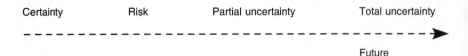

Figure 8.5   *Definition of risk*

Source: Hargitay and Yu (1993).

Certainty is where there is precise knowledge of the outcome, risk is a situation where alternate outcomes are identified together with a definite statement of the probabilities of such outcomes. Partial uncertainty is where alternative outcomes can be identified but without the knowledge of the probabilities of such outcomes. Total uncertainty is where even the alternative outcomes cannot be identified. Thus if risk is regarded as the extent to which the actual outcome of an action or decision may diverge from the expected outcome, an action or decision is risk-free when the consequences are known with certainty. To a rational investor/developer who is averse to risk, the possibility of a lower than expected return has more importance than the possibility of a higher than expected return; the former case is therefore termed the downside risk.

Definitions of risk may be descriptive or analytical. Descriptive definitions are related to sources and elements of risk and are used for classification of projects on the basis of the risk associated with them; they may also be used to determine the risk premium for use in a discount rate. Analytical definitions provide definitions of risk in terms of probability or variability: that is, the probability of loss; the probability that the investor will not receive the expected or required rate of return; the deviation of realised return from the expected return; and the variance or volatility of returns (Hargitay and Yu 1993). Portfolio Theory also tells us that total risk will have two components, systematic and unsystematic risk, as shown in Box 8.2.

COMPONENTS OF RISK	
Systematic risk	Unsystematic risk (or specific risk)
• Caused by factors which affect *all* projects/investments. • e.g. Changes in general economic/ political/social environment. • Investor has no control.	• Affects only a particular investment • e.g. Way a project has been financed, so more debt, more risk. • Investor has limited control by taking the appropriate investment decisions.

Box 8.2   *Components of risk from portfolio theory*

Systematic risk may have a number of elements: these relate to, say, variations in the market, business cycles, inflation and financial interest rates. Unsystematic risk will cover elements such as business risk (associated with the product, markets, strategy), financial risk (associated with financial structure: see Chapter 13 on finance), liquidity risks, and other specific risks related to the industrial sector in which the project takes place, the nature of the property and its location. Investment risks are concerned with future events which by their nature are uncertain. A rational approach to risk associated with the development process must include a strategy for dealing with risk, such as:

(i)   recognition and definition of risk and its various components;
(ii) quantification and measurement of risk;
(iii) the analysis of risk
(iv) a response to risk.

In a risk/return trade-off, the risks associated with an investment project must be adequately compensated for by the expected returns generated. A suitable combination of discounting and probability criteria is the best solution (Hargitay and Yu 1993). In investment decision-making, risk is defined as the extent to which the actual outcome of a decision may diverge from the expected outcome. Statistical measures such as measures of standard deviation and variance can be used as the absolute measure of variability of the actual outcome and the expected outcome. The methods of risk analysis indicated can thus be classified in detail as shown in Box 8.3.

RISK ANALYSIS	
Methods which attempt a description of the riskiness of a project	Methods which attempt the incorporation of perceived risk in appraisal models
• expected value/variance methods (mean variance method) • sensitivity analysis • scenario testing • simulations • beta analysis	• risk adjusted discount rate method (RADR) • certainty equivalent method • sliced income approach

Box 8.3   *Risk analysis*

Detailed analysis of these approaches is beyond the scope of this book, and you are referred to the following texts for an introduction to this rapidly developing area: Byrne and Cadman(1984); Baum and Crosby (1995) Dubben and Sayce (1991); and Hargitay and Yu (1993). The descriptive methods of risk analysis have been outlined elsewhere in this text in relation to sensitivity testing, scenarios and simulations. The mean variance rule is used in projects and suggests that project A is preferred to project B where at least one of the following situations arises:

(i)   the expected return of A is greater than B and A's variance is less than or equal to B (expected return $A > B$, variance $A \leq B$);

(ii)   the expected return of A is equal to or greater than B and A's variance is less than B's (expected return of $A \geq B$, variance $A < B$).

The variance is a statistical measure of dispersion around the mean expected value and is a measure of risk, as discussed earlier. For a background to these statistical measures see Hargitay and Yu (1993) or Brown (1991). Finally, amongst these descriptive measures is beta analysis. This concerns Modern Portfolio Theory and the earlier discussion of systematic and unsystematic risk. For further reading on this you are again referred to Hargitay and Yu (1993) and Brown (1991). The methods which attempt to incorporate risk into appraisal models are discussed in detail in Baum and Crosby (1995) and I will outline a brief summary of these methods here:

Risk adjusted discount rate (RADR)

The market interest rate or discount rate,

$$I = (1 + i)(1 + d)(1 + r) - 1$$

where i is the time preference allowance
d is the inflation premium
r is the risk premium

The risk-free rate (RFR) is a function of i and d only so that:

$$I = (1 + RFR)(1 + r) - 1$$

In practice the equation used is

$$I = RFR + r \quad \text{(Risk-free rate + risk premium)}.$$

The effective difference is small (Isaac and Steley 1991). The use of the risk-adjusted rate implies more return is required to compensate for more risk, but the problem is the estimation of how much.

Certainty equivalent techniques

This approach uses the statistical techniques of the mean and standard deviation to indicate the position where a risk-averse investor would be able to avoid the downside risk. Taking a normal statistical distribution as shown in Figure 8.6, ±1 standard deviation of the distribution from the mean will incorporate 66% of the range of outcomes, and the downside risk in this situation is defined as the area below the curve, more than 1 standard deviation less than the mean. This area will incorporate only 17% (half the balance) of the distribution. Using this position, the distribution tells us that the investor has an 83% chance of bettering the position. Thus in this approach the mean and standard deviation is calculated and, at this risk-averse position, noted above, is used in the analysis (the mean expected value − 1 standard deviation). In practice this expected value will be calculated from the probability calculation shown earlier.

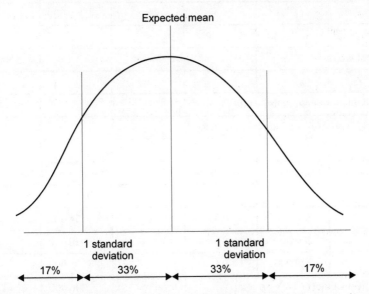

Figure 8.6 *Distribution under a normal curve (the downside risk is the 17% of outcomes on the left side of the diagram below the curve)*

The certainty equivalent approach is in five stages:

1. Calculate the expected value:

$$\text{Expected value } (\bar{r}) = \sum (p \times \hat{r})$$

where p = the probability of the sample
and $\hat{r}$ = each sample outcome

2. Calculate the variance

$$\text{Variance } (\sigma^2) = \sum (p)(\hat{r} - \bar{r})^2$$

3. Calculate the standard deviation

$$\text{Standard deviation (population)} = \sqrt{\text{variance}} = \sigma$$

4. Calculate certainty equivalents
5. Re-do the calculation with certainty equivalent variables.

The calculation which follows is done with the aid of a spreadsheet structure; note the layout and note that there may be rounding differences as the spreadsheet is working to more precise figures not visible in the figures displayed in the example.

Example 8.8: Application of certainty equivalent approach

INVESTMENT VALUATION					
Income				£200 000	
YP perp @	8	%		12.5	
Capital value					2 500 000
(1) Calculate the expected value					
The two variables are income and yield					
Income:	outcome	probability =		sample outcome	
	$\hat{r}$	p		$(p \times \hat{r})$	
	180 000	0.3		54 000	
	200 000	0.6		120 000	
	220 000	0.1		22 000	
Expected value $(\bar{r}) = \sum (p \times \hat{r})$			total	196 000	

Yield:	outcome	probability =		sample outcome	
	$\hat{r}$	p		$(p \times \hat{r})$	
	0.07	0.1		0.007	
	0.08	0.5		0.04	
	0.09	0.4		0.036	
Expected value $(\bar{r}) = \sum(p \times \hat{r})$			total	0.083	
(2) Calculate the variance					
Income:					
outcome	expected			probability	
$(\hat{r})$	value $(\bar{r})$	$(\hat{r} - \bar{r})$	$(\hat{r} - \bar{r})^2$	p	$p(\hat{r} - \bar{r})^2$
180 000	196 000	−16 000	256 000 000	0.3	76 800 000
200 000	196 000	4 000	16 000 000	0.6	9 600 000
220 000	196 000	24 000	576 000 000	0.1	57 600 000
Variance $(\sigma^2) = \sum(p)(\hat{r} - \bar{r})^2$					144 000 000
Yield:					
outcome	expected			probability	
$(\hat{r})$	value $(\bar{r})$	$(\hat{r} - \bar{r})$	$(\hat{r} - \bar{r})^2$	p	$p(\hat{r} - \bar{r})^2$
0.07	0.083	−0.013	0.000169	0.1	0.0000169
0.08	0.083	−0.003	0.000009	0.5	0.0000045
0.09	0.083	0.007	0.000049	0.4	0.0000196
Variance $(\sigma^2) = \sum(p)(\hat{r} - \bar{r})^2$					0.000041
(3) Calculate the standard deviation					
Income: s.d. $= \sqrt{\text{variance}} = \sigma$				12 000	
Yield: s.d. $= \sqrt{\text{variance}} = \sigma$				0.006403	

(4) Calculate certainty equivalents					
	= expected value − standard deviation				
Income:	196000	−12000	=	184 000	
Yield:	0.083	+ 0.006403	=	0.089403	
(for the yield the risk is of a higher yield/lower YP/less value so it is the upper end of the range we do not want = expected value + standard deviation)					
(5) Reinsert values in calculation					
INVESTMENT VALUATION (CERTAINTY EQUIVALENT)					
Income				£184 000	
YP perp @	8.940312	%		11.2	
Capital value					2 058 094

Sliced income approach

This approach develops risk adjustment and certainty equivalent techniques to provide an overall method which may be suitable for property appraisal. Like the hardcore method or layer approach (see Isaac and Steley 1991, and Chapter 6), it distinguishes layers of income which are less risky (core income) and more risky (top slice income). The guaranteed income could thus be valued at a risk-free rate whilst the overage or top slice income (calculated with the hardcore/layer method) is then discounted at a highly risk-adjusted rate. The top slice income is calculated by comparing the expected value of the total income stream with the level of the risk-free core income. Baum and Crosby (1995) suggest that this method can be used in situations where a core rental is guaranteed, or with turnover rents where there is a core element with an addition which is profit or turnover related. In development valuations the concept could be applied in partnership arrangements; the various slices as shown in the approaches would have differing risk levels (Isaac 1996). A summary of the possible advantages and disadvantages of the various steps of risk analysis drawn from Baum and Crosby's work (1995) are set out in Box 8.4 opposite.

A summary of approaches to risk analysis is set out in Box 8.5 overleaf.

REFERENCES

Baum, A. (1987) 'An Approach to Risk Analysis', Henry Stewart Conference, *Property Investment Appraisal and Analysis*, Cafe Royal, London, 1 December.

Baum, A. and Crosby, N. (1988) *Property Investment Appraisal*, Routledge, London.

Baum, A. and Crosby, N. (1995) *Property Investment Appraisal*, Routledge, London.

Brown, G. (1986) 'A Certainty Equivalent Expectations Model for Estimating the Systematic Risk of Property Investments', *Journal of Valuation*, vol. 6, no. 1, pp. 17–41.

Brown, G. R. (1991) *Property Investment and the Capital Markets*, E. & F.N. Spon, London.

Butler, D. and Richmond, D. (1990) *Advanced Valuation*, Macmillan, London.

LEVELS OF RISK ANALYSIS			
Level of analysis	Examples	Advantages	Disadvantages
1. Sensitivity analysis	includes: scenario testing, analysis of expected returns, probability, simulation	investor retains decision responsibility	no simple decision rule, range of results
2. Risk-adjusted discount rate	RADR, certainty equivalent techniques, sliced income approach	provides an objective decision rule	decision made by subjective risk adjustment, investment advisors may replace the risk/ return indifference of investor with own attitudes
3. Mean-variance analysis	coefficient of IRR/ NPV variation	has separate measures of risk and return, investor can be more subjective about risk/return trade-off	deals with individual project risk rather than portfolios
4. Portfolio analysis	beta analysis	deals with the effect on a port-folio of invest-ments of carrying out the project	difficult to estimate betas (which are the measures of systematic risk)

Box 8.4   *Levels of risk analysis*

AN APPROACH TO RISK ANALYSIS: A SUMMARY

Baum suggests that there are four levels of risk analysis that can be used:

(i)   Sensitivity analysis.
(ii) Risk adjustment techniques.
(iii) Mean variance criterion.
(iv) Portfolio risk analysis.

Sensitivity analysis involves the changing of the variables from the best estimates. For instance, the effect of a 10% change in a variable can be contrasted with the effect of a 10% change in another variable. Thus the results are checked against the product of individual changes to determine how the changes in the inputs will affect changes in the final result. This form of sensitivity analysis will indicate those variables which are most sensitive to change in the sense that they will affect the final result more.

   Risk adjustment techniques can include the adjustment of the discount rates to account for risk. For instance, an increase of 2% could be used in the investment decision to indicate risk. In **certainty equivalent techniques**, the approach uses assigned probabilities to alternative capital values and costs. Standard deviations are calculated. Using statistical techniques in a normal distribution of results, it is expected that 67% of the results will fall within one standard deviation from the mean of the results. Thus the equation is calculated using the variables at the position one standard deviation below the mean. This conservative approach is intended to convert the variable risky estimates into relatively certain ones. A third type of risk adjustment technique is the **sliced income approach** which can adopt different interest rates for the layers of income. A guaranteed income could be discounted at a risk-free rate, whereas the average or additional bonus would be discounted at a higher rate than the overall risk-adjusted discount rate.

   The **mean variance criterion** can be used to choose between two investment arrangements by adopting the rule that project A is chosen if the NPV of A is greater than the NPV of B and the risk of A is less than the risk of B. The risk is a separate measure using the standard deviation of the data. The approach to this analysis is to list the possible net present values of the cash flow using a matrix of the key variables; for instance, in an investment valuation this could be growth in income against the yield on the resale valuation. If there are three possible outcomes for each of the two variables, then the matrix will be 3×3 having 9 different cases. The assigned probability is 1 in 3×1 in 3 or $0.333 \times 0.333 = 0.1111$. Using this probability as the expected value of the NPV can be calculated and the standard deviation can also be calculated from the data. The decision rule for choosing between two similar projects is thus dependent on the mean variance criterion where the expected NPV is the measure of return and the standard deviation is a measure of risk. Where there are a number of possible present values, then a Monte Carlo simulation can be used.

   In **portfolio analysis** investments are chosen which are advantageous in their effect on risk and return on the total investors' portfolio.

Box 8.5   *An approach to risk analysis: a summary*

Source: Baum (1987).

Byrne, P. and Cadman, D. (1984) *Risk, Uncertainty and Decision Making in Property Development*, E. & F.N. Spon, London.

Chapman, C. B. (1991) 'Risk', in P. Venmore-Rowland, P. Brandon and T. Mole (eds), *Investment, Procurement and Performance in Construction*, RICS, London.

Darlow, C. (ed) (1988) 'Valuation and Development Appraisal', *Estates Gazette*, London.

Dixon, T. J., Hargitay, S. E. and Bevan, O. A. (1991) *Microcomputers in Property*, E. & F.N. Spon, London.

Dubben, N. and Sayce, S. (1991) *Property Portfolio Management: An Introduction*, Routledge, London.

Estates Gazette (1995), 'Mainly for Students: Spreadsheets and Valuations', *Estates Gazette, 21* January, pp. 116–19.

Flanagan, R. and Norman, G. (1993) *Risk Management and Construction*, Blackwell, Oxford.

French, N. (1994) Editorial: 'Market Values and DCF', *Journal of Property Valuation and Investment*, vol. 12, no. 1, pp. 4–6.

Hargitay, S. E. and Sui-Ming, Yu (1993) *Property Investment Decisions*, E. & F.N. Spon, London.

Isaac, D. (1996) *Property Development: Appraisal and Finance*, Macmillan, London.

Isaac, D. and Steley, T. (1991) *Property Valuation Techniques*, Macmillan, London.

Lumby, S. (1991) *Investment Appraisal and Financing Decisions*, Chapman & Hall, London.

Marshall, P. (1991) *Development Valuation Techniques, Research Technical paper*, RICS, London.

Mollart, R. (1988) 'Computer Briefing: Monte Carlo Simulation using Lotus 1-2-3', *Journal of Valuation*, vol. 6, no. 4, pp. 419–33.

Mollart, R. (1994) 'Software Review: Using @Risk for Risk Analysis', *Journal of Property Valuation and Investment*, vol. 12, no. 3, pp. 89–94.

Morley, S. (1988a) 'Financial Appraisal – Cashflow Approach', in C. Darlow (ed.), *Valuation and Development Appraisal*, Estates Gazette, London.

Morley, S. (1988b) 'Financial Appraisal – Sensitivity and Probability', in C. Darlow (ed.), *Valuation and Development Appraisal*, Estates Gazette, London.

Pearce, B. (1989) 'Forecasting: An Overview', paper in seminar: *Application of Forecasting Techniques to the Property Market*, RICS/SPR Seminars, Spring 1989.

Schiller, R. (1994) 'Comment: The Interface between Valuation and Forecasting', *Journal of Property Valuation and Investment*, vol. 12, no. 4, pp. 3–6.

9   Investment Risk

9.1   INDIVIDUAL RISK

Risk is a major determinant of return. Modern Portfolio Theory sees the investment decision as a trade-off between risk and expected return; see Figure 9.1. Much research in property risk has been devoted to the application of measures, already devised for equity investment, to the property market and these are related to portfolio risk analysis which is covered in the following chapters. Waldy (1991) suggests that the main argument for considering single asset risk to be equally as important in practice is that most investors in the UK are not able to diversify away the individual property element of risk adequately. Aspects of risk analysis have already been discussed in Chapter 8. Waldy suggests there is a hierarchy of these approaches, starting with the intuitive approach used in traditional valuation for the assessment of the all risks yield (ARY) which is assessed in accordance with the risk profile of the property; the ARY is thus an implicit valuation which is open to criticisms of subjectivity. Explicit approaches used in discounted cash flow appraisals include sensitivity analysis and scenario testing. Sensitivity analysis measures the effect upon capital value by a change in variable inputs to the calculation. Scenario testing postulates situations by assigning appropriate values to the variables to test for different scenarios. Risk-adjusted discount rates provide for a premium to reflect risk; certainty equivalent techniques through probability and the removal of downside risk calculates risk-free cash flows which can be capitalised using the risk-free rate of return. Probability analysis is inherent in these calculations. The problems associated with this area of risk analysis include the continuous distribution of variables, skewness of samples and serial correlation between cash flows.

Lack of certainty regarding the expected return results in the devaluation of the return. Sources of risk in a property investment decision may arise from: tenant risk; sector risk; structural risk; legislation risk; taxation risk; planning risk; and legal risk (Baum and Crosby 1995). Morley (1988) suggests the following aspects of risk in property investment: rental value and rental growth; yield on sale and timing of sale; age and obsolescence; lease structure; liquidity; management costs; taxation and inflation. He also cites the fact that risk analysis is a major factor in property development.

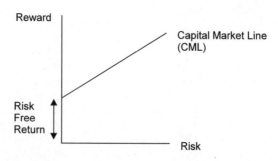

Figure 9.1   *The relationship between risk and reward*

Financial management theory suggests three broad categories of risk: business, financial and liquidity risk. Business risk is due to the uncertainty of future income flows, based on the nature of the firm's business. Financial risk is risk arising from the method of financing of an investment. Liquidity risk is the uncertainty introduced by the availability/ access to the secondary market for an investment. Another way of analysing risk is to look at the effect of risk on money income and real income. This depends on whether the investment is inflation proof or inflation prone. Thus this analysis is looking at the risk of inflation affecting cashflows. Money risk is the risk of variation in monetary income flows. Real risk is the risk of variation in real income flows. Examples of real and monetary risks are shown in Table 9.1.

Table 9.1   *Real and monetary risks*

Level of risk	Real	Monetary
Low	Index linked gilts	Fixed interest gilts
	Equities	Bank deposits
	Property	Index linked gilts
	Bank deposits	Property equities
High	Fixed interest gilts	

Source: Baum and Crosby (1995).

Risk can attach to a single property or a portfolio of property or investments. Markowitz (1952) developed a basic portfolio model which suggested that risk can be reduced within a portfolio by combining assets whose returns demonstrated less than perfect positive correlation (i.e. a spread of risk). Property as an investment is prone to both unsystematic and systematic risks. Unsystematic or specific risk relates to individual investment and by diversifying this is reduced in the portfolio. Systematic risk relates to the market and cannot be diversified away. The market risk is quantified as β (beta) and this measures the sensitivity of income movements of the portfolio relative to movements in the market. A β (beta) of 1.5 would mean that if rents in the sector fell 1% the rental level of the portfolio would fall 1.5%. Thus the effect of a balanced portfolio is to reduce but not remove property investment risk.

The rational investor seeks to maximise return, but often return is not the only criterion. Factors such as capital and income growth can be incorporated into the calculation by the use of DCF techniques, but others like liquidity and ease of management present more difficulty; these are dealt with by intuitive policy decisions. Risk analysis is a standard management technique and if property investment is to compete with other media, and these techniques are needed. Increased knowledge of statistical techniques and the use of computers enable the analysis to be completed with ease. Risk is defined in many ways, but for a property investment it is the level of probability that a required return, measured in terms of capital value and income, will be achieved. Over time, the variance of actual return from expected return (the volatility) can be measured and used to help determine probability levels. Risk is about the interaction of future returns, it can give rise to a number of possible results and different chances that any particular outcome will result. The degree to which actual performance may exceed the expected performance is called the upside potential, whilst the amount by which it falls below expectation is the downside risk. It is with the latter concept that investors are most concerned, particularly with an investment being funded by borrowed money. Upside potential is regarded as the 'added bonus' over and above the return targeted. The distinction between risk and uncertainty is that risk is concerned with variances and probabilities, with variations in return usually calculated in terms of standard deviations, a measure of the dispersion of returns around the mean. The term standard deviation is explained below; the greater the standard deviation, the more widely the returns are spread, the greater the risk and vice versa. Uncertainty is different in that no probability can be ascribed to the probable outcome; the assessment must remain qualitative not quantitative, although investors may feel fit to deal with such situations by the use of other criteria such as a payback technique.

Risk evaluation aids the decision-making process, and helps the investor answer the following questions:

(i)   What is the expected rate of return or the most likely outcome?
(ii)   What is the probability of making a loss as measured against a target return, cost of borrowing or alternative investment return? Alternatively what is the probability of exceeding the target?
(iii)   What is the variability or spread of returns in relation to the expected return? Low volatility (risk) is traded off against return.

9.2   TYPES OF RISK

The types of risk which may be encountered by an investor are summarised in the following paragraphs and relate to risk attached to the income flow, future outgoings, capital value and market value.

Income flow

Any investment other than a government stock carries the risk of default; with equities, the size or frequency of the dividend is not secure. With property, the risk of default on rack rented investments will depend on the strength of the covenant; in the case of reversionary property, risk is attached to the projected income flow, voids and size. With leasehold properties, there are problems of dilapidation claims. Many appraisals of property especially in the boom years of the 1980s had built in explicit expectation of rental growth, the amount depending on the age and type of property and projected demand. Growth can be built into the capitalisation rate; a lower rate means more risk because of risk that the growth rate will not be achieved. Risk of not achieving target returns is greater with low yielding property.

Future outgoings

Risk is very relevant to direct property investment. Even with a new unit let on full repairing and insuring (FRI) terms, there is a strong possibility that technology and fashion change can affect a property sufficiently so that premature obsolescence can set in. This will mean a large future expense not reflected in the original appraisal. Any property at risk from obsolescence will need to build in estimates of future refurbishment in the initial investment appraisal. Other expected outgoings are structural failures due to inherent defects, unforeseen legal costs and government legislation such as the Counter Inflation Act 1973 which led to a rent freeze.

Capital value

The capital value depends on the expected income flow; this reflects the level of likely outgoings, but even without this changing, the capital value can vary with the yield. Capital value predictions may prove inaccurate because of general imperfections in market knowledge, lack of comparable transactions and the secrecy surrounding deals. There may also be valuation errors (see Chapter 6); the difference in valuation can affect the return significantly with an error of $\pm 10\%$.The fact that values are not tested in the market with the frequency that gilt or equity transactions take place leads to uncertainty regarding capital value.

Market value

The valuation is normally carried out to open market value (OMV) defined by the Statement of Asset Valuation Practice and Guidance Notes provided by the RICS (1992), now superseded by the new 'Red Book'(RICS 1995). Frequently, however, the price that the investment actually realises is very different, due to the strength of the market at the moment of sale or due to the presence of a special purchaser. The pressure for some institutions to realise their assets means that the price may be less then the theoretical value. Other risks may be associated with legislation, obsolescence, inflation, legal risk, and timing risk.Timing is critical to obtain the optimum return. In an unsecured position, or an out-of-town shopping situation, the rental value could be hard to predict and the appropriate capitalisation rate yet more difficult. Another risk is the holding period; the longer the project life, the greater the uncertainty attached to the likely income flows.

Techniques used to manage risk in the individual asset

The approaches used to manage risk include payback, expected net present value (ENPV), normal distribution theory, simulation, sensitivity analysis and risk adjustment techniques, certainty equivalent and sliced income approaches. The main approaches are covered in this book but you are also referred to Hargitay and Yu (1993). The assessment of risk in practice is limited. Waldy (1991) examined risk perception by practitioners and found they envisaged risk in terms of individual sources such as voids or depreciation rather than in investment terms. The results indicated that investors appeared more concerned about single asset risk than portfolio risk. About 90% of the respondents to his survey did not measure risk, those that did used scenarios, sensitivity analysis and probability. Waldy concluded that it would seem prudent for investors to undertake far more analysis, and by making greater use of DCF techniques, such as sensitivity analysis, to seek to improve their intuitive 'feel'. For the near future, he concluded, they could follow Hargitay (1983) who considered scenarios to be a reasonable interim approach to incorporating risk into property appraisal, pending the resolution of the problems attached to complex probabilistic models.

9.3   PRINCIPLES OF RISK

If decisions are made in an environment where the future is uncertain then decision-making involves taking a risk. Risk is related to return but it is important to distinguish between risk and uncertainty. Whereas risk can be assessed in terms of its probability and therefore insured against or allowed for, this is not possible with uncertainty. Risk also needs to be distinguished in its application to an individual asset or to a portfolio of assets. Risk relating to a portfolio is more concerned with investment strategy and portfolio analysis, and this is discussed later. Allowance for risk can be applied in a number of ways. Firstly it can be applied to the discount rate used in the calculation, or secondly it can be applied to the cash flow which arises from the investment. In the first case, for instance, if a risk-free rate is 5% and the risk premium is 2% then this premium could be added to the risk-free rate to give a discount rate of 7%, which is therefore appropriate for the risk taken. If the risk is applied to the cash flow, then this flow has to be varied within a range of acceptable values and thus the output of the calculation can be assessed accordingly. The result can be found by using a statistical analysis assigning probability to the incidence of the cash flows and thus the result can even be more accurately defined. Investors are offered a high return from an investment as a reward or compensation for taking the risk involved. In an ideal situation the market could publish a list of interest rates related to the level of risk involved instead of an investor being faced with a single market rate. Such an approach would ignore the problems of how to identify the degree of risk associated with a particular investment. Even if the project's risk level could be measured, how could the corresponding market discount rates be identified?

Expected utility model

The nature of the investors' decision relates to the decision made by investors. Decision-making by investors is assumed to follow four basic axioms (Lumby 1991). These axioms, which are statements which appear logical and true, are termed as such because they do not require proof. The basic behaviour of investors when making decisions is:

(i)   Investors are able to choose between alternatives by ranking them in some order of merit, so they are able to make a decision.

(ii)   Any such ranking of alternatives is 'transitive' so if alternative A is preferred to B and alternative B to C, then alternative A must be preferred to C.

(iii)   Investors do not differentiate between alternatives which have the same degree of risk, their choice is dispassionate in that it is based solely upon consideration of the risk involved rather than on the nature of alternatives available.

(iv)   Investors are able to specify for any investment, whose returns are uncertain, an exactly equivalent alternative which would be just as preferable but would involve a certain return, so for an decision involving risk an investor would be able to specify a certainty equivalent.

These axioms can be used to construct a utility function which can act as a model of the investor's risk attitudes. Investors in making decisions are assumed to maximise their individual expected utility index, a measure of the utility of the return. This utility function is shown in Figure 9.2; the utility index is arbitrary in terms of the scale but the shape of the function is important. The return is shown along the x axis. The utility function can be used to indicate how a choice can be made between alternative risky projects, with the investor aiming to achieve maximum utility in the circumstances. An example of the calculation of an individual choice using a utility function is shown in Example 9.1.

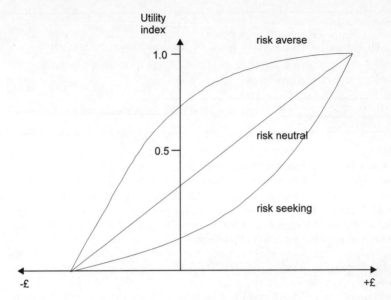

Figure 9.2   *Utility functions illustrating attitudes to risk*

Source: Lumby (1991).

Example 9.1: Calculation of expected utility (from Lumby 1991)

Investment A	Investment B
Expected return:	Expected return:
Possible return × probability of return	Possible return × probability of return
−£1000 × 0.3 = −£300	+£500 × 0.2 = + £200
+£2000 × 0.4 = + £800	+£1500 × 0.6 = + £900
+£5000 × 0.3 = + £1 500	+£2500 × 0.2 = + £500
Expected return + £2 000	Expected return + £1 500
Expected utility:	Expected utility:
$E[U(\text{Inv A})] = 0.3 \times U(-£1\,000) +$	$E[U(\text{Inv B})] = 0.2 \times U(+£500) +$
$0.4 \times U(+£2\,000) +$	$0.6 \times U(+£1\,500) +$
$0.3 \times U(+£5\,000)$	$0.2 \times U(+£2\,500)$

The estimated utility of the investment can be taken from the individual utility function which would look like the upper curve in Figure 9.2, which is concave to the x axis (risk averse). If a detailed figure were available it would be possible to measure off a utility against a given return. −£1 000 return would be say 0.28 on the utility index and so on. Thus the following expected utilities can be estimated.

Expected utility:	Expected utility:
$$E[U(\text{Inv A})] = (0.3 \times 0.28) +$$ $$(0.4 \times 0.8) +$$ $$(0.3 \times 1) = 0.704$$	$$E[U(\text{Inv B})] = (0.2 \times 0.59) +$$ $$(0.6 \times 0.74) +$$ $$(0.2 \times 0.85) = 0.732$$
As $E[U(\text{Inv B})] > E[U(\text{Inv A}]$ the individual will select investment B in order to maximise utility.	

In example 9.1, the investor chooses B because, being risk averse, the individual judges that the risk/expected return combination is superior. The shape of the concave function for the investor is an important part of the analysis; it will be difficult to calculate individual functions in the investment market place and even more problematic to aggregate them. The concave utility function of the risk-averse investor shows the function is a quadratic equation of the form:

$$U(x) = a + bx - cx^2$$

The use of the utility function is a base for building the portfolio theory. Portfolio theory is developed in the context of the risk-averse individual investor concerned to combine shareholdings in several different quoted companies. The investor's aim is assumed to be a maximisation of return given a specified level of risk. Such a portfolio is termed efficient, minimising risk for a given level of expected return. This analysis was extended to Modern Portfolio Theory (MPT) which concerns the decisions made by an investor wishing to construct an efficient portfolio of investments, and the Capital Asset Pricing Model (CAPM) which utilises the theory for financial management decision-making, for instance the cost of capital and capital structures.

9.4   THEORY OF RISK

Risk is defined in many ways, but for a property investment it is the level of probability that a required return, measured in terms of capital value and income, will be achieved. Over time, the variance of actual return from expected return (the volatility) can be measured and used to help determine probability levels. Risk is about the interaction of future returns, and can give rise to a number of possible results with different chances that any particular outcome will result. In a world where the future is uncertain, decision-making involves taking a risk. Investments offer the expectation of high returns from the investor as a reward or compensation for taking the risk involved; in this case the perfect capital market does not just display a single interest rate but a continuum of interest rates. The problems associated with this are the calculation of the risk associated with any investment, and how the capital markets will price this risk in terms of the interest rates charged.

We have seen that the axioms mentioned in the previous section could be used to build a model of investors' risk attitudes. This model would be based on the utility functions of individual investors and assumes that the investors make investment decisions to achieve their aim of maximising their own utility. A utility index function can be constructed for individual investors. The measures of utility shown on the utility index are

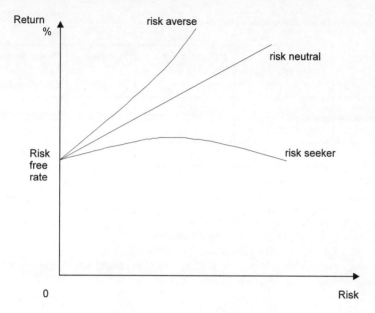

Figure 9.3   *Risk/return trade-off*

arbitrary but can still be used in assessing the individual utility function. Risk-averse individuals have utility curves which are convex to the origin of the graph (point 0 in Figure 9.3). If the individual has a certainty equivalent value equal to the project's expected value, the utility function would be a straight line, and if the value is greater and the investor is risk-seeking then the curve is concave to the origin. Thus the risk-indifference curves shown in Figure 9.2 can be adapted to show the return expected in the market and the actual trade-off of risk and reward as shown in Figure 9.3.

The utility function may be used to indicate how an investor chooses between alternative risky projects. This choice is made on the basis of maximising utility. The following sections will develop the concepts of risk and return.

Return

Over a single period the investment return can be seen to be:

$$\frac{\text{Selling price less purchase price plus income}}{\text{Purchase price}}$$

This would be net selling prices less any transaction costs and a gross selling price including transaction costs. This approach uses a single period to avoid problems of discounting the sums; this could be any period but usually measures of return are made on an annual basis. These returns are historic and, it should be noted, may not be of use in assessing future returns. To calculate the return you need to estimate the future selling price and income; this is not usually a single estimate but a range of estimates, as in Example 9.2.

Example 9.2: Range of probable estimates

Market	Investment selling price (£m)	Income p.a. @ 10% (£m)	Probability	Probable return (income × probabilities)
At start	1.0	0.10		
Boom	1.3	0.13	0.25	0.325
Growth	1.1	0.11	0.50	0.455
Slump	1.03	0.103	0.25	0.2575
Expected	1.1325		1.00	0.11325

Notes: (i)   Income is 10% of selling price;
       (ii) Expected return is income x probability;
       (iii) Total expected return is sum of probabilities;
       (iv) Investment selling price × 10% = total expected return, investment selling price = total expected rent × 100/10.

A calculation of this sort is limited because it only allows for three different possible returns on the investment and cannot account for intermediate returns or those outside the limits made. This is a crude representation of a probability distribution. The probability distributions in the example are symmetrical around the mean. If the returns are symmetrical, that is evenly distributed around the most likely outcome; this is a normal distribution shown graphically in Figure 9.4.

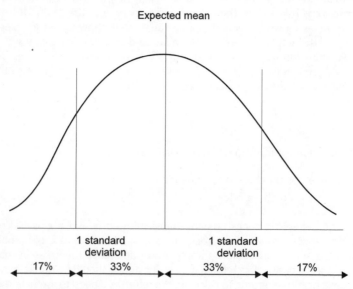

Expected mean

1 standard deviation   1 standard deviation

17%   33%   33%   17%

Figure 9.4   *Distribution under a normal curve (the downside risk is the 50% of outcomes to the left of the expected mean, the upside potential to the right)*

A normal distribution can be described in two ways:

- The mean: this is a measure of the central tendency of the return, more strictly the arithmetic mean or expected return;
- The variance: this is a measure of the dispersion of the returns around the mean (known as σ^2), the square root of the variance is the standard deviation (σ).

If the returns are not distributed symmetrically, the distribution is asymmetrical or skewed, a third measure of skewness is thus required. The mean and the variance can be shown by the equation:

Mean: $E(r) = \sum r_i p_i$

Variance: $\sigma^2 = E(r^2) - (Er)^2$

$$= \sum r_i^2 p_i - \left(\sum r_i p_i\right)^2$$

The symbol $\sum$ is a greek symbol which means sum; it indicates that the string of numbers following should be added together. Strictly speaking, in this calculation the sum symbol should be:

$$\sum_{i=1}^{n}$$

Examples 9.3 and 9.4 show how the expected return and the variance of return are calculated:

Example 9.3: Calculation of expected return

Return		Probability		$r_i p_i$
r_i		p_i		
35%	×	0.3	=	10.5%
20%	×	0.4	=	8.0%
5%	×	0.3	=	1.5%
			$E(r) = \sum r_i p_i$	20.0%

Example 9.4: Calculation of the variance of returns

(Return)^2		Probability		$r_i^2 p_i$
r_i^2		p_i		
1225	×	0.3	=	375.5
400	×	0.4	=	160.0
25	×	0.3	=	7.5
			$E(r^2) = \sum r_i p_i$	535

Risk

The expected return in example 9.3 is 20%: this is the arithmetic mean return or average. The actual return may, however, vary between 35% and 5%. The measure of range may indicate dispersion and thus risk, but would not indicate the numbers of the samples occurring at the extremes, even if the expected return and the range are the same for two distributions. Thus, if there are more frequent extreme readings in an investment A than B then B would be the choice. This is a measure of kurtosis which indicates how peaked or flat the normal distribution is. Thus an additional measure is required for the normal distribution which gives an indication of the dispersal of returns not just the range. The dispersal is indicated by the variance and standard deviation; standard deviation is especially useful as it is in the same units as other expected returns. The risk of an investment can be measured by the variance or standard deviation of the possible return around the expected return. The greater the dispersion, the greater the risk the greater the standard deviation or variance. If there is a normal distribution we can use the calculation of the area under the curve as a better indication of risk than the standard deviation because, statistically in a normal distribution, there is a 66.67% chance that the actual return will lie between ± 1 standard deviation from the mean (in the example $20 \pm 11.62\%$) and a 95% chance of it lying between ± 2 standard deviations (in the example $20 \pm 23.24\%$).

Downside risk

Risk-averse investors are not too worried about their investment doing better than expected (the upside potential) but they are more likely to be worried by the investment doing worse (downside risk). The chance of upside potential is part of the reward for taking this risk. The downside risk could be very important if the distribution is asymmetrical. A symmetrical distribution measures both the upside and downside risk well, but if the distribution is not symmetrical, it is not much use. The dispersion calculation is then averaging two different risk types. It is possible to use the distribution of each half, thus relating it to each risk type. This is called a semi-variance which measures the distribution of each half distribution.

Risk and expected utility

The risk equation can summarised as follows:

$$U(x) = a + bx - cx^2$$

Expected utility: $\quad E[U(r)] = a + bE(r) - cE(r^2)$

but variance $\quad\quad\quad = \sigma^2 = E(r^2) - E(r)^2$

$\therefore \quad\quad\quad\quad\quad -cE(r^2) = -c\left[\sigma^2 + E(r)^2\right]$

Thus expected utility: $\quad E[U(r)] = a + bE(r) - c\sigma^2 + cE(r)^2$

Thus the expected utility produced by an investment is determined by the three risk attitude constants (a, b, c) and two of the characteristics of the probability distribution of the investment's return: the expected return $(E(r)$ and $E(r)^2)$ and the variance of returns (σ^2). The more uncertain the actual return on the investment , the greater will be the value of the variance and the less will be the value of the utility expected from the investment by the investor. This is what would be expected of a risk averse investor.

There are two important assumptions made in this analysis. Firstly, the variance is acceptable as a measure of risk as long as the probability distribution of possible returns is symmetrical. If it is asymmetrical then, besides the mean and variance, a measure of the skew would be required. Furthermore, neither standard deviation nor variance would then provide an adequate measure of downside risk. The skew is the greatest problem in the analysis. Intuition tells us that investment returns must be skewed as the maximum downside risk in an investment in a limited liability company is 100% but the upside potential can quite easily exceed that. The point is that only 100% of the investment can be lost. However this may be the situation in limited liability, but often in practice within property investment, other properties are offered as collateral and personal guarantees given. There is thus often a situation where more than 100% is lost depending on the liabilities. The second assumption is that the conclusions only hold if the investors' utility functions do follow the quadratic form developed earlier. There is some evidence to suggest that investors' utility curves may exhibit both convexity and concavity so they may be risk-seekers or risk-averse depending upon the size of invest-ment under consideration. If the utility functions of investors have a more complex form than that of a simple quadratic equation and if returns are asymmetrical, then the measurement of risk is likely to be more complex. Finally, if investors are to maximise their utility and are risk-averse they would make the following decisions to be rational:

(i)   if two investments have the same return, they choose the one with less risk;
(ii)   if two investments have the same risk, they choose the one with more return.

This analysis does not tell us, however, whether the return is sufficient for the investor and cannot distinguish the choice between an investment with high return/risk and another with low return/risk. In order to identify the degree of risk involved and the corresponding capital market interest rate, you need portfolio theory. The analysis in this chapter will not indicate a project's absolute desirability (accept/reject) but only provide a comparative analysis with another project.

REFERENCES

Baum, A. (1987) 'An Approach to Risk Analysis', Henry Stewart Conference, *Property Investment Appraisal and Analysis*, Cafe Royal, London, 1 December.

Baum, A. and Crosby, N. (1995) *Property Investment Appraisal*, Routledge, London.

Baum, A. E. (1989) 'A Critical Examination of the Measurement of Property Investment and Risk Appraisal', *Discussion Paper Series*, no. 22, University of Cambridge, Department of Land Econ-omy, April.

Brown, G. (1987) 'A Certainty Equivalent Expectations Model for Estimating the Systematic Risk of Property Investments', *Journal of Valuation*, vol. 6, no. 1, pp. 17–41.

Brown, G. R. (1991) Property Investment and the Capital Markets, E. & F.N. Spon, London.

Byrne, P. and Cadman, D. (1984) *Risk, Uncertainty and Decision Making in Property Development*, E. & F. N. Spon, London.

Chapman, C. B. (1991) 'Risk', in P. Venmore-Rowland, P. Brandon and T. Mole (eds), *Investment, Procurement and Performance in Construction*, RICS, London.

Hager, D. P. and Lord, D. J. (1985) *The Property Market, Property Valuations and Property Performance Measurement*, Institute of Actuaries.

Hargitay, S. E. (1983) 'A Systematic Approach to the Analysis of the Property Portfolio', Unpublished PhD thesis, University of Reading (quoted in Waldy 1991).

Hargitay, S. E. and Sui-Ming Yu (1993) *Property Investment Decisions*, E. & F.N. Spon, London.

Isaac, D. and Steley, T. (1991) *Property Valuation Techniques*, Macmillan, London.

Lumby, S. (1991) *Investment Appraisal and Financing Decisions*, Chapman & Hall, London.

Markowitz, H. (1952) 'Portfolio Selection', *Journal of Finance*, vol. VII, no. 1, March, pp. 77–91.

Markowitz, H. (1959) *Portfolio selection: Efficient Diversification of Investment*, John Wiley, New York.

Morley, S. (1988) 'Financial Appraisal – Sensitivity and Probability', in C. Darlow (ed.) *Valuation and Development Appraisal*, Estates Gazette, London.

Morley, S. J. E. (1988) 'The Analysis of Risk in the Appraisal of Property Investments', in A. R. MacLeary and N. Nanthakumaran (eds), *Property Investment Theory*, E. & F.N. Spon, London.

Royal Institution of Chartered Surveyors (RICS) (1992) *Statement of Asset Valuation Practice and Guidance Notes*, RICS, London.

Royal Institution of Chartered Surveyors (RICS) (1995) *RICS Appraisal and Valuation Manual*, RICS, London.

Waldy E. B. D. (1991) 'Single Asset Risk' in P. Venmore-Rowland, P. Brandon and T. Mole (eds), *Investment, Procurement and Performance in Construction*, RICS, London.

10 Investment Performance and Portfolio Strategy

10.1 INVESTMENT MANAGEMENT PRINCIPLES

Because of the nature of property as an investment, which has been detailed in earlier chapters, there is a great need to manage it effectively. Generally larger investment amounts are being dealt on the market and the collectivisation of savings into the financial institutions has led not only to their growth but also their need to be accountable. Proper management of property investment is part of this need, coupled with the requirements to match the efficient management of other asset classes, if property is to be treated as a significant player in the investment portfolio. Some property investment managers concentrate on opportunities which require management and active development, redevelopment or refurbishment; others are content to hold fully let prime investment properties on institutional leases and almost treat the investment as a paper investment with little active management. The main problems of property as an investment have been summarised as the lotting problem (the size and indivisibility of lots for sale); illiquidity; the need for management; and the complexity of financing development (Dubben and Sayce 1991). These areas all require effective management. The investment decision will relate to the amount of property within the institutional portfolio. To compete with gilts and equities the property portfolio will need to consider the proportion of the property investment placed in different sectors. For instance, some commentators in the past have made generalised statements suggesting that the ideal pension fund portfolio could be around 50% retail, 30% office and 20% industrial. This chapter will indicate some of the complexities of such a decision.

Blundell and Ward (1987) have described a multi-factor model, using methods of portfolio allocation and applied a multi-index approach to portfolio decision-making to enable investors to explore the effects of changing their allocation decisions. In the allocation of funds within a mixed-asset portfolio or between different types of property within a wholly property orientated portfolio, strategic decisions are important in affecting investment performance. Strategic property decisions would determine the proportion of the total portfolio devoted to property and the allocation of funds to different types of property. Key investment strategies of the UK property industry focus on the spread between types of property and location, the overall policy being to avoid too many eggs in too few baskets or to 'buy the index' (generate returns at the level of the main property index). These strategies are based on the concepts arising from portfolio analysis and the works of Markowitz (1952) and Sharpe (1964). The basis of this analysis are the assumptions that:

(a)   investors are risk averse, i.e. they will require a higher return to compensate them for greater risk;
(b)   risk can be measured by analysing the likely divergence between the returns from a portfolio and its expected return; and,

(c)   investors, when considering whether not to buy an asset, will be rationally concerned with the net effect on their portfolio and will not consider the risk of the asset in isolation from other assets held.

In the words of Markowitz:

Two objectives however, are common to all investors . . . :
1.   *They want 'return' to be high. The appropriate definition of 'return' may vary from investor to investor. But, in whatever sense is appropriate, they prefer more of it to less of it.*
2.   *They want this return to be dependable, stable, not subject to uncertainty.*
(Markowitz 1991, p. 6)

Portfolio theory is dealt with in more detail in Chapter 11 but portfolio strategies are developed in this chapter. Readers may wish to read Chapter 11 first if they have no knowledge of portfolio theory and find some of the discussion here difficult.

10.2   OBJECTIVES AND STRATEGIES

Dubben and Sayce (1991) suggest that there are four criteria in particular that an individual or institution would use to select a property:

(i)   Do the particular characteristics of the investment satisfy the investment needs of the investor in terms of security, growth and other aspects?
(ii)   Is the price to be paid reasonable in all the circumstances?
(iii)   Is the property suitable in respect of the portfolio balance?
(iv)   If the need to alter the portfolio changes, will the property be readily saleable?

The last point is very important in this analysis. Investors are unlikely to purchase a property where there is little chance of a ready market at the estimated time of disposal. The point here is the forecasting of the market at the time of disposal. Innovative investments are thus unlikely to attract investors, as an established record of demand for space and rental growth may be lacking.

Sweeney (1988) tested the viability of the percentage investment of the portfolio in property by using the risk/return characteristics of various asset classes and calculating the mean return and standard deviation for property, gilts and shares over the period 1978–87. Here the standard deviation of the returns is used as a surrogate for risk, as it calculated from the variability of return about the mean return. These mean returns and standard deviations are shown in Table 10.1.

Table 10.1   *Risk/return for various assets classes*

Asset	Property	Gilts	Shares
Mean return (%)	17.54	15.68	26.40
Standard deviation (%)	7.20	1.35	13.15

Source: Sweeney (1988).

Sweeney then looked at portfolios of various mixes of assets, and using the Markowitz mean-variance analysis derived the standard deviation and mean returns for various asset mixes. The low risk portfolio she derived had 70% in property which suggested that property within the portfolio lowered the overall risk of the portfolio. She found the lowest standard deviation for the portfolio mixes tested had 60% in property whereas the high risk portfolios were low in property. This arose because of the correlation between the asset classes. In an analysis of the Richard Ellis Property Market Indicators against gilts and shares she found that the reason why gilts and equities in a portfolio increased risk was that the gilts and equities were correlated whereas gilts and shares had a negative correlation with property, but this was not significant. These findings are summarised in Table 10.2.

Table 10.2   *Correlation between asset classes 1978–87*

	Property	Gilts	Shares
Property	1.0	−0.38	−0.17
Gilts		1.0	0.78
Shares			1.00

Note: The correlation coefficient varies between 0 (not strong) and 1 (strong) and may be positively or negatively (− in table) correlated.
Source: Sweeney (1988).

At the time of writing (1996) there had been a net disinvestment in property in the market, down from £173m to £71m for the financial institutions (*Estates Gazette* 1996b). The quarterly net property investment for the third quarter is set out in Figure 10.1, this

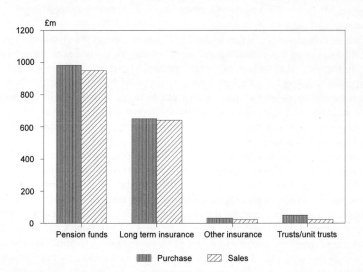

Figure 10.1   *Net investment by financial institutions in property, 3rd quarter 1996*

Source: *Estates Gazette* (1996b).

showed that the disinvestment was discontinuing and the net investment is calculated as the difference in purchases and sales for the various financial institutions. This study showed the insurance companies and unit trusts being very active in the market.

A research study earlier in the year by the Investment Property Forum and the *Estates Gazette* (*Estates Gazette* 1996a) had provided an indication of investors' intentions in the sector, with a large proportion intending to disinvest from the office sector (80%). The return for 1995 reflected a weaker performance for property: 4.1% returns against 24% for equities and 18% for gilts. Investors were still keen to be in property and gave the following reasons: relative price in relation to other assets; the pattern of property performance; risk diversification; and opportunities for proactive management. Investors were looking for, firstly, retail investment, especially in the regions (North West, West Midlands and Scotland), and, secondly, industrial investments in the South East and Midlands. The market was showing an increase in yield difference between primary and secondary yields. The yields quoted are shown in Table 10.3.

Table 10.3   *Current yields April 1996*

Sector yield	Office	Business parks	Retail shop units	Retail warehouses	Shopping centres	Industrial	Distribution
Prime rack-rented	6.6	7.2	5.6	7.0	7.0	8.2	7.8
Secondary	9.4	9.4	7.8	8.6	9.0	10.4	9.6

Byrne and Lee (1995) have reaffirmed the case for property in the portfolio; by analysing the affects of de-smoothing (discussed later) and through the application of Modern Portfolio Theory, they make a case that property in the portfolio could be higher than at present. This is done by constraints on asset weighting and adjusting the property data for appraisal bias.

The use of risk analysis techniques and computers have assisted in the application of theory to developing the optimal portfolio composition. Using a scenario-assisted data approach, Matysiak (1993) has coupled the portfolio framework with a scenario general input approach. Using an optimiser type of analysis he has identified the broad strategies, targets, and appropriate balances of portfolio holdings. Modern investment theory shows that investors make allocation decisions based on a trade-off between risk and expected return. Different combinations of individual assets may be held in such a way that the highest possible return for the given, smallest, levels of risk may be achieved, known as efficient diversification. Readily available computer software, known as an optimiser, can calculate how much of each asset should be held in order to achieve an efficiently diversified portfolio. To perform the calculations, the necessary inputs are: expected return on each asset, the uncertainty of this return as measured by the assets' variability (standard deviation) and the extent to which each pair of assets is expected to co-vary as measured by their correlation coefficient. Given these inputs it is possible to derive risk and return profiles for different portfolios of assets holdings by the use of an optimiser. Byrne and Lee (1994) used spreadsheet optimisers to combine assets to provide 'efficient' portfolios which were then connected to provide a Markowitz 'efficient frontier' (see Chapter 11).

10.3 PROPERTY PERFORMANCE AND MEASUREMENT

The measurement of property performance is difficult; the evaluation of a property investment is based on changes in the capital value of the investment flow, the income generated by the investment. Unlike the markets in equities and gilts where prices can be discovered in the market and prices change rapidly, there is no centralised market place for property. Property, unlike other elements of an investment portfolio, may be unique in its nature and location, the property may not be regularly revalued and if the property has not been tested in the market, there will be no specific evidence to go on. The valuation of property often involves the use of comparable evidence, in terms of rental value, yields and capital value of a combination, and these figures are often based on the accumulation of historic data on which comparable evidence can be amassed. It is thus extremely difficult to assess future trends from this data and estimate changes in the property cycle, especially important in the downturn phase of the property cycle. In order to encourage investment in property and justify its inclusion in portfolios of mixed assets, it is important to be able to compare property returns with returns on the other major asset classes, equities and gilts.

Dubben and Sayce (1991) quote some research carried out by them to indicate the use of quantitative measurement techniques by property investment managers. Their sample of 70 investment managers had four major areas of conclusions, relating to methods of performance measurement, performance targets, the frequency of performance review, and the assessment of risk, and these conclusions are discussed later in the chapter. With regard to the methods of performance measurement, they found that the internal rate of return was the usual technique used but that many respondents could not distinguish between time-weighted rate of return (TWRR) and money-weighted rates of return (MWRR).

Hall (1981) suggested that the portfolio can be examined on the basis of:

- Income/cost
- Income/value
- Value/cost
- Income growth
- Rental value growth
- Rental value/income
- Time-weighted total return
- Money-weighted total return.

However, he felt that to produce all the figures would provide too much information and thus be counterproductive.

There is thus a need to establish objectives for portfolio performance. These objectives will be relevant to any portfolio and are grouped in three categories:

(i) *League tables or inter-fund comparisons*
   Overall results need to be contrasted with one another to examine the reasons for variation in the results but each fund has to be assessed over the same time-scale and the same footing. League tables are best suited to unit trusts and bonds which produce regular prices for their units. For pension funds there may be different objectives.

(ii)   *Measurement against external yardsticks like inflation or alternative forms of investment*
More practical than (i), this requires an overall review of performance.

(iii)   *Internal assessments which are likely to produce management information for subsequent action in the portfolio*
The detailed breakdown and analysis of the entire portfolio between individual properties, not only shows the global effect of holding property but identifies the strategies and weaknesses. The information for this requires the valuation of each property at the beginning of the period chosen or its cost if it is acquired subsequently.

Having decided to apply an appropriate strategy, the strategy for measurement of the portfolio should reflect the information required. The most logical method is to view the portfolio initially as a single entity and break it down into composite parts, as shown in Figure 10.2.

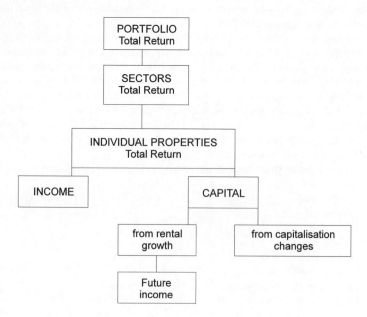

Figure 10.2   *Performance measurement strategies*

Source: Hall (1981).

Methods of measurement

Yields have already been explored in Chapter 5. The measure of return is the amount of capital growth or rental income from an investment purchased or valued, over time. There are two ways of assessing the return: by money-weighted rates of return (MWRR) or time-weighted rates of return (TWRR). MWRR is calculated by discounting income and expenditure over time to calculate the IRR or NPV. The return can be broken down to quarterly or weekly periods. The MWRR is the discount rate which equates the initial outlay and the cash flows at the date they occur to the final value of the investment. The weakness of the MWRR as a measure of a portfolio's comparative performance is that it is very sensitive to the timing and size of new investments. This is important in a portfolio of direct property investment as such funds are generally growing quickly (Hetherington 1980). TWRR is calculated every time a cash flow occurs. Each time there is a rental income or expenditure, returns are calculated at this point. An introduction to the calculation of MWRR and TWRR is outlined below and detailed in the next two sections.

Calculation of MWRR and DCF

Assuming income is received quarterly:

$$C = R_1 + \frac{R_2}{1+r} + \frac{R_3}{(1+r)^2} \text{ etc} \ldots \frac{R_n}{(1+r)^{n-1}} + \frac{V}{(1+r)^n}$$

where C = the initial value of the investment
r = quarterly return
R = rental income per quarter (R_1 for the first quarter and so on)
V = final value of property at the end of the measured period

Approximately

$$R = \frac{V_1 - V_0 + C}{V_0}$$

where R = total return over the period
V_1 = capital value at the end of the period
V_0 = capital value at start of period
C = rental income over the period

This calculation is not time-weighted; there is no discounting.

Calculation of TWRR

This needs the calculation to be performed each time there is a cash flow, and the formula is:

$$R = \frac{V_1 - V_0 + C}{V_0}$$

This formula has been used above to find the approximate MWRR for the whole period, but if the formula is used per quarter and the results for each quarter are linked together, the results would be a time-weighted rate of return. (Dubben and Sayce, 1991)

Money-weighted rate of return

The MWRR is the interest or discount rate which equates the sum of all the realised cash flows and the capital value of the asset at the end of a holding period to the initial capital outlay or the capital value of the asset at the beginning of the holding period. This equates to the internal rate of return (IRR) in a discounted cash flow calculation. The rate of return will be dependent on the size and the time of occurrence of realised cash flows:

$$CV_{t-1} = \frac{CV_t}{(1 + r_m)^n} + \sum_{i=1}^{n} \frac{C_i}{(1 + r_m)^i}$$

This equation is to be solved for r_m where:

r_m is the internal rate of return or the money-weighted rate of return;
C_i is the net realised cash flow for a sub-period i;
CV_{t-1} is the capital value of the asset at the beginning of the holding period or the initial capital outlay;
CV_t is the capital value of the asset at the end of the holding period.
(Hargitay and Yu 1993)

Time-weighted rate of return

This is the geometric mean of rates of return achieved in each sub-period contained in the holding period. For each sub-period the rate of return is defined as:

$$r_i = \frac{CV_i - CV_{i-1} + C_i}{CV_{i-1}} = \frac{CV_i + C_i}{CV_{i-1}} - 1$$

where r_i is the rate of return for the sub-period i;
C_i is the net cash flow in sub-period i;
CV_i is the value of the asset at the end of sub-period i;
CV_{i-1} is the value of the asset at the beginning of sub-period i.
(Hargitay and Yu 1993)

Additional capital injections are to be included into the cashflow and also into the capital at work. If the lengths of the sub-period are short, the usual procedure is to include this additional input into CV_{i-1}.

$$\text{Since} \quad 1 + r_i = \frac{CV_i + C_i}{CV_{i-1}}$$

the geometric mean of n sub-period rates of return is:

$$1 + R_T = \left[(1 + r_1)(1 + r_2) \ldots (1 + r_n) \right]^{\frac{1}{n}}$$

$$R_T = \left[{}^n\pi_{i=1}(1 + r_i) \right]^{\frac{1}{n}} - 1$$

This equals the weighted average where the weights are based on the lengths of individual sub-periods; if the time periods are equal then:

$$t_1 = t_2 \ldots = t_n$$

$T = n.t$ and therefore all sub-period returns will be weighted equally. The computed result will not be affected by the timing of the cash in- and out-flows (Hargitay and Yu 1993).

Example 10.1: calculate MWRR and TWRR

Property asset:
Purchase price   £100 000
Net income   £10 000 pa
Value end of year 1   £125 000
Sale price end of year 2 £145 000

Calculate MWRR:

Year	Expenditure	Income	Net cash flow
0	−100 000		−100 000
1		10 000	10 000
2		10 000 + 125 000	135 000
		IRR (MWRR)	21.3%

Calculate TWRR:

Year 1: $CV_0 = £100\,000,\ C_1 = £10\,000,\ CV_1 = £125\,000$

$$r_1 = \frac{£125\,000 + £10\,000 - £100\,000}{£100\,000} = 0.35$$

Year 2: $CV_1 = £125\,000,\ C_2 = £10\,000,\ CV_2 = £145\,000$

$$r_2 = \frac{£145\,000 + £10\,000 - £125\,000}{£125\,000} = 0.24$$

TWRR $= R_T$, for a 2-year period $(1 + R_T)^2 = (1 + r_1)(1 + r_2)$

$(1 + R_T)^2 = (1 + 0.35)(1 + 0.24)$

$R_T = (1.674)^{1/2} - 1 = 0.294 = 29.4\%$

Comparison of the alternative measures of the rate of return

The money-weighted rate of return is a variant of the internal rate of return (IRR). MWRR uses only realised cash flows. In the MWRR the effects of the fluctuations of the capital value of the asset over the holding period will not be reflected. The IRR is a kind of long-term interest rate which assumes that cash flows are reinvested at a uniform rate. These rates are extremely sensitive to the size and timing of cash flows. Since the managers of portfolios do not have control over the timing and size of the flow of funds, this comparison could be misleading. The TWRR is the geometric mean of sub-period rates of return and provides a time profile of investment performance which reflects the effects of fluctuations in capital values as well as periodic cash flows. The short-term rates of sub-period returns provide a better, direct and immediate comparison with contemporary alternative investment opportunities than a long-run rate of return. On the other hand, the TWRR will not be influenced by the timing of cash flows or the timing of changes in capital values. The TWRR assumes reinvestment at short-term rates which prevail at the time of the in- or outflows of monies. The assumption of reinvestment at short-term interest rates has the important advantage of reflecting, more realistically, the relative values of cash flows in contemporary market situations (Hargitay and Yu 1993).

Use of quantitative measurement techniques

Dubben and Sayce (1991) carried out a survey to find the usage of quantitative measurement techniques using a sample of 70 fund managers. This survey has already been discussed briefly earlier, but, in detail, the results were grouped under four headings:

Methods of property performance measurement

IRR was found to be the usual method; some managers could not distinguish between TWRR and MWRR.

Performance targets

Managers will usually look at other performance measures when evaluating property. Most look at alternatives as a guide only, rather than a target. The range of alternatives used as a target or benchmark varies from a specially created target fund to the indices produced by large firms (JLW, Weatheralls, IPD). The use of gilts as a benchmark is widespread (some used index-linked stock whilst other used long or medium dated). The use of equity indices was less favoured but some used the FTSE 100 index.

The frequency of performance review

The time-horizon of investors (the time-scale over which returns are measured) has shortened in recent years, with investors who traditionally are prepared to take a long-term view preoccupied with short-term returns. This short-termism is reflected in the frequency of review found in the study with some respondents reviewing their performance on a very regular basis, sometimes even quarterly.

The assessment of risk

There was some assessment of risk found in the study, generally using the risk-adjusted discount rate or 'risk premium'.

10.4 PORTFOLIO CONSTRUCTION

The principle of diversification is a rule which has established itself amongst investors generally and investors in property portfolios specifically, but there are few empirical studies which relate the size of the property portfolio with the level of risk. The reason for this is that it is difficult to obtain time series data on a reliable sample of properties (Brown 1991). The issue of how many properties an investor should hold to diversify risks is obviously a key one. From portfolio theory it can be seen that the variations in property returns can be split into two parts, systematic and unsystematic risk. The reduction of risk in the portfolio is thus the reduction of unsystematic risk in the portfolio. As the portfolio increases in size and approaches the size of the market, the variation in portfolio returns should approach the systematic level. As the portfolio size increases so the portfolio variance should approach the average covariance for all stocks. Research has shown that portfolios of between 15 and 20 properties can obtain most of the reduction in risk. By holding about 30 properties and assuming that the portfolio is not unduly influenced by large value properties, it is possible to diversify down to the systematic risk level. Assuming average properties and equal weighting, the degree of risk reduction has been shown to be in the region of 62–73% depending on the sector and about 68% at the portfolio level. Comparable figures in the UK stock market are in the region of 50%. High levels of risk reduction are due to the low correlation of returns that exist between individual properties. The unequal weights and small numbers associated with property portfolios does not mean that their performance from period to period will be heavily influenced by factors specific to individual properties as opposed to market-wide factors; the only way that the market can significantly affect portfolio performance is by holding very large numbers of properties. The risk in each sector can be seen from the Betas attached to each sector. Brown (1991) took annual returns data on seven portfolios of different sizes collected over the period 1978–83 and regressed them on to the returns from the Richard Ellis Property Market Indicators over the same period. The estimated betas for each sector are shown in Table 10.4.

Table 10.4   *Estimated betas for each sector measured relative to the property market (1978–83)*

Sector	Beta
Office	0.943
Retail	1.041
Industrial	0.850

Source: Brown (1991).

Thus retail is shown as the most volatile and thus risky with industrial least risky. On this basis investors will be expecting a higher level of return from retail property.

It is in fact very difficult to achieve portfolios of property which are highly diversified. Investors in property will find it impossible to select a portfolio capable of tracking an index. The average-sized portfolio of 30 properties has a considerable amount of residual risk still to be diversified away. For a portfolio that could be used as an index, thousands of properties would be required to provide a portfolio which would be a good proxy for market movements. Many commercially available indices utilise only a few hundred properties, thus a considerable amount of residual risk remains in these indices. In addition there is the problem caused by smoothing (this arises because of the infrequent nature of valuations) which causes properties which do not have synchronous values to be included in the index.

Thus performance of individual properties is affected by the unsystematic components of risk, and market effects make only a small contribution in explaining returns. If the holding period is long there is a decline in systematic risk; if the portfolio is actively managed then as the systematic risk declines, so will the return. Unsystematic components of risk in the property are aspects such as location of the property; this factor operates to provide a low correlation coefficient between properties and thus reduces risk. Over reasonable holding periods, there is little advantage in diversification of the portfolio across different sectors as similar levels of risk reduction can be obtained by diversification within a single sector. If investors can forecast positive abnormal returns for an individual sector, then that sector will provide a better risk/reward trade-off by diversifying amongst properties in that sector. if the investor is unable to forecast abnormal returns, then, although investors should pursue a policy of diversifying, such a policy will not have the results envisaged.

Property as an asset class

In considering the structure of the portfolio one should also consider the correlation of returns in property with other asset classes. Brown (1991) carried out empirical studies related to the relationship of returns to other asset classes. In the period January 1979–December 1982, he found that equally weighted and value weighted portfolios exhibited low and negative correlation with gilts. As the holding period of investments increases so does the correlation coefficient, suggesting greater relationship. There is a low correlation between properties and the FT All Share Index. The relationship with the property share index is much higher and increases with the holding period. A high correlation between property and the Retail Price Index (RPI) indicates the ability of property to act as a hedge against inflation. In 1988 Richard Ellis tested the hypothesis that the property market moves counter-cyclically to equities and gilts and is thus a good prospect for the diversification of a portfolio. This study was initially discussed in Chapter 1, and found:

(i)   *Very limited similarity* between property returns and equities (0.10 correlation coefficient);
(ii)   *no similarity* between property returns and gilts (0.03 correlation coefficient);
(iii) gilts and equity returns were *more in line* (0.44 correlation) (Barter 1988).

Returns follow a distribution which is approximately log normal. There is a low correlation between individual returns and this shows the market responds more to specific factors than general market movements. This evidence indicates that property has an important part to play in the mixed-asset portfolio where long-term passive strategy not only implies diversification but also hedging.

Risk reduction in a portfolio can be expressed as a percentage of the change in standard deviation from the average σ_p to the systematic or market risk level $\sigma_s = RR$.

$$RR = \frac{\sigma_p - \sigma_s}{\sigma_p} = 1 - \frac{\sigma_s}{\sigma_p}$$

$$RR = 1 - \varphi_{p,m}$$

Thus risk reduction is a function of the correlation structure $\varphi_{p,m}$ that exists between the property and the market.

$$average\ risk\ p = \sigma_p = \frac{\sigma_s}{1 - RR}$$

Average risk is likely to vary between 15 and 47% depending on market conditions (Brown 1991). An analysis for the different property sectors is shown in Table 10.5.

Table 10.5 *The estimation of average property risk for each sector based on a market risk rate of 8%*

Sector	Average property risk (%)
Office	23.78
Retail	32.59
Industrial	29.33
Portfolio	27.50

10.5 PORTFOLIO STRATEGY

Property portfolios are held for a number of different objectives. For example they are usually held for long-term investment, but other aspects, such as short-term speculation or charitable purposes, may compromise that objective. In addition, much of the stock of property is owner-occupied and the objectives of owner-occupation, where a property forms an inherent part of the operation of a firm and thus its profitability, will mean a divergence of objectives from the normal investment return. Institutional investors like pension funds may be compromised compared to the traditional objectives of, say, profit maximisation or wealth creation in a corporate entity. It is now generally considered that maximisation of shareholders' wealth by increasing the value of shares is better than strict profit maximisation as a goal criterion of a firm. Pension funds seek to maximise cash flow for the provision of funds for members in retirement; the timing of such flows may not accord with profit maximisation at any particular point in time. In public companies, higher returns may result in increased dividends but this may not be as useful as building up assets and thus share price to generate funds and make larger profits in the future.

Portfolio strategies are based on the proposal that underpriced properties can be recognised. This idea is based on the analysis of the market and specifically the efficient market hypothesis. Analysis of the market has determined that it is efficient at the weak form level and on this basis merely tracking past movements will give no guide to future movements. Technical analysis suggests that prices increase because of increased risk being taken on with an investment. Fundamental analysis looks at the specific factors which contribute to the value of the asset and identifies if the asset is underpriced. Property portfolios tend to be poorly diversified, thus abnormal returns are due to luck, inside information or superior forecasting ability (Brown 1991). Some forecasting ability can be utilised in an active–passive strategy. This suggests that the process is in two parts. The first part is to create a portfolio which tracks an index, thus all specific risk is eliminated through diversification and thus the returns are more in line with the index. The second part of the strategy is to identify assets which have an intrinsic value different to the current market value.

Underpriced property

The problem of the strategy is thus how to identify underpriced property. If market information is generally available then prices have already impounded values. Without a formal theory of market equilibrium it is doubtful whether research can identify underpriced properties except by chance. The market only rewards investors for taking on that part of risk which cannot be diversified away; that is, systematic or market risk. The purpose of the analysis is to identify abnormal returns on an *ex-ante* basis. The ability to identify underpriced properties depends on how well the information can be processed. Consensus information will not identify underpriced property except by chance. The approach uses comparables; the estimated beta for properties is an historic beta and therefore the expected beta is needed. It is possible to use a certainty equivalent model to find the expected beta, and one corrected for valuation error will be the best estimate of market risk. By using a riskless rate of return, if the slope of the security market line is known then it is possible to work out underpriced and overpriced property. This is shown in Figure 10.3.

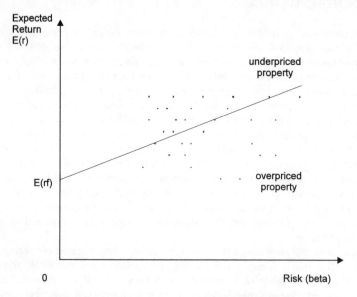

Figure 10.3   *Underpriced and overpriced property*

This approach can be developed by analysing a large sample of properties at a single point in time. By plotting the expected returns against risk and analysing the results using regression analysis, it is possible to identify property which is underpriced. Valuations contain some error or noise; the valuation model used is the equated yield model assuming property is valued part-way through the rent review period.

$$V_0 = \frac{a[1 - (1 + r)^{-n}]}{r} + \frac{R(1 + g)^n}{r(1 + r)^n}\left[\frac{(1 + r)^p - 1}{(1 + r)^p - (1 + g)^p}\right]$$

This equation assumes V_0 is known along with the lease structure and growth and thus it is possible to solve for the expected rate of return r. n is number of years since review and p is the rent review pattern.

Allocation of funds

The key questions a portfolio strategy will ask is:

- What percentage of funds should be put into property?
- What percentage of funds should go into each sector?

The key to these problems is the correlation between each asset class. Property exhibits a low correlation with every sector except the Retail Price Index. Property portfolios exhibit low correlation with the FT Property Share Index; this is because property shares are highly geared so equity returns are more likely to be in line with the FT all share index. The correlation coefficient between property shares and equities means that there is little diversification benefit from investing in property shares and incorporating them into a portfolio of equities. The 1990s were an important era in the development of commercial property as a serious asset class. New skills are required by those in the market. The traditional skills in the property market can be contrasted with those involved in asset allocation – what Barber (1995) refers to as the difference between stock picker and asset allocators. The skills of assets allocation will assist variation in return of the various funds. Barber gives details of the variations in the returns on the market indicated by the various indices, as shown in Table 10.6.

Table 10.6   *1994 Property returns: market variation (%)*

Index	IPD (annual)	IPD (monthly)	Richard Ellis	Jones Lang Wootton
Retail	12.8	16.8	11.2	14.4
Industrial	11.2	16.0	15.7	14.4
Office	10.6	12.3	12.1	15.2

Source: Barber (1995).

Although the indexes do give different results and rankings, there is little difference between the performances of the different sectors. The precise balance in each of the indices is influenced by the nature of the portfolio used for the index. In such conditions the ability to choose good stock is as vital to returns as the variation between sectors. Thus both activities can be seen to be valuable: the surveyors who stress stock picking, against the assets allocators who promote the pursuit of correct portfolio distribution between office, retail and industrial. These roles are important, as in 1994 institutional weighting of property began to rise to around 5–6%, an event not seen since 1979 (Barber 1995).

So what makes for a good strategy? IPD analysed the top 20 performing funds and found that they were generally more active in the market than the average and were more exposed to the growth areas. The study took place in 1996 and the areas were seen to be retail warehousing, provincial industrial investments and a mixture of other sectors including areas like agricultural, residential and leisure. The top performers also watched their backs whilst being exposed, in the sense that their portfolios have lower rent voids and smaller exposure to over-rented property. In respect of the top-performers' activity, Ian Cullen of IPD was quoted as saying: 'This did give the lie to some of the anecdotal evidence that says if you leave things alone and minimise buying and selling, you will probably outperform' (Catalano 1996, p. 44).

Finally an important part of the strategy must be regular valuations of property. Valuations can become quickly dated and a proactive strategy must rely on up-to-date valuations. The accuracy of those valuations is another matter, and much debate has gone on since Hager and Lord (1985) published their paper to the Institute of Actuaries criticising the accuracy of valuations. In response to this criticism, even at the time, Reid (1985) was saying that the annual valuation of an investment portfolio was an essential prerequisite to active management. This may help to counter the belief commonly held, that valuers are conservative in their approach and consistently undervalue.

An alternative approach to portfolio strategy has been suggested by Eichholtz *et al.* (1995), who suggest that the usual top-down approach to portfolio allocation involves, first, the decision as to how much to allocate to each broad asset category, and second, a decision on an optimal strategy within each asset category. In part, this involves the management of risk through diversification within the asset category. For real estate portfolios, the conventional approach to defining diversification categories is to use property type and geographical region. Returns on different property types are believed to be driven by different economic factors: for example, offices by office employment, shops by retail sales, and industrial properties by manufacturing output. Similarly, there should be differential performance across regions within each property type. But the regions used are usually administrative regions based on geographic boundaries rather than functional regions. The suggestion is that regions should be grouped by their economic base and therefore the economy underlying the property market within the unit of analysis becomes more homogenous.

10.6   PORTFOLIO PERFORMANCE MEASUREMENT AND PROPERTY INDICES

So what makes for good performance in a portfolio? Brown (1991) has suggested four questions that need to be asked in this respect:

(i)   How well has the portfolio performed relative to a property index?
(ii)   Is it possible to outperform the index?
(iii)   How many properties are required in the portfolio to ensure the portfolio is well diversified?
(iv)   Is it possible to achieve high levels of diversification?

In measurement of performance, the measurement will need to take into account the aims and of objectives of the investor. The objectives of holding a portfolio can range from pure speculation, to mainstream investment, and on to charitable objectives. There is also the difference between the aims of the institutional investors and the occupier as investor. The difference between these viewpoints might well be the difference between holding a portfolio of properties for investment and holding properties for use. The privity of contract issue is one where the institutional investor as landlord, and the business occupier, perhaps a multiple retail occupier, would have different views on the appropriate legal framework in which their respective economic activities operate. From a business occupier's point of view it is not the property as an investment which is important but the use of the building in the portfolio which contributes to the overall profitability of the company.

In a study of real estate investment trusts (REITs) in the USA, Redman and Manakyan (1995) found that the risk-adjusted performance of a trust is based on its financial ratios (gross cash flow, leverage, asset size), the regional location of its properties and the type of real estate investment. More specifically, they found performance was better in those funds which has invested in the western USA, in healthcare properties and in secured mortgages, indicating the growth areas in US property.

Property performance measurement

In the post-war years there has been increased involvement by institutional funds in property which has encouraged the need to appraise performance. The application of targets to investment situations requires a detailed appraisal of property performance. The need to measure performance is in turn reflected by the following requirements:

- The need to compare performance with a target return.
- The need to compare performance with important external economic indicators. For instance, the rate of inflation will determine the real return.
- The need to check property performance against competing investments such as equities or gilts. Lack of performance will result in switching from one media to another.
- The need for a comparison of portfolio performance. The need to check internally and with competing funds, which sectors are performing well and which portfolios are performing well
- The need to maximise portfolio return and balance investment returns to ensure maximisation of growth sectors.
- The need to match risks with returns.

The portfolio return should reflect the risk involved. A spread of investments may involve a spread of risks and the portfolio should be analysed accordingly. Measurement is required to actively manipulate the portfolio in accordance with the strategy required. Methods of measurement include: yield; capital appreciation; rental growth; time or money-weighted returns; DCF analysis.

Measuring market performance

Market reports of surveying and financial firms can assist in providing data to examine the performance of the property sector but note that the conclusions have to be viewed in the light of the data used. Generally the data are based on institutional property, that is sectors of the property market in which the institutions have an interest, with conventional leases and also generally considered prime in respect of tenant, construction, location, design, etc. The data may or may not be classified on a regional basis. Locational variations are important even within regions. Portfolios may be weighted or adjusted to accord with typical institutional portfolios. The time-periods covered by surveys may be arbitrary and of insufficient length for trends to be determined. Because of the rental relationship with capital, value movements in one variable may be offset by the other and thus overall returns may be unaffected or different. The rent passing may not reflect actual rents. To improve its market analysis and comparison with other asset classes, the Investment Property Databank (IPD) has brought its annual index into line with gilt and equity measurements. The model for the index is calculated on the assumption of

Table 10.7   *Property performance measures*

Name	Organisation	Measure	Frequency	Base date
Jones Lang Wootton	Surveyors	The Property Index	Annual Quarterly	June 67–77 June 77
Hillier Parker	Surveyors	ICHP Property Market Indicators – Rates of Return	Annual Semi-annual	Dec 72–76 Dec 76
The WM Company Ltd	Independent performance measurement organisation	(i) Pension Fund Service (PFS) (ii) Annual Review Property Portfolio Service	Annual Annual	Mar 75 Mar 80
The Wyatt Company	Consulting actuary	Survey of Pooled Pension Funds	Quarterly	Dec 75
Morgan Grenfell Laurie-Corporate Intelligence Group	Surveyors and business consultants	The MGL-CIG Property Index	Annual	Dec 77
Richard Ellis[a]	Surveyors	The Richard Ellis Monthly Index (REMI)	Annual Monthly	Mar 79–86 Dec 86
Weatherall Green & Smith.	Surveyors	The Quarterly Property Index	Quarterly	Dec 79
Combined Actuarial Performance Service (CAPS)	Performance measurement organisation	CAPS General Report	Annual	Dec 79
Mercer Fraser	Consulting actuary	UK Pooled Pension Fund Survey	Annual	Dec 79
The Property Index	Group of four surveying practices[b]	The Property Index	Annual	Mar 80
Property Investment Databank Ltd (IPD)	Independent performance measurement organisation, index producer and research database	(i) IPD Annual Review and Property Investors Digest (ii) IPD Monthly Index	Annual Monthly	Dec 80 Dec 86
Property Research Database (PRD)	Research Database comprising data from various sources[c]	No published measures	Quarterly	Dec 80

[a] Capital and rental growth only is given between 1979 and 1986. Annual total returns are published monthly from December 1987.
[b] Group comprises Healey & Baker, Hillier Parker, Jones Lang Wootton and Richard Ellis.
[c] Data from Healey & Baker, Hillier Parker, Jones Lang Wootton, Richard Ellis and Prudential Portfolio Managers.
Source: Morrell (1991).

continuously accrued income, whereas the traditional valuation model assumes the income is received annually in arrears. Most leases state that income should be received quarterly in advance, but, in reality, income is often a continuous flow. Using data going back to 1971, the new calculation should result in an average annual improvement of 0.3% p.a because the old system failed to take into account the possibility of reinvesting income collected throughout the year (Baillie 1997).

Property indices can be classified into three types: whole fund indices, indices derived from specific index portfolios, and indices based on data drawn from specific locations. These indices are generally disaggregated into capital or capital growth indices, rental or rental growth indices or total return indices (Hargitay and Yu 1993). The Morgan Grenfell Laurie/Corporate Intelligence Group (MGL/CIG) Property Index is an example of a whole fund index. The index is composed of indices for property values, total return and income return and is based on actual funds who are willing to provide the information. The actual calculation is carried out by linking the period figures together, weighting the portfolio on the basis of value. Special index portfolios include the Investment Property Databank (IPD), The Jones Lang Wootton (JLW) Property Index, the Richard Ellis (RE) Property Market Indicators and the Weatherall Green and Smith (WGS) Quarterly Property Index. These providers create notional market portfolios by aggregating selected properties into large representative portfolios; the JLW Index, for instance, measures the increases in capital and rental values in a representative institutional portfolio. This approach differs from the whole fund approach in that data from individual properties is included in the fund which in turn is used to construct the index. Indices based on data drawn from specific locations are used to reflect changes in rental levels. These are assembled at collection points in the regions of the UK and are used in the Investors Chronicle/Hillier Parker Rent Index and the Healey and Baker Rental Growth Index, for instance. A summary from Morrell (1991) shows the different performance measures in use in 1991 in Table 10.7.

Sector correlation

To maintain the risk of the portfolio at the desired level then the beta should equal 1. There is no advantage in diversifying across different property sectors as opposed to within one sector. The reason for diversification across sectors in property is a hedging strategy, to take advantage of any hypothetical changes and to cope with illiquidity. An analysis of property investment performance across property sectors has been provided by Jones Lang Wootton over a long period and is contained in Table 10.8.

Table 10.8 *Average returns and risk for property 1961–81*

Sector	Average return	Standard deviation
Industrial	17.4	9.5
Retail	14.6	11.8
Industrial	14.1	11.0

Source: Jones Lang Wootton, in Brown (1991).

This table shows that the highest returns were in the industrial sector but this also has the lowest risk. The reason for this anomaly is because of the regularity of abnormal profits in this sector over the period studied, and this factor is analysed by Brown (1991).

Smoothing in property indices is caused by serial correlation which exists in a time series of returns created from property valuations. This smoothing is introduced through two effects:

(i)   Valuers do not respond to new information on the valuation of property, this results in a conservatism to changing values;

(ii)   Valuations in an index are not carried out at the same time. The result is a moving average and smoother returns. In the series the standard deviation is understated and implies the property market carries less risk. It is possible to use an approach suggested by Blundell and Ward (1987) to remove the serial correlation.

The conversion of monthly or quarterly standard deviations to their annual equivalents thus presents few problems if the underlying returns are serially uncorrelated. If, however, the same procedure is used to convert serially correlated returns then the annual equivalent risk measure may be seriously understated. Brown and Matysiak (1996b) used continuous rates of return and provided an allowance for serial correlation in order to make the conversion workable over any interval.

Performance measurement

If investors are prepared to pay a premium for bearing risk then risk must play an important part in explaining performance. Hager and Lord (1985) questioned the ability of valuers to arrive at similar views. The function of valuation models is to establish whether individual properties offered for sale are under or overpriced relative to their equilibrium market value.

The common models are:

$$E(v_t) = f\left[\frac{E(a, r, g)}{\phi_t}\right]$$
$$= f\left[\frac{E(a, y)}{\phi_t}\right]$$

where $E(v_t)$ = expected value at time t, a = income, g = growth rate, r = required return, y = yield, ϕ_t = information available at time t.

The expected value of a property is thus a function of expected income, required return and growth; the latter two combine to give a yield, all subject to a subset of information which depends on location, lease structure, tenant, reversion, quality of building, voids, and so on. So there is a distribution of valuations dependent on the probabilities assigned to each variation.

Property performance measurement is required for a number of reasons: investors want to know how the portfolio is performing against various criteria; the performance is also required for comparison by portfolio managers with other competing portfolios. Brown (1991) suggests that the three reasons for undertaking performance measurement are communication, accountability and research. The objectives of performance measurement are thus external, to measure the performance against preset targets like the market or other funds, or internal, to measure the performance of investment properties against one another to balance the portfolio. Performance measurement seeks to answer questions like:

(i)   What returns have been achieved?
(ii)   How do the returns compare with other portfolios and assets?
(iii)   Has the timing of purchases and sales been good, for instance purchases in a rising market?
(iv)   Has the selection of investments been good, for instance the selection of underpriced property?
(v)   Can good performance be achieved consistently?
(vi)   What is the risk profile of the portfolio?
(vii)   How well diversified is the portfolio?
(viii)   How are the returns arising, from skill or by chance?

Performance measurement requires measurement of the rates of return; the choice of benchmark against which to make a comparison; and, the analysis of the results.

Measurement of returns

It is important to use the correct calculation. There is a difference between money-weighted and time-weighted rates of return and these arise when there are cash flows into and out of the portfolio. These approaches were discussed earlier in the chapter but are revised here using the equations and comments provided by Brown (1991):

Time-weighted rate of return (TWRR)

This is the geometric mean rate of return.

$$TWRR = \sqrt[n]{(product\ of\ internal\ rates\ of\ return\ for\ n\ periods)} - 1$$
$$= \sqrt[n]{(r_1 r_2 r_3 \ldots r_n)} - 1$$

Money-weighted rate of return

This is the internal rate of return of the portfolio (IRR).

$$\frac{V_n}{(1 + MWRR)^n} = V_1$$

where V_n is the value for the nth period
           V_1 is the value for the first period.

TWRR remains the same, but in a rising market MWRR > TWRR and in a falling market MWRR < TWRR. It is important in the analysis to differentiate between discrete and continuous rates of return:

Discrete rates of return $r_t = \dfrac{v_t - v_{t-1} + a}{v_{t-1}}$

Continuous rates of return $r_t = \ln\left[\dfrac{v_t + a}{v_{t-1}}\right]$

where v_t and v_{t-1} are values at the beginning and end of a period and a is the income received. ln is the natural logarithm.

Continuous rates of return are better. The MWRR is sensitive to timing so relative skill is not measured. The TWRR is neutral to timing so is more appropriate; if MWRR > TWRR the timing of the investment into the portfolio is good, if MWRR < TWRR then the timing of the investment into the portfolio is poor. The calculation of the TWRR involves two common methods, the exact method and the linked IRR. Using the exact method there needs to be a valuation every time there is a cash flow and these flows need to be precisely dated to produce an accurate measure. The calculation of the MWRR also requires the precise dating of cash flows but has the advantage that it requires only two valuations, at the beginning and at the end of the period. So TWRR = continuous time-weighted rate of return:

$$TWRR = \frac{1}{t_f - t_0} - \left[\ln\left(\frac{v_f}{v_0}\right) - \sum \ln\left(\frac{v_j + c_j}{v_j}\right) \right]$$

where c_j = nth amount of jth cash flow
v_0 = initial value of the portfolio
v_f = final value of the portfolio
v_j = value of the portfolio immediately before the jth cash flow
$t_f - t_0$ = time in years from beginning to end of period under consideration
ln is the natural logarithm

This procedure calculates the continuous IRR (MWRR) for each sub-period when a cash flow occurs and then takes the average by weighting each return by the length of its corresponding sub-period. Difficulties arise in the dating of the cash flow; valuation must accord with income flow and this is expensive. If valuations are carried out at less frequent intervals and timings change, then there are errors, so there is a need to use a linked IRR method. The linked IRR method divides the time-span over which the time-weighted rate of return is estimated into sub-periods. Knowing the value of the portfolio at the beginning and end of each period, together with the timing and amount of each of the cash flows into or out of the fund, it is possible to compute the IRR for each sub-period. The TWRR calculates by taking an average of the IRRs assuming they are continuously compounded on an annual basis; the weight used for each sub-period is the length of the period. Approximation does produce errors, these problems mean that, in practice, the mean fund concept is used. Using the mean fund concept, the value of the property is known at the beginning and end of each period but there are no valuations at the time of any intermediate cash flows. The principle involved is to measure the IRR adjusted for average capital employed during the period. The formula is:

$$r = \sum_i \frac{\left[M_{i_n} - M_{i_{n-1}} - C_{i_n} + I_{i_n} \right]}{\left[M_{i_{n-1}} + C_{i_n}(1 - t_i) \right]}$$

where M_{i_n} = capital value of property i at period n
$M_{i_{n-1}}$ = capital value of property at period (n − 1)
C_{i_n} = capital expenditure on property i at period n
$t_{i.}$ = timing of expenditure C_i as a proportion of total period from (n − 1) → n.

(Brown 1991).

The alternative to this is to substitute half the capital expenditure in the denominator rather than weight.

$$r = \sum_i \frac{\left[M_{i_n} - M_{i_{n-1}} - C_{i_n} + I_{i_n}\right]}{\left[M_{i_{n-1}} + \frac{1}{2}C_{i_n}\right]}$$

Both methods provide a money-weighted IRR which is used as a proxy for the TWRR. Errors in reported returns using this method could be in the region of 0.5% p.a.

Performance measurement is concerned with the difference between what was expected and what is achieved. By estimating market risk at the beginning of the measurement period using the basic risk measure, it is possible to establish the appropriate risk-adjusted rate of return which can then be compared with the realised return on the portfolio. The risk-adjusted return calculated in this way is the benchmark return. Abnormal returns equals actual returns less expected returns. Abnormal returns can be considered as a return due to selectivity and it can be split into two components, part due to diversity and the remainder due to net selectivity. Most of the abnormal returns from property portfolios can be attributed to net selectivity. We would expect this, as property portfolios tend to be poorly diversified; most of the return is dependent on selection ability or creative management.

Comparison of property indices

There are not enough sales to generate indices; the heterogeneity of the market means that data is thin when applied to property regions and types. Sales recorded over a year cover too broad an aspect of market movements; there are too few to provide a reliable index even at an aggregate level. The use of a valuation-based index is thus necessary but suffers from accuracy of valuation (the question as to whether values are a good proxy for prices was discussed in Chapter 6) and secondly the limitations of a smoothed time series. Valuations tend to generate a smoothed time series; it is possible to detect serial correlation in indices based on valuations. The reasons for this are that appraisals are based on comparable evidence of rent levels and yields which do not coincide with the date of valuations; also valuations in practice are not carried out on a single day. However, the evidence on which purchasers are making their bids is exactly the same as that of the valuers, and it seems reasonable to suggest that the market itself follows a smoother time series than that of equities, where synchronised and almost immediate information is available to dealers. A property index based on prices would be likely to demonstrate similar smoothing. The limitation imposed by the finding that valuation-based indices demonstrate serial correlation is, however, largely confined to the area of comparison of the volatility of property returns with those of equities or gilts. Here there is undoubtedly a danger that the use of valuation-based indices will suggest that property is a less risky asset than the other two asset classes. Asset allocation models based on comparisons of volatilities must therefore be handled with extreme caution. Analysis within the property market is less problematic. Other data limitations relate to property as managed assets. There is a need to record the capital and revenue expenditure drawn from accounting records and the times of cash flows must be recorded precisely to calculate accurate record on capital employed (Godson 1991). Commercial property indices record market trends not market movements. Abnormal performance is based on biased evidence unless the returns from the benchmark index and the subject portfolio are serially uncorrelated (Brown and Matysiak 1995). Two indices of monthly figures are published by IPD and Richard Ellis Investment. Comparison of each is based on the need to see if they are tracking the market. Other indices can be analysed on the criteria of average total returns, standard deviation and serial correlation. Where periods used by indices are comparable, the average returns are of the same order, although there is a significant difference in range in the annual standard deviation of returns of these indices, which have been computed on an annual basis, and those computed quarterly or monthly. A comparison of the average returns and standard deviations of property indices is shown in Table 10.9.

Table 10.9   *Comparison of property indices*

Index	Frequency	Dates	Average returns (% p.a.)	Annual standard deviation
WGS-Total returns	A	Dec 79–Dec 88	14.72	8.83
The property index	A	Mar 81–Mar 89	13.79	10.02
MGL-CIG index	A	Dec 78–Dec 88	16.04	7.14
JLW	A	Jun 67–Jun 68	15.23	10.13
HP	A	May 73–May 88	20.01	17.78
JLW	A	Mar 82–Dec 88	12.07	4.15
IPD	M	Dec 86–Dec 89	20.28	4.23

Note: See Table 10.7 for details of the various indices.
Source: Brown (1991).

The existence of monthly property indices helps to integrate property into the financial markets. The problems arise if fund managers decide to adjust the values of some properties in line with changes in the index; this will induce serial correlation. The problem of serial correlation as we have seen is for the standard deviation to be understated, thus underestimating risk. Brown and Matysiak (1996) have suggested the introduction of a real time index despite the fact there is in existence a wide range of existing indices. The real-time index is an index updated continuously, like a stock market index, reflecting the arrival of new information. Derivative markets in property are another reason for introducing the real-time index. These markets require volatility to encourage investors to take positions, and if current indices do not accurately monitor the true volatility of the property market then the introduction of new products will be limited. The real-time property index will be of considerable value in asset allocation, performance measurement and the assessment of the underlying value of traded paper assets like property unit trusts and property shares. Current indices which are most frequently used are those provided by IPD and Richard Ellis (RE). The IPD monthly index consists of over 2000 properties and has a market value of £4.4 billion. Although the IPD index is large, its distributional characteristics are such that the measures provide a tilted view of the market (Brown and Matysiak 1996). Furthermore, given the time it takes to collate the data, the release dates of the index numbers take place some time after the index reporting dates. The RE index is similar; currently available best practice reflects a trade-off between an acceptable sample and the administration involved in profiling the figures within an acceptable time scale. Also the IPD and RE monthly indices are highly smoothed; they are really tracking trends in the market rather than discrete changes. Thus changes in capital growth of the index are highly predictable. To construct a real-time index there are a number of approaches:

- indices using cross-sectional explanatory variables;
- indices based on underlying movements in the market;
- repeat sale/valuation regression-based indices;
- indices based on market derived valuation data.

A good index will be accepted by the market and monitor true property market movement; require minimal data input; be easy to produce; be impartial; not make use of confidential data; provide useful information for the market as a primary goal; be updated rapidly and be published quickly.

10.7 PORTFOLIO ANALYSIS

Portfolio analysis is not just a simple measurement tool but a powerful research technique; this guides strategic planning and operational management. Some of the decisions which will have to be made by the portfolio manager include:

(i)   the required balance between capital and income return;
(ii)   the acceptable level of risk;
(iii)   the allocation of funds to sectors and property types;
(iv)   the size of holdings;
(v)   the method of funding;
(vi)   the regional distribution of assets;
(vii)   the selection of individual properties (Godson 1991).

Godson suggests the analysis of a portfolio has been described as a simple logical sequence based on the appraisal of the pattern of investment in the portfolio and the assessment of the funds structure whilst then focusing on the results of the portfolio as a whole and its constituent parts in terms of good and bad performance. Such an analysis would sequentially deal with the matters in the following paragraphs.

Fund size and patterns of investment

This would include the timing and allocation of investment and factors such as whether there was passive or proactive management of the portfolio.

Fund structure

This is the asset mix in different sectors, the percentage of portfolio value in retail, office, industrial and other types compared to the index average (in this example the IPD average). Table 10.10 shows the IPD averages for September 1996.

Table 10.10   *IPD Index Composition*

	Retail	Office	Industrial	All properties
Total capital value (£m)	2154.4	1390.2	883.0	4449.8
Capital value (%)	48.4	31.2	19.8	100.0
Total rental value (£m)	169.4	109.5	82.0	363.0
ERV (%)	46.7	30.2	22.6	100.0
No. of properties	1251	586	413	2263
Proportion by capital value (%)				
Central London	4.9	24.4	0.0	10.0
Suburban London	7.3	10.6	10.9	9.1
Rest SE	22.9	29.8	43.5	29.1
East Anglia and SW	14.7	11.4	15.7	13.8
Midlands and Wales	19.1	7.8	14.1	14.6
North England and Scotland	31.2	16.0	15.9	23.4

Source: IPD (1996b).

Property type

This requires an analysis of property types in the portfolio and a comparison of the percentage value to the IPD average. For each property type the percentage of value in the fund is compared to the benchmark of the IPD portfolio. This breaks down property types into more detailed components such as single shops, shopping centres, retail warehouses, other retail, London offices, regional offices, industrial/office, warehouse, manufacturing, sites, and other. This analysis can then be extended to look at the regional distribution of assets. It can also be extended to look at the size distribution of investments which may be important in order to liquify assets. The medium sized ones will sell faster and are therefore disposed of quicker in difficult circumstances, leaving an imbalance of large properties which then needs to be addressed. The analysis can also be further extended to assess the level of development and construction activity in the portfolio and the balance of sites to completed investments.

Measures of performance

The criteria for the measures include:

(i)   performance in absolute and relative terms; relative to the market, relative to funds of a similar types or relative to other types of investment;

(ii)   results in nominal or real terms;

(iii)   short- or long-term performance;

(iv)   money- or time-weighted returns;

(v)   the volatility or risk associated with the fund's returns.

The annual results and long-term performance of the funds are shown in terms of total returns. For each year the range of returns can be shown and the funds performance mapped on it, as in Figure 10.4.

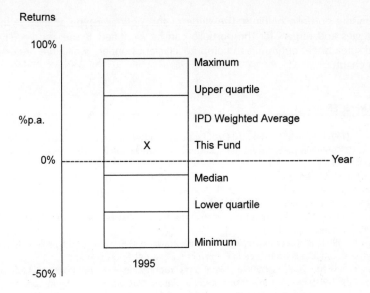

Figure 10.4   *IPD box plot display showing fund performance*

Volatility of returns

The total risk includes the systematic risk associated with the volatility of the market and the specific risk of the individual asset. By regressing the returns of the individual asset against those of the market the regression coefficients (betas) may be used as a measure of the systematic risk, and the standard deviation of the error terms about the regression line acts as a measure of specific risk. This principle can be extended to measure portfolio risk by regressing fund returns against those of the market. Portfolio risk will be minimised by the selection of an asset mix which reflects that of the market.

Diagnostic analysis

This involves a breakdown and analysis of the constituent parts of the contribution made to overall returns by the constituent parts; capital and income contributions, sources of capital growth, the impact of transactions and developments, and, the contribution of sector weightings to the fund's relative return (a comparison as to whether a good return had been due to the heavy weighting of the fund in the best performing sectors of the market – the sector components, or the above average performance of the fund's own properties in each sector relative to the market norm for that sector – the property component).

Further research

As discussed earlier in the book, Matysiak (1993) has suggested that a portfolio framework coupled with a scenario approach to general inputs is an effective approach to optimising portfolio holdings. The value of this optimiser-type analysis is that broad strategies and targets for the portfolio can be identified. Byrne and Lee (1994) have used spreadsheet optimisers to compute 'efficient frontiers' which are discussed in the next chapter.

REFERENCES

Baillie, R. (1997), 'New IPD Index Will Deal Property a Better Hand', *Estates Gazette*, 11 January, p. 40.

Barber, C. (1995) 'Property Investment: Returning from the Edge of the Abyss' *Property Week*, 20 April, p. 14.

Barter, S. L. (1988) 'Introduction', in S. L. Barter (ed.), *Real Estate Finance*, Butterworths, London.

Blundell, G. F. and Ward, C.W. R. (1987) 'Property Portfolio Allocation: A Multi-factor Model', *Land Development Studies*, vol. 4, pp. 145–56.

Brown, G. (1986) 'Property Investment and Performance Measurement: A Reply', *Journal of Valuation*, vol. 4, no. 1, pp. 33–44.

Brown, G. (1991) 'Property Index', in P. Venmore-Rowland, P. Brandon and T. Mole (eds), *Investment, Procurement and Performance in Construction*, E. & F.N. Spon, London.

Brown, G. and Matysiak, G. (1996a) 'A Real-time Property Index', *Estates Gazette*, 13 July, pp. 128–30.

Brown, G. R. (1991) *Property Investment and the Capital Markets*, E. & F.N. Spon, London.

Brown, G. R. and Matysiak, G. (1995) 'Using Commercial Property Indices for Measuring Portfolio Performance', *Journal of Property Finance*, vol. 6, no. 3, pp. 27–38.

Brown, G. R. and Matysiak, G. A. (1996b) 'A Note on the Periodic Conversion of Measures of Risk', *Journal of Property Research*, vol. 13, no. 1, pp. 13–16, March.

Byrne, P. and Lee, S. (1994) 'Computing Markowitz Efficient Frontiers using a Spreadsheet Optimiser', *Journal of Property Finance*, vol. 5, no. 1, pp. 58–66.

Byrne, P. and Lee, S. (1995) 'Is There a Place for Property in the Multi-Asset Portfolio', *Journal of Property Finance*, vol. 6, no. 3, pp. 60–81.

Catalano, A (1996) 'The Leaders of the Pack', *Estates Gazette*, 4 May, p. 44.

Dubben, N. and Sayce, S. (1991) *Property Portfolio Management: An Introduction*, Routledge, London.

Eichholtz, P. M. A., Hoesli, M., MacGregor, B. D. and Nanthakumaran, N. (1995) 'Real Estate Portfolio Diversification by Property Type and Region', *Journal of Property Finance*, vol. 6, no. 3, pp. 39–59.

Estates Gazette (1996a), 'Thumbs up for property', *Estates Gazette*, 20 April, p. 41.

Estates Gazette (1996b), 'Investment Funds Give Thumbs Up to Property', *Estates Gazette*, 28 September, p. 56.

Evans, P. and Jarrett, D. (1988), 'Institutional Investors' Intentions', *Estates Gazette*, 18 June, pp. 24–6.

Fairchild, S. (1992) 'Methods of Portfolio Analysis', Conference paper: *The Theory and Practice of Portfolio Analysis*, RICS, 23 October.

Godson, V (1991) 'Methods of Portfolio Analysis', in P. Venmore-Rowland, P. Brandon and T. Mole (eds), *Investment, Procurement and Performance in Construction*, E. & F.N. Spon, London.

Hager, D. P. and Lord D. J. (1985) *The Property Market, Property Valuations and Property Performance Measurement*, Institute of Actuaries.

Hall, P. (1983) 'Property Performance Measurement' in C. Darlow (ed.) *Valuation and Investment Appraisal*, Estates Gazette, London.

Hall, P. O. (1981), 'Alternative Approaches to Performance Measurement', *Estates Gazette*, 19 July, pp. 935–8.

Hargitay, S. E. and Sui-Ming Yu (1993) *Property Investment Decisions*, E. & F.N. Spon, London.

Hetherington, J. (1980) 'Money and Time-Weighted Rates of Return', *Estates Gazette*, 20/27 December, pp. 1164–5.

International Property Databank (IPD)(1996a) *Annual Index: 1995*, IPD Ltd.

International Property Databank (IPD)(1996b) *Monthly Index*, IPD Ltd., September.

Lizieri C. and Finlay, L. (1995) 'International Property Portfolio Strategies: Problems and Opportunities', *Journal of Property Valuation and Investment,* vol. 13, no. 1, pp. 6–21.

Markowitz, H. (1952) 'Portfolio selection', *Journal of Finance,* no. 7, pp. 77–91.

Markowitz, H. (1959) *Portfolio selection: Efficient Diversification of Investment,* John Wiley, New York.

Markowitz, H. (1991) *Portfolio selection: Efficient Diversification of Investment,* Blackwell, Cambridge, Massachusetts.

Matysiak, G. A. (1993) 'Optimising Property Portfolio Holdings: A Scenario-Assisted Approach', *Journal of Property Finance,* vol. 4 nos. 3/4, pp. 68–75.

Matysiak, G. and Venmore-Rowland, P. (1994) 'Appraising Commercial Property Performance', *Cutting Edge Conference,* RICS, 3 September.

Morley, S. J. E. (1988) 'The Analysis of Risk in the Appraisal of Property Investment', in A. R. MacLeary and N. Nanthakumaran (eds) *Property Investment Theory,* E. & F.N. Spon, London.

Morrell, G. D. (1991) 'Property Performance Analysis and Performance Indices: A Review', *Journal of Property Research,* vol. 8, pp. 29–57.

Newell, G. and Worzala, E. (1995) 'The Role of International Property in Investment Portfolios', *Journal of Property Finance,* vol. 6 no.1 , pp. 55–63.

Redman, A. L. and Manakyan, H. (1995) 'A Multivariate Analysis of REIT Performance by Financial and Real Asset Portfolio Characteristics', *Journal of Real Estate Finance and Economics,* vol. 10 no. 2, March, pp. 169–75.

Reid, I. (1985) 'A Response to Hager/Lord', *Estates Gazette,* 6 April, pp. 19–20.

Sharpe, W. F. (1964) 'Capital Asset Prices: A Theory of Market Equilibrium Under Conditions of Risk', *Journal of Finance,* vol. 19, pp. 425–42.

Sweeney, F. (1988) '20% in Property – A Viable Strategy', *Estates Gazette,* 13 February, pp. 26–8.

Sweeney, F. (1989) 'A Property Market without Frontiers', *Estates Gazette,* 2 September, pp. 20–2 and 30.

11 Portfolio Theory

11.1 INTRODUCTION: FINANCIAL THEORY

In the last 30 years a branch of applied microeconomics was developed and specialised into modern finance theory. It is important to understand some of the advances in this theory and how they underpin the principles of property investment. It is not within the range of this text to provide details of the theory or any extensive discussion and you are referred to one of the specialist texts. This summary, for instance, uses an approach from *Financial Theory and Corporate Policy* (Copeland and Weston 1988). The beginning of the separate development of modern finance theory was with Markowitz's work in the 1950s when he was developing portfolio theory, which is now applied in the selection of investment portfolios (Markowitz 1952, 1959). In addition, Modigliani and Miller were working on capital structure and gearing at this time. Modern finance theory emphasises the analytical and quantitative skills of management rather than a descriptive approach to the understanding of finance. However, you should appreciate that, in a text of this nature, a descriptive approach is appropriate at this level and thus the application of theory is limited. Copeland and Weston (1988) suggest that there are six seminal and internally consistent theories on which modern finance theory and investment is founded. These are listed below together with brief explanations. All these theories attempt to answer the common problem related to economics: 'How do individuals and society allocate scarce resources through a price system based on the valuation of risky assets'?

  (i)   Utility theory – the basis of rational decision-making in the face of risky
         alternatives – how do people make choices?
  (ii)   State preference theory
  (iii) Mean-variance theory and the capital asset pricing model
  (iv)   Arbitrage pricing theory
  (v)   Option pricing theory
  (vi)   Modigliani–Miller theorems
  (vii) Market efficiency

Utility theory shows how people make choices. State preference theory, mean variance theory, arbitrage and option pricing theory describe the objects of choice. Combining the theory of choice with the objects of choice shows how risky alternatives are valued. If correctly assigned, asset prices should provide the appropriate indicators for resource allocation. Modigliani–Miller theory asks 'Does the method of financing have any effect on the value of assets, particularly the firm?'

Utility theory

In Figure 11.1, utility theory suggests that investors maximise expected utility as their preferred outcome. This can be done by selecting the best combination of risk and return. The indifference curves for a number of assets (1–4) for a risk-averse investor are shown as functions of risk and return. $E(R)$ represents mean return. The standard deviation of return (often represented as σR) shows how expected return can vary and represents risk (see Figure 11.2).

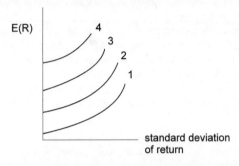

Figure 11.1 *Utility theory*

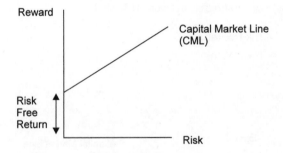

Figure 11.2 *The relationship between risk and reward*

State preference theory

Prices of investments represent the aggregate risk preference of individuals and firms. The development of state preference theory provides a means to determine the optimal portfolio decisions for individuals and the optimal investment rules for firms in a world of uncertainty. In a perfect capital market a set of prices for market securities can be derived. These prices are determined by:

(i)   individual time preference for consumption and the investment opportunities of firms;

(ii)   probability beliefs concerning pay-offs which are dependent on the assumptions of the scenarios possible at the time of the pay-off (state contingents);

(iii)   individual preferences toward risk and the level of non-diversible risk in the economy.

Mean-variance theory

This theory combines the theory of investor choice (utility theory) with the objects of investor choice (the portfolio opportunity set) to show how risk-averse investors wishing to maximise expected utility will choose their optimal portfolios. Measures of risk and return can be combined with probability to show the risk and return for a portfolio of risky assets, called portfolio theory.

From this theory two theoretical models can be derived that enable us to price risky assets in equilibrium; these are the Capital Asset Pricing Model (CAPM) and the Arbitrage Pricing Theory (APT). In the CAPM the appropriate measure of risk is the covariance of returns between the risky asset in question and the market portfolio of all assets. The CAPM is a useful conceptual framework for capital budgeting and the cost of capital. Although the model is not perfectly validated by empirical tests its main implications appear correct:

    (i)   that systematic risk β (beta) is a valid measure of risk;
    (ii)   that the model is linear;
    (iii) the trade-off between return and risk is positive.

The CAPM is shown graphically in Figure 11.3, where:

$$R_F \qquad = \text{risk-free return}$$
$$E(R) \qquad = \text{mean return}$$
$$\text{beta or } \beta \quad = \text{risk}$$

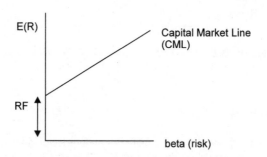

Figure 11.3   *The capital market line*

The CAPM says that the required rate of return on any asset is equal to the risk-free rate of return plus a risk premium. The risk premium is the price of risk multiplied by the quantity of risk. In the terminology of the CAPM, the price of risk is determined by the slope of the line, the difference between the expected rate of return on the market portfolio and the risk-free rate of return. The quantity of risk is called Beta (β).

Arbitrage pricing theory

Arbitrage Pricing Theory (APT) is more general than the CAPM discussed above. It suggests that many factors, not just the market portfolio, may explain asset returns. For each factor the appropriate measure of risk is the sensitivity of asset returns to changes in the factor. For normally distributed returns the sensitivity is analogous to the beta or systematic risk of the CAPM. APT can be applied to cost of capital and capital budgeting problems.

Option pricing theory

The theory assumes that all financial assets are contingent claims. For example, ordinary shares are really a call option on the value of the assets of a firm. Similarly, other securities may also be thought of as options. Option prices are functions of five parameters: the price of the underlying security, its instantaneous variance, the exercise price of the option, the time to maturity and the risk-free rate. All variables are observable except the instantaneous variance; this is the variation of the rate of return on the underlying asset – the holder of a call option will prefer more variance in the price of the stock as this will increase the probability that the price of the stock will exceed the exercise price and this will thus be of some value to the call holder. The option price does not, in this theory, depend on either individual risk preferences nor the expected rate of return on the underlying asset (options are discussed further in Isaac 1994).

Modigliani–Miller theorems

The cost of capital is used as a basis for a rate of return. This rate needs to be defined so that a project's returns can be assessed against required criteria. For a firm the main criterion is usually taken as whether the project improves the wealth position of the current shareholders of the firm. The original Modigliani–Miller theorems have been extended using the CAPM so that a risk-adjusted cost of capital may be obtained for each project. When the expected cashflows of the project are discounted at the correct risk-adjusted rate, the result is the net present value (NPV) of the project. In a world without taxes the value of the firm is independent of its capital structure. With the introduction of corporate and personal taxes the firm is unaffected by the choice of financial gearing. However, although no completely satisfactory theory has yet been found to explain the existence of an optimal capital structure, casual empiricism suggests that firms behave as though it does exist. Thus the estimated weighted average cost of capital can be calculated using a target capital structure. Empirical evidence suggests there is a gain from being geared.

Market efficiency

The hypothesis of capital market efficiency says that the prices of securities instantaneously and fully reflect all available relevant information. Capital market efficiency relies on the ability of arbitrageurs (dealers who capitalise on dealing in assets which are over- or under-valued on the market) to recognise that prices are out of line and to make a profit by driving them back to an equilibrium value consistent with available information. In an efficient market securities will be traded at correct prices. This provides confidence to investors and the best allocation of funds.

For a stock market to be perfect, the following conditions need to apply:

(i)   The market needs to be frictionless without transaction costs and taxes. No constraining regulations limiting freedom of entry and exit for investors and companies seeking funds. All shares should be perfectly marketable.

(ii)   All services in the market should be provided at the average minimum cost, with all participants price takers.

(iii) All buyers and sellers should be rational expected utility maximisers.

(iv)   There should be many buyers and sellers.

(v)   The market should be efficient from an informational point of view; information should be costless and received simultaneously by all individuals.

No market satisfies all these conditions. It is possible to relax some of the assumptions and still have an efficient market. The assumptions of costless information, a frictionless marketplace and many buyers and sellers are not necessary conditions for the existence of an efficient capital market. The capital market approach used in finance theory is important in respect of financial decisions made; the approach is only tenable if markets are efficient. If markets are efficient then the market prices will reflect the effects of decisions made in the market. The market price is the present value of future returns expected by the participants in the market discounted at a rate which reflects the risk-free rate and an appropriate risk premium. The stock market is essentially a secondary market — a place to buy and sell established securities. The influence of the market on sources of new capital is very high. The conditions necessary for efficiency in the capital markets are not as stringent as those defined by a perfect capital market. The efficient market requires that the dealing costs are not to be too high; that the relevant information is available to a largish number of participants and finally, that no individual dominates the market. If people disagree on individual judgements on future returns, this will lead to transactions. The sum of the transactions process will produce unbiased valuations in an efficient market. Such a market is a 'fair game' one. If it is a fair game then *ex-post* gains or losses cannot be predicted *ex-ante*.

Capital market theory

Capital Market Theory relates to the Capital Asset Pricing Model and to Arbitrage Pricing Theory. The theory is about discounting risky cashflows. The theory has a number of important aspects which are covered point by point:

(i)   How is risk measured?

The risk is related to an asset (we can use a company stock for ease of understanding). It relates to the variability of returns, measured by their variance or standard deviation. This is applicable to a single asset or security.

(ii) How is risk measured in a portfolio of securities?

Investors generally hold diversified portfolios; we are thus interested in the contribution of a security to the risk of the entire portfolio. Because a security's variance is dispersed in a large diversified portfolio, the security's variance/standard deviation no longer represents the security's contribution to the risk of a large portfolio. In this case, the contribution is best measured by the security's covariance with the other securities in the portfolio. For example, if a stock has high returns when the overall return of the portfolio is low and vice versa, the stock has a negative covariance with the portfolio. It acts as a hedge against risk, reducing the risk of the portfolio. If the stock has a high positive covariance, there is a high risk for the investor.

(iii)   What is the measure of diversification?

β (beta) is the appropriate measure of the contribution of a security to the risk of as large portfolio.

(iv)   What is the criteria for holding an investment?

Investors will only hold a risky investment if its expected return is high enough to compensate for its risk. There is a trade-off between risk and reward. The expected return on a security should be positively related to the security's Beta. Expected return on a security =

Risk-free rate + (beta×(Expected return on market portfolio - Risk-free rate))

The term in brackets is positive so the equation relates the expected return on a security as a positive function of its beta. This equation is the basis of the Capital Asset Pricing Model (CAPM). The Arbitrage Pricing Theory (APT) also derives a relationship between risk and return but not in this form. The APT draws basically the same conclusions but makes assumptions that the returns on securities are driven by a number of market factors.

Capital asset pricing model

$$\bar{R} = R_F + \beta(\bar{R}_M - R_F)$$

Where $\bar{R}_M$ is the expected return on the market, $\bar{R}$ is the expected return on the security, R_F is the risk-free rate, and Beta is the measure of risk. Beta is a measure of the security's sensitivity to movements in an underlying factor, a measure of systematic risk. Systematic risk affects a large number of assets and is also called market, portfolio or common risk. Diversifiable risk is a risk that affects a single asset or small group of assets; this is also called unique or unsystematic risk. The total risk for an individual security held in a portfolio can thus be broken down:

Total risk of individual security =
portfolio risk + unsystematic or diversifiable risk.

Total risk is the risk borne if only one security is held. Portfolio risk is the risk still borne after achieving full diversification. Portfolio risk is often called systematic or market risk. Diversifiable, unique or unsystematic risk is that risk which can be diversified away in a large portfolio.

Gearing and the cost of capital

The expected return on any asset depends on its beta. If a project has a beta risk similar to the firm then it can be used in the CAPM. If a project's beta is different then it should be used in assessing the return or else the average beta of similar projects in the industry. The beta of the company is determined by the revenue cycle, operating gearing and financial gearing (Ross *et al.* 1993).

The cost of capital is the weighted average of the firm's cost of equity and debt. If the cost of equity is r_S and the cost of debt is r_B the total cost of capital $=$

$$\frac{S}{S+B}r_S + \frac{B}{S+B}r_B$$

where S is the percentage of equity to total capital and B is the percentage of debt to total capital.

Operating gearing is based on the differences between fixed and variable costs; one cost alters with the quantity of output and the other does not. If there are higher fixed costs and lower variable costs then there is a higher operating gearing defined as:

$$\frac{\text{Change in EBIT}}{\text{EBIT}} \times \frac{\text{Sales}}{\text{Change in sales}}$$

EBIT $=$ earnings before interest and taxes. Operating gearing measures the percentage change in EBIT for a given percentage change in sales; operating gearing increases as fixed costs rise and variable costs fall (see Chapter 13 for a further discussion on operating gearing).

Financial gearing is the extent to which a firm relies on debt. A highly geared firm means it has to make interest payments regardless of the firm's sale or income. So this is a fixed cost of finance. The risk (β) of an asset or of a company is reflected by its cost of capital and is determined by its capital structure; thus:

The firm's $\beta = \beta$ of ordinary shares if the firm is only financed with equity, otherwise:

$$\beta \text{ asset} = \frac{\text{Debt}}{\text{Debt} + \text{Equity}} \times \beta \text{ debt} + \frac{\text{Equity}}{\text{Debt} + \text{Equity}} \times \beta \text{ equity}$$

β debt is very low and in practice can be assumed to $= 0$

Thus:

$$\beta \text{ asset} = \frac{\text{Equity}}{\text{Debt} + \text{Equity}} \times \beta \text{ equity} = \textit{Equity gearing} \times \textit{Risk of equity}$$

Because $\dfrac{\text{Equity}}{\text{Debt} + \text{Equity}}$ must be < 1 for a geared firm, it follows β asset $< \beta$ equity.

β in an ungeared firm must be less than the β of equity in an otherwise identical geared firm.

Efficient markets

Efficient markets suggest that current market prices reflect available information. If valuations are a good proxy for prices then valuations should reflect all known information. There are several forms of market efficiency: weak-form; semi-strong and strong. If markets are efficient, they can process the information available and the information is thus incorporated into the price of the security. Thus systems for playing the market cannot succeed, abnormal returns cannot be expected. The definition of the types of market depends on the information the market uses to determine prices:

- *Weak-form* – incorporates the past history of prices and is efficient with respect to these prices. So stock selections based on patterns of past stock price movements are no better than random choice.
- *Semi-strong form* – this market makes use of all publicly available information; this is reflected in the price of stocks, thus investors will not be able to outperform the market by using the same information.
- *Strong-form efficiency* – the market has available all information and uses all the available information that anyone knows about the stocks, including inside information to price the stocks.

Evidence from different financial markets supports the weak-form and semi-strong efficiency but not the strong form. Thus it is still not possible for the investor to use available information to beat the market; the share prices therefore conform to a 'random walk'. Efficient markets enable us to say something about the way assets should be priced. If the market is a fair game, investors should be compensated for that part of the total risk that cannot be reduced by diversification. An efficient market implies valuers are doing a good job impounding information into valuations (Brown 1991).

Capital structure

In a no-tax world, Modigliani and Miller suggest that the value of the firm is unaffected by gearing. But with taxes the firm's value is an increasing function of gearing. The expected rate of return is related to gearing, and before taxes:

$$r_S = r_O + \frac{B}{S}(r_O - r_B)$$

where r_S is the cost of equity, r_O is the cost of equity in an ungeared firm, r_B is the cost of debt; $S =$ percentage of equity, B is percentage of debt to total capital.

11.2 PORTFOLIO ANALYSIS

Quantitative measures can be allocated to concepts of risk and return. Returns are measured by expected cashflow returns but risks are measured by standard deviation and variance; the standard deviation is not actually risk but a surrogate for risk. An example of risk diversification can be seen in Example 11.1.

Example 11.1: Portfolio risk and return

		Opportunity A	Opportunity B
Return %	x	3 or 7	9 or 1
Probability of each return	$\bar{x}$	0.5	0.5
Expected return	x	5	5
Variance %	σ^2	4	16
Standard deviation %	σ	2	4

Variance $= \sigma^2$ and is the sum of the differences between the return and the expected returns squared and divided by the number of returns:

$$\sigma^2 = \frac{\sum (x - \bar{x})^2}{n}$$

For opportunity A,

$$\sigma^2 = \frac{(3 - 5)^2 + (7 - 5)^2}{2} = 4, \text{ thus } \sigma = 2.$$

For opportunity B,

$$\sigma^2 = \frac{(9 - 5)^2 + (1 - 5)^2}{2} = 16, \text{ thus } \sigma = 4.$$

Both opportunities have the same expected return but differ in risk. B has a greater variance than A and is therefore more risky. Rational decision-makers faced with two projects of the same return will take one with less risk. If the investor invests in both, let us assume that the projects are inversely correlated. Assume the decision-maker invests 2/3 of funds in A and 1/3 in B. The expected return on the portfolio is the weighted average of the returns on the individual opportunities, using the fraction of the funds in each as weights:

$$ER_p = \sum x_i (Ei)$$

where ER_p is the return on the portfolio, x_i is the proportion invested in opportunity i, and E_i is the expected return on opportunity i. $ER_p = 2/3(5) + 1/3(5) = 5$. The expected return is the same as if one had directly invested in A or B. However the risk of the portfolio is reduced if A and B are inversely correlated. When A is a high return, then B is low and vice versa.

A high: $ER_p = 2/3(7) + 1/3(1) = 5$
B high: $ER_p = 2/3(3) + 1/3(9) = 5$

The risk of the portfolio is 0 ($\sigma = 0$).

Combining two risky opportunities, the decision-maker has achieved a risk-free return. The situation has arisen because the opportunities are inversely correlated (coefficient of correlation = −1) and the proportion of funds invested in each was determined on this basis. The effect is based on diversification and is an example of the statement that risk can be diversified away. For a single opportunity, it is necessary to consider the expected return and variance; for two or more opportunities, it is necessary to consider the expected return and variance; for two or more opportunities, it is necessary additionally to consider their interactive risk. This is covariance and this is discussed in greater detail later in the chapter. The analysis of investment using portfolio analysis assumes the investor's assets are a collection of different property assets. The key criterion is the relationship of one property asset to other property assets in the portfolio not the consideration of risk in respect of the single property. In the situation of an uncertain future, investment decisions need to look forward and thus have to consider expectations of return and risk. These two elements then have to be quantified. The key to quantitative analysis is to use the concept of expected return for returns and standard deviation (σ) or variance (σ^2) for risk. These latter measures are not risk in themselves but a surrogate for risk.

The concept that diversification leads to risk reduction is the basis of modern portfolio theory. This reduction occurs when the investment returns are not perfectly correlated. Perfect positive correlation of investments will look like Figure 11.4.

Perfect positive correlation

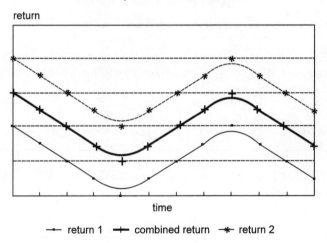

$-\!\!\!\bullet\!\!\!-$ return 1 $-\!\!\!+\!\!\!-$ combined return $-\!\!\!*\!\!\!-$ return 2

Figure 11.4   *Perfect positive correlation of investment returns*

Perfect negative correlation will be thus smoothing out the variations in return as shown in Figure 11.5. In practice it will be difficult to find investments whose returns are perfectly negatively correlated, because despite the nature of the investments, they will, as a group, tend to respond in the same way to external influences, either macroeconomic or related to the investment class more directly. Thus it is difficult to create a risk-free portfolio. Portfolio theory is essentially concerned with risk, the theory states that the risk relating to a portfolio of investments may be reduced through diversification.

Perfect negative correlation

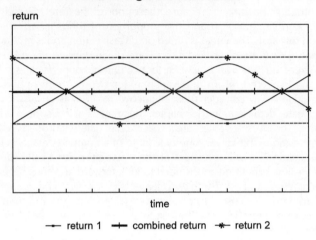

Figure 11.5 *Perfect negative correlation of investment returns*

An example of how this may occur is taken from Dubben and Sayce (1991):

Example 11.2: Diversification in a two-asset portfolio

Assume a two-asset portfolio with three investments to choose from. Investment *A* is a low-risk investment, *B* and *C* are both volatile. 50% of funds will be invested in each investment.

Expected return:

Investment	Return			Average return	Standard deviation
	Optimistic	Average	Pessimistic		
A	12	10	8	10	1.63
B	20	10	0	10	8.16
C	0	10	20	10	8.16

A risk-averse investor would choose investment *A*, the volatility measured by the standard deviation is the least. However, if the investor wishes to combine two investments, the returns will be equal to the average of the returns for each investment chosen.

Combined portfolio:

Investment	Return			Average return	Standard deviation
	Optimistic	Average	Pessimistic		
$(A+B)/2$	16	10	4	10	4.89
$(A+C)/2$	6	10	14	10	3.26
$(B+C)/2$	10	10	10	10	0

By any combination the average return remains unchanged, but by combining B and C the risk has been totally eliminated without any reduction in the average return. To combine in this way is obviously the optimal solution. Portfolio theory answers the questions of how to eliminate risk without loss of return.. The reason why risk is taken out is that the investments were negatively correlated. If the investments are positively correlated then diversification will not always reduce risk, but if returns are linked other than in perfect correlation then diversification can lead to some effective risk eduction. In practice it is difficult to find investments with perfect negatively correlated returns because no matter what the nature of the investment, nearly all will react to the economic forces in similar ways; it is thus regarded as very difficult to create a risk-free portfolio.

11.3   MODERN PORTFOLIO THEORY

Modern investment theory shows that investors make allocation decisions based on a trade-off between risk and expected return. The development of a quantitative theory took place in the 1950s when Markowitz wrote a number of articles and books on the subject of portfolio management. The theories were applied to investment in stock-market shares and bonds. Markowitz suggested that investors should select portfolios on the basis of mean and variance or alternatively mean and semi-variance. Semi-variance seemed the more plausible measure of risk but posed greater computational difficulties (Markowitz 1952). Portfolio theory assumes an investor is both rational and risk-averse and as such has a number of choices of investments to construct a portfolio. Investment opportunities involve risks and reward, and an efficient frontier can be constructed where combinations of investments will have a given level of risk and return and at the efficient frontier will be the best possible risk–reward combinations: see Figure 11.6. Markowitz showed that assets in a portfolio can be combined to provide an 'efficient' portfolio that will give the highest possible level of portfolio return for any level of portfolio risk as measured by the variance or standard deviation; these portfolios are thus connected to generate the 'efficient frontier' (Markowitz 1952, 1959). The approach which follows, used to explain the theory, is based on Lumby (1991) which is recommended as an initial text to deal with Modern Portfolio Theory.

Portfolios which have a combination below this efficient frontier will not be maximising the efficient trade-off, according to the investor's preference. Having established an efficient frontier it is now necessary to decide where along the frontier the investor will choose a portfolio. This choice will depend on attitude to risk and on whether the investor will wish to minimise risk at the expense of return or be prepared to take a

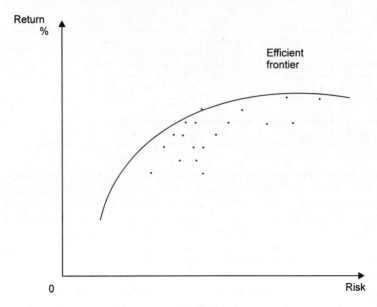

Figure 11.6   *The efficient frontier*

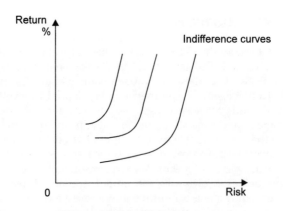

Figure 11.7   *Indifference curves*

higher risk to achieve maximum return. Institutional investors may tend to be risk-averse whilst private or specialist investors may be able to accept higher risk profiles. This risk/return trade-off is shown by the investor's utility function, which is an indifference curve shown in Figure 11.7. These indifference curves can be developed for the utility curves discussed in Chapter 9 and shown in Figure 9.2.

The curve represents a frontier of the highest acceptable level of risk for a given return. The curve to the left side is the most acceptable. The indifference curves are super-imposed on the efficient portfolio diagram and the optimal choice will be that at which the indifference curve touches the efficient frontier (point X) in Figure 11.8.

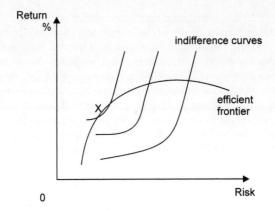

Figure 11.8   *Indifference curves and the efficient frontier*

Plotting the efficient frontier is very complex. To plot it, it is necessary not only to calculate future expected returns and variance but the correlation between each pair of investments. This measure is the covariance. To calculate the correlation between each pair, it is necessary to quantify the co-variance by the formula:

$$Cov_{AB} = \sum_{1}^{n} [A_r - \bar{A}_r][B_r - \bar{B}_r] P_r$$

where A_r = expected return

$\bar{A}_r$ = average expected return A
(the same for B)

P_r = probability of each return being achieved

The correlation between two investments is:

$$Corr_{AB} = \frac{Cov_{AB}}{\sigma_A \sigma_B}$$

If an investor's risk profile is known, then, given a number of investment opportunities with different risk/return profiles, it is possible to calculate the combination which will be optimal for the investor. Byrne and Lee (1994) have used a spreadsheet optimiser to compute the efficient frontier. Although the mathematics is complex for the calculation it is now possible to use a spreadsheet optimiser using matrix methods for the portfolio calculation.

The Capital Asset Pricing Model (CAPM) is an extension of Markowitz's mean-variance theory. CAPM is developed from Modern Portfolio Theory (MPT) but with three major additions: firstly, the concept of a risk-free investment is introduced; secondly, a notional market portfolio is used; and thirdly, an efficient market is assumed to exist. Investment portfolios can thus be constructed with a knowledge of expected outcomes and covariance using the arithmetic means of the component investments; the variances of those investments and the covariance of the expected returns. The expected return is found from a weighted average of investments that make up the portfolio; the risk of the portfolio is, however, less than the weighted average risk of constituents. This reduction of risk can be seen from the following portfolio consisting of two risky assets. The concept of both assets being defined as risky is important in this context because the analysis goes on later to discuss the introduction of a risk-free asset in the analysis. This portfolio consists of two investments A and B with a total investment assumed to be 1 with x being invested in A. Thus in a two-asset portfolio; the expected return is given by:

$$E(r_p) = xE(r_A) + (1 - x)E(r_B)$$

The risk is given by:

$$\text{variance } \sigma_p^2 = x^2\sigma_A^2 + (1 - x)^2\sigma_B^2 + 2x(1 - x)\text{Cov}(r_A, r_B)$$

Cov is the covariance of the returns between investment A and investment B; it measures the degree to which the variability of returns tends to move in the same way. Covariance can be positive or negative: Positive covariance indicating that the returns are moving in the same way and negative covariance in the opposite direction. The range is from $+1$ to -1 as with coefficients of correlation on which it is based; the nearer the covariance is to ± 1 the stronger the positive/negative covariance. The reduction in risk in the portfolio is the effect of the third term in the equation above, so the further from $+1$ (i.e. toward -1) the smaller will be this term's contribution to the risk of the portfolio. When this third term $= +1$ (perfect positive correlation between the two investments) then the portfolio risk is the weighted average of the component investments' risks and reduces as the value of this term reduces. The effect of risk and return and the composition of the portfolio can be seen from Figure 11.9.

When perfectly negatively correlated, the graph appears as a dogleg; when positively correlated, as a single line. Variations between appear as a nonlinear function between

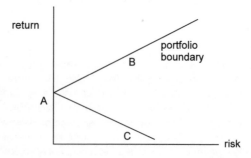

Figure 11.9   *Two-asset portfolio, assets negatively correlated*

the lines. Positions higher on the graph allowing greater return for the same risk are preferred. For instance take the case of two perfectly negative correlated investments. Investment combinations *AB* are preferred to *AC* because along *AB* increased returns are obtained for the same levels of risk. Options along the portfolio boundary *AB* are said to dominate *AC*. If we take a case between the perfect correlations, then the portfolio will be a nonlinear curve increasing its values from the origin, and the number of options in a two-investment portfolio will be represented by the umbrella shape as in Figure 11.10.

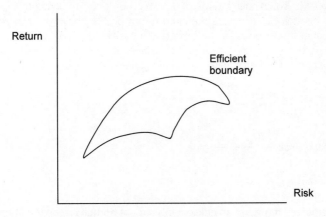

Figure 11.10   *Two-asset portfolio, general case*

The boundary to the north-west will be the efficient boundary here. The analysis shows that at the point where the utility curves of the investor touch the efficient frontier then the investor's utility will be maximised, and this has already been shown in Figure 11.4. The addition of a risk-free investment such as government bonds or stocks produces a linear relationship identifying the risk–riskless efficiency boundary which has been shown in Figure 11.1. The addition of borrowing and lending facilities extends the frontier; the borrowing rate will determine the position of the capital market line, the relationship between risk and reward. As the number of investments is increased in the portfolio so risk reduces, but it will do so only to a defined limit. This remaining risk is called non-diversifiable risk whereas the rest is diversifiable risk. Risk is analysed in the market by the Capital Market Line (CML). The slope of the CML is:

$$\frac{\left[E(r_M) - r_F\right]}{\sigma_M}$$

where:

$$E(r_M), \sigma_M, r_F$$

are the expected return of the market portfolio, the risk of the market portfolio and the risk-free return respectively. The slope of the CML is the risk/return relationship in the market. So if:

$$E(r_M) = 16\%$$

$$\sigma_M = 3\%$$

$$r_F = 10\%$$

$$\text{Market price of risk} = \frac{16\% - 10\%}{3\%} = 2\%$$

Thus the CML would have a slope of $+2$, and thus for every percentage point of risk taken, the investor can expect a premium return of 2% above the risk-free rate. An investor taking on 4% of risk in a portfolio will receive $10\% + (4 \times 2\%) = 18\%$. The return to a portfolio will thus consist of the risk-free return plus the market risk indicated above. So for an efficient portfolio 'j' (lying along the CML) the equation is:

$$E(r_j) = r_F + \frac{\left[E(r_M) - r_F\right]}{\sigma_M}\,\sigma_j$$

$$\text{let market risk } \frac{\left[E(r_M) - r_F\right]}{\sigma_M} = \lambda$$

$$\text{then } E(r_j) = r_F + \lambda\sigma_j$$

So the expected return on an efficient investment portfolio is the risk-free return plus the risk premium and the risk premium is the product of the portfolio risk and the market price of risk. This approach is only applicable to efficient portfolios lying along the CML. The market price of risk compensates the investor for additional non-diversifiable risk; no reward is paid for diversifiable risk.

11.4   CAPITAL ASSET PRICING MODEL

The CML leads us to conclusions that the capital markets display a linear risk–expected return relationship of the type:

$$E(r_j) = r_F + \lambda\sigma_j$$

This relationship, as we have seen, is not based simply on the total risk of individual investments (the variability of their possible returns) but on just one part of that risk, the non-diversifiable risk. The market will not provide a reward (in terms of an increased expected return) for that part of an investment's risk that could be eliminated by holding it as part of a well-diversified portfolio (Lumby, 1991). The relationship can also be applied to individual assets to develop a share price valuation model which could be used as an asset valuation model for property. The price model when used to look at the investment in shares of individual companies (or individual property investments), rather than portfolios, is called the Capital Asset Pricing Model (CAPM) and it is thus based on the conclusions of Modern Portfolio Theory (MPT). The model has a number of unrealistic assumptions, as did MPT, but it does appear adequate in its analysis. The analysis shows that different combinations of individual assets may be held in such a way that the highest possible return for a given level of risk may be achieved, known as efficient diversification. Readily available computer software, known as optimisers, can calculate how much of each asset should be held in order to achieve an efficiently diversified portfolio. To perform the calculations the necessary inputs are: expected return on each asset, the uncertainty of these returns as measured by the assets' variability (standard deviation) and the extent to which each pair of assets is expected to covary as measured by their correlation coefficient. Given these inputs it is possible to derive risk and return profiles for different portfolios of assets holdings by the use of optimisers (Matysiak 1993).

The Capital Market Line (CML) function provides an expression for the return that can be expected from an efficient portfolio investment with lending or borrowing at the risk-free rate of return. It can also be used to derive the expected return on an inefficient investment, such as a risky portfolio other than the market portfolio or, more importantly, an investment in the shares of a single company. To derive the expression for the expected return on an inefficient investment (e.g. on the shares of an individual company or a single property). Lumby (1991) uses the following approach:

The analysis of the risk and expected return of a two-asset portfolio that the risk is given by the expression:

$$\sigma_p = \sqrt{x^2\sigma_A^2 + (1 - x^2)\sigma_B^2 + 2x(1 - x)\sigma_A\sigma_B\varphi_{A,B}}$$

The risk-reduction effect of diversification results from the correlation coefficient; as we have seen, the further away the correlation coefficient is from $+1$, the greater is the risk-reduction effect. This expression shows that portfolio risk is made up of three elements. The first element, given by the term:

$$x^2\sigma_A^2$$

is the contribution that investment A makes independently to the portfolio. The second element:

$$(1 - x^2)\sigma_B^2$$

is investment B's independent contribution to portfolio risk. However, the third element:

$$2x(1 - x)\sigma_A\sigma_B\varphi_{A,B}$$

comprises two identical parts and represents the contribution made to the risk of the portfolio by the two investments jointly, determined by their tendency to covary. Because investment A covaries with investment B in an identical fashion to how investment B covaries with investment A, there are two identical parts to the third element. Within each part, the term:

$$\sigma_A\sigma_B\varphi_{A,B}$$

is known as the covariance of returns between investments A and B, and represents the non-diversifiable risk that each investment contributes to the portfolio. So when the correlation coefficient is $+1$, there is no risk reduction effect. This is because the total risk of each investment would be all non-diversifiable. So, when

$$\varphi_{A,B} = +1$$

the portfolio risk expression becomes:

$$\sigma_p = \sqrt{x^2\sigma_A^2 + (1 - x^2)\sigma_B^2 + 2x(1 - x)\sigma_A\sigma_B}$$

which simplifies to:

$$\sigma_p = x\sigma_A + (1 - x)\sigma_B$$

That is, the portfolio risk is just a weighted average of the risk of the portfolio components. However, when

$$\varphi_{A,B} < +1$$

then not all the total risk of each investment is non-diversifiable. Some of it can be diversified away, and so:

$$\sigma_p < x\sigma_A + (1 - x)\sigma_B$$

which is the risk-reduction effect of diversification. Furthermore, from the discussion of the capital market line, the expression for the expected return from an efficient portfolio was derived as:

$$E(r_p) = r_F + \lambda\sigma_p$$

where all the portfolio's risk (σ_p) consisted of non-diversifiable risk derived from the portfolio's holding of the market portfolio. From this expression can be derived an expression for the return on an inefficient investment, such as the shares in company S:

$$E(r_s) = r_F + \lambda\sigma_s\varphi_{s,m}$$

This is the general expression for the expected return from any non-'efficient portfolio' investment and is termed the securities market line (the SML). To summarise, the capital market line is similar to the securities market line. The CML indicates the return on an efficient portfolio and has two elements, the risk-free return and the risk premium for holding the investment. The risk premium is the product of the market price for risk and the risk taken on by the particular efficient portfolio chosen. The risk of the market portfolio is non- diversifiable by definition, so the risk premium is only for non-diversifiable risk. The security market line is the same. For instance, a company's share risk consists of two elements: the risk-free return and the risk premium. The premium is based on the non-diversifiable risk of shares in the company. Non-diversifiable risk is systematic risk, whereas diversifiable risk is unsystematic risk. The SML expression gives the return an investor should expect from any efficient investment given the level of systematic risk. This relationship is known as the Capital Asset Pricing Model or CAPM. The return on shares is the risk-free return plus a risk premium. The risk premium is derived from the market price of systematic risk and the systematic risk levels of shares. For company A:

$$E(r_A) = r_F + \left[\frac{E(r_M) - r_F}{\sigma_M}\right]\sigma_A\varphi_{A,M}$$

In this equation $E(r_M)$ could be the return on the FTSE market whilst r_F is the return on government stock. There are three elements which are difficult to calculate. These are:

$$\sigma_M, \sigma_A, \varphi_{A,M}$$

These are combined together and termed the beta value of the share, so:

$$E(r_A) = r_F + \left[E(r_M) - r_F\right]\beta_A$$
$$\text{where } \beta = \frac{\sigma_A\varphi_{A,M}}{\sigma_M}$$

which equals the systematic risk of company A divided by the total risk of a market portfolio (all systematic risk). The beta value is an index of the amount of the company's systematic risk relative to the market portfolio, indicating the degree of responsiveness of the expected return on the shares relative to movements in the expected return on the market. For instance, assume company A has the following:

$$\sigma_A = 10\%$$
$$\varphi_{A,M} = 0.7$$
$$\sigma_M = 5\%$$
$$\text{then } \beta = \frac{10\% \times (0.7)}{5\%} = 1.4$$

A has systematic risk of $10\% \times (0.70) = 7\%$, and as the market portfolio only has 5% of systematic risk, company A has 40% more systematic risk than the market portfolio, $7\% - 5\% = 0.4$ or 40% (Lumby 1991). Shares with a beta value > 1 will tend to out-perform the return on the market portfolio and low beta shares will underperform. This applies to rises and falls in price, and therefore high/low beta shares will exaggerate the market movements. Beta values indicate the expected change in a share's return relative to a change in the return on the market portfolio. They cannot indicate the expected return on a share relative to the expected return on the market portfolio; for this, one needs to know the risk-free return. The components of a portfolio, the beta values and expected returns of individual investments can be aggregated by a weighted average of the component investments. Beta can be measured by movements in share price relative to changes in the state of the economy. This relationship could be used to measure systematic risk or beta value. Historic returns on the FTSE, used as a surrogate for the market portfolio, can be plotted on a scatter diagram against the corresponding return on the shares of a particular company. A linear regression line (a line of best fit) is plotted through the data to provide a market model. The slope of the line is the volatility of shares relative to the return on a market portfolio. If the slope is greater than 1 then the shares are more volatile and the slope of the regression line represents beta. There is evidence to suggest that the value of beta is stable over the short term, certainly up to 5 years, although there is a tendency over time for shares with high or low beta to move to a beta of 1. This analysis of beta values for individual shares can be equally applied to the returns and volatilities of movements in returns of property investments.

The CAPM can generate the appropriate discount rate for a project, $E(r_{project})$, having taken into account the systematic risk of the investment project. This would be of the form:

$$E(r_{project}) = r_F + [E(r_M) - r_F]\beta_{project}$$

(Lumby 1991).

However, the CAPM is a single period return whereas the rate for an NPV calculation is a multi-time period rate. If the risk-free return and the excess over market return remains constant over the life of the project, then the single period CAPM model can be used safely in multi-time period analysis. If there is volatility in the excess market return, an annual yield to redemption on government stocks with the same period to maturity as the life of the project can be used as an estimate of the risk-free return. If there is a problem in identifying the value of a projects's beta then the beta value of the industry in which the project could be classified can be used as a surrogate for the beta value of the project. The industry beta value would simply be an average (weighted by market value) of the beta values of the firms within that industry. In projects there will be a need to identify the systematic risk. Systematic risk refers to the degree of sensitivity to macro-economic changes. The greater the degree to which cash flows are sensitive to macro-economic changes, the greater their systematic risk and the greater the project's beta value. The reverse is true of cash outflows; the lower the sensitivity of cash outflows to macroeconomic changes, the lower the degree of systematic risk.

REFERENCES

Brown, G. R. (1991) *Property Investment and the Capital Markets*, E. & F. Spon, London.
Byrne, P. and Lee, S. (1994) 'Computing Markowitz Efficient Frontiers using a Spreadsheet Optimiser', *Journal of Property Finance*, vol. 5, no. 1, pp. 58–66.
Copeland, T. E. and Weston, J. F. (1988) *Financial Theory and Corporate Policy*, Addison-Wesley, Wokingham.
Dubben, N. and Sayce, S. (1991) *Property Portfolio Management: An Introduction*, Routledge, London.
Hargitay, S. E. and Sui-Ming Yu (1993) *Property Investment Decisions*, E. & F.N. Spon, London.
Isaac, D. (1994) *Property Finance*, Macmillan, London.
Isaac, D. and Steley, T. (1991) *Property Valuation Techniques*, Macmillan, London.
Lumby, S. (1991) *Investment Appraisal and Financing Decisions*, Chapman & Hall, London.

Markowitz, H. (1952) 'Portfolio Selection' *Journal of Finance*, vol. VII, no. 1, March, pp. 77–91.

Markowitz, H. (1959) *Portfolio Selection: Efficient Diversification of Investment*, John Wiley, New York.

Markowitz, H. (1991) *Portfolio Slection: Efficient Diversification of Investment*, Blackwell, Cambridge, Massachusetts.

Matysiak, G. A. (1993) 'Optimising Property Portfolio Holdings: A Scenario-Assisted Approach', *Journal of Property Finance*, vol. 3, nos. 3/4, pp. 68–75.

Pike, R. and Neale, B. (1993) *Corporate Finance and Investment*, Prentice Hall, London.

Ross, S. A., Westerfield, R.W. and Jaffe, J. F. (1993) *Corporate Finance*, Irwin, Boston.

Sharpe, W. F. (1964) 'Capital Asset Prices: A Theory of Market Equilibrium Under Conditions of Risk', *Journal of Finance*, vol. XIX, no. 3, September, pp. 425–42.

12 Securitisation

12.1 DEFINITIONS

- **Securitisation** is the creating of tradeable securities from a property asset.
- **Unitisation** is also the creation of a tradeable security but the aim in this case is to parallel a return comparable to direct ownership.

This distinction may sound confusing but it is based on an analysis relating to debt and equity investments. To begin with, one must consider a single property rather than a portfolio. For a single property, if we divide the interest into a number of holdings, then we divide the equity, and this is unitisation. If we divide the interest and add debt securities, in the way a company may have shares and loan stock, this is securitisation. In fact securitisation is rather like imposing a corporate finance structure on a property, that is, a single-asset property company, but this approach simplifies matters because it is important to understand the objectives of securitisation and unitisation, which will differ from the operation of a property company. From the above, securitisation thus includes unitisation and can be used as a general term incorporating unitisation and this will be done here except when discussing securitisation historically or when the securitisation of the equity alone is considered. The distinction between securitisation and unitisation is shown in Figure 12.1.

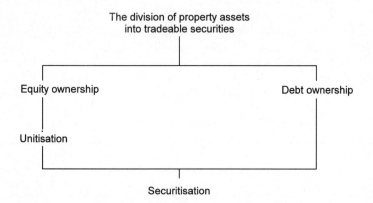

Figure 12.1 *Securitisation and unitisation*

The distinction of a single property is important to this analysis. If a portfolio of properties is considered, then unitisation is basically akin to property units, as in an authorised property unit trust, whilst securitisation of a portfolio would be a property company's shares and loanstock/debentures. A matrix of options will clarify this, as shown in Figure 12.2.

Securitisation

	Equity	Dept
One Property Asset	Unitisation Securitisation	Securitisation
Portfolio of Assets	Unit trusts Shares in a Property Company	Mortgage Backed Securities Loan Stock/Debentures in a Property Company

Figure 12.2 *Securitisation matrix*

A further analysis was used in the past by the Barkshire Committee (Barkshire 1986) related to the distinction between the unitised property market (in which the investor gets a percentage interest in the ownership of the property investment) and property income certificates (where an investor gets a percentage income that the investment produces). This distinction of structure is not very useful and confuses the elements of debt and equity. Nevertheless, as another structure for clarification, the framework is outlined in Table 12.1.

The vehicles originally conceived for unitisation and/or securitisation were:

- Single Property Ownership Trusts (SPOTs)
- Single Asset Property Companies (SAPCOs)
- Property Income Certificates (PINCs).

From Table 12.1 it can be seen that SPOTs, because they only deal with equity, are vehicles for unitisation whereas SAPCOs and PINCs can be securitised. To summarise, securitisation in general is the conversion of an asset into tradeable securities (these are certificates of ownership or rights to income). In the property context used here, securitisation is the conversion of a single property and the tradeable securities may be debt

Table 12.1 *Unitisation and securitisation vehicles*

Vehicle	Ownership		Securitisation of equity (Unitisation)	Securitisation of debt (Total Securitisation)
SPOTs	Direct	} Unitised property market	Yes	No
SAPCOs	Direct		Yes	Yes
PINCs	Income owned		Yes	Possible
				(Initially unitised but debt securities could be added.)

or equity based. Unitisation is included in securitisation but specifically refers to the securitisation of the equity interest. In its simplest form this unitisation will provide a share of the rental and capital growth with no obligation of management. This approach contrasts to property share ownership in the sense that, with unitisation, the investor selects specific property assets in which ownership is held rather than having to accept an existing managed portfolio. In this respect, Barter, writing in 1988, suggested the income yield which could arise from unitisation (which, because of its tax transparency will be the equivalent of investing directly in property) may be twice the dividend yield from property company shares (Barter 1988).

12.2 HISTORY

The pattern of investment in commercial property has changed substantially over the post-war period. There has been a collectivisation of savings and the property investment market has become dominated by the major institutions, the insurance companies and the larger pension funds. This has been less so in recent years where property investment and development has been funded by banks and by raising equity in property companies. Problems with the ownership of property investment have arisen because of the lack of liquidity in the market. There are difficulties in transferability; extended negotiations are necessary to achieve matched deals. Other investment media such as quoted shares have a centralised market and do not experience these problems. Further problems with illiquidity have been experienced in terms of the increasing size of investments available. A number of recent property developments are too large to fit neatly within the portfolio of existing institutions. Institutions would not commit a large proportion of their available funds to a single-property investment where this may be contrary to existing policy or where over-commitment to one project may increase risk within the portfolio related to the balance of the investments. The number of potential purchasers for a larger investment (say more than £20 million) is thus limited and this will affect the price of the asset. The problem of illiquidity will affect the demand, supply and value of large projects because of the way the asset is traded.

Other problems with large investments may relate to situations where a partial disposal is required or where developers may wish to retain the investment but recoup some of the project cost. There is also a lack of opportunity to spread investment portfolios by incorporating larger buildings which because of location and prestige may be attractive assets. Finally, there will be problems associated with the valuation of such properties by traditional methods where comparable evidence is lacking, and a bulk discount relating to size or a discount reflecting the lack of ease of transferability, especially important in the event of a forced sale, will need to be incorporated.

For a long period, indirect investment in property shares and unit trusts has been readily available to investors and to some extent has addressed the problems of illiquidity. For a long period until recently, property unit trusts (PUTs), where they were unauthorised, had not been able to invest in real property. Exempt unauthorised unit trusts could not under previous law (the Prevention of Fraud (Investment) Act 1958) be openly offered for sale to the public. The result is that only the main institutions had been involved in this form of investment. Property bonds existed but also suffered from illiquidity problems and some contained provisions which delayed repayment of investments for up to 6 months. Property share investment has been popular since the Second World War and the growth of property investment companies over this period has been a major factor in the property market. Property company share ownership suffers from three major difficulties. Firstly, there is a tax problem relating to double taxation of income (the shares are not tax transparent). Secondly, there is no purity of investment, in that the portfolios of properties can be large, varied and changing and it is therefore difficult to identify the asset ownership related to the share ownership. Finally, the net asset values are discounted on the stock market in respect of property investment companies, whilst property trading companies are valued on the assessment of future income probability, which may not readily relate to existing asset values.

As indicated earlier, three major vehicles had originally been suggested to deal with the problems. For simplicity these structures have been considered as single-asset property companies (SAPCOs), single-property ownership trusts (SPOTs) and property income certificates (PINCs). In the first two cases, the single-property vehicles are divided up on the basis of ownership of the asset. In the case of SPOTs, the interest is divided up into equity units which are identical; in the case of SAPCOs, the division is by securitisation, the layering of negotiable interests in the investment on a risk/reward basis and including debt as well as equity interests. Different interests are thus created in relation to the assets in much the same way as companies are financed through a variety of corporate funding techniques. Finally, PINCs differ from the previous two vehicles in that they provide ownership rights to the income arising from the investment rather than direct investment in the asset. Other vehicles which have been considered are property unit trusts (PUTs) and mortgage-backed securities (MBS) which are common in the USA.

Mortgage-backed securities had developed in the residential market originally. They enabled a Building Society or specialist mortgage lender to raise funds using a pool of mortgages as collateral, the strength of which meant that the issue received a high credit rating. MBS allows the issuer to repackage their mortgage assets for sale in capital markets, freeing up capital for additional loans. Subsequent to the Building Societies Act 1986 the Building Societies have been committing funds to the commercial property sector, although there have been some bad experiences in their investments. Despite this, the presence of Building Societies in the market may accelerate the take up of MBS issues (Savills 1989).

Objectives of securitisation: a summary

Securitisation:

(i)   Provides for liquidity in the market and, associated with this, the need to keep values up by increasing the size of the market and speeding up the time taken for transactions.

(ii)   Assists in the diversification of risk. Securitisation provides a range of opportunities to have a mixed portfolio and to invest in different development proposals more precisely. Securitisation offers the ability also to invest in debt and equity security, in themselves having different risk profiles.

(iii)   Provides the opportunity to avoid the management of property which occurs with direct ownership and to leave the task to the more skilled and experienced.

(iv)   Provides tax transparency and avoids the double taxation which exists with property company shares.

(v)   Provides a more flexible financial structure to encourage debt instruments and thus gearing situations, making the funding market more flexible for the sale of the developer's interest or part interest and provides a better opportunity for refinancing development funds with long-term investment.

12.3   PROBLEMS IN THE DEVELOPMENT OF SECURITISATION

A number of statutory and legal constraints have stalled the development of securitisation in the property field. These basically relate to legal ownership, financial disclosure, tax and share listings.

Legal ownership

The Law of Property Act 1925 basically reduces the number of legal owners to four. Where there are more than four, then separation must be made between legal owners and those receiving the beneficial interests. If those joining together form a trust for sale or a partnership then both of these structures have important limitations and, in respect of the latter, the risk of unlimited liability. Really, only a company or a unit trust, where the asset is held by trustees on trust for members holding units, are suitable vehicles for securitisation of a single property (RICS 1985).

Financial disclosure

Before 1986 the Prevention of Fraud (Investments) Act 1958 prevented dealings of the public in unauthorised unit trusts. The Department of Trade and Industry would not authorise trusts made up of property assets because of the perceived illiquidity and lack of diversification of interests. The Financial Services Act 1986 introduced 'collective investment schemes' for property, and authorised property unit trusts (APUTs) have now been established. Single-property schemes could now be promoted under this legislation.

Taxation

Tax transparency is defined as the ability through securitisation to achieve the same level of net after-tax return as would be achieved through direct ownership. The primary objective of securitisation was to avoid the double taxation that shareholders in property companies suffer. This relates to both capital gains tax and income tax and is discussed in Chapter 3.

Share listing

The Stock Exchange would not permit the listing of single-property vehicles and thus there was no ready market for the shares. In May 1987 the International Stock Exchange permitted listing of single-property schemes.

12.4 THE VEHICLES

Single-property ownership trusts (SPOTs)

This was envisaged as a vehicle rather like an existing property unit trust but would involve investment in a single-property asset. The trust would be authorised and would enable multiple direct ownership in a property or financial terms no less favourable than those available for single direct ownership in property (RICS 1985). SPOTs involve a trustee holding the legal title to the property, with the trust deed providing details of the operating framework for the scheme. Income accruing to the trust as a result of rents received passes straight to the investor (unit holder). Rental income is secured by the covenant of the tenant and by the form of lease agreement. Thus the vehicle is a trust which could be floated on the stock exchange; management is through trustees who retain the ownership; there are no debt interests. SPOTs require the law to be changed to achieve tax transparency; the Inland Revenue classed them as unauthorised unit trusts and thus liable to corporation tax (Savills 1989). In 1988 the Treasury confirmed it would not grant SPOTs tax transparency and thus the vehicle is in abeyance (Barter and Sinclair 1988).

Single-asset property companies (SAPCOs)

A SAPCO is a company structure rather like a property company, only in this case the company holds a single property rather than a portfolio. SAPCOs can be listed on the Stock Exchange but suffer from the same problems as a property company in that they are not tax transparent. SAPCOs are the best examples of complete securitisation, and an example is given later. SAPCOs fulfil the opportunities of securitisation by providing various financial instruments such as debt, preferred equity and equity secured on a single asset, in order to access the widest possible pool of investment capital and thereby enhance liquidity through tradeability. Layers of securities of different characteristics are created to appeal to different classes of investor who will be looking for different returns and notes (Gibbs 1987, p.350).

Property income certificates (PINCs)

A PINC is a tradeable share. The share represents a right to the income arising from rent and capital appreciation of the single-property asset. It has the benefit of tax transparency and the ability to be listed. Debt instruments can be issued to create gearing. A PINC is a composite security encompassing two elements:

    (i)   the right to receive a share of the property's income;
    (ii)   an ordinary share in a company which exercises control and management.

   A PINC is a limited liability equity share in a tax-transparent single-asset property company. The structure for a 80% flotation, where the developer or vendor retains 20%, is shown in Figure 12.3.

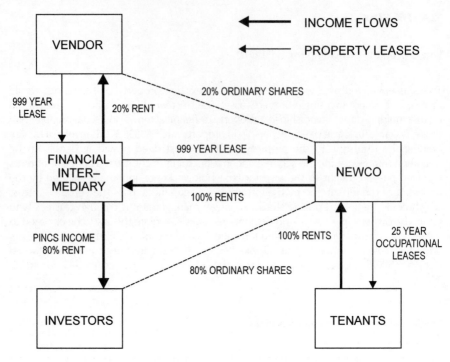

Figure 12.3   *PINCs Structure*

Source: Orchard-Lisle (1987).

12.5   ISSUES IN SECURITISATION

Problems of Valuation of the Units

The units may change hands at a discount to the asset value as perceived by the valuer and will thus mirror the market movement of shares in property investment companies. The possibility of discount runs counter to the views of the organisers of the market, who suggest that there should be a premium on the price of units because of liquidity. By taking the whole and dividing it into smaller units, the increased liquidity should avoid any bulk discount on the whole and thus trade at a premium to the value. The initial value may vary; the issue price will reflect the market conditions. There will be problems of revaluation in the sense of when these should take place and by whom. The significance is that, like company accounts, there needs to be an adjustment of market value. The valuation here will be the assessment of profit and net asset value (NAV) through the company accounts. Periods for revaluation could be 1 year or 5 years. There may be problems for the valuation profession in the sense that there may be less need for valuations of properties generally but still the need for these revaluations. The basis of valuation may be different here to reflect the discount and the increased liquidity.

Problems of management of the units

The managers of the units will need to make decisions relating to the sale of the asset, refurbishment and financial management. For instance:

(i)   They will need to provide maintenance and sinking funds.
(ii)   They will need to decide on any programme for refurbishment.
(iii)   They will have to provide guarantees to perform and to protect the investor's interests.

Problems of marketability

The problems of marketability will depend on demand, premiums and discount trading, the size of the market and alternative investments including property shares.

Size and membership of the market

There needs to be a critical mass for the market to operate properly. The net worth of the members of the market will need to be decided both for market-makers and others. The initial fee and subsequent membership fee will need to be decided. There needs to be a diversity of investors, otherwise the market can be manipulated by one party. The surveyor will have a role here in the provision of financial services. The initial number of properties will have to be agreed. There is a debate as to whether freehold or long-leasehold properties should be unitised.

Conflicts of interests and insider trading

Rent review considerations involving the tenant and landlord's surveyors may give rise to conflicts of interest. The unit holders may be tenants, as well, of buildings which are securitised or comparable buildings from which market evidence in negotiations can be derived. 'Chinese Walls' (which establish clear divisions of information so that inside information obtained in one area of the firm cannot be used elsewhere) will need to be established within firms to prevent transactions on the basis of insider information; what constitutes insider information may be difficult given the nature of the property market. Disclosure of property information, including structural defects and dangerous materials, will be necessary.

12.6 EXAMPLE OF SECURITISATION (from Gibbs 1987)

Case study: Billingsgate, Lower Thames Street, EC2
Joint developers: London & Edinburgh Trust
                         S & W Berisford

    £20 million raised internally   (30% construction cost)
    £44 million raised on market   (70% construction cost)

The money raised on the market was non-recourse borrowing from a syndicate of banks. Finance for the construction and letting was to be repaid on resale or refinancing.

Valuation:
Let to Samuel Montagu on a 35-year lease with 5-year upward-only reviews.

Rental	£ 5 000 000
Yield	6.2%
Capital Value	£79 000 000

London & Edinburgh Trust sold out interest to S & W Berisford who in turn did not wish to hold a £79 million investment.

Securitisation solution:
3 layers of security:

(i)   *Debt security*

£52.5 million of $6\frac{5}{8}$% deep discounted first mortgage bonds expiring 2006 offered at 32.5% discount. (This represents a gross redemption yield of 10.6% which was 1.15% over the yield provided by Treasury 13.5% 2004–2008, the equivalent gilt.) This raised £35.5 million.

(ii)   *Preferred equity security*

£25.8 million cumulative preferred equity shares of 1p each at a price of 100p per share. Shareholders were guaranteed 30.2% of the rental income to be paid as dividends (on the basis that the current rent showed a 5.9% return). The gross dividend rises to 20% p.a. by year 2000 from the initial 5.9%.

(iii)   *Ordinary equity security*

The rest was kept as ordinary shares. These are highly geared. There was no dividend entitlement till the next review. The shareholders get a 69.56% increase in rental and capital growth. The value of the shares is £79 million, less debt and preferred equity = £17 million.

   There was little investor interest in the shares despite the booming market at the time in City Offices and the massive leap in rents expected at the next rent review. In September 1988, Berisford made a bid for the outstanding preference shares and now controls more than 50%. The Billingsgate experience may have damaged prospects for further SAPCOs (Savills 1989).

12.7   LIQUIDITY AND SECURITISATION

The vehicles discussed above have floundered for a number of reasons: the inability to be listed and problems of developing a market that is rapidly changing. Securitisation does offer an approach to counter the illiquidity of the market and will return once the market generally has picked up. Securitisation and liquidity will provide certainty about market price but will mean that investors will no longer have direct control.

The RICS in their research have provided the following advantages for holding a single property in multiple ownership:

(i)   to stimulate investment in large urban renewal projects;
(ii) to enable small investors to enter the market;
(iii) to create a vehicle which would supplement the involvement of the major institutions in the market;
(iv) to introduce liquidity to the benefit of all classes of investor;
(v)   to open a wider range of property investment opportunities and enable an investor to spread risk through a tax neutral vehicle (Maxted 1988).

A survey by Rydin *et al.* (1990) asked a number of financial institutions about the prospects for a unitised property market. The respondents considered unitised property as a substitute for direct property holding and not as a substitute for equities or gilts. The need for an active market was stressed before they would become involved. The main criteria stated for the emergence of an active unitised market were:

(i)   Choose quality properties;
(ii) Install active management to ensure capital growth.

In the analysis 43% considered the opportunities for gearing unimportant, thus were satisfied with a unitised rather than a completely securitised market (Rydin *et al.* 1990). The response of those surveyed as to what they believed unitisation acted as a substitute for in alternative investments, is shown in Figure 12.4.

Christopher Jonas (1995) has suggested that:

Illiquidity is one of the major drawbacks inherent in property investment. At a time when the pensions and life regulatory regime is increasing valuation and solvency requirements, property does not sit comparably in many portfolios. (Jonas 1995, p. 52)

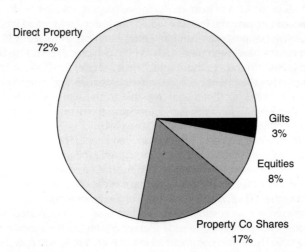

Figure 12.4   *Unitisation: Substitution of other investments (%)*

Source: Rydin *et al.* (1990).

Jonas's view is that a paper security should be provided to enable institutional investors to be exposed to the market without the associated cost of direct ownership, and he suggests the principle criteria to judge the success of any new security would be:

- one which gives the owner as nearly as possible a share in the whole of the rental income and the whole of the capital value of a building;
- one which can be issued within existing tax and regulatory rules; and
- one which would quickly attract a following among market-makers so that a fully liquid market was available to investors daily through third-party market-makers.

At the end of 1995 it was estimated that there were over 400 commercial properties in the UK each with a capital value above £40m, a combined value of around £30 billion or one-seventh of the total value of UK commercial property. Investors cannot generally afford to buy these investments, and those who can are worried about aspects of liquidity when alternative asset classes offer better opportunities. Regulations under the Pensions Act 1995 may provide a further disincentive to fund investment in property. A minimum funding requirement under the Act will mean that funds must match assets and liabilities closely. The proposed basis for valuing the liabilities is by reference to the yields on UK equities and gilts, depending on the maturity of the pension scheme. Property does not appear to figure highly in the arrangements for these regulations (Goodwin 1995). The need for liquidity has become even more apparent, and a number of approaches have been suggested which involve new types of stock-exchange-quoted property investments and derivative financial products which base their returns on indices of property market performance. Commercial property investment trusts have also been considered, with tax breaks where investors buy pools of property assets rather than single buildings. Unlike property companies, investment trusts are exempt from tax on capital gains, so tax-exempt investors such as pension funds can swap buildings for shares without a tax penalty. The model for the initiative is based on the US Real Estate Investment Trust market which is valued at £38 billion and is used as a way for pension funds in the USA to gain access to the property market. A similar market in the UK is restricted because the Treasury would not historically extend investment trust benefits to commercial property (London 1996). Attempts to recreate US investment trusts by other means have been tried, such as PUTs (which can be quoted on the Stock Exchange and benefit from tax advantages). These vehicles, however, are not ideal for commercial property investment because unlike companies and investments trusts the unit trust is open-ended, so the capital available to the fund expands and contracts depending on the demand for units; if investors want to sell units when property values fall then it can be difficult to sell buildings to raise cash.

In 1995 the Investment Property Forum produced a report on property securitisation. In it they argued for the establishment of a securitised property market. By comparison with successful securitised markets in the USA, Australia and Belgium, they showed the relative failure of successful securitisation exercises in the UK. In a serious lobbying of the government they, the RICS and other members of the property profession were insistent that in order to create a successful market, an instrument was required which was tax neutral, tradeable and available to a wide market. In the US, the market in Real Estate Investment Trusts (REITs), which commenced in the early 1960s, was now a sizeable one, as was the market in Australia for Australian Listed Property Trusts (ALPTs) (Investment Property Forum 1995). The report suggested that securitisation would address the con-straints of the direct property market in terms of liquidity, divisibility, problems of management and costs, price signalling (a traded securities market place with real time price information provides immediate indication of value and performance), risk control, information transparency, investment timing, diversification and breadth of investment opportunity. The recommendations of the report were:

- An approach should be made to HM Treasury to seek Government agreement to accepting income and capital gains tax neutrality for a Stock Exchange tradeable pooled property vehicle. Such an approach needs to have the widespread support of the property industry through its representative bodies and institutions.
- The approach to HM Treasury will need to be accompanied by an assessment of the likely tax revenue implications of the introduction of securitised property vehicles. A study undertaken by the RICS in 1993 in relation to single properties concluded that the introduction of tax transparency for SPOTs would be revenue positive in overall terms.
- The existing DTI regulations which apply to single properties will need amendment to encompass pooled property vehicles.
- An approach should be made to the London Stock Exchange to permit the existing rules relating to the listing of single properties to be extended to pooled securitised property vehicles.
- The precise vehicle/vehicles which might be most suitable which must address the needs for tax neutrality, Stock Exchange promotion, trading and regulation, should be left open at this stage for discussion with HM Treasury. Such vehicles could involve:
  - The extension of the OEIC (Open ended investment company) regime to include tax neural and listable direct property trusts and,
  - The extension of the criteria which govern Investment Trusts to include direct property.

The definitions of securitisation used in the report are summarised in Box 12.1.

In 1996 the Government changed the rules to allow both Authorised Property Unit Trusts (APUTs) and Housing Investment Trusts (HITs) to trade on the stock market. The RICS has written subsequently to the Treasury to set out its concern that other countries, particularly Belgium and the Republic of Ireland, have securitised vehicles and that, in the absence of appropriate vehicles in the UK, a securitised market in UK property could be run from Brussels, Dublin or elsewhere (CSM 1996).

Robinson (1996) has argued that portfolios are undiversified in property because the investment vehicles which would allow agents to cheaply, quickly and conveniently modify their exposure to property (and thus allow an efficient transfer of risk from those who want less exposure, like households, companies and banks, to those who want more such as institutional investors), do not exist. He argues that current investment vehicles offer only a limited exposure to the property market and says that Real Estate Investment Trusts in the USA have limited use because:

- certain classes of property (e.g. residential) may not be held by investment companies;
- prices of REITs are correlated with the stock market rather than the property market thus rendering them ineffective as hedging instruments.

DEFINITIONS OF SECURITISATION

Property Equity Securitisation – The conversion of property assets into tradeable paper securities. Property Unitisation refers to vehicles based on a unit structure (e.g. property unit trusts) rather than securities.

Property Debt Securitisation – The conversion of property assets into tradeable paper debt securities, now commonly applied to property debentures (a long-established instrument), zero coupon and deep discount bonds, residential property mortgages and, more recently, the refinancing of portfolios of commercial property mortgages into rated tradeable paper and the securitisation of income-producing portfolios through a financial instrument.

Debt/Equity Instruments – Tradeable paper debt securities which provide investors with an option at a future date either to redeem their debt securities for a predetermined cash sum or to convert them into new equity shares in the company owning the underlying property assets.

Synthetics and Derivative Instruments – A *synthetic* is a tradeable instrument which is designed to track the performance characteristics of a benchmark index on a one-to-one basis.

A *derivative* is a tradeable instrument which comprises either a futures contract or an option agreement to buy or sell a given commodity at a pre-specified date in the future at a predetermined exercise price.

A *futures* contract is a legally binding contract where the parties to the transaction are bound to give and take delivery of the commodity (or a cash settlement when an index or synthetic is involved) at the expiry date. Usually these contracts are tradeable during the life of the contract.

An *option* contract is similar to a futures contract, but differs in that the purchaser of the option to buy (or sell) has the option and not the legal obligation to buy (or sell).

Box 12.1   *Definitions of securitisation*

Source: Investment Property Forum (1995).

As an alternative, the establishment of a market in property derivatives (futures, forwards, options, etc.) directly linked to property price indices is suggested, thus assisting in portfolio construction because of an inverse correlation with bonds and low correlation with equities. Investors could lay off risks in many ways using derivatives, and property companies could hedge their exposure. Property companies are often trapped between high gearing, rising interest rates and falling asset prices in an illiquid market; property derivatives could be used to hedge these exposures and thereby reduce the equity capital required to support any project. Institutional investors could modify their exposure to property without the costs and uncertainties of transacting in the 'cash' market. The inclusion of commercial property results in a better risk-return trade-off. The advantages of derivatives are summarised as:

- Transaction costs would be lower.
- The time of execution of transactions with derivatives could be chosen with more precision by the investor. Even those investors who prefer strategic holdings of physical property would find derivatives useful, as they would allow the investor to maintain exposure to property until transactions in the physical market could be effected.
- Because they derive from broad-based property indices, derivative securities would offer property investment in a diversified form, even for a limited outlay.
- They remove the need for property management.

In 1994 BZW launched its Property Income Certificates (PICS1), a simple instrument which pays a return pegged to the income and returns registered by Investment Property Databank's index. The first issue of £150m attracted 43 investors, composed of UK pension funds, insurance companies and property companies as well as some overseas buyers. The second version of PICS (PICS2) was launched in July 1995 and dealt with two of the drawbacks of the first launch. PICS1 could not be bought and sold on the open market although Barclays did undertake to arrange trades on a matched bargain basis. PICS2 was only be sold to professional investors like financial institutions, but can be subsequently traded by a listing on the London Stock Exchange as a Barclay debt security. The second problem with PICS1 was that it carried a 12% discount on the income return, and investment managers, worried about the performance relative to the IPD index, considered this to be too large a discount to the index. PICS2 pays the full return registered by IPD, less an annual charge of 0.15% of the capital value for expenses (Catalano 1995). BZW has now launched a forward contract based on the Investment Property Databank's annual capital growth index called PIFs. These are over-the-counter (OTC) forward contracts, where one party agrees to buy and another agrees to sell an asset (the IPD Annual Capital Growth Index) at a certain time in the future for a certain price. The contract is settled at the expiry date, one or two years on, by a cash payment, made between the two counter- parties, according to the percentage rise, or fall, in the IPD index. Barclays Bank will initially act as a counter-party to all PIF transactions and BZW market-makers will quote bid/offer prices on Reuters. A futures contract is simply an exchange-traded forward contract (Catalano 1996b).

This requirement for liquidity in the investment market was shown in a recent survey by solicitors Cameron Markby Hewitt (1996). Liquidity was a major concern of respondents to the survey, who suggested the following provisions to deal with liquidity, (in order): having a central property register; up-to-date 'log books' to be maintained by vendors; shorter and less complex occupational leases; and sellers to provide detailed warranties and a full certificate of title. Log books should include not only management information such as tenancy schedules, payment records, arrears, service charge accounts, progress of rent reviews and turnover rent computations, but also copies of summaries of the title and occupancy documentations (Bourne 1995).

Amongst the new products required in the market by respondents to the Cameron Markby Hewitt survey, were, in order:

(i)   Securitisation or unitisation of property with full tax transparency.
(ii)   Tax-effective products which enable the property investor to generate funds in other areas without disposing of the property (e.g. a forward sale of rental flow or capital allowances).
(iii)   Property investment companies which pursue full benchmarking.
(iv)   Property futures based on a recognised property index.

The need for securitisation is international because of the global nature of finance and investment. In Australia there are already securitised instruments but in a study of investors' attitudes, Newall and Fife (1995) found that the underlying assumptions and expectations of investors in Australia concerning the need for liquidity matched those in the UK; but specifically related to Australia, investors in the survey provided the following conclusions:

(i)   The principal benefit of property securitisation was seen as the ability to access physical property assets which would otherwise be beyond prudent investment levels;

(ii)   There was a desire for investment liquidity and the use of securitised property as an effective portfolio management tool to obtain geographic and property type diversification and allocation benefit.

(iii)   Unit trusts were the preferred method of securitised property investment with listed property trusts being the preferred trust format.

REFERENCES

Barkshire, R. (1986) *The Unitised Property Market*, Working Party of the Unitised Property Market, London, February.

Barter, S. and Sinclair, N. (1988) *Securitisation* in S. L. Barter (ed), *Real Estate Finance*, Butterworths, London.

Bourne, T. (1995) 'Accelerating Towards Best Returns', *Estates Gazette*, 10 June, pp. 44-5.

Cameron Markby Hewitt (1996) 'The Future of Investment Property', *Property Update*, Cameron Markby Hewitt, Summer.

Catalano, A. (1995) 'Property Paper Chase', *Estates Gazette*, 1 July, p. 52.

Catalano, A. (1996a) 'An Industry Hungry for Change', *Estates Gazette*, 18 May, p. 44.

Catalano, A. (1996b) 'MEPC Taps US Market with $225m Bond Issue', *Estates Gazette*, 18 May, p. 43.

Chartered Surveyor Monthly (CSM) (1996) 'RICS Presses Treasury on Securitisation', *CSM*, October, p. 7.

Gibbs, R. (1987) 'Raising Finance for New Development', *Journal of Valuation*, vol. 5, no. 4, pp. 343–53.

Goodwin, M. (1995) 'A Recipe for Liquifying Property', *Chartered Surveyor Monthly*, November/December, pp. 28–9.

Investment Property Forum (1995) *Property Securitisation*, IPF, London.

Jonas, C. (1995) 'Liquidity and Property', *Estates Gazette*, 3 June, p. 52.

Lennox, K. (1996) 'Future Perfect', *Estates Gazette*, 24 August, p. 30.

London, S. (1996) 'Lure of the property magnet', *Financial Times*, 23 September, p. 19.

Maxted, B. (1988) *Unitisation of Property*, College of Estate Management, Reading

Newall, G. and Fife, A. (1995) 'Major Property Investors Attitudes to Property Securitisation', *Journal of Property Finance*, vol. 6, no. 1, pp. 55–63.

Orchard-Lisle, P. (1987) 'Financing Property Development', *Journal of Valuation*, vol. 5, no. 4, pp. 343–53.

Robinson, G (1996) 'Derivatives: Filling a Gap in the Market', *Estates Gazette*, 2 November, pp. 179–81.

Royal Institution of Chartered Surveyors (RICS) (1985) *The Unitisation of Real Property*, RICS, London.

Rydin, Y., Rodney, W. and Orr, C. (1990) 'Why Do Institutions Invest in Property', *Journal of Property Finance*, vol. 1, no. 2, pp. 250–8.

Savills (1989) *Financing Property 1989*, Savills, London.

Whitmore, J. (1993) 'Debt Securitisation to Aid the Market', *CSW-The Property Week*, 28 January, p. 15.

13 Financial Management

13.1 PROPERTY ACCOUNTS

For investment appraisal, a knowledge of property accounts is essential. This provides the analysis of the corporate entity and can be used to analyse the strength of tenants, business partners and companies which are being invested in. This chapter provides an outline of financial management for these purposes.

Company financial statements

A company's financial statements are contained in the reports sent to their shareholders. The reports provide details of the operations of the company. It contains a Chairman's review which looks at the preceding year and prospects for the future. There is also a Director's Report which comments on such matters as profits, dividends, fixed assets and finance, and includes the report of the auditors and a summary of the accounting policies of the company which can be useful in the analysis of the position of the firm. Accounting policies are important in the property sector in respect of asset valuation and there will be different bases according to whether a property company is an investment or a trading company. Attached to the report are the financial statements. These financial statements would be:

- the profit and loss account;
- the balance sheet;
- notes to the accounts;
- current cost accounts;
- a statement of source and applications of funds;
- a statement of value added.

The balance sheet and the profit and loss account are the main statements of the financial situation of the company. The balance sheet would be for an individual or group of companies, but if there were a parent company then this may be included in addition. The main accounts would be in accordance with historic cost conventions, but current cost accounts would attempt to take into account inflation of asset values. It is useful to remind ourselves at this stage, of those particular groups who need to use published accounts, because it is their need for information which will have to be satisfied. These are set out in Box 13.1.

The balance sheet

The balance sheet lists the balances of assets and liabilities as at the accounting date. As a result of the EEC's fourth directive on company accounts, balance sheets are now to be in a standardised form. The balance sheets are built up from three categories of entry: assets, liabilities and shareholders' funds. Thus total assets are equal to the sum of

WHO ARE THE USERS OF PUBLISHED ACCOUNTS?

The equity investor group including existing and potential shareholders and holders of convertible securities, options or warrants.

The loan creditor group including existing and potential holders of debentures and loan stock, and providers of short-term secured and unsecured loans and finance.

The employee group including existing, potential and past employees.

The analyst–adviser group including financial analysts and journalists, economists, statisticians, researchers, trade unions, stockbrokers and other providers of advisory services such as credit rating agencies.

The business contact group including customers, trade creditors and suppliers, and, in a different sense, competitors, business rivals, and those interested in mergers, amalgamations and takeovers.

The government including tax authorities, departments and agencies concerned with the supervision of commerce and industry, and local authorities.

The public including taxpayers, ratepayers, consumers, and other community and special interest groups such as political parties, consumer and environmental protection societies and regional pressure groups (Westwick 1980).

Box 13.1   *The users of published accounts*

the shareholders' funds plus liabilities if one looks at the balance sheet from the point of view of the company; alternatively from a shareholder's view, one can see that the difference between assets and liabilities is the shareholders' funds.

> *Business view:*   assets = shareholders' funds + liabilities
>
> *Shareholder's view:*   assets − liabilities = shareholders' funds

Fixed assets + Net current assets (current assets less current liabilities) = Capital employed (shareholders' funds + long-term liabilities). This is a modification of the business view taking current liabilities to the asset side of the equation.

The balance sheet model of the firm is set out in Figure 13.1 to clarify these concepts.

Profit and loss account

Whilst the balance sheet is for a particular moment, a profit and loss account is for a year ending on the accounting date: it is the result of the year's activities. The profit is shown before and after tax. Profit attributable to minority interests arises from investment in other companies amounting to 50% or less of ownership, and these profits are now allowed to be consolidated in the sheet. The accounts also show the proportion of profit distributed and retained. To grow, a company will need to increase its assets. The balance sheet shows that assets = liabilities plus shareholders' funds, so that the ways to grow would be to increase liabilities (borrow more) or increase shareholders' funds. There are two ways of increasing the shareholders' funds: by issuing more shares or ploughing back profits. Ploughing back profits is not necessarily the cheapest source of long-term funds for the company and it also restricts the payment of dividends.

Balance Sheet Model of the Firm

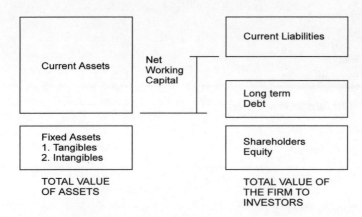

Figure 13.1 *Balance sheet model of the firm*

Source: Ross et al. (1993).

Examples of a balance sheet and a profit and loss account

Balance sheet as at 31 March 1993		
	£000	£000
Fixed assets		
(Investment properties for property companies)		3000
Land and buildings for occupation		400
Plant and machinery		200
Fixtures and fittings		200
		3800
Current assets		
Stocks (Trading properties for property companies)	3000	
Debtors	100	
Cash	100	
	3200	
Current liabilities		
Bank overdraft	400	
Trade creditors	600	
	1000	
Net current assets		2200
Total assets less current liabilities		6000

continued overleaf

Balance sheet continued

Capital and reserves

Issued share capital	2000
Revenue reserves	1000
Capital reserves	1000
Shareholders' interest	4000

Long-term liabilities (over one year)

Loans	2000
Total long-term capital	6000

Source: Adapted from Asch and Kaye (1989).

Notes to balance sheet:

The following notes refer to an ordinary trading company; notes relating to the peculiarities of property companies are in brackets.

Fixed assets

Assets were normally valued at historic cost for an ordinary company. Land and buildings were shown at original cost less depreciation in normal accounts, but because this does not reflect worth, companies now revalue to market value. Depreciation is an annual allowance for wear and tear and reduces the balance sheet valuation; it is deducted from profit as a cost. (For a property company, the valuation should be market value for an investment property, or the lower of cost and realisable value for a property in the course of development but intended as an investment property – that is intended as a fixed asset.) Fixed assets are intended to be permanent features of the company's assets; current assets are turned into cash usually within one year. Plant and machinery and fixtures and fittings are shown at cost less depreciation. The valuation of property assets for inclusion in a company's accounts were discussed in Chapter 5.

Current assets

Stocks are valued at cost. (For a property company, properties to be traded are stocks and are valued at the lower of realisable value or cost. Cost includes the expenses paid out on a property since purchase, and interest.)

Current liabilities

These are the amounts due to creditors within 1 year. The balance of current assets less current liabilities is called the net working capital.

Capital and reserves

Issued share capital is the amount paid in by the shareholders when they originally bought the shares in the company. Reserves arise because profits are not distributed to shareholders but ploughed back in the company; these are called revenue reserves. Revenue reserves have to be distinguished from capital reserves which arise on the revaluation of assets and which then may give rise to a surplus. (Capital reserves are especially important in property companies, arising from revaluation of the assets rather than profits from rents or trading.)

Long-term liabilities

These are amounts owed by the company at a future date, longer than one year.

Profit and loss account for the year ended 31 March 1993

		£000	£000
Turnover			10000
less cost of sales (direct costs)			6500
Gross profit			3500
less (indirect costs)	Administration expenses	1000	
	Selling and distribution costs	200	
	Interest on loans	150	
			1350
Net profit before tax			2150
Corporation tax			750
Profit on ordinary activities after tax			1400
Extraordinary item after taxation			200
Profit for the year			1200
Dividends			600
Transfer to reserves			600

Source: Asch and Kaye (1989).

Notes to profit and loss account:

Whereas the balance sheet reveals the state of affairs of the company at one point in time, the profit and loss account shows how much net cash has been generated by activities over the accounting period by matching the expenditure of the year against the revenues. The cost of sales is the cost of raw materials, production or direct labour, power, and other factory costs. An extraordinary item is one which is unusual in terms of size and frequency. They are infrequent and thus need to be omitted when considering profit trends over a period of years. For instance, a large profit may have been made from disposal of part of the business, an event which is unlikely to occur again and which distorts the profit figure for that year.

Basic accounting concepts

The financial statements are produced and based on accounting concepts. Four rules or concepts are observed in all published accounts unless it is otherwise stated. These rules are:

- The going concern concept;
- The accruals concept;
- The consistency concept;
- The prudence concept.

The going concern concept assumes that the business will be continuing its activities for the foreseeable future on a similar scale. Thus the values attaching to assets and liabilities in the Balance Sheet reflect going concern values. This concept is important in property asset valuation for accounts purposes. The accruals concept says that it is vital for an accurate assessment of profit and loss for the accounting period to compare costs and benefits accurately. It is important to assign costs and financial returns to the period incurred, which may not be the same time period when money costs are incurred or financial returns received. For instance, if a sale has legally taken place, whether or not cash has been received from the customer for the goods delivered, the transaction will be taken as a sale and included as part of the sales revenue appearing in the profit and loss account. The consistency concept is necessary so that approaches to the formulation of the accounts remain the same and so valid comparisons and analysis can be made against previous results and with other companies. The prudence concept covers the attitudes of dealing with costs and revenues; it is the cautious way an accountant approaches the problem unless it is certain. Based on the above concepts, the Companies Acts makes it a legal requirement that a company's Balance Sheet should show a true and fair view.

Techniques for analysis

The analysis of company accounts involve the initial consideration of three problems:

- (i)   Is the company making a satisfactory profit?
- (ii)   Is the company short of cash or cash rich?
- (iii) What should be the source of long-term funds?

These problems relate to profitability, liquidity and capital structure and are as applicable to individual property projects as they are to property companies or any firm. The techniques applied are based on relationships between the elements in the financial statements (financial ratios) and rates of return (yields). The area of capital structure is of major interest in financing arrangements and has parallels in the financial construction of property projects.

Profitability measures

The key ratios used to analyse the profitability of an enterprise are:

- (i)   Trading profit as a percentage of turnover.
- (ii)   Profit before interest and tax as a percentage of average capital employed.

(iii) Earnings per share, either basic (based on issued share capital) or fully diluted (based on authorised share capital, which is the total share capital that can be issued).

(iv) Dividend per share.

(v) Number of times covered – that is, the number of times a dividend is covered by earnings. This is also a measure used by property managers to assess the security of a tenant by calculating the number of times the rent is covered by the net profit of the tenant company.

(vi) Assets per share – the asset backing of shares based on the value of the net assets divided by the number of shares. There has been much discussion in this area in relation to the share price of property investment companies, as one would expect the asset value per share to relate to the market price of the share. However, traditionally the market has discounted the net asset values of property investment companies historically by an average of approximately 20%. The discount is measured by

$$\frac{\text{Share price} - \text{Net asset value per share}}{\text{Net asset value per share}} \times 100\%$$

(Isaac and Woodroffe 1987)

Return on investment

This is defined as

$$\frac{\text{Profit}}{\text{Assets}} \times 100\%$$

Thus profit is looked at as a percentage of capital, and this is further influenced by two further ratios comprising the profit margin (profit as a percentage of sales) and the rate of asset turnover (sales dividend by assets).

$$\frac{\text{Profit}}{\text{Assets}} = \frac{\text{Profit}}{\text{Sales}} \times \frac{\text{Sales}}{\text{Assets}}$$

or:

Return on capital = Profit margin × Turnover.

The return on capital may vary from one industry to another but wider variations may be found in the profit margin and rates of turnover. For instance, a return of 20% could be achieved by a high profit margin and a low turnover (the corner shop) or low profit margin and high turnover (the supermarket piling the goods high and selling cheap).

A sector comparison should show the capital-intensive industries with long production cycles would have a low rate of turnover but a high profit margin. From the key ratios above, a number of subsidiary ratios relating costs or assets to sales can be formulated. Depending on the use to which the ratio is put, the definition of profit and assets will differ. Generally a wider view of company performance is taken:

$$\text{Return on capital} = \frac{\text{Profit before tax, interest and dividends}}{\text{Total capital employed}}$$

The comparison of profitable ratios enables firms within a sector to be compared against one another and for the various sectors to be compared.

Liquidity and cash flows

As well as being profitable, it is also important that a company should be liquid. A profitable and fast-expanding company may find that it has tied up its profits in fixed assets, stocks and debtors and that is has difficulty paying its debts as they fall due. There are two main ratios to examine the liquidity of a company, the liquidity ratio and the current ratio.

The liquidity ratio is also called the acid test ratio because it is a most important test. It is the ratio of liquid assets to current liabilities and a 1:1 ratio means that a company has sufficient cash to pay its immediate debts. Liquid assets are defined as current assets excluding stocks of goods which cannot be quickly turned into cash. In effect, liquid assets are debtors, cash and any short-term investments like bank deposits or government securities. A company can survive with a liquid ratio of less than 1:1 if it has an unused bank overdraft facility.

The other test of a company's liquidity is the current ratio which includes stocks and work in progress, on the grounds that stocks eventually turn into debtors and then into cash itself. It is calculated by relating all current assets to current liabilities. A norm of 2:1 is generally regarded as being satisfactory but this will depend on the norm for a particular industry.

Thus:

Liquidity ratio = Liquid assets : Current liabilities

Current ratio = Current assets : Current liabilities

Gearing ratio and interest cover

Two important measures of financial analysis are the gearing ratio and interest cover.

The gearing (or leverage) ratio is the ratio of debt to shareholders' funds. This could be expressed as the ratio of debt to net operating assets, and this is the approach used in most economic texts, but normally in the market it is stated as:

$$\text{Gearing ratio} = \frac{\text{Debt (borrowings)}}{\text{Shareholders' funds}}$$

also known as the debt to equity ratio.

Interest cover is the profit available to pay interest charges.

$$\text{Interest cover} = \frac{\text{Profit before interest and tax}}{\text{Net interest}}$$

Example:

	Co. A	Co. B
Balance Sheet	£m	£m
Net operating assets	100	100
Financed by: Debt	20	80
Shareholders	80	20
	100	100
Profit and Loss Account		
Operating profit	15.0	15.0
Less interest payable @ 10%	(2.0)	(8.0)
Profit before tax	13.0	7.0
Tax @ 35%	(4.55)	(2.5)
Net profit	8.45	4.5
Gearing ratio	$\dfrac{20}{80} = 25\%$	$\dfrac{80}{20} = 400\%$
Interest cover	$\dfrac{15}{2} = 7.5$ times	$\dfrac{15}{8} = 1.88$ times

The gearing ratio is used to compare levels of debt between companies. Interest cover indicates the safety margin before profits become inadequate to cover the interest charge. Gearing and interest cover are used by lenders to determine whether a company's borrowings are at a reasonable level and whether it is prudent to lend more.

Investors are concerned with the company's capacity to absorb a down in profit without having to sell assets in possibly unfavourable market conditions. Also gearing is a measure of the potential to finance expansion without recourse to the shareholders which would depress share price. If a company requires additional debt to fund a new project the resultant gearing effect may depress share price and restrict flexibility to respond to future opportunities. There is thus pressure to record the project, the asset and debt, off balance sheet.

Financial gearing and operational gearing

This section is based on the analysis of Asch and Kaye (1989). Many organisations have some control over production methods – that is, they can use either a highly automated process with its associated high fixed costs, but low variable costs, or alternatively, a less-automated process with lower fixed costs, but higher variable costs. If the enterprise chooses to use a high level of automation, its break-even point is at a relatively high sales level and changes in the level of sales will have a magnified effect on profits. In other words, the degree of operating gearing is high. This is the same effect as that produced with financial gearing, in that the higher the gearing factor, the higher the break-even sales volume and the greater the impact on profits. The degree of operating gearing can be defined as the percentage change in operating profits associated with a given percentage change in sales volume. Operating gearing can be calculated using the following formula:

$$\text{Degree of operating gearing} = (S - VC)/(S - VC - FC)$$

where S represents the level of sales (quantity × value), VC is total variable cost, and FC is total fixed cost. For example, let us suppose that a firm has a level of sales of £100 000, total variable costs of £50 000 and total fixed costs of £20 000. Its degree of operating gearing would be:

$$(100\,000 - 50\,000)/(100\,000 - 50\,000 - 20\,000) = 1.67 \text{ or } 167\%$$

Therefore, if sales increase by 100 per cent, profit increases by 167 per cent. Operating gearing affects earnings before interest and taxes (EBIT), whereas financial gearing affects earnings after interest and taxes, that is, the amount available to equity holders in the company. Financial gearing will intensify the effects on earnings available to equity after the effect of operating gearing has been taken into account.

The degree of financial gearing can be defined here as: the percentage change in earnings available to equity that is associated with a given percentage change in earnings before interest and taxes (EBIT). That is the change in equity return relative to overall return before tax. An equation has been developed for calculating the degree of financial gearing:

$$\text{Degree of financial gearing} = EBIT/(EBIT - I)$$

where $EBIT$ is earnings before interest and taxation, and I is interest paid (which is the return to debt capital, so $EBIT - I$ is the return to equity capital). Thus in the earlier example, we can compute the degree of financial gearing if we now assume that further debt is required involving interest payments (I) of £5000. The degree of financial gearing would be:

$$30\,000/(30\,000 - 5000) = 1.2 \text{ or } 120\%$$

If EBIT were to increase by 100 per cent this would result in an increase of 120 per cent in the amount available to equity. We can combine operating and financial gearing to reveal the overall effect of a given change in sales on earnings available to the owners as follows (which in effect merely reflects the addition to the interest cost to fixed costs):

$$\text{Combined gearing effect} = (S - VC)/(S - VC - FC - I)$$

which for our example would be:

$$(100\,000 - 50\,000)/(100\,000 - 50\,000 - 20\,000 - 5000) = 2 \text{ or } 200\%$$

Therefore, if sales change by 100 per cent this would cause the earnings available to equity investors to change by 200 per cent. In this example, the combined gearing effect of 2 was obtained from a degree of operating gearing of 1.67 and financial gearing of 1.2, but clearly other combinations would have produced the same effect. It is possible to make trade-offs between financial and operating gearing. The concept of the degree of gearing allows an organisation to predict the effect of change in sales on the earnings available to ordinary shareholders, in addition to revealing the interrelationship between financial and operating gearing. The concept can be used to predict, for example, that a decision to finance new plant and equipment with debt may result in a situation where a small change in sales volume will produce a large variation in earnings, whereas a different operating and financial gearing combination may reduce the effect on earnings.

Analysing a property company: a summary

In order to analyse a property company, its accounts and finances, the following criteria will be important:

(i) *Net asset value per share*
If the net assets are £10m and the issued share capital is 5m shares at £1 each, then the net asset value per share is £10m/5m, i.e. £2 or 200p per share.

(ii) *Gearing*
If the shareholders' funds are £5m and the debt capital is £3m, then the gearing is £3m/£5m, i.e. 0.66 or 66%.

(iii) *Composition of interest rates in the debt*
What is the percentage of variable rate loans to total loans? A company with a lot of debt with floating rates may find its share price suffering, especially in a period of volatile interest rates.

(iv) *Valuation of assets*
When were they last valued? Property companies are meant to value their properties internally annually and have an external independent valuation every five years.

(v) *Comparison of the amount of properties shown at cost* (development properties in the process of being developed) *with the amount shown at value* (investment property).
This analysis gives an indication of the level of development activity.

(vi) *The legal interests* in properties held
The breakdown of properties into freeholds, long leaseholds and short leaseholds can give an indication of the type and amount of income arising and the nature of the reviews.

(viii) *Comparison of profit*
A year on year comparison excluding extraordinary items is a valuable analysis.

(ix) *Capital*
How is it financed, what capital commitments are there?

(x) *Contingent liabilities*
Has the company guaranteed the borrowing of associate companies which increases its liabilities? Are there any off-balance sheet transactions? (Adapted from Brett 1990a).

13.2 PROPERTY ACCOUNTS: ISSUES

Capitalisation of interest for property companies

One aspect of financial reporting attracts more adverse comment than others. This is the process of capitalising interest into the cost of property developments rather than treating it as an expense. Thus the cost increases the asset value in the balance sheet rather than reducing the profit in the profit and loss account. The difference between capitalising and expensing interest can have a high impact on the reported results and net assets of business during the development period. It is somewhat surprising that generally accepted accounting practice in the UK permits both policies (Smee 1992) The capitalisation of borrowing costs into most types of property development appears a logical and appropriate policy. Interest is a development cost and is no different from construction and land costs in this respect. The policy of capitalising interest is mandatory in the USA and looks set to become so elsewhere in the world.

The arguments against capitalisation are set out in Exposure Draft (ED) 51 (ASC 1990) and are briefly:

- (i)   It is illogical to treat finance costs as a period expense normally and then treat them as a cost during the period of construction and reverting to treating them as a period expense once the asset is complete, as finance costs are probably continuing to be incurred.
- (ii)   Borrowing costs are often for the whole enterprise and allocation of cost to a particular fixed asset will be arbitrary.
- (iii) Capitalisation of borrowing costs results in similar fixed assets carrying different levels of interest. A highly geared company will carry its fixed assets at a higher amount than one which is not.

Smee (1992) suggests that capitalisation results in a proper matching of income and capital return with the development expenditure, and best reflects, from an accounting view, the management's judgement of a project's viability rather than being creative accounting.

Goodwill

When a company acquires a business, it often seeks to write off the goodwill against capital reserves to avoid having to amortise the goodwill in its profit and loss account. The company can thus increase net profit and earnings per share. On resale of the business, the company can record a greater gain as the original price will not reflect the additional sum paid for goodwill. After 23 January 1992 the profit and loss account on the date of disposal should be determined by reference to the attributable amount of purchase goodwill where this has not previously been charged to the profit and loss account. This ruling was made by the Urgent Issues Task Force set up by the Accounting Standards Committee and the Accounting Standards Board (Ryland 1992).

Structure of financial statements: reporting in financial statements

The Accounting Standards Board (ASB) has issued an exposure draft on financial statements – this requires additional matters to be included in the statements to make it more difficult for companies to inflate net profits and earnings per share. The ASB requires each company to prepare a cash flow statement as part of their financial statements for accounting periods ending after 23 March 1992 (Ryland 1992).

Valuation of assets

Through time, the value of investment property will increase and the upward revaluation will create a surplus, being the difference between the open market value and its historic cost. This gain (loss) can be dealt with in three ways:

(i)   It can be passed through the profit and loss account as ordinary, exceptional or extraordinary item.

(ii)   If the company's articles prevent the option (i), then the gain can be transferred to the capital reserve.

(iii)   It can be shown in a separate capital profit and loss account. This is best practice, to place gains or losses in a proper reserve and show it in the accounts as a capital profit and loss account which thus makes a distinction between realised and unrealised surpluses (Purdy 1992).

Information in property company accounts

In May 1990 chartered accountants Stoy Hayward and researchers from the University of Reading set up a panel of experts to look at the provision of information in property company accounts and the main areas of problems relating to loans and interest, the nature of the assets and joint ventures. The recommendations of the panel are listed below:

(i)   Property company accounts should be placed in context, in terms of: what has happened over the year; how the company has been performing over the last five years; a view of the future and what accounting policies are used.

(ii)   More details should be included about loan arrangements, the payment of interest and the capitalisation of interest.

(iii)   An analysis of properties should be included showing their use as either trading stock, investment properties or development properties.

(iv)   A list of properties with a worth greater than 5% of the total property portfolio should be included.

(v)   An external revaluation, on an open market basis should be carried out in accordance with the guidelines of the Royal Institution of Chartered Surveyors.

(vi)   All revaluation gains or losses should be passed into a property revaluation reserve, shown in the accounts as a capital profit and loss account which distinguishes between realised and unrealised amounts.

(vii)   Details of costs and revenues from all developments relating to, and details of, all joint ventures should be included (Purdy 1992).

13.3   THE REGULATION OF ACCOUNTS

There are several sources of regulation with which statutory accounts have to comply. These are:

(i)   The Companies Acts: these describe the principles which should be followed in preparing statutory accounts. They indicate that accounts should show a true and fair view. The Companies Acts also set out the detailed disclosure requirements.

(ii)   The accounting profession publishes SSAPs (Statements of Standard Accounting Practice) and these cover accounting and disclosure.

(iii) If the company is listed, the Stock Exchange specifies mandatory disclosure requirements.

The company accounts are independently examined by the auditor who has to report to the shareholders that the accounts show a true and fair view and are properly prepared in accordance with the Companies Act. Auditors are under a professional obligation to ensure the accounts comply with SSAPs. If the accounts do not accord with the regulations, the auditor must state this in his report unless, in exceptional circumstances, he concurs with a departure from an SSAP. This seldom happens. If the auditor is going to qualify the accounts he will discuss this with the directors and often they will amend the accounts to avoid qualification. The auditor will also advise of any failure to observe the relevant requirements of the Stock Exchange.

13.4   OFF-BALANCE SHEET FUNDING

Off-balance sheet funding has become common in the last few years because there is less equity and more debt in the balance sheets, small developers have limited equity resources and banks have become more competitive, flexible and innovative in their lending. In the 1980s banks contrived with the lenders to encourage off-balance sheet funding for their own marketing. Also in the UK, the SSAPs have never been intended to be applied mechanistically but intended to set out the broad principles which are to be applied in drawing up accounts. There is thus a tendency for the broad approach of the SSAPs to be ignored and for some property lenders to pursue accounting treatments which while consistent with the letter of accounting standards may be at variance with their spirit.

Examples of off-balance financing are provided by Peat (1988) and these are set out and discussed in the following paragraphs:

(i)   Controlled non subsidiary

If a developer sets up a debt-financed subsidiary to undertake a project the consolidated balance sheet of the parent company would have to show the debt of the subsidiary. An alternative is to form a company which is not technically a subsidiary within S.736 of the Companies Act 1985. A company is a subsidiary of another if the latter is a member of the company and controls the board. If the parent company has only the right to appoint half the board but its directors each have two votes whilst the others have one, it will not control the composition of the board although it will effect almost total control. Similarly a company is a subsidiary of another if the latter holds more than half its equity share capital in terms of nominal value. The technique in this respect is for a company to own shares which represent no more than half of the nominal value of the share capital but give a right to, say, 99% of the company's profits. The company would not technically be a subsidiary, even though its 'parent' enjoyed 99% of its profits, as referred to previously, and effectively controlled the board. This kind of structure is called a diamond structure.

Example of a 'diamond structure':

The definition of a subsidiary set out in S.736 of the Companies Act 1985 provides that a company is a subsidiary of a parent company only if:

(i)   The parent is a member of the board and controls the board of directors of the subsidiary.
(ii) The parent company holds more than half the nominal value of the equity share capital of the subsidiary.
(iii) The subsidiary will be regarded as a subsidiary of the parent, if it is itself a subsidiary of a subsidiary of the parent.

The diamond structure set out in Figure 13.2 avoids the definition of subsidiaries indicated in the previous paragraphs.

Diamond Structure

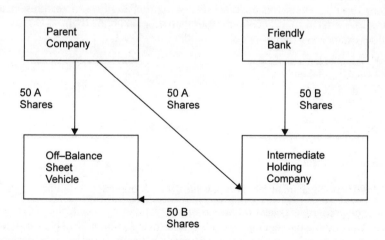

Figure 13.2   *Off-balance sheet funding: diamond structure*

A and *B* shares have the same number of votes except on a vote to appoint directors. The holders of the *A* shares have the right to appoint three directors without reference to the holders of the *B* shares; similarly the *B* shareholders have the right to appoint three directors without reference to the holders of the *A* shares. However at Board meetings of the off-balance sheet vehicle (the quorum for which requires an *A* director) the *A* directors each have six votes while the *B* directors have one each. Rights to dividends and returning capital on a winding up may be split so that the *A* shareholders received 99% and the *B* shareholders 1%.

Although the parent receives nearly all the profit and can control decisions because the membership of the board is 50:50 it was not considered under the Companies Act 1983 to be a subsidiary; the fact that the directors appointed by the parent carry a majority of the votes which may be cast at board meetings is not addressed in this legislation.

This diamond structure also means that the parent does not hold more than half of the nominal value of the equity share capital. *A* and *B* shares are equity share capital within the meaning of the Act. Equity share capital is defined as the issued share capital excluding capital which carries rights to participate beyond a specified amount in the distribution. In this example there is no specified amount as a ceiling. Although the dividend right of the *A* shares is far greater than that of the *B* shares, the definition of a subsidiary requires that the measure of the relative weight of the shares is to be their nominal value.

A similar result to above could be arranged by having the *B* shares of the off-balance sheet vehicle held by the bank, but the structure above exists for tax reasons. For example, it may be necessary to ensure that the off-balance sheet vehicle and its parent would be treated as falling within the same group for group relief purposes or for corporation tax on capital gains, or it may be necessary to minimise the stamp duty payable on transfers of property between the parent and the off-balance sheet vehicle.

Prior to the publication of the draft SSAP on Accounting for Special Purpose Transactions (Exposure Draft 42), most accountants held that it was not permissible to consolidate a company which was not a legal subsidiary, thus a note to the accounts would disclose these interests. This approach is not appropriate if the notes present a view contradictory to the main accounts rather than supplementing them.

Other examples of off-balance sheet funding are:

- sale and leaseback;
- lease and finance leaseback;
- sale and repurchase;
- options;
- joint ventures;
- non-recourse debt.

(ii) Sale and leaseback

If sale and leaseback are at fair market values, the accounting transaction is as follows:

- the property is taken off balance sheet;
- the net sale proceeds are included as cash or debtors in the balance sheet;
- the profit or loss is recognised (difference between net sale proceeds and value in accounts) and,
- the rent payable is charged to profit over term of the lease.

Variations in this may include put and call options where the seller has a right to buy back the property at a predetermined price (preserving an interest in the capital growth of the asset) and the lender has a put option to require the seller to repurchase at the same price (protecting the lender from capital losses). Accounting for leases is dealt with in SSAP 21. This distinguishes between a finance lease and a standard lease. A finance lease is defined as 'a lease that transfers substantially all the risks and rewards of ownership of an asset to the lessee'. Any other lease is an operating lease. In property a lease is likely to be an operating lease where:

(a) There are regular rent reviews to a market rent.
(b) There is a reversion of the asset to the landlord on the expiry of the lease. Thus the landlord takes the risk/rewards of the rental income and the capital appreciation.

The categorisation of the leaseback as a finance or operating lease determines whether the asset and the related financing can be taken off-balance sheet. This can only really be done if the lease is an operational lease; the presumption with other leases is that they are finance leases on the basis that the lessee has uninterrupted use of the property. If the lease is a finance lease then under the provisions of SSAP 21 it will need to be capitalised by the lessee, the property asset is included in the balance sheet at its fair value, and the obligation to pay rentals is included as a liability of a similar amount, or alternatively the sale proceeds can be included on the balance sheet as a liability.

(iii) Sale and repurchase

This comprises two agreements, one for sale and one for the repurchase, entered into simultaneously. The price payable to repurchase will be the sale price plus interest. The intended effect is that the seller's balance sheet after sale and before repurchase includes the sales proceeds but neither the property nor the obligation to repay (the debt is taken off balance sheet). It is not likely that the auditors would accept that the property and obligation to repay should be off balance sheet because the seller (repurchaser) retains substantially all the beneficial interest in the property. A more sophisticated approach has been used by house builders to finance showhouses and can take the finance off balance sheet:

Example of sale and repurchase:

(a) The builder sells the completed showhouses to the financier.
(b) The financier grants the builder a right to use houses for a fee which equals the interest on funds advanced by the financier.
(c) The builder undertakes to sell the showhouses as an agent for the financier.
(d) The builder retains from sale proceeds an agency fee equal to the excess sale proceeds over the amount due to the financier.

The critical difference here is that the sold houses are unlikely to revert to the housebuilder nor will he probably have to make good any shortfall in sale proceeds. The builder will guarantee that the houses will be sold in a certain period of time and he will make good the shortfall, but the time period and the values included in the agreement would be such that he would be unlikely to have to do so. The builder may also report a profit in the period he enters into the sale agreement rather than waiting for the actual sale.

(iv)   Options

Property transactions frequently involve the grant of options to purchase a property. The accounting profession has no prescribed rules for options. Options are often used as an alternative to secured borrowings and to create off-balance sheet structures, as with buy-back options in sale and finance leaseback.

Example of an option arrangement:

The direct purchase of a property may look like:

Equity	£1m
Debt	£9m
Value	£10m

These elements could be shown on a balance sheet. As an alternative a bank could purchase the property on the investor's behalf for £10m and the investor could pay £1m for an option to purchase the property at some future time for a predetermined price. The predetermined price equals the purchase price plus the bank's interest and other costs less rent received. The bank will have a put option, if the value declines, to force the investor to acquire the property for the same amount as the purchase price. The idea is to take the asset and debt of the balance sheet because here it appears that the beneficial ownership has been acquired by the financier. However, as before, because the investor has the cost/benefits of the option, the option will be shown in the accounts with disclosure of the contingent obligation under the put option. More strictly it would be viewed that the effect of the option, because of the likelihood of repurchase, is to, in effect, purchase the property.

(v)   Lease and finance leaseback

This is a variant of the sale and leaseback and is a useful means of structuring the finance of a property which is going to be developed by a developer.

A manufacturer acquires a site on which to build a building for his own use; the finance agreement with the bank might be:

- manufacturer grants the bank a lease for 25 years, no premium and peppercorn rent;
- bank enters into contract with a builder to build the warehouse;
- bank leases back building to manufacturer for 25 years. No premium is paid, rents reimburse the bank for development costs and interest.

This approach is a finance one rather than an attempt to obtain an accounting advantage. Thus the property and the obligation to pay would be on the balance sheet. This approach is motivated by tax considerations, the desire for the bank to obtain the benefit of capital allowances. This benefit (reducing the bank's tax) will be shared with the manufacturer as it will be reflected in the lower rentals payable under the leaseback.

(vi)   Joint ventures

Joint ventures are reflected in the accounts of the parent companies (the joint venturers) as an investment asset, at the cost of the investment plus investor's share of profits; the borrowings of the joint venture company, however, may not appear.

(vii)   Non-recourse debt

Lenders' rights are restricted to a charge over a particular asset which is pledged as security. Some suggestions, especially by bankers, are that non-recourse debt in the balance sheet be netted against the asset it is financing. These suggestions reflect the bankers' and lenders' primary interest in the balance sheet, which in their case is used to determine whether there are sufficient assets available to repay future and existing debt. Netting off of non-recourse debt is not generally an acceptable approach as accounts extend beyond just credit and liquidity assessment.

Recent moves to account for off-balance sheet transactions

Exposure draft (ED) 42 says that transactions should be accounted for in accordance with their economic substance, having regard to their effect on the enterprise's assets and liabilities. ED42 as incorporated in the Companies Act 1989, affects the off-balance sheet vehicles described above dramatically. For instance:

- *Controlled non-subsidiary* — should be accounted for as a subsidiary.
- *Sale and leaseback* — would be treated as a borrowing transaction and the terms of arrangement need to be reworded.
- *Lease and finance leaseback* — unaffected.
- *Sale and repurchase* — need to clearly account for transaction as borrowing.
- *Options* — transaction or arrangement should be accounted for on the basis of the likelihood that the option will be exercised, that is if it is probable that it would be exercised. Probable is assumed to be a situation where the non-exercise would be highly unlikely. This would be the case where two options, one to sell and one to buy, exist.
- *Joint ventures* — if a joint venture is a genuine sharing of risk and reward, a participant who has an interest of 50% or less will not need to disclose separate joint venture asset and borrowing on the parent companies' balance sheets.
- *Non-recourse debt* — it is not appropriate to offset the asset against its liability. If the accounts are used solely for lending decisions, there may be a basis for netting off. Assets and liability should be separate categories in the balance sheet (Peat 1988).

Implementation of the EEC Directive on Company Law

This deals with group accounts; it deals with voting rights and problems discussed with the diamond structure. There is a new definition of subsidiary. It is a subsidiary if the parent holds a participating interest in the subsidiary, and either:

(i)   exercises a clear influence over the subsidiary, or
(ii)   the subsidiary and parent are managed on a unified basis.

Overall there is still the requirement that the accounts present a true and fair view.

13.5   OFF-PROFIT AND LOSS ACCOUNT FINANCING

This approach basically charges operating costs directly to shareholders rather than in the profit and loss account. Share option renumeration, for instance, where directors and employees receive share options rather than income, is a dilution of share capital not charged to profit and loss account. Another example is convertible loan stock which has a lower interest rate but gives the holder rights to convert to equity at a fixed price (Peat 1988). Other structures which provide off-profit and loss account financing are:

Deep discount debentures

These bonds are issued at a lower rate of interest, which may remain at this level or be stepped up. The accruals concept of accounting (see earlier in the chapter) should mean that revenues and expenses should be matched for the appropriate time period. The real rate of interest should be thus accounted for over the life of the bond, which reflects the use of the loan over the period, and this should be taken out of profit.

Share premium accounts

There is a need to credit the share premium account when the proceeds of an issue of shares exceeds the nominal value. At the same time one is able to write-off costs of the issue of shares and debentures including commission and discounts against the account. It is possible therefore to write off the deep discount of a bond against the share premium account. The appropriate method should be to amortise the discount through the profit and loss account (as notional interest) then transfer (by way of a movement of reserves) an amount from the share premium account to retained profits.

Redeemable convertibles

These are redeemable, convertible loan stock. The interest coupon is lower than on the conventional convertible and this is compensated for by the inclusion of a redemption option. If the share price does not increase sufficiently to make conversion worthwhile, the holder may opt for redemption at a premium over issue price, and this has an appropriate return to compensate. The issue is, should the potential redemption premium be accrued and charged to the profit and loss account as interest to the date when it may be exercised? The approach should be that the potential premium should be accrued and charged to the profit and loss account rather than held as a contingency for a possible claim.

Convertible preference shares

These issues have the same problems as redeemable loan stock. Convertible issues are usually bonds, but convertible preference shares with a redemption premium option have been issued. The preference shares thus convert to ordinary shares under this procedure, but if the price is low they can be redeemed with a premium to make up for the low yield. Systematic accrual should be made through the profit and loss account for the potential redemption premium however remote its potential redemption appears to be.

Debt with equity warrants

This is an issue of debt with equity warrants, which are rights to subscribe for shares at fixed price. These warrants are redeemable: that is, the amount paid for the warrant is repayable if the warrant is not exercised. The debt instruments and the warrants are traded separately. The objective is (as for convertible debt) to secure lower interest rates for the debt issued. Thus to account properly for this the proceeds from the issue should be allocated between debt and the warrants and accounted for separately. If the warrant is redeemable, accrual should be made through the profit and loss account for potential redemption.

REFERENCES

Accounting Standards Committee (ASC) (1990) *Exposure Draft 51, Accounting for Fixed Assets and Revaluations*, ASC, May.

Asch, D. and Kaye, G. R. (1989) *Financial Planning: Modelling Methods and Techniques*, Kogan Page, London.

Barkham, R. J. and Purdy, D. E. (1992) 'Financial Company Reporting: Potential Weaknesses', *Journal of Property Valuation and Investment*, vol. 11, no. 2, pp. 133–44.

Brett, M. (1990a) *Property and Money*, Estates Gazette, London.

Brett, M. (1990b) *How to Read the Financial Pages*, Hutchison, London.

Calachi, R. and Rosenburg, S. (eds) (1992) *Property Finance, An International Perspective*, Euromoney Books, London.

Isaac, D. and Woodroffe, N. (1987) 'Are Property Company Assets Undervalued', *Estates Gazette*, London, 5 September, pp. 1024–6.

Peat, M. (1988) 'The Accounting Issues', in S. L. Barter (ed.) *Real Estate Finance*, Butterworths, London.

Pike, R. and Neale, B. (1993) *Corporate Finance and Investment*, Prentice Hall, London.

Purdy, D. E. (1992) 'Provoking Awareness through the Provision of Relevant Information in Property Company Accounts', *Journal of Property Finance*, vol. 3, no. 3, pp. 337–46.

Ross, S. A., Westerfield, R. W. and Jaffe, J. F. (1993) *Property Finance*, Irwin, Boston.

Ryland, D. S. (1992) 'Changes in Accounting Rules', *Journal of Property Finance*, vol. 3, no. 1, pp. 28–37.

Smee, R. (1992) 'Capitalisation of Interest for Property Companies', *Journal of Property Finance*, vol. 3, no. 1, pp. 13–22.

Westwick, C. A. (1980) *Property Valuation and Accounts*, Institute of Chartered Accountants in England and Wales, London.

14 Forecasting and Research

14.1 RESEARCH

In their report on commercial property in the UK economy, Currie and Scott (1991) concluded that commercial property represented an important sector of the economy and had a major influence on the rest of the economy. They were surprised that despite this importance, property received relatively little attention from economic commentators and policymakers. A key conclusion of the report was that the current state of statistics in the sector was poor for commercial property, a situation which contrasted with the level of statistical data in the private housing market which was well documented. A number of various areas of research are now being developed. Areas of research sponsored by the RICS include the relationship of property cycles to business cycles. In addition, interest has been created by the opening of Eastern Europe and the property markets in that region. In terms of valuation principles and methods, further research has continued into portfolio investment and the development of existing appraisal methods which are dealt with in more detail below.

Lizieri and Richards (1992) suggest that there are three categories of research into property investment that are being developed:

(i) The development of measures of property performance at an individual property or portfolio level and in terms of a benchmark market indicator. Hence the development of commercial property indices.

(ii) The forecasting of activity at a variety of levels, from macroeconomic forecasts, through national property market trends, to detailed analysis at sector, region and town level.

(iii) The combination of performance measurement and the forecasting of results to establish portfolio strategies: that is, the diversification of the portfolio, the management of property as a financial asset and the buy/sell decision.

In evaluating property investment a vital step is the establishment of a market performance benchmark. There have been calls for a reduction in the number of indices used and the establishment of a 'single definitive index' but investors may have different benchmark requirements. The investment manager will tend to seek to identify the risk/return profile of any given portfolio and set it against appropriate benchmarks.

Property in a portfolio context

The valuation of properties in a traditional way, building by building, is now seen as an inadequate approach, as investors are exposed to localised property markets and the wide swings of local prices. Such volatility is controlled in other investment portfolios, such as shares, and these techniques are now being introduced to commercial property portfolios. The use of modern portfolio theory which was discussed in some detail previously has been debated at some length because of the range of possible properties and markets. The right choice of investment for the portfolio is even more important in property than it may well be in competing investment markets like equities and gilts. The general feeling is that most property portfolios are badly diversified. Also, property portfolios demand active management unlike other investment media. If there is no active management, then the choice of properties for the portfolio might be negated anyway. The performance of a portfolio in comparison with an index is difficult to chart. Property portfolios after all need to be analysed, not only in terms of return, but also in terms of risk. Findings from the Investment Property Databank (IPD) have shown that diversification is only possible in large funds with an excess of 250 properties where patterns of performance or volatility do not deviate markedly from the market norms. However, it has been possible for small funds in the region of 30 or 40 properties to achieve higher levels of return over the last ten years or so without a higher than average volatility. However, for the smaller fund, such a result cannot be guaranteed. The conclusion of the IPD evidence is that the complexity of the asset class and the illiquidity of the market contribute to the difficulty of achieving low-risk, well-diversified, portfolios without large and expensive asset bases.

Research into valuation methods

The RICS has commissioned a number of reports which looked into valuation methods. These included the residual valuation, the profits methods, the contractor's method and reversionary valuations.

The cost approach to valuation

In a paper presented at a valuation techniques seminar on the 13 March 1992, Connellan (1992) suggested that the calculation of value on a cost basis usually concerns three categories of building. These are *precisely similar, simple* or *modern substitute*. He suggested that these categories be replaced by three alternative categories, being *reconstructed, modified reconstructed* and *radical alternative*. Depreciation is defined as the loss of real existing use value of a capital asset. In depreciation the age/future life method is the most commonly used method, which assumes straight line depreciation. It is generally agreed that this must be a wrong approach.

The Depreciated Replacement Cost is defined by Gross Replacement Cost (GRC) × Depreciation Factor (DF) = Net Replacement Cost (NRC).

$$DF = \frac{\text{Estimated future life of building}}{\text{Age} + \text{Estimated future life of building}} = \frac{\text{Remaining life}}{\text{Total life}}$$

The conclusion is that cost-base valuations are the best available sources for *no-market* properties. However, the comment is made that the guidance notes and information papers provided by the Asset Valuation Standing Committee are not as useful as they might be, as the advice is too theoretical and does not give much practical guidance.

Profits method

Colborne (1992) has carried out some research into the Profits Method of valuation. She suggested that there are three different approaches:

(i)   Total capitalisation;
(ii)   Dual capitalisation/super profit;
(iii) Capitalised (discounted) earnings.

The total earnings method of valuation is based on the net operating profit (profit before interest and tax) x a multiplier to give a valuation. In the dual capitalisation method, the profit figures are taken for the last three to five years. The net profit is capitalised separately from the goodwill. The various approaches to the profit method are comparable and use the sustainable net profit for valuation. The basic differences are firstly, the division of the net profit as a return from the building and tenant; and secondly, a discount rate used over a limited time period as against the use of a Years Purchase.

The valuation of reversionary freeholds

In his RICS research, Crosby (1992) suggests that the major criticism of contemporary approaches is that they do not forecast growth and that they subjectively choose a discount rate. He suggests that using the implied rental growth rate analysis will reduce the subjectivity. There is a debate between academics over which type of model makes the best use of available evidence: the growth explicit model using comparable transactions to assess an implied growth rate after subjectively choosing a discount rate or, alternatively, the growth explicit model using the objectively found equivalent yield from comparable transactions and then applying it subjectively to properties to be valued. The view is that the subjective element in contemporary methods has less effect on the possible range of solutions than the subjective element in conventional approaches. This is still, however, a minority view. The market valuation of reversionary freehold property is generally carried out by conventional growth implicit techniques but the research showed that not all were using the same conventional approach. Crosby, in his paper, indicates that in the future he perceives a demise of the traditional term and reversion approach. These aspects have already been discussed in some detail earlier in the book.

Portfolio analysis

There are two areas of financial theory which have had some impact in the areas of property investment valuation and appraisal, and these areas relate to market efficiency and the Capital Asset Pricing Model.

Market efficiency

Market efficiency theories as applied to property markets say that the price of property investments should reflect all available information in the market. Dealers in the market should recognise when prices are out of line and accordingly will make a profit by buying or selling and thus driving the price back to equilibrium values consistent with all available information. Thus in an efficient market, property will be traded at the correct prices. This situation will provide confidence to the investors involved and ensure the best economic allocation of funds. It is likely that the property market is efficient in what is described as a weak-form level, which means that the market reflects the past history of prices and is efficient in respect of these. It may not, however, use all the information available as signified by higher levels of efficiency called strong forms. As access to market information becomes more restricted, it is likely that the market will progressively become more inefficient so there is more likelihood of dealers earning abnormal returns. Brown (1991) suggests that the efficiency of the market is difficult to test with valuation models which are based on the comparison method. Although this method does give a guide to the potential price in the market place, it does not indicate whether the property is under- or over-priced in its economic sense (that is, relative to future income and risk). Conventional evaluation models are thus unable to answer this question as they have no economic reference to market equilibrium.

Capital asset pricing model (CAPM)

The CAPM as developed in capital market theory helps us to understand the relationships of risk and return in an investment. The CAPM can give us an indication of how to measure risk. If the risk is related to a single-property asset, it relates to the variability of returns, and this is measured statistically by their variants or standard deviation. As applied to risk in a portfolio of properties, we are interested here in the contribution of a property to the overall risk of the entire portfolio. Because a property's variance in return is dispersed in a large diversified portfolio, the single-property's variance no longer represents its contribution to the risk of a large portfolio. In this case, contribution is measured by the property's covariance with the other properties in the portfolio. For instance, if a property has high returns when the overall return of the portfolio is low, and vice versa, the property has a negative covariance with the portfolio. It acts as a hedge against risk reducing the risk of the portfolio. If the property has a higher positive covariance, there is a high risk for the investor. In the CAPM the measure of risk is called Beta. The criteria for holding an investment in a portfolio can be defined in terms of the property's Beta. Thus investors will only hold a risky property if its expected return is high enough to compensate for its risk. There is thus a trade-off between the risk and the reward of future income. The expected return on a property is positively related to the property's Beta or risk. The model gives the formula that the expected return on an asset for a period is equal to the riskless rate of return plus a variable which reflects risk. This variable is Beta multiplied by the difference between the expected return on the market portfolio minus the risk-free rate. Beta here is the systematic risk. This systematic risk is still borne after achieving full diversification.

Cost of capital

The analysis of the CAPM can be combined with the notion of the contribution of debt and equity finance in the purchase costs for the asset. This then provides some background to gearing which is the relationship of debt capital to total capital in the purchase of the property asset. As debt returns are usually defined by the provider of debt whereas equity return is a surplus, this form of analysis can more clearly define the actual returns on property by differentiating between the debt and equity returns.

Portfolio research

The assessment of the portfolio needs an analysis of the forces driving performance and their impact on return. This process involves breaking down the overall figure for total return into the component parts of capital return and income. The question that arises in the analysis of the portfolio is at what level of the portfolio should this analysis commence: at sector level or perhaps broken down to subcategory, sector/region or even individual properties? Fairchild (1992) suggests two techniques which assist in this analysis: firstly, attribution analysis, which explains why a fund has out- or under-performed the benchmark chosen by being able to pinpoint the strong or weak performing parts of the portfolio and assess the impact of strategy; secondly, risk analysis, which involves a part of Modern Portfolio Theory (MPT) as already discussed in previous chapters and by using the Capital Asset Pricing Model (CAPM) some useful insights are provided in the analysis. Lee (1991) identifies the main areas of Modern Portfolio Theory where research should be directed:

- What is the risk of property?
- The use of 'appraisal' rather than 'transaction' data in analysis portfolio returns in a portfolio context which has led to an underestimation of risk in property because of the smoothing of data (discussed in Chapter 6).
- Sector or geographical diversification.
- International diversification especially with regard to Europe and the common European currency.

The use of index models in portfolio analysis has enabled analysts to relate portfolio risks between investments through the movements in the general market index. Index models not only simplified the calculations but provided more information about individual and portfolio risk/return characteristics. Lee says these can be simply summarised by three statistics obtained by regressing the returns of the investment against the returns of the market index; these measures are:

- *Alpha*: which measures the return you would get on average if there was no change in the index, i.e. the return independent of the market.
- *Beta*: measures the sensitivity of the individual or portfolio relative to the market; i.e. is the investment more or less risky than the market?
- *R Squared*: how diversified the individual investment portfolio is relative to the market (the correlation coefficient).

Betas and correlations of investment returns were discussed in Chapters 10 and 11.

14.2 COMPUTER TECHNIQUES

In addition to databases to provide the evidence and analysis for valuation and property transactions, the spreadsheet is also a critical tool to be used by a valuation surveyor in calculations. The spreadsheet was introduced generally at the beginning of the 1980s.

The spreadsheet consists of a computer program which displays on the computer screen a number of cells. Each cell is given a location rather like a map reference and these co-ordinates provide an address in which to put input data and a means by which the relationship between each of the cells can be described. By knowing the addresses of the various cells, by installing data within the cells and by instructing the computer in a relationship between the cells, it is possible to build up a complex calculation across a number of cells and obtain an answer to the calculation. The power of the spreadsheet is its ability to recalculate instantly when one or a number of the inputs into the cells are changed. The investment calculation can thus be changed to allow access of a number of 'what if' scenarios. It may also be used with the input of very simple data to ensure that the calculation process that has been put into the spreadsheet is correct before elaborate calculation. The use of the spreadsheet comes into its own when considering developments in valuation methods, particularly when dealing with discounted cash flow calculations and attempting to apply growth rates to variables or risk probabilities as discussed earlier. The development of the spreadsheet came mainly in the area of accounting where it can be seen that the tool was very powerful in managing the complex financial transactions as contained in the accounts of companies and being able to give solutions for the final accounts.

Computer software is critical for property investment appraisal; in addition to databases to provide the evidence and analysis for valuation and property transactions, the spreadsheet is also an important tool to be used by valuation surveyors in calculations.

The application of spreadsheets to portfolio analysis has already been mentioned in Chapter 10 on portfolio theory; for instance, different combinations of individual assets may be held in such a way that the highest possible return for a given level of risk may be achieved, known as efficient diversification. Readily available computer software, known as an optimiser, can calculate how much of each asset should be held in order to achieve an efficiently diversified portfolio. To perform the calculations the necessary inputs are: expected return on each asset, the uncertainty of these returns as measured by the assets' variability (standard deviation), and the extent to which each pair of assets is expected to co-vary as measured by their correlation coefficient. Given these inputs it is possible to derive risk and return profiles for different portfolios of assets holdings by the use of optimisers (Matysiak 1993). Byrne and Lee (1994) used a spreadsheet optimiser to compute the efficient frontier. Although the mathematics is complex for the calculation, it is now possible to use a spreadsheet optimiser using matrix methods for the portfolio calculation.

Expert systems

Expert systems are models and simulations which are at the leading edge of sophistication. These models and simulations attempt to copy decision-making processes in certain contexts by asking questions of the data provided, in the same way that an enquiring professional might. This process simulates the thought and decision-making processes of the brain so that appropriate responses are made in the same way. Expert systems, if appropriately modelled, can avoid subjectivity of some decision-making and appraisal. On the other hand, there is no allowance for subjectivity and wider consideration which may improve the quality of the decision made.

14.3 FORECASTING

Forecasting techniques

In an overview of forecasting, Brian Pearce (Pearce 1989) suggests that there are a number of key decisions which will indicate the forecasting method to use. The methods may be subjective versus objective. Subjective methods use processes not explicitly specified by the researcher. They are also naive versus causal methods. Naive methods, for instance, use historic patterns to project into the future while causal methods go beyond the variable of interest to ask why? Finally there are linear versus classification methods. Without wishing to go into great detail in the approaches, the resultant analysis can be grouped as follows:

Method	Forecasting techniques
Subjective	Judgmental
Objective – Naive	Extrapolation
Objective – Causal – Linear	Econometric
Objective – Causal – Classification	Segmentation

Investment trends

Investment fund managers must seek to identify trends in the market and capitalise on the market movements. Innovations in developments and thus major property investments include the development of major shopping and leisure centres: for example, shopping areas at Lakeside in Thurrock and the Metrocentre in Newcastle. Leisure parks range in concept from the amusement park approach of Legoland or Alton Towers, to marinas like St Katherine's Dock or Port Solent, to holiday leisure concepts such as Center Parcs. Dubben and Sayce (1991) suggest that these developments have arisen from US influences both in design and concept, and also include the idea of the 'festival market place' epitomised by the approaches to festival sites in Liverpool and South Wales but conceptualised by the original ideas of the waterfront projects in Baltimore and Boston. The plan for the Millennium site at the Greenwich Peninsular on the Thames is another development of this approach. The influence of the US in terms of its investment finance and international business corporations also has effect. The internationalisation of capital has internationalised finance; financial structures have been introduced into the markets of the UK from their conception in the US. US firms in the City of London and elsewhere have had influence on the quality of premises demanded and the technology provided. They have had influence on the nature of the lease, requiring shorter more flexible lease structures with appropriate break clauses. They have also had influence in the efficient utilisation of space and in requiring efficient facilities management, warranties and service guarantees. Many offices in Central London are now technologically obsolete because of the lack of provision or flexibility in space to accommodate trunking, service, electronic and computer provision, The need for facilities management to handle the provision of a high-tech environment including the IT provision is now ever more apparent.

It is not just the Americans who are influencing the investment market in the UK. Relaxation in the statutory requirements of Japanese pension funds led to investment in the UK. Other significant investors in the UK are from Scandinavia, Germany and the Netherlands who are looking to diversify their portfolios. The deregulation of the Stock Exchange in 1986 enabled a much freer and active investment market to be developed. The move to the single European market (1992) and a single currency will also ease capital flows across borders in the European Union, avoiding problems of currency risk, when exchange rates move adversely and affect the profitability of foreign investment cash flows.

Investment from Far East investors has also been evident, especially in the high-class residential markets. The economies of the Far East are developing rapidly and thus cash-rich individual investors have been looking for appropriate investments, and this, coupled with the movement of cash from Hong Kong prior to 1997 (the return of the territory to China) has meant significant influence on sections of the property market, especially central London high-class apartments.

The provision of residential premises is of course dependent on the nature of the occupants, family size, demography, and so on. The breakdown of the conventional nuclear family has led to smaller family units with increased one-parent units. This has not led to a lesser demand, as housing provision is in demand from these units as well as single occupiers, thus the numbers occupying properties are falling. As more people remain or become single, through choice or old age and loss of their immediate families, the demand holds up, including demand in an aging population for sheltered, safe and convenient provision. Childless couples, in many cases with double incomes, have the ability and taste for larger properties, adding to conventional demand. The working population will become less as the number of older persons increases coupled with earlier retirements. The economically active will also vary more in their make-up, jobs are becoming more fixed- or short-term, part-time employment is increasing, and flexible employment or non-employment is evident. Job losses for male breadwinners has happened at the same time as increased employment of wives. The nature of the working population will have an effect on the location and design of work premises to accommodate its changing characteristics.

14.4 STATISTICAL ANALYSIS

Statistical analysis has already been covered in some detail in Chapter 9 on risk; here we analyse some key points only. The application of mathematics and statistics to economic theory is called econometrics; more precisely it is the discipline which attempts to establish quantitative relationships between economic variables with the aid of statistical methods. The methods used to establish the relationship are essentially those of statistical analysis and in particular regression analysis.

The econometric process can be viewed as a five-stage process (Hetherington 1989):

  (i)   Definition of the problem: the economic system. Model building or forecasting revolves around establishing relationships between the dependent variable and the independent variable which often represents supply or demand in the economic situation.

  (ii) Establishing the quantitative relationship: the equation. Regression analysis is the most popular device to establish the equation between the dependent variable(s) and the independent variable(s).

(iii)   Validate and redefine the equation:

–   how good is the fit of the equation?
–   is it statistically significant?
–   can any of the independent variables be discarded?
–   is the equation well defined – are there any essential variables missing?
–   are the underlying assumptions to the methodology satisfied?

(iv)   Interpretation of the results and their sensitivity. How sensitive are the dependent variable(s) to movements in the index (variable(s))? The interest is in the profile as well as the level of response; for instance:

–   is the effect lagged?
–   is the effect one-off?
–   does the effect fade, or increase with time, or is it consistent?
–   have the independent variable(s) had the same effect over time?

(v)   Application – forecasting.

The methods which can be applied in such econometric analysis include moving averages, simple linear regression, multiple linear regression, simultaneous equations, time-series analysis and non-linear models. The use of statistical and econometric approaches in property analysis is limited. Gallimore and West (1992) argue that the comparable approach to market valuation is essentially non-statistical and suggest the use of multiple regression analysis (MRA) to evolve equations or models which will predict the relationship between a collection of property characteristics and their market value. A MRA model is essentially an equation used to predict the value of property. A model based on a simplistic additive structure is limited because it does not allow for the incorporation of elements, such as location, which have influence across a number of factors, nor does it enable expression of the varying relationship within some factors (such as the way in which the price per m^2 of house varies with house size), whilst a multiplicative model is capable of overcoming these problems. As an example only, Gallimore and West suggests a house pricing model takes the form:

$$Market\ value = b0 \times House\ size^{b1} \times b2^{Central\ h} \times b3^{Garage} \times b4^{Location\ 1} \times b5^{Location\ 3}$$

Here $b0$ is a constant, a starting value which is then modified through multiplication by the other variables; $b1$ is a coefficient which transforms the size of the house into a multiplier. Because it is created as an exponential coefficient, this multiplier reflects not only the influence of house size but also the non-uniform nature of this influence as noted above. Central heating and garage have either the value 1 or 0 indicating their presence or not; $b2$ and $b3$ reflect the percentage adjustment due to each. Locational factors are included here, adjustment is for locations 1 and 3, location 2, say, being omitted as it is the 'standard'. Neither additive nor multiplicative models are appropriate to reflect the influences actually operating in property pricing. To achieve this it is necessary to use a hybrid equation which cannot be solved directly using linear MRA but needs a trial and error process of non-linear MRA or a procedure known as adaptive estimation (or feedback). Gallimore and West suggest the lack of statistical techniques in the property market is not because there is a problem of application of techniques but that property valuers are unwilling to embrace an overly statistical interpretation of market data. Other commentators have rejected the move to econometrics:

the current uncertainty hovering over the property industry is not the result of an inexor-
able economic dynamic dooming the industry to damaging booms and slumps. Rather,
the property industry is having to learn to operate in new, riskier times.

(Guy and Harris 1994, p. 1)

Guy and Harris argue that whilst recognising that changing property development conditions require a re-evaluation of research strategies, they question the 'econometric shift' property research has taken and suggest the introduction of a demand-orientated research strategy which they say is vital to the success of new 'flexible' property business. They indicate that research from its inception has been supply-led, not addressing the structure of demands in terms of spatial or temporal segmentation, which has led to the provision of buildings inappropriate to users' needs. The dominance of the financial institutions in the market has reinforced this, and property research has adopted a reductionist approach to analysis that has made it ever more dependent on fewer and fewer variables. They pose the question: should prediction be the goal of research or should we be striving for more comprehension and explanation? Thus research should respond to continuous segmented change not tides of development, and there is a need to determine a more managed development pattern in which the profile of new building more closely matches the pattern of demand.

Brown (1995) presents an opposite view in defence of rigorous quantitative analysis and states a number of points in his argument:

(i)   Economic theories developed in finance literature have strong economic underpinnings which are equally valid in the property sector. Portfolio theory, for example, was never drafted solely in terms of the equity markets. It is a general theory which applies to the combination of risky assets. Rejection of these ideas results from a misunderstanding of the issues involved.

(ii) Theories of valuation developed in finance can be extended to property and be developed to explain many of the valuation anomalies which occur in the market. For example, rent reviews can be considered an option. So can undeveloped land. Taken in this context, it opens up a completely different way of looking at the theory of valuation. (For a discussion of options, see Isaac 1994.)

(iii) A good understanding of property as an investment asset can only be developed through examining hard data. This, however, needs to be supported by economically valid models. *Ad hoc* views of the market can do a lot of harm.

(iv) A true appreciation of the market can only be achieved through an understanding of the problems associated with the data. Much of the data available in the property sector suffer from severe problems of accuracy. This inevitably means that the data need to be subject to rigorous econometric analysis before they can be used. If poor data are used in an analysis then the results may be inconclusive.

REFERENCES

Antui, A. (1995) 'Multiple Regression in Property Analysis', *Estates Gazette*, 11 February, pp. 144–6.
Brown, G. R. (1991) *Property Investment and the Capital Markets*, E. & F.N. Spon, London.
Brown, G. R. (1995) 'Editorial', *Journal of Property Finance*, vol. 6, no. 1, pp. 3–4.

Byrne, P. and Lee, S. (1994) 'Computing Markowitz Efficient Frontiers using a Spreadsheet Optimiser', *Journal of Property Finance*, vol. 5, no. 1, pp. 58–66.

Colborne, A. (1992) 'Profits Method', paper presented at RICS valuation techniques seminar, 13 March 1992.

Connellan, O. (1992) 'Cost Approach to Valuation', paper presented at RICS valuation techniques seminar, 13 March 1992.

Crosby, N. (1992) *Reversionary Freeholds: UK Market Valuation Practice*, RICS.

Currie, D. and Scott, A. (1991) *The Place of Commercial Property in the UK Economy*, London Business School, January.

Dixon, T. (1994) 'The Benefits of Property Research', *Chartered Surveyor Monthly*, November/December, pp. 28–9.

Dubben, N. and Sayce, S. (1991) *Property Portfolio Management: An Introduction*, Routledge, London.

Fairchild, S. (1992) 'Methods of Portfolio Analysis: A Critical Review', Conference paper, *The Theory and Practice of Portfolio Analysis*, RICS, 23 October.

Gallimore, P. and West, R. (1992) 'Statistical Techniques: Time for Reassessment', *Estates Gazette*, 26 September, pp. 143–4.

Guy, S. and Harris, R. (1994) 'Property in a Risk Society: Towards Marketing Research', Presentation: *New Directions Series*, Society of Property Researchers, RICS, 5 October.

Hetherington, J. (1989) 'Econometrics – A Route to Forecasting', Seminar paper: *The Application of Forecasting Techniques to the Property Market*, Society of Property Researchers/Royal Institution of Chartered Surveyors Technical Seminars, Spring.

Isaac, D. (1994) *Property Finance*, Macmillan, London.

Lee, S. L. (1991) 'Emerging Concepts for the Management of Portfolios and the Role of Research', Conference paper: *Property in a Portfolio Context*, Society of Property Researchers/Royal Institution of Chartered Surveyors Technical Seminars, Spring.

Lizieri, C. and Richards, P. (1992) 'Property Research: Investment', *Estates Gazette*, 11 January, pp. 77 and 103.

Matysiak, G. A. (1993) 'Optimising Property Portfolio Holding: A Scenario-Assisted Approach', *Journal of Property Finance*, vol. 3, nos. 3/4, pp. 68–75.

Pearce, B. (1989) 'Forecasting: An Overview', Seminar paper: *The Application of Forecasting Techniques to the Property Market*, Society of Property Researchers/Royal Institution of Chartered Surveyors Technical Seminars, Spring.

Property Week (1994) 'JLW Review Reveals Most Positive Business Confidence Since 1989', *Property Week*, 21 April 1994, p. 10.

SPR/RICS (1991) *Property in a Portfolio Context*, Society of Property Researchers/Royal Institution of Chartered Surveyors Technical Seminars, Spring.

Bibliography

Accounting Standards Committee (ASC) (1990) *Exposure Draft 51, Accounting for Fixed Assets and Revaluations*, ASC, May.

Adams, A. (1996) 'What Differentiates Grades of Agricultural Land?' *Chartered Surveyor Monthly*, July/August, p. 43.

Albert, D. and Watson, J. (1990) 'An Approach to Property Joint Ventures', *Journal of Property Finance*, vol. 1, no. 2, pp. 189–195.

Antui, A. (1995) 'Multiple Regression in Property Analysis', *Estates Gazette*, 11 February, pp. 144–6.

Asch, D. and Kaye, G. R. (1989) *Financial Planning: Modelling Methods and Techniques*, Kogan Page, London.

Baillie, R. (1997), 'New IPD Index Will Deal Property a Better Hand', *Estates Gazette*, 11 January, p. 40.

Balchin, P. and Bull, G. (1987) *Regional and Urban Economics*, Harper and Row, London.

Bank of England (1994a) *Quarterly Bulletin*, vol. 34, no. 3, August.

Bank of England (1994b) *Quarterly Bulletin*, vol. 34, no. 4, November.

Bank of England (1996) *Quarterly Bulletin*, vol. 36, no. 4, November.

Barber, C. (1995) 'Property Investment: Returning from the Edge of the Abyss', *Property Week*, 20 April, p. 14.

Baring, Houston and Saunders (1991) *Property Report*, Baring, Houston and Saunders, London, November.

Barkham, R. J. and Purdy, D. E. (1992) 'Financial Company Reporting: Potential Weaknesses', *Journal of Property Valuation and Investment*, vol. 11, no. 2, pp. 133–44.

Barkham, R. J., Ward, C.W. R. and Henry O.T. (1995) 'The Inflation-Hedging Characteristics of UK Property', *Journal of Property Finance*, vol. 7, no. 1, pp. 62–76.

Barkshire, R. (1986) *The Unitised Property Market*, Working Party of the Unitised Property Market, London, February.

Barras, R. (1994) 'Property and the Economic Cycle: Building Cycles Revisited', *Journal of Property Research*, vol. 11, no. 3, winter, pp. 183–97.

Barter, S. L. (1988) 'Introduction', in S. L. Barter (ed.), *Real Estate Finance*, Butterworths, London.

Barter, S. and Sinclair, N. (1988) 'Securitisation', in S. L. Barter (ed.), *Real Estate Finance*, Butterworths, London.

Baum, A. (1987) 'An Approach to Risk Analysis', Henry Stewart Conference, *Property Investment Appraisal and Analysis*, Cafe Royal, London, 1 December.

Baum, A. (1994) 'Quality and Property Performance', *Journal of Property Valuation and Investment*, vol. 12, no. 1, pp. 31–46.

Baum, A. and Crosby, N. (1988) *Property Investment Appraisal*, Routledge, London.

Baum, A. and Crosby, N. (1995) *Property Investment Appraisal*, Routledge, London.

Baum, A., Crosby, N. and MacGregor, B. (1996) 'Price Formation, Mispricing and Investment Analysis in the Property Market. A Response to "A Note on 'The Initial Yield Revealed: Explicit Valuations and the Future of Property Investment'"', *Journal of Property Valuation and Investment*, vol. 14, no. 1, pp. 36–49.

Baum, A. E. (1988) 'Depreciation and Property Investment Appraisal', in A. R. MacLeary and N. Nanthakumaran (eds), *Property Investment Theory*, E & F N Spon, London.

Baum, A. E. (1989) 'A Critical Examination of the Measurement of Property Investment and Risk Appraisal', *Discussion Paper Series*, no. 22, University of Cambridge, Department of Land Economy, April.

Baum, A. E. and Schofield, A. (1991) 'Property as a Global Asset', in P. Venmore-Rowland, P. Brandon and T. Mole (eds), *Investment, Procurement and Performance in Construction*, RICS, London.

Beveridge, J. (1988) 'The Needs of the Property Company', in S. L. Barter (ed.), *Real Estate Finance*, Butterworths, London.

Beveridge, J. A. (1991) 'New Methods of Financing', in P. Venmore-Rowland, P. Brandon and T. Mole (eds), *Investment, Procurement and Performance in Construction*, RICS, London.

Blundell, G. F. and Ward, C. W. R. (1987) 'Property Portfolio Allocation: A Multi-Factor Model', *Land Development Studies*, vol. 4, no. 2, pp. 145–56.

Bourne, T. (1995) 'Accelerating Towards Best Returns', *Estates Gazette*, 10 June, pp. 44–5.

Bowie, N. (1982) 'Depreciation: Who Hoodwinked Whom?', *Estates Gazette*, 1 May, pp. 405–11.

Bowie, N. (1988) 'More Thoughts on the Market', *Estates Gazette*, 3 December, pp. 26–8.

Bramson, D. (1988) 'The Mechanics of Joint Ventures', in S. L. Barter (ed.), *Real Estate Finance*, Butterworths, London.

Brett, M. (1983a) 'Growth of Financial Institutions', in C. Darlow (ed.), *Valuation and Investment Appraisal*, Estates Gazette, London.

Brett, M. (1983b) 'Indirect Investment in Property', in C. Darlow (ed.), *Valuation and Investment Appraisal*, Estates Gazette, London.

Brett, M. (1989) 'Characteristics of Property', *Estates Gazette*, 21 January, p. 14.

Brett, M. (1990a) *Property and Money*, Estates Gazette, London.

Brett, M. (1990b) *How to Read the Financial Pages*, Hutchison, London.

Brett, M. (1991a) 'How Property Futures Work', *Estates Gazette*, 18 May, p. 71.

Brett, M. (1991b), 'Property and Money: Mortgages which Convert into Property', *Estates Gazette*, 17 August, p. 28.

Britton, W., Davies, K. and Johnson, T. (1990) *Modern Methods of Valuation*, Estates Gazette, London.

Brown, G. (1986) 'Property Investment and Performance Measurement: A Reply', *Journal of Valuation*, vol. 4, no. 1, pp. 33–44.

Brown, G. (1987) 'A Certainty Equivalent Expectations Model for Estimating the Systematic Risk of Property Investments', *Journal of Valuation*, vol. 6, no. 1, pp. 17–41.

Brown, G. (1991) 'Property Index', in P. Venmore-Rowland, P. Brandon and T. Mole (eds), *Investment, Procurement and Performance in Construction*, E & F N Spon, London.

Brown, G. and Matysiak, G. (1996) 'A Real-Time Property Index, *Estates Gazette*, 13 July, pp. 128–30.

Brown, G. R. (1991) *Property Investment and the Capital Markets*, E. & F.N. Spon, London.

Brown, G. R. (1995) 'Editorial', *Journal of Property Finance*, vol. 6, no. 1, pp. 3–4.

Brown, G. R. and Matysiak, G. (1995) 'Using Commercial Property Indices for Measuring Portfolio Performance', *Journal of Property Finance*, vol. 6, no. 3, pp. 27–38.

Brown, G. R. and Matysiak, G. A. (1996) 'A Note on the Periodic Conversion of Measures of Risk', *Journal of Property Research*, vol. 13 no. 1, pp. 13–16, March.

Butler, D. (1995) *Applied Valuation*, Macmillan, London.

Butler, D. and Richmond, D. (1990) *Advanced Valuation*, Macmillan, London.

Byrne, P. and Cadman, D. (1984) *Risk, Uncertainty and Decision Making in Property Development*, E. & F.N. Spon, London.

Byrne, P. and Lee, S. (1994) 'Computing Markowitz Efficient Frontiers using a Spreadsheet Optimiser', *Journal of Property Finance*, vol. 5, no. 1, pp. 58–66.

Byrne, P. and Lee, S. (1995) 'Is There a Place for Property in the Multi-Asset Portfolio', *Journal of Property Finance*, vol. 6, no. 3, pp. 60–81.

Cadman, D. and Catalano, A. (1983) *Property Development in the UK – Evolution and Change*, College of Estate Management, Reading.

Calachi, R. and Rosenburg, S. (eds), (1992) *Property Finance, An International Perspective*, Euromoney Books, London.

Cameron Markby Hewitt (1996) 'The Future of Investment Property', *Property Update*, Cameron Markby Hewitt, Summer.

Catalano, A. (1995) 'Property Paper Chase', *Estates Gazette*, 1 July, p. 52.

Catalano, A. (1996a) 'MFR Threat to Property Overdone, Says Research', *Estates Gazette*, 13 January, p. 57.

Catalano, A. (1996b) 'Property in the Pensions Balance', *Estates Gazette*, 13 January, pp. 62–3.

Catalano, A. (1996c) 'Foreign Wallet Open in the UK', *Estates Gazette*, 27 January, pp. 66–7.

Catalano, A. (1996d) 'Different Strokes', *Estates Gazette*, 9 March, p. 139.

Catalano, A. (1996e) 'The Leaders of the Pack', *Estates Gazette*, 4 May, p. 44.

Catalano, A. (1996f) 'An Industry Hungry for Change', *Estates Gazette*, 18 May, p. 44.

Catalano, A. (1996g) 'MEPC Taps US Market with $225m Bond Issue', *Estates Gazette*, 18 May, p 43.

Catalano, A. (1996h) 'Property with no Inflation', *Estates Gazette*, 8 June, p. 46.

Cavanagh, E. (1996) 'Design: Hot Tin Roof But Not a Cat in Sight', *Estates Gazette*, 2 November, pp. 108–9.

Central Statistical Office (CSO) (1992) *Financial Statistics: Explanatory Handbook*, CSO, December.

Central Statistical Office (CSO) (1993a) *Financial Statistics*, CSO, September.

Central Statistical Office (CSO) (1993b) *Housing and Construction Statistics*, CSO, September.

Central Statistical Office (CSO) (1994a) *Financial Statistics*, CSO, November.

Central Statistical Office (CSO) (1994b) *Economic Trends*, HMSO, London.

Central Statistical Office (CSO) (1995) *UK Economic Accounts*, no 8, HMSO, London, January.

Central Statistical Office (CSO) (1996a) *Annual abstract of statistics: 1996 Edition*, HMSO, London.

Central Statistical Office (CSO) (1996b) *Financial Statistics*, CSO, November.

Chapman, C. B. (1991) 'Risk', in P. Venmore-Rowland, P. Brandon and T. Mole (eds), *Investment, Procurement and Performance in Construction*, RICS, London.

Chartered Surveyor Monthly (CSM) (1995a) 'Finding Your Way into the New Red Book', *CSM*, October, p. 22.

Chartered Surveyor Monthly (CSM) (1995b) 'Finding Your Way into the New Red Book', *CSM*, November/December, pp. 20–2.

Chartered Surveyor Monthly (CSM) (1995c), 'Mallinson Delivers a Yorker', *CSM*, November/December, p. 48.

Chartered Surveyor Monthly (CSM) (1996a) 'The Variable Value of Property Investment Valuation Reports', *CSM*, April, pp. 38–9.

Chartered Surveyor Monthly (CSM) (1996b) 'RICS Presses Treasury on Securitisation', *CSM*, October, p. 7.

Chesterton Financial (1995) *Property Lending Survey*, Chesterton Financial, London, February.

Chesterton Financial/CSW (1993) *Property Confidence Barometer*, Chesterton Financial, London, July.

Cleaveley, E. S. (1984) *The Marketing of Industrial and Commercial Property*, Estates Gazette, London.

Colborne, A. (1992) 'Profits Method', paper presented at RICS valuation techniques seminar, 13 March 1992.

Colliers (1987) 'Unitisation: Elaborate Experiment or Worthwhile and Much Needed Solution?', *International Review*, no. 20, Colliers International Property Consultants.

Connellan, O. (1992) *Cost Approach to Valuation*, paper presented at RICS valuation techniques seminar, 13 March 1992.

Copeland, T. E. and Weston, J. F. (1988) *Financial Theory and Corporate Policy*, Addison-Wesley, Wokingham.

Cox, C. (1996) 'Contract Farming or Letting with a Farm Business Tenancy', *Chartered Surveyor Monthly*, July/August, pp. 44–5.

Crosby, N. (1991) 'Over-Rented Freehold Investment Property Valuation', *Journal of Property Valuation and Investment*, vol. 10, no. 2, pp. 517–24.

Crosby, N. (1992) *Reversionary Freeholds; UK Market Valuation Practice*, Research paper, RICS, London.

Crosby, N. and Goodchild, R. (1992) 'Reversionary Freeholds: Problems with Over-Renting', *Journal of Property Valuation and Investment*, vol. 11, no. 1, pp. 67–81.

CSW-The Property Week (1993a), '25 year lease', *CSW-The Property Week*, 10 June, pp. 24–5.

CSW-The Property Week (1993b), 'New Research Reveals Market Pattern', *CSW-The Property Week*, 28 October, p. 13.

Currie, D. and Scott, A. (1991) *The Place of Commercial Property in the UK Economy*, London Business School, January.

D. J. Freeman (1994) *The Language of Property Finance*, D.J. Freeman, London.

Darlow, C. (ed.), (1983) *Valuation and Investment Appraisal*, Estates Gazette, London.

Darlow, C. (ed.), (1988a) *Valuation and Development Appraisal*, Estates Gazette, London.

Darlow, C. (1988b) 'Corporate and Share Capital Funding', in C. Darlow (ed.), *Valuation and Development Appraisal*, Estates Gazette, London.

Darlow, C. (1988c) 'Direct Project Funding', in C. Darlow (ed.), *Valuation and Development Appraisal*, Estates Gazette, London.

Darlow, C. (1988d) 'The Supply and Sources of Finance', in C. Darlow (ed.), *Valuation and Development Appraisal*, Estates Gazette, London.

Davidson, A.W. (1989) *Parry's Valuation and Investment Tables*, Estates Gazette, London.

Davis, Langdon and Everest (1996) 'Cost Model: Offices of the Future', *Procurement, Building*, September, pp. 13–20.

Dawson, A. (1995) 'Finance: Picking a Path Through the Hedges', *Estates Gazette*, 11 March, pp. 46–7.

Debenham, Tewson and Chinnocks (1984) *Property Investment in Britain*, Debenham, Tewson and Chinnocks, London.

Dixon, T. (1994) 'The Benefits of Property Research', *Chartered Surveyor Monthly*, November/December, pp. 28–9.

Dixon, T. J., Hargitay, S. E. and Bevan, O. A. (1991) *Microcomputers in Property*, E. & F.N. Spon, London.

DoE (Department of the Environment) (1994a) *Housing and Construction Statistics 1982–1993 (Great Britain)*, HMSO, London.

DoE (Department of the Environment) (1994b) *Housing and Construction Statistics (Great Britain)*, June quarter 1994, part 2, HMSO, London.

Drivers Jonas/IPD (1988) *The Variance in Valuations*, Drivers Jonas Research Department, London, Autumn.

DTZ Debenham Thorpe (1993) *Money into Property*, DTZ Debenham Thorpe, London, August.

DTZ Debenham Thorpe (1996) *Money into Property*, DTZ Debenham Thorpe, London, September.

Dubben, N. and Sayce, S. (1991) *Property Portfolio Management: An Introduction*, Routledge, London.

Edgington, D. (1996), 'What Drives Japanese Property Investors?', *Chartered Surveyor Monthly*, March, p. 32.

Eichholtz, P. M. A., Hoesli, M., MacGregor, B. D. and Nanthakumaran, N. (1995) 'Real Estate Portfolio Diversification by Property Type and Region', *Journal of Property Finance*, vol. 6, no. 3, pp. 39–59.

Enever, N. and Isaac, D. (1995) *The Valuation of Property Investments*, Estates Gazette, London.

Estates Gazette (1995a), 'Mainly for Students: Spreadsheets and Valuations,' *Estates Gazette*, 21 January, pp. 116–119.

Estates Gazette (1995b), 'Rent-Free Periods and Valuation', *Estates Gazette*, 13 May, pp. 143–4.

Estates Gazette (1995c), 'Property Cycles Explained', *Estates Gazette*, 25 November, pp. 147–8.

Estates Gazette (1996a), 'Tenants are Lukewarm on New Lease Code of Practice', *Estates Gazette*, 6 January, p. 40.

Estates Gazette (1996b), 'The New Red Book', *Estates Gazette*, 6 January, pp. 96–7.

Estates Gazette (1996c), 'Thumbs Up for Property', *Estates Gazette*, 20 April, p. 41.

Estates Gazette (1996d) 'Industry Profile: Fashion Retailing', *Estates Gazette*, 6 July, pp. 58–60.

Estates Gazette (1996e) 'Leisure Development', *Estates Gazette*, 20 July, pp. 103–5.

Estates Gazette (1996f) 'Industry Profile: Food and Drink Industry', *Estates Gazette*, 27 July, pp. 41–2.

Estates Gazette (1996g) 'Teleworking Threat to Office Demand', *Estates Gazette*, 31 August, p. 28.

Estates Gazette (1996h) 'PPG6 Causes Drop in Retail Park Proposals', *Estates Gazette*, 21 September, p. 41.

Estates Gazette (1996i), 'Investment Funds Give Thumbs Up to Property', *Estates Gazette*, 28 September, p. 56.

Estates Times (1993) 'Swaps Not Cash', *Estates Times*, 19 November, p. 24.

Evans, P. and Jarrett, D. (1988), 'Institutional Investors', Intentions', *Estates Gazette*, 18 June, pp. 24–6.

Evans, P. H. (1993) 'Statistical Review', *Journal of Property Finance*, vol. 4, no. 2, pp. 75–82.

Fairchild, S. (1992) 'Methods of Portfolio Analysis', Conference paper: *The Theory and Practice of Portfolio Analysis*, RICS, 23 October.

Findlay P. N. and Tyler, J. B. (1991) 'The Performance Measurement of Property Investment', *Journal of Property Investment and Valuation*, vol. 9, no. 4, pp. 295–316.

Fisher, I. (1930) *The Theory of Interest*, Porcupine Press, Philadephia.

Flanagan, R. and Norman, G. (1993) *Risk Management and Construction*, Blackwell, Oxford.

Fraser, W. (1996), 'A Schematic Model of the Commercial Property Market', *Chartered Surveyor Monthly*, January, pp. 32–3

Fraser, W. D. (1993) *Principles of Property Investment and Pricing*, Macmillan, London.

Freedman, C.. (1996a) 'Design for life', *Estates Gazette*, 14 September, pp. 122–3.

Freedman, C. (1996b) 'Local loyalties', *Estates Gazette*, 5 October, pp. 104–5.

French, N. (1994) 'Editorial: Market Values & DCF', *Journal of Property Valuation and Investment*, vol. 12, no. 1, pp. 4–6.

French, N. (1995) 'Property – love it or leave it', *Estates Gazette*, 7 October, pp. 126–7.

French, N. and Ward, C. (1995) 'Valuation and Arbitrage', *Journal of Property Research*, vol. 12, no. 1, pp. 1– 11, Spring.

Gallimore, P. (1996) 'Confirmation Bias in the Valuation Process: A Test for Corroborating Evidence', *Journal of Property Valuation and Investment*, vol. 13, no. 4, pp. 261–273.

Gallimore, P. and West, R. (1992) 'Statistical Techniques: Time for Reassessment', *Estates Gazette*, 26 September, pp. 143–4.

Gibbs, R. (1987) 'Raising Finance for New Development', *Journal of Valuation*, vol. 5, no. 4, pp. 343–53.

Gibson, G. and Carter, C. (1995) 'Is Property on the Strategic Agenda?', *Chartered Surveyor Monthly*, January, pp. 34–5.

Godson, V. (1991) 'Methods of portfolio analysis' in P. Venmore-Rowland, P. Brandon and T. Mole (eds), *Investment, Procurement and Performance in Construction*, E. & F.N. Spon, London.

Goodwin, M. (1995) 'A Recipe for Liquifying Property', *Chartered Surveyor Monthly*, November/December, pp. 28–9.

Guy, G. (1994), *The Retail Development Process: Location, Property and Planning*, Routledge, London.

Guy, S. and Harris, R. (1994) 'Property in a Risk Society: Towards Marketing Research', Presentation: *New Directions Series*, Society of Property Researchers, RICS, 5 October.

Hager, D. P. and Lord D. J. (1985) *The Property Market, Property Valuations and Property Performance Measurement*, Institute of Actuaries.

Hall, P. (1983) 'Property Performance Measurement', in C. Darlow (ed.), *Valuation and Investment Appraisal*, Estates Gazette, London.

Hall, P. O. (1981), 'Alternative Approaches to Performance Measurement', *Estates Gazette*, 19 July, pp. 935–8.

Hargitay, S. E. (1983) 'A Systematic Approach to the Analysis of the Property Portfolio', Unpublished PhD thesis, University of Reading (quoted in Waldy 1991).

Hargitay, S. E. and Sui-Ming Yu (1993) *Property Investment Decisions*, E. & F.N. Spon, London.

Hetherington, J. (1980) 'Money and Time-Weighted Rates of Return', *Estates Gazette*, 20/27 December, pp. 1164–5.

Hetherington, J. (1989) 'Econometrics – A Route to Forecasting', Seminar paper: *The Application of Forecasting Techniques to the Property Market*, Society of Property Researchers/Royal Institution of Chartered Surveyors Technical Seminars, Spring.

Hiatt, C. (1996) 'Irrestible Lure of Green Fields', *Estates Times*, 21 June, p. 13.

Hunt, J. (1996) 'Teleworking Poised to Rise Sharply by 2000', *Property Week*, 1 June, p. 7.

Hutchinson, N. (1996), 'Variations in the Capital Values of UK Commercial Property', *Chartered Surveyor Monthly*, April, pp. 40–1.

Investment Property Databank (IPD) (1992) *Annual Review: 1993*, IPD Ltd., London, December.
International Property Databank (IPD) (1996a) *Annual Index: 1995*, IPD Ltd.
International Property Databank (IPD) (1996b) *Monthly Index: September*, IPD Ltd., September.
Investment Property Forum (1995) *Property Securitisation*, IPF, London.
Isaac, D. (1986) 'Corporate Finance and Property Development Funding: An Analysis of Property Companies' Capital Structures with Special Reference to the Relationship Between Asset Value and Share Price', Unpublished thesis, Faculty of the Built Environment, South Bank Polytechnic, London.
Isaac, D. (1994) *Property Finance*, Macmillan, London.
Isaac, D. (1996) *Property Development; Appraisal and Finance*, Macmillan, London.
Isaac, D. and Steley, T. (1991) *Property Valuation Techniques*, Macmillan, London.
Isaac, D. and Woodroffe, N. (1987) 'Are Property Company Assets Undervalued', *Estates Gazette*, 5 September, pp. 1024–6.
Isaac, D. and Woodroffe, N. (1995) *Property Companies: Share Price and Net Asset Value*, Greenwich University Press, London.
Jack, S. (1996) 'Ever Increasing Circles', *Estates Gazette*, 5 October, pp. 108–9.
Jenkins, S. (1996), 'Valuations still Highly Variable', *Estates Times*, 15 March, p. 2.
Jennings, R. B. (1993) 'The Resurgence of Real Estate Investment Trusts (REITs)', *Journal of Property Finance*, vol. 4, no. 1, pp. 13–19.
Jonas, C. (1995) 'Liquidity and Property', *Estates Gazette*, 3 June, p 52.
Jones Lang Wotton (1989) 'The Glossary of Property Terms', *Estates Gazette*, London.
Keogh, G. (1994) 'Use and Investment Markets in British Real Estate', *Journal of Property Valuation and Investment*, vol. 12, no. 4, pp. 58–72.
Law, D. and Gershinson, J. (1995) 'Whatever Happened to ERP?', *Estates Gazette*, 16 September, pp. 164– 5.
Lawson, D. (1995) 'Inflated opinions: Barber White Inflation report', *Property Week*, 16 March, pp. 20–1.
Lee, S. L. (1991) 'Emerging Concepts for the Management of Portfolios and the Role of Research', Conference paper: *Property in a Portfolio Context*, Society of Property Researchers/Royal Institution of Chartered Surveyors Technical Seminars, Spring.
Lennox, K. (1995) 'Moving with the times', *Estates Gazette*, 27 May, pp. 50–1.
Lennox, K. (1996a) 'IPD Annual Index: Down But Not Out', *Estates Gazette*, 30 March, p. 52.
Lennox, K. (1996b) 'Thumbs Up for Property: IPF/EG survey', *Estates Gazette*, 20 April, p. 41.
Lennox, K. (1996c) 'Valuations – Winners and Losers', *Estates Gazette*, 27 April, p. 60.
Lennox, K. (1996d) 'Future Perfect', *Estates Gazette*, 24 August, p. 30.
Lennox, K. (1996e) 'Property on the Up', *Estates Gazette*, 7 September, pp. 50–1.
Lizieri, C. and Finlay, L. (1995) 'International Property Portfolio Strategies: Problems and Opportunities', *Journal of Property Valuation and Investment*, vol. 13, no. 1, pp. 6–21.
Lizieri, C. and Richards, P. (1992) 'Property Research: Investment', *Estates Gazette*, 11 January, pp. 77 and 103.
Lizieri, C. and Venmore-Rowland, P. (1991) 'Valuation Accuracy: A Contribution to the Debate', *Journal of Property Research*, vol. 8, no. 2, pp. 115–22.
London, S. (1996) 'Lure of the Property Magnet', *Financial Times*, 23 September, p. 19.
Lumby, S. (1991) *Investment Appraisal and Financing Decisions*, Chapman & Hall, London.
Mackmin, D. (1994) *The Valuation and Sale of Residential Property*, Routledge, London.
Mallinson, M. (1988) 'Equity Finance', in S. L. Barter (ed.), *Real Estate Finance*, Butterworths, London.
Markowitz, H. (1952) 'Portfolio Selection', *Journal of Finance*, vol. VII, no. 1, March, pp. 77–91.
Markowitz, H. (1959) *Portfolio Selection: Efficient Diversification of Investment*, John Wiley, New York (also second printing (1970) Yale University Press, New Haven, Conn.).
Markowitz, H. (1991) *Portfolio selection: Efficient Diversification of Investment*, Blackwell, Cambridge, Massachusetts.
Marriott, O. (1962) *The Property Boom*, Hamish Hamilton, London.
Marshall, P. (1991) *Development Valuation Techniques*, Research Technical Paper, RICS, London.

Matysiak, G., Hoesli, M., MacGregor, B. and Nanathakumaran, N. (1995) 'Long-Term Inflation-Hedging Characteristics of UK Commercial Property', *Journal of Property Finance*, vol. 7, no. 1, pp. 50–61.

Matysiak, G. and Venmore-Rowland P. (1994) 'Appraising Commercial Property Performance', *Cutting Edge Conference*, RICS, 3 September.

Matysiak, G. A. (1993) 'Optimising Property Portfolio Holding: A Scenario-Assisted Approach', *Journal of Property Finance*, vol. 3, nos.3/4, pp. 68–75.

Maxted, B. (1988) *Unitisation of Property*, College of Estate Management, Reading.

McGregor, B., Nanthakumuran, N., Key, T. and Zarkesh, F. (1994) 'Investigating Property Cycles', *Chartered Surveyor Monthly*, July/August, pp. 38–9.

McIntosh, A. and Sykes, S. (1985) *A Guide to Institutional Property Investment*, Macmillan, London.

Melzack, H. (1990) 'Sheds Checklist', *CSW Business and Industrial Space Supplement*, *Chartered Surveyor Weekly*, 26 July, p. 42.

Millington, A. F. (1984) *An Introduction to Property Valuation*, Estates Gazette, London.

Millman, S. (1988) 'Property, Property Companies and Public Securities', in S. L. Barter (ed.), *Real Estate Finance*, Butterworths, London.

Mollart, R. (1988) 'Computer Briefing: Monte Carlo Simulation using Lotus 1-2-3', *Journal of Valuation*, vol. 6, no. 4, pp. 419–33.

Mollart, R. (1994) 'Software Review: Using @ Risk for Risk Analysis', *Journal of Property Valuation and Investment*, vol. 12, no. 3, pp. 89–94.

Morgan, P. and Walker, A. (1988) *Retail Development*, Estates Gazette, London.

Morley, S. (1988a) 'Financial Appraisal – Cashflow Approach', in C. Darlow (ed.), *Valuation and Development Appraisal*, Estates Gazette, London.

Morley, S. (1988b) 'Financial Appraisal – Sensitivity and Probability', in C. Darlow (ed.), *Valuation and Development Appraisal*, Estates Gazette, London.

Morley, S. (1996) 'The Future for Offices', *Estates Gazette*, 3 August, pp. 76–8.

Morley, S. J. E. (1988) 'The Analysis of Risk in the Appraisal of Property Investment', in A. R. MacLeary and N. Nanthakumaran (eds), *Property Investment Theory*, E. & F.N. Spon, London.

Morrell, G. (1995) 'Property Indices: A Coming of Age', *Journal of Property Investment and Valuation*, vol. 13, no. 3, pp. 8–21.

Morrell, G. D. (1991) 'Property Performance Analysis and Performance Indices: A Review', *Journal of Property Research*, vol. 8, pp. 29–57.

Newall, G. and Fife, A. (1995) 'Major Property Investors' Attitudes to Property Securitisation', *Journal of Property Finance*, vol. 6, no. 2, pp. 8–19.

Newall, G. and Worzala, E. (1995) 'The Role of International Property in Investment Portfolios', *Journal of Property Finance*, vol. 6, no. 1, pp. 55–63.

Norton, M. D. (1988) 'Market Analysis and Project Evaluation', in C. Darlow (ed.), *Valuation and Development Appraisal*, Estates Gazette, London.

Orchard-Lisle, P. (1987) 'Financing Property Development', *Journal of Valuation*, vol. 5, no. 4, pp. 343–53.

Paribas Capital Markets (1993a) *European Equity Research: Rodamco*, Banque Paribas Nederland NV., October.

Paribas Capital Markets (1993b) *Monthly Property Share Statistics*, Banque Paribas, November.

Paribas Capital Markets (1995a) *Prospects for the Property Sector*, Banque Paribas, January.

Paribas Capital Markets (1995b) *UK Property Sector Review 1*, Banque Paribas, March.

Pearce, B. (1989) 'Forecasting: An Overview', Seminar paper: *The Application of Forecasting Techniques to the Property Market*, Society of Property Researchers/Royal Institution of Chartered Surveyors Technical Seminars, Spring.

Peat, M. (1988) 'The Accounting Issues', in S. L. Barter (ed.), *Real Estate Finance*, Butterworths, London.

Peto, R., French, N. and Bowman, G. (1996) 'Price and Worth: Developments in Valuation Methodology', *Journal of Property Valuation and Investment*, vol. 14, no. 4, pp. 79–100.

Pike, R. and Neale, B. (1993) *Corporate Finance and Investment*, Prentice Hall, London.

Plender, J. (1994) 'Exploring foreign markets', *Estates Gazette*, 26 November, p. 68.

Property Journal (1996) 'PPG6 Makes Progress But Introduces New Problems Says BPF', *Property Journal*, British Property Federation, July, p. 3.

Property Week (1994) 'JLW Review Reveals Most Positive Business Confidence Since 1989', *Property Week*, 21 April 1994, p. 10.

Pugh, C. (1991) 'The Globalisation of Finance Capital and the Changing Relationships between Property and Finance', *Journal of Property Finance*, vol. 2, no. 2, pp. 211–5 and no. 3, pp. 369–79.

Pugh, C. and Dehesh, A. (1995) 'International Property Cycles: The Causes', *Chartered Surveyor Monthly*, January p. 33.

Purdy, D. E. (1992) 'Provoking Awareness through the Provision of Relevant Information in Property Company Accounts', *Journal of Property Finance*, vol. 3, no. 3, pp. 337–46.

Ratcliffe, J. (1978) *An Introduction to Urban Land Administration*, Estates Gazette, London.

Rayner, M. (1988) *Asset Valuation*, Macmillan, London.

Redman, A. L. and Manakyan, H. (1995) 'A Multivariate Analysis of REIT performance by Financial and Real Asset Portfolio Characteristics', *Journal of Real Estate Finance and Economics*, vol. 10, no. 2, March, pp. 169–75.

Rees, W. H. (ed.), (1992) *Valuation: Principles into Practice*, Estates Gazette, London.

Reid, I. (1985) 'A response to Hager/Lord', *Estates Gazette*, 6 April, pp. 19–20.

Rich, J. (1994) 'The Wonderland of OMVs, ERPs and DAVs', *Estates Gazette*, 26 November, pp. 153–5.

Richard Ellis (1986) 'Development Finance', *Property Investment Quarterly Bulletin*, Richard Ellis, London, April.

Riley, M. and Isaac, D. (1994) 'Property Lending Survey 1994', *Journal of Property Finance*, vol. 5, no. 1, pp. 45–51.

Riley, M. and Isaac, D. (1995) 'Property Lending Survey 1995', *Journal of Property Finance*, vol. 6, no. 1, pp. 67–72.

Robinson, G. (1996) 'Derivatives: Filling a Gap in the Market', *Estates Gazette*, 2 November, pp. 179–81.

Ross, S. A., Westerfield, R. W. and Jaffe, J. F. (1993) *Corporate Finance*, Irwin, Boston.

Royal Institution of Chartered Surveyors (RICS) (1985) *The Unitisation of Real Property*, RICS, London.

Royal Institution of Chartered Surveyors (RICS) (1992) *Statement of Asset Valuation Practice and Guidance Notes*, RICS, London.

Royal Institution of Chartered Surveyors (RICS) (1994) *Understanding the Property Cycle: Economic Cycles and Property Cycles*, RICS, London, May.

Royal Institution of Chartered Surveyors (RICS) (1995a) *RICS Appraisal and Valuation Manual*, RICS, London.

Royal Institution of Chartered Surveyors (RICS) (1995b) *Rental Valuation of Commercial Lease Inducements*, consultative document, RICS, London.

Royal Institution of Chartered Surveyors (1995c) *Valuation of Development Land*, RICS, London, January.

Rydin, Y., Rodney, W. and Orr, C. (1990) 'Why Do Institutions Invest in Property', *Journal of Property Finance*, vol. 1, no. 2, pp. 250–8.

Ryland, D. (1991) 'Authorised Property Unit Trusts', *Estates Gazette*, London, 9 November, pp. 163–4.

Ryland, D. S. (1992) 'Changes in Accounting Rules', *Journal of Property Finance*, vol. 3, no. 1, pp. 28–37.

S. G. Warburg Securities (1993) *U.K. Property: Review of 1992 and Prospects for 1993*, S. G. Warburg, London.

S. G. Warburg Research (1993) *U.K. Property: Monthly Review*, S. G. Warburg, London, November.

Salway, F. (1987) 'Building Depreciation and Property Appraisal Techniques', *Journal of Valuation*, vol. 5, no. 2, pp. 118–24.

Savills (1989) *Financing Property 1989*, Savills, London.

Savills (1993a) *Financing Property 1993*, Savills, London.

Savills (1993b) *Investment and Economic Outlook*, Savills, London, Issue 3, October.

Scarrett, D. (1991) *Property Valuation: The Five Methods*, E. & F.N. Spon, London.

Schiller, R. (1990) 'International Property Investment: The Importance of Debt', *Estates Gazette*, 24 February, pp. 22–4.

Schiller, R. (1994) 'Comment: The Interface between Valuation and Forecasting', *Journal of Property Valuation and Investment*, vol. 12, no. 4, pp. 3–6.

Schiller, R. (1996) 'Town-Centre Winners and Losers', *Estates Gazette*, 13 July, pp. 134–5.

Scott, I. P. (1992) 'Debt, Liquidity and Secondary Trading in Property Debt', *Journal of Property Finance*, vol. 3, no. 3, pp. 347–55.

Scrimgeor Vickers & Co (1986) *United Kingdom Research, Annual Property Report*, Scrimgeor Vickers & Co, London.

Seeley, I. H. (1996) *Building Economics*, Macmillan, London.

Sexton, P. and Laxton, C. (1992) 'Authorised Property Unit Trusts', *Journal of Property Finance*, vol. 2, no. 4, pp. 468–75.

Sharpe, W. F. (1964) 'Capital Asset Prices: A Theory of Market Equilibrium Under Conditions of Risk', *Journal of Finance*, vol. XIX, no. 3, September, pp. 425–42.

Sieracki, K. (1993) 'U.K. Institutional Requirements for European Property', *Estates Gazette*, July 17, p. 116.

Simmons, M. (1996) 'My Perfect Office', *Estates Gazette*, 14 September, pp. 108–10.

Smee, R. (1992) 'Capitalisation of Interest for Property Companies', *Journal of Property Finance*, vol. 3, no. 1, pp. 13–22.

SPR/RICS (1991) *Property in a Portfolio Context*, Society of Property Researchers/Royal Institution of Chartered Surveyors Technical Seminars, Spring.

Sweeney, F. (1988) '20% in Property – a Viable Strategy', *Estates Gazette*, 13 February, pp. 26–28.

Sweeney, F. (1989) 'A Property Market without Frontiers', *Estates Gazette*, 2 September, pp. 20–22 and 30.

Sykes, S. G. (1983) 'The Assessment of Property Risk', *Journal of Valuation*, vol. 1, pp. 253–267.

Tarbert, H. (1995) 'Is Commercial Property a Hedge Against Inflation? A Cointegration Approach', *Journal of Property Finance*, vol. 7, no. 1, pp. 77–98.

Taylor, S. (1996), 'Privity and Property Lending', *Estates Gazette*, 2 March, pp. 119–20.

UBS Global Research (1993) *UK Equities: Property Perspective*, UBS Ltd, January.

UBS Global Research (1995) *UK Property Service: Company Ranking by Market Capitalisation*, UBS, London, January.

Venmore-Rowland, P. (1991) 'Vehicles for Property Investment', in P. Venmore-Rowland, P. Brandon and T. Mole (eds), *Investment, Procurement and Performance in Construction*, RICS, London.

Waldy E. B. D. (1991) 'Single Asset Risk', in P. Venmore-Rowland, P. Brandon and T. Mole (eds), *Investment, Procurement and Performance in Construction*, RICS, London.

Watson, C. J., Billingsley, P., Croft, D. J. and Huntsberger, D. V. (1990) *Statistics for Management and Economics*, Allyn and Bacon, Boston.

Westwick, C. A. (1980) *Property Valuation and Accounts*, Institute of Chartered Accountants in England and Wales, London.

Whitmore, J. (1993) 'Debt Securitisation to Aid the Market', *CSW-The Property Week*, 28 January, p. 15.

Whitmore, J. (1994), 'RICS Identifies the Property Cycle', *Property Week*, 12 May, p. 4.

Woodroffe, N. and Isaac, D. (1987) 'Corporate Finance and Property Development Funding', *Working Paper of the School of Applied Economics and Social Studies*, Faculty of the Built Environment, South Bank Polytechnic, London.

Worzala, E. (1994) 'Overseas Property Investments: How Are They Perceived by the Institutional Investor?', *Journal of Property Valuation and Investment*, vol. 12, no. 3, pp. 31–47.

Wright, M. G. (1990) *Using Discounted Cash Flow in Investment Appraisal*, McGraw-Hill, London.

Yuen Ka Yin, McKinnell, K. and Isaac, D. (1988) The Unitisation of Real Property in Hong Kong, unpublished research paper, Hong Kong University/University of Greenwich.

Index